Conducting Scientifically Crafted Child Custody Evaluations

DI019348

To my children, Madeline, Robbie, and Stevi:
Through their eyes and smiles, the wondrous meaning
of family love is expressed every day.

To the children of divorce:
May their parents never lose sight of their children's
need for family love in their journey through life.

Conducting Scientifically Crafted Child Custody Evaluations

Jonathan W. Gould, Ph.D.

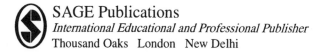

SAGE Publications
International Educational and Professional Publisher
Thousand Oaks   London   New Delhi

Copyright © 1998 by Sage Publications, Inc.

All rights reserved. No part of this book may be reproduced or utilized in any form or by any means, electronic or mechanical, including photocopying, recording, or by any information storage and retrieval system, without permission in writing from the publisher.

For information:

 SAGE Publications, Inc.
2455 Teller Road
Thousand Oaks, California 91320
E-mail: order@sagepub.com

SAGE Publications Ltd.
6 Bonhill Street
London EC2A 4PU
United Kingdom

SAGE Publications India Pvt. Ltd.
M-32 Market
Greater Kailash I
New Delhi 110 048 India

Printed in the United States of America

Library of Congress Cataloging-in-Publication Data

Gould, Jonathan W., 1953–
    Conducting scientifically crafted child custody evaluations /
by Jonathan W. Gould.
        p.   cm.
    Includes bibliographical references and index.
    ISBN 0-7619-1100-6 (cloth: acid-free paper)
    ISBN 0-7619-1101-4 (pbk.: acid-free paper)
        1. Custody of children—United States. 2. Evidence,
Expert—United States. 3. Forensic psychiatry—United States. I. Title.
KF547 .G68 1998
346.7301'73—ddc21   98-19718

This book is printed on acid-free paper.

98 99 00 01 02 03 04 7 6 5 4 3 2 1

Acquiring Editor:	Jim Nageotte
Editorial Assistant:	Fiona Lyon
Production Editor:	Sherrise M. Purdum
Production Assistant:	Karen Wiley
Typesetter/Designer:	Rebecca Evans
Indexer:	Juniee Oneida
Cover Designer:	Candice Harman

Contents

Preface

I am a private practitioner actively engaged in the practice of forensic psychology. I am not an academic. It has been years since I have had the privilege and luxury of spending my days thinking about concepts and reading journals. My days today are filled with clinical treatment, forensic evaluations, writing, and training. When the day is done, I come home to my wonderful family, which is the rudder of my life.

As a private practitioner, I sometimes lose touch with the awesome amount of material that is published in my chosen field. Trying to keep up with managed care requirements and the paperwork resulting from a busy clinical and forensic practice challenges my meager organizational and administrative skills.

I introduce you to my professional life as a private practitioner, in part, to let you know that I do not spend my days researching and writing and thinking about civil forensic mental health in the ivory tower world of academics. Would that I could! Instead, I live it. I practice it. And I have learned through experiencing my growth as well as observing that of my colleagues that the majority of people engaging in child custody evaluations do not understand the relationship between the legal system and behavioral science.

When, as mental health professionals, we offer services to the court through the performance of child custody evaluations, we need to understand that it is our work product that needs to fit into the legal system, not the other way around. We need to craft both our behavior and our work product to fit the requirements for the admissibility of scientific evidence.

We also need to remember that custody recommendations offered by evaluators are works in progress. All families are dynamic, growing systems. Divorced families also are dynamic, growing systems with inter- and intrafamilial variables that challenge those who live within the transitioned family. As evaluators, we need to remember that the evaluation process often occurs at a time when the family system is in chaos—parents are living apart and children are trying to rediscover their balance, their safety, and their security. The picture of a particular family is surely not a "Kodak moment." It may not even be an accurate snapshot of how the family will function once the disarray turns into a lifestyle.

The purpose of this volume is to help practitioners, teachers, and students integrate the multifaceted components of behavioral science literature and the law into a unified approach to child custody evaluations. The behavioral science literature is rich with conceptual and empirical work examining a plethora of areas relevant to children's adjustment to separation and divorce. There is a growing literature about the use of standard interview protocols and psychological tests in a forensic context. Finally, there is increasing professional awareness of the applicability of federal and state rules of evidence to the written and verbal testimonial information offered by mental health professionals.

The main cord that binds this book is the commitment to craft child custody evaluations into empirically based, scientifically crafted, legally admissible documents that optimally serve the court. It is my firm belief that through better crafted reports that have their basis in behavioral science literature, mental health professionals can provide the best possible service to those for whom we toil: the children of divorce.

Acknowledgments

No family man can write a book without the support and hard work of his spouse and children. No one has earned her place in this section more than my wife, Debra. She held down the fort, and she rechanneled our children's energies when they sought me out to play and I had to focus on writing instead. She graciously read and reread chapter after chapter, to the point where she is probably a pretty competent evaluator herself! All my love and thanks go to her, first and foremost. Thanks also go to my agent, Alan Witmann. I cannot think of a better mentor or sage about the publishing business than Alan. His honor, integrity, and wisdom helped me through many frustrating rejections before Sage Publications took a chance on someone new. The person at Sage who saw some merit in my work was Jim Nageotte. A patient man with helpful advice and clear thoughts, Jim has guided this work from Charlotte to Thousand Oaks to your hands.

The people in Charlotte who have helped challenge my thinking about child custody and the law are many. Among those most influential are De Kirkpatrick, PhD; Katie Holliday, Esq.; Marcia Jarrell; Billie Maitland, PhD; Lisa Bell, Esq.; The Honorable William Jones; The Honorable Jane Harper; The Honorable Yvonne Mims Evans; and my practice partners: Randy Wall, PhD; Rick Deitchman, PhD; Phyllis Marsh, MA; and Elizabeth Meadows, MSW.

Finally, there is my good friend who got me involved in custody evaluations with a serious eye toward integrating law and mental health—attorney Joe LaMonaca. There is no way to thank someone for opening up a world of experience rich with growth and opportunity. My arguments, discussions, and work with Joe have challenged my work to a higher level.

ONE

Introduction

Decisions about parenthood are decisions about the unquan-
tifiable, unmeasurable things of the heart.

Leslie Ellen Shear (1996, p. 440)

Forensic child custody evaluations are in their infancy. We are just now beginning to organize a coherent literature and methodology about how to interview, assess, report, and testify. If we look at evaluations as a field of professional endeavor, mental health professionals have been somewhat poorly
skilled at identifying the developmental factors of most importance *at each
stage of child development* that need to be measured in an evaluation. We are
often worse at clearly presenting that information to the court. We have
struggled with the task of conceptualizing and researching characteristics that
define positive parenting capacity. As with so many other things in life, mental health professionals are able to identify *negative* parenting characteristics,
but they struggle with defining and examining what defines positive parenting capacity; added to these profoundly difficult concerns is the complex
challenge of describing a healthy interaction between a child's developmental
characteristics and the parent's parenting capacity to determine the best fit.
We are only now learning how to build a solid framework.

This book humbly undertakes the awesome task of compiling the literature on major aspects of child custody evaluation into a coherent, logically
integrated format to be used in the practical application of forensic child custody evaluations. There is no attempt to portray this as *the* definitive word
because the field is dynamic; growing; and, on a daily basis, being redefined
through research, case law, and theoretical reformulation. Based upon available literature, this book represents the state of the art today.

I offer three separate ideas for your consideration. The scientific literature about the effects of divorce on children, adults, and family systems needs
to be better integrated into child custody reports so that we may better serve
the children of divorcing families. I have always been curious as to why books

1

QUICK REFERENCE   **Areas of Responsibility for the
Forensic Child Custody Specialist**

- Responsibility to children
- Responsibility to the courts
- Responsibility to the highest ethical and professional practice standards

---

on child custody evaluation did not spend more time describing the tenuous, frightened world of the child whose family is in transition. Understanding—indeed, picturing—a 7-year-old child's emotional upheaval over losing her safety and security through the process of divorce and then having to be subjected to a forensic evaluation is a painful reality. Those of us who engage in forensic child custody evaluations must remember to *never lose sight of the child*. Our evaluation is focused on finding what is in the child's psychological best interests. There is no cookbook, no convenient plastic overlay that can work for every child. Our ethical responsibility and, in my judgment, our moral charge is to use every means available in providing a state-of-the-art assessment of the child, the parents, and the resulting fit.

The second idea is that custody evaluators need to take seriously the criteria for the admission of expert testimony in legal proceedings. It is predicted that the recent holding from the U.S. Supreme Court decision in *Daubert v. Merrell Dow Pharmaceuticals*, 1135. Ct. 2786 (1993) will set a higher, more scientific standard for custodial evaluations. The *Daubert* holding has redefined judicial standards for qualifying experts and examining their methods and procedures (Goodman-Delahunty, 1997). Its relevance for custody evaluators is that our methods and procedures may need to meet a higher standard of judicial scrutiny.

The third idea is the ethical standard that forensic mental health professionals are required to perform at the *highest* level of their professional competency (Committee on Ethical Guidelines for Forensic Psychologists, 1991). Child custody evaluations are an interdisciplinary undertaking, drawing on academic and applied knowledge from such areas as psychology, law, sociology, and family studies. They are also public works that directly affect the lives of children and their families. Yet there has been a hesitancy among professionals to adequately or properly address child custody evaluations with an up-to-date, integrated understanding of the behavioral science literature.

Mental health professionals have been slow in responding to the need for more empirically based, rationally constructed interview and assessment protocols designed to guide the evaluation process. In the words of Black and

Cantor (1989), "Most custody determinations are made poorly. . . . Arrangements for a child's custody can be a staggeringly complex task. Some investigators make custody decisions badly, too many others fall back on convenient presumptions to avoid making decisions at all" (pp. xi-xii).

These three ideas about our responsibility to children, our responsibility to the courts, and our responsibility to maintain the highest of professional standards form the philosophical backbone of this book.

Children and the Custody Process

More than one million children per year are involved in their parents' divorce proceedings (Hoffman, 1991). This has resulted in many children's futures being decided by the courts. As their mothers and fathers fight over where the children will sleep, who will take them during Christmas, and which school district offers greater possibilities for growth and development, the children are left adrift in a sea of confusion. They are torn by feelings of betrayal, disloyalty, and bewilderment.

The security and safety of home life, which *should* be the inalienable right of every child, has suddenly become a whirlwind of questions and fear. Children are deeply affected by the breakup of their family. Their lives are profoundly altered by the anger, disappointment, and failure that characterizes their parents' marital breakdown. The child feels a loss of control over his or her environment. Suddenly, there is a group of strangers with whom they must talk, tests to take, and a judge who talks about choosing between mommy and daddy.

The current judicial system attempts to find justice in a fundamentally unjust situation. Children of divorce want their parents to kiss and make up. They do not want to live a life divided between every other weekend and Tuesday nights at Dad's. They want their parents to stop pretending to be mad at each other and to live together again.

Of course, parents seldom reconcile once divorce action has been filed. Marriages end, and children living in those marriages learn quickly—unfairly, maybe—that the world is changing constantly. For many children, this change teaches them their world is unsafe, insecure, and unstable. They learn that parents leave, relationships end, and loving someone—in the carefree, open, wonderful way that children love parents—can be dangerous. These children hold tightly within themselves their feelings of love, security, and importance. They have learned that to give their love so freely, so innocently, so fully to their mother and father has resulted in one of their parents leaving. Some children blame themselves for the marital breakup. Others blame their parents. Still others blame "mommy's boyfriend" or "daddy's girlfriend."

It is an awesome task to protect these children and make judgments about their best interests. We—the judges, lawyers, and mental health professionals involved in custody determinations—are only journeymen in the lives of these people. We hope our training, wisdom, and clarity of observations may provide accurate and appropriate information useful in making determinations about what will be in a child's best interest. They are, in the end, only judgments. They are not truths. They are not facts.

The very nature of our legal system places each professional in peculiar situations. Lawyers are asked to advocate for a particular side in a divorce case regardless of their personal belief about the fitness of the parent to serve the best interest of the child.

Mental health professionals are asked to offer opinions based upon limited data collected under exceptional circumstances. Each of us knows that the parent being evaluated is putting his or her best foot forward. Each child is being influenced, subtly or otherwise, to communicate a desire to live with one parent or the other. Our job is *not* to be swayed by who we like or dislike but by the relevant factors contributing to a positive environment for the child. The temptation to allow our countertransference to impose itself on the process is, at times, powerful. We are, after all, human beings with likes, dislikes, and personal opinions. However, our professional responsibility is to be driven by the data, not by our whims.

Finally, the judges, who are motivated by their sincere and passionate concern for social order and responsibility, are asked to render judgement about the best interests of the child despite not knowing the child. Theirs is the supreme balancing act, listening for information and relevant facts within a sea of game-playing, positioning, and accumulation of irrelevant facts made to look important.

The shame of it all is that if the marriage had remained viable, there would be no question about who is the better parent. Parenting values, skills, limitations, and advantages would be wrapped up tightly in family functioning. Mother and father would balance each other's strengths and weaknesses. The divorce, however, forces decisions about who is the better parent upon the family as it grapples with its reorganization after divorce.

Most married parents live with the positives and negatives of their spouse's parenting skills. Custody disputes force us to develop simplified lists of parenting pros and cons for each spouse. From this list, the judge is asked to choose which parent is "better." The legal system forces us to lose sight of how the intact family system balanced its strengths and weaknesses, and it compels us to make judgments about who is the better parent during the most tumultuous period in this family's life. Most of us know that dividing what was previously a whole results in something less than whole. The kids lose. The parents lose. And, in a far greater sense, our society loses because we

QUICK REFERENCE   **Changes in Forensic**
                   Child Custody Practice

Child custody evaluators need to be familiar with numerous changes in a
variety of different applied and academic disciplines.

• Changes in mental health practice
• Changes in civil forensic mental health practice
• Maintenance of a current library of research, practice, and case law
• Comprehension of rules governing expert witness testimony applied
  to mental health professionals
• Proficiency in court protocol
• Awareness of and sensitivity to protecting the civil rights of parents
  and their children

raise children who have skewed ideas about maleness, femaleness, family life,
and marriage.

Yet in determining where children should live, and with whom, we cannot
turn to the people whose interests are most highly prominent—the parents.
There is a built-in conflict of interest. Few parents would be bold enough to
provide the court with an honest evaluation of their parenting abilities and
skills if it put at risk either their relationship with their children or their custodial rights.

So, it is left, in large part, to the mental health professionals who have
been used by the courts to help determine appropriate placement for children
of divorce. Mental health professionals who conduct child custody evaluations must remain objective and provide compassionate yet unbiased and
thorough investigations into the psychological needs of the child.

> Considering what is at stake in making such decisions, the mental health pro-
> fessional carries a heavy responsibility to provide an evaluation that is at once
> compassionate and dispassionate, soundly based and firm but not inflexible.
> The quality of a child's life hangs in the balance. (Schutz, Dixon, Linden-
> berger, & Ruther, 1989, p. xi)

One of the fastest growing areas of professional involvement is child custody dispute resolution. Whether through mediation interventions, divorce
counseling, or child custody evaluations, mental health professionals find
themselves more involved in the divorce process than ever before. There are
several factors that drive the need for continued education and reformulation

of the custody evaluation process. Listed below are some of the reasons that the knowledge base for forensic custody evaluations needs to be revised continually.

Changes in Mental Health Practice

Forensic child custody evaluations are an area of increasing participation by mental health professionals. Two forces appear to be driving this change. First, mental health professionals who have traditionally engaged in clinical practice are finding that the downward pressure on costs resulting from managed care is forcing many to seek more diversified practice opportunities. Currently, forensic work is not subject to the cost containment measures of more traditional clinical work. The bottom line is that there is money available for services without interference from outside monitoring agencies telling clinicians how to practice their trade.

Second, courts are seeking expert opinions more often from mental health professionals on a wide range of psycholegal issues. An expert child custody evaluator can provide valuable information to the trier of fact upon which relevant custody and visitation decisions are made.

With increasing participation comes increasing exposure and liability. The fastest growing area of psychological malpractice suits is child custody work. In large part, this is the result of well-intentioned clinicians stepping into the forensic arena without understanding the complex differences between clinical and forensic work. The result is the unknowing violation of professional practice guidelines and ethical principles as well as litigants' civil rights.

Changes in Forensic Practice

There has been an explosion of information about the role and responsibilities of the forensic mental health professional. The economics and business of forensic practice differ significantly from those of clinical practice. The forensic specialist needs to follow the ethical principles and professional code of conduct guiding his or her respective professional behavior *and more*.

The role of the forensic specialist is qualitatively different from that of the clinician, yet it is only recently that these differences have received conceptual and empirical examination (Greenberg & Shuman, 1997; Weissman, 1991a). Forensic child custody specialists are expected to respect and follow the recommendations of their profession with regard to how to conduct themselves and their work product. For example, in the field of psychology, the competent specialist is directed by the American Psychological Association's (APA; 1994) "Guidelines for Child Custody Evaluations in Divorce Proceedings" and the "Specialty Guidelines for Forensic Psychologists" (Committee on Ethical Guidelines, 1991).

Of particular importance is the position taken by the "Specialty Guidelines" on professional responsibility: "Forensic psychologists have an obligation to provide services in a manner consistent with the *highest* [italics added] standards of their profession. They are responsible for their own conduct and the conduct of those individuals under their direct supervision" (Committee on Ethical Guidelines, 1991, p. 657).

The professional responsibility that forensic practitioners have to themselves, their clients, their profession, and the public at large is to perform at the highest level of competence. This is an awesome responsibility to carry. It means that we carry an obligation for maintaining state-of-the-art knowledge about research, practice, case law, and a variety of other critically important psycholegal factors.

Skilled forensic evaluators are expected to be knowledgeable and proficient in other types of forensic evaluations that may frequently accompany child custody evaluations. Specifically, knowledge of the issues, methods, procedures, and research pertaining to evaluation of sexual abuse within the context of child custody assessment is important. Therefore, one needs to be conversant with specialty and practice guidelines such as those published by the American Professional Society on the Abuse of Children (APSAC, 1995a, 1995b). There are also guidelines governing the evaluation of child and adolescent sexual abuse (American Academy of Child and Adolescent Psychiatry, 1988, 1997).

Changes in Research

The forensic specialist needs to be aware of changes in the literature in areas of child development, family systems, blended families, stepfamilies, custody and visitation outcome research, case law, and psycholegal precedents. For example, there is literature about the concept of the psychological parent (Ainsworth, 1979; Lamb, 1987)—how children at different developmental levels need to be matched with the parent whose demonstrated parenting capacities match the children's unique needs (Bray, 1991). There are changes in the role of fatherhood (Gould & Gunther, 1993) that have created changes in the constellation of the family (Blankenhorn, 1995). There is a rapidly expanding literature examining, among other critical factors, the effects of different custody/visitation arrangements on children's adjustment (Johnston, 1995) and on parental adjustment (Rohman, Sales, & Lou, 1987); a typology of domestic violence in custody disputes (Johnston & Campbell, 1993); parental alienation (Gardner, 1985, 1992, 1997); suggestibility of children's memory (Ceci & Bruck, 1995; Doris, 1991); clinical and forensic decision making (Borum, Otto, & Golding, 1993; Seman & Baumgarten,

1995); forensic interviewing techniques (Black & Cantor, 1989; Gardner, 1989b; Schutz et al., 1989); forensic use of psychological tests (Greenberg & Moreland, 1996); admissibility standards of scientific evidence (Goodman-Delahunty, 1997); move away concerns (Shear, 1996; Weissman, 1994); true sexual abuse allegations (Myers, 1994); false allegations of sexual abuse in custody disputes (Faller, 1993; Gardner, 1992); data-gathering and assessment tools designed for custody evaluations (Ackerman & Schoendorf, 1992; Bricklin, 1984, 1990); parenting styles (Maccoby & Mnookin, 1992); and visitation structures for high-conflict, postdivorce families (Garrity & Baris, 1994).

The competent child custody evaluator is responsible for maintaining a current library of literature addressing the major issues commonly presented for assessment.

Changes in Rules Governing Expert Witness Testimony

Among the most profound transformations affecting child custody evaluators are the rules governing expert witness testimony (Goodman-Delahunty, 1997). In *Frye v. United States,* 293F. 1013, D.C. Cir. (1923), the Supreme Court ruled that expert witness testimony was admissible when the data or techniques have been shown to have gained general acceptance in the scientific community.

In 1993, the Supreme Court again ruled on the admissibility of expert and scientific evidence. The new standard, referred to as the *Daubert* standard, held that judges are responsible for determining the degree to which the proffered evidence and its consistency and compliance with an underlying theory of science and scientifically based methods of assessment have been examined (Golding, 1994).

Some forensic scholars might argue, and rightly so, that the *Daubert* standard applies only to federal courts. State and local courts are still free to use the *Frye* standard. Others argue that *Daubert* applies only to pure science and not to social science, such as psychology or social work (Faigman, 1995). The important point for forensic specialists is that the standard of acceptable methodology is beginning to reflect our profession's long-held value of and belief in the use of empirically derived, scientifically based, psychometrically sound tools for the evaluation of human behavior (Goodman-Delahunty, 1997).

For too long, child custody evaluations have had the tinge of fiction presented as fact. Each of us has read reports (maybe even written a few, too) in which the majority of data presented were drawn from clinical interviews with no outside confirmation. Instead of using a multitrait-multimethod approach to data gathering, the evaluator presents a conclusion to the court

---

QUICK REFERENCE **Sample of Research Areas to Consider in Child Custody Practice**

- Children's adjustment to divorce
- Parental adjustment to divorce
- Changing role of fathers
- Economic impact of divorce on single-parent families
- Stepfamilies
- Blended families
- High-conflict, postdivorce families
- Domestic violence factors
- Suggestibility of children's memory
- Forensic interviewing techniques
- Forensic use of psychological tests
- Forensic decision-making variables
- Never-married parents
- Move away factors
- Parental alienation
- True and false allegations of sexual abuse
- Parenting styles
- Children's temperament
- Visitation structures in families of differing levels of conflict

---

based upon his or her *clinical* judgments derived from a single 2-hour interview with each parent, a 1-hour visit with each child, and an MMPI-2.

Under the *Daubert* standard, custody evaluators may be called upon to demonstrate to the court how the data gathered from the MMPI-2 and standard forensic interview protocols are related to psycholegal judgments about parenting capacity.

Court Protocol

Understanding how mental health professionals should interface with the legal system is a complex issue. The competent child custody evaluator will understand how to handle a referral properly, how to request a court appointment, and whether or not to address the ultimate issue. Do you know how to respond properly to a subpoena? Do you need an attorney of your own when you are deposed? Have you studied the literature about when to testify and how to testify? Are you prepared for cross-examination about the standardization procedures of the MMPI-2? Judicial protocol sometimes varies from jurisdiction to jurisdiction; are you familiar with protocol in each of the surrounding counties in which you work? It may also vary from judge to judge within the same jurisdiction. Are you familiar with differences among judges for whom you testify?

Parental and Child Civil Rights

A final area of preparation is exploring the civil rights of parents and children during a custody evaluation. With whom do you share information about the assessment? How is that information properly shared? For example, if a noncustodial parent brings his son into your office for an evaluation during Christmas vacation because he is concerned about possible maltreatment at the custodial home, do you accept the assessment? If you decide not to perform an evaluation, is it acceptable practice to see the child in therapy to ascertain the alleged level of maltreatment so that the father has some basis for filing a complaint with the custodial parent's state Department of Social Services? Do you know the rules in your state?

Summary

Undertaking competent forensic child custody evaluations is not simply an extension of clinical evaluation and decision making into a new forum. It is an intricate, sophisticated methodology integrating a large number of varying disciplines, each with its own literature base, conceptual frameworks, practice guidelines, and tests and measures.

The undertaking of these evaluations is an exciting area of professional growth and development, and it comes with an awesome responsibility—to keep up with the explosion of literature and methodological innovations through advanced training seminars, journal reading, professional consultation, and interdisciplinary collaboration.

TWO

The Role of the Forensic Child Custody Evaluator

Forensic psychologists have an obligation to provide services in a manner consistent with the *highest* standards of their profession.

Specialty Guidelines for Forensic Psychologists
(emphasis added)

Over the past three decades, classic gender-based concepts of parental fitness (i.e., tender years doctrine and maternal preference) have been replaced with custodial considerations of the best interest of the child. The result has been an increasing pressure placed on the courts to make decisions about custodial responsibility that accurately reflect the best interest doctrine. Mental health professionals have been asked by the court to play a much more frequent and important role in providing information about the best psychological interests of the child (Goodman-Delahunty, 1997), yet little empirical research has guided the mental health professional in offering such opinions. As a result, the role of the forensic evaluator in child custody assessments has come under attack.

These attacks have come from professionals outside mental health as well as from within and entail multiple concerns. One concern is that the roles of clinician and forensic evaluator are poorly understood and often confused (Greenberg & Shuman, 1997). Dual role relationships are explicitly unethical, yet many mental health professionals engage in clinical treatment that is presented to the court as a forensic evaluation product. A second concern is that the opinions offered by forensic mental health professionals routinely exceed the limitations of empirically derived scientific knowledge (Melton, Petrila, Poythress, & Slobin, 1987). Third, evaluators both *use inappropriate*

QUICK REFERENCE   **Criticisms of the Child Custody Evaluation Process**

- Confusion between forensic and clinical roles
- Recommendations often exceed the data
- Recommendations often based on absent or faulty reasoning
- Inappropriate use and interpretation of assessment techniques
- Poor integration of data with established child development research
- Poorly written reports, confusing the data with the inferences drawn from those data
- Providing testimony that exceeds the limits of the data, goes beyond current empirical research, or is beyond the professional competencies of the testifying expert

assessment tools as well as inappropriately use assessment techniques and then present opinions to the court based on irrelevant, faulty, or invalid inferences (Brodzinsky, 1993; Heilbrun, 1995). A fourth criticism is the frequent lack of integration of established child development research into custodial recommendations. Another criticism is the poor quality of evaluation reports. Few evaluators prepare reports in which the observed behavioral data are clearly distinguished from the inferences drawn from that data, leaving the reader to guess where the observational data end and the inferences and conclusions begin. A sixth concern is that the testimony we provide to the court under the guise of science is too often based on intuition and clinical experience rather than empirical research. These opinions are often presented with a misleading degree of certainty, leading to the belief that our conclusions are far more valid than they really are.

There is a small, yet emerging literature addressing critical factors in custody evaluation, empirically determined factors associated with the best psychological interests of the child (Rohman et al., 1987), use and misuse of psychological testing (Brodzinsky, 1993; Heilbrun, 1995), impact of law reforms on custody determinations, and changes in visitation patterns (Kelly, 1994). There are also empirical and conceptual works examining the standards of professional practice (Ackerman & Ackerman, 1996, 1997; Keilin & Bloom, 1986), application of single-subject design concepts to custodial assessment (Schutz et al., 1989), assessment of parental capacity framed within the psycholegal concept of a competency assessment (Grisso, 1988), and structured behavioral assessment procedures (Marafiote, 1985).

Clinical Versus Forensic Roles

Recently, attention has been paid to the distinction between the roles of the clinician and the forensic specialist. This section reviews the relevant literature concerning the role of the forensic evaluator and provides a conceptual framework from which to develop your professional role.

Defining the Role of the Forensic Evaluator

What is the proper role of a forensic child custody specialist? Historically, there was little distinction between the ways in which mental health professionals conducted themselves in clinical settings and legal arenas. Over the past decade, there has been a growing concern about delineating the separate role of the clinician from that of the forensic evaluator. This is due, in part, to the emergence of forensic mental health as a unique specialty. For example, within the field of professional psychology, forensic psychology is a hybrid—part psychology, part law. As a means of guiding forensic specialists toward professional behavior that enhances the subspecialty's professional standards, status, and credibility, a set of aspirational guidelines was established (Committee on Ethical Guidelines, 1991). Its goal was to improve the quality of forensic psychological services (and may be useful to all disciplines involved in forensic mental health services) offered to individual litigants and the legal system.

Specialty Guidelines for Forensic Psychologists

The "Specialty Guidelines for Forensic Psychologists" (Committee on Ethical Guidelines, 1991) define forensic psychology as

> all forms of professional psychological conduct when acting, with definable foreknowledge, as a psychological expert on explicitly psycholegal issues, in direct assistance to the courts, parties to legal proceedings, correctional and forensic mental health facilities, and administrative, judicial, and legislative agencies acting in an adjudicative capacity. (p. 657)

Those considered within the aspirational definition are "psychologists who regularly engage in the practice of forensic psychology" (Committee on Ethical Guidelines, 1991, p. 657). Psychologists brought into a legal matter and who were not informed at the time of the delivery of professional mental health services that their efforts would be part of a legal proceeding are not considered acting in a forensic role. There are many experts in forensic ethics who would insist that a clinician *should* be able to anticipate how his or her professional services may become involved in a legal proceeding, and he or she has an obligation to conduct him- or herself in a manner consistent with the role of forensic specialist (Committee on Ethical Guidelines, 1991).

I believe that the spirit as well as the intent of the Guidelines is to make clear that *any* professional behavior having even the remotest chance of entering the legal system is bound to conform itself to the highest standards of forensic practice. Two reasons guide this belief. The first is that we have an obligation never to do harm. Mental health professionals who provide professional services that ultimately are used in a legal proceeding have an obligation to possess a "fundamental and reasonable level of knowledge of the legal and professional standards that govern their participation as experts in legal proceedings" (Committee on Ethical Guidelines, 1991, p. 658). Without such fundamental knowledge, it is possible that we may inadvertently compromise a person's civil rights, provide inadmissible testimony, or harm the therapeutic relationship. We may offer opinion testimony that reflects clinical intuition but does not conform to the admissibility of scientific evidence and therefore cannot be supported under the scrutiny of legal examination.

When we enter a professional relationship in which the object of our professional services is an individual involved in a custody dispute, we *always* (yes, I said *always*!) have an obligation to understand the legal, ethical, and professional implications of our involvement, our professional product, and our public statements. We need to know the formal legal boundaries governing our testimony. Different states often have different laws and statutes governing expert witness testimony. There are local rules as well as informal, court-specific rules in different jurisdictions. What may be considered useful to one judge may be considered an infringement of judicial authority in another (e.g., providing of testimony about the ultimate issue).

A cursory perusal of current malpractice allegations against psychologists indicates that the second most frequent category *and* the fastest growing area of complaints lies in forensic child custody work. This is due, in part, to increasing numbers of mental health professionals stepping into the forensic arena with little or no training. There are few, if any, professional gatekeeper functions that identify those professionals competent to engage in forensic evaluations or provide testimony to the court. One's forensic competence is often discovered *during* testimony or upon submission of a professional work product.

Ours is an increasingly litigious society, and zealous clinicians are often too willing to provide testimony to the court that supports their patient's contention in a lawsuit. Such behavior is clearly inappropriate. Our proper role is to provide testimony that will assist the trier of fact to understand the evidence or determine a fact. Forensic specialists do not take sides. We do not give testimony specifically designed to offer support for one side or the other. We advocate an objective, data-driven opinion. We not only clearly describe to the court the theoretical foundation, empirical data, and inferences that lead us to our conclusions, but we also offer reasoning about alternative, competing hypotheses that may also fit the data.

Differences Between Therapeutic Care and Forensic Examination Relationships

There are a number of critical differences between the role of the clinician and that of the forensic specialist. The different roles require different conceptual models revolving around the patient-therapist relationship and the forensic specialist-litigant relationship. The reader is referred to Greenberg and Shuman's (1997) excellent article for a more detailed explanation. In their article, Greenberg and Shuman identify 10 differences between a clinical-therapeutic role and that of a forensic examiner (see Table 2.1).

Whose Client Is the Patient/Litigant?

In the case of the clinician, the client is the patient. The clinician ultimately is answerable to the patient. It is the patient who hires the clinician and decides whether to use (or continue to use) such services.

The forensic examiner has the court as his or her client. He or she is hired by the court or by an attorney. The party being evaluated is the attorney's client, not the evaluator's. The examiner ultimately is answerable to the court.

Having the court or an attorney as a client maintains a distance between the examiner and the litigant that is not present in a patient-therapist relationship. The legal definition of what is to be evaluated is determined by the attorney or the court. The exchange of monies is between the attorney or court and the examiner. The exchange of work product is between the examiner and the attorney or court.

Who Holds the Privilege?

The constitutional right to privacy includes a psychotherapist-patient relationship (*In re Lifschutz*, 1970). The privilege is owned by the patient, *not* the therapist. When a patient releases a therapist from the privilege, the therapist is allowed to share the information the patient has released to some specified third party.

There is no patient-therapist privilege in a forensic evaluation. There is no therapist, and there is no patient. There is a forensic evaluator who, after being hired by a court or attorney, examines the litigant. The relationship that does exist is between litigant and attorney. It does not extend to any relationship the forensic evaluator has with the litigant.

When the examiner is hired by one side in a legal dispute, the examiner's relationship may be governed by attorney work product privilege. Again, the privilege is owned by the attorney, *not* the forensic examiner. When the

TABLE 2.1 Irreconcilable Differences Between Therapeutic Care and Forensic Examination Relationships

	Therapeutic Care	Forensic Examination	Basic Conflict
1. Whose client is patient/litigant?	Mental health practitioner	Attorney or court	Role
2. Relational privilege governing disclosure in each relationship	Therapist-patient	Attorney-client or attorney-work product privilege	Role
3. Cognitive set and evaluative attitude of each expert	Supportive, accepting, empathic	Neutral, objective, detached	Role
4. Nature and degree of alliance in each relationship	Helping relationship, allies; rarely adversarial	Evaluative relationship; frequently adversarial	Role
5. Differing areas of competency of each expert	Therapy techniques for treatment of the impairment	Forensic examination techniques relevant to the legal claim	Foundation
6. Nature of the hypotheses tested by each expert	Diagnostic criteria for the purpose of therapy	Psycholegal criteria for the purpose of legal adjudication	Foundation
7. Amount and control of structure in each relationship	Patient-structured and relatively less structured than forensic examination	Examiner-structured and relatively more structured than therapy	Foundation

8. Scrutiny applied to information used in the process and the role of historical truth	Based mostly on information from person being treated, with little external scrutiny of that information by the therapist	Litigant information supplemented with and verified by collateral sources and scrutinized by the examiner, adversaries, and the court	Foundation
9. Goal of each professional in each relationship	Therapist attempts to benefit the patient by working within the therapeutic relationship	Examiner advocates for the results and implications of the evaluation for the benefit of the court	Role
10. Impact of each relationship of critical judgment by expert	Basis of relationship is the therapeutic alliance, and critical judgment is likely to impair that alliance	Basis of relationship is evaluative, and critical judgment is less likely to cause serious emotional harm	Role

SOURCE: Adapted with permission from Greenberg and Shuman (1997). Copied with permission from Greenberg and Brodsky (in press), *The Civil Practice of Forensic Psychology*. Washington, DC: American Psychological Association.

examiner is appointed by the court, the privilege is held by the court rather than the forensic examiner.

Attitudes and Beliefs Toward the Patient/Litigant

How we approach the individual with whom we are working is an important step in the establishment and maintenance of a productive relationship. The clinician approaches the patient with an attitude of support, acceptance, compassion, unconditional positive regard, and lack of judgment. The beliefs of the clinician are often focused on helping the patient to change, to learn new behaviors, or to improve some aspect of his or her life.

The forensic evaluator approaches the litigant with an attitude of objectivity, detachment, and impartiality. The forensic examiner is neutral in feeling and attitude toward the litigant. His or her job is not to help change the litigant's current situation but to make a dispassionate, objective assessment of the issue at hand and to communicate those facts and opinions to the court.

This is not to say that we treat litigants poorly. We treat them with respect and understand the exceptional emotional challenges they may face in enduring a custody challenge. However, no matter how strongly we may feel on a personal level about the issues at hand, no matter how much we may like the litigants on one side and dislike the litigants on the other side, it is imperative that our professional attitude and beliefs focus us on a neutral, impartial, objective, fair, and dispassionate evaluation.

In those instances—rare as they may be—when we may lose our professional perspective and find our personal feelings intruding into the evaluation, we have an ethical obligation to withdraw, inform the court or attorney, and possibly refund fees already paid. These issues would be best discussed with the chairperson of the state psychological association's ethics committee, other forensic colleagues, or other professionals from whom you seek advice.

Different Areas of Competence

The clinician is expert in therapy techniques. He or she is also expert in differential diagnosis and treatment of different clinical categories of behavior. The focus is on change and the patient's subjective report of improvement.

The forensic evaluator is expert in evaluation techniques relevant to psycholegal categories of behavior that are directly related to the legal claim. The focus is on discovery of facts and the objective reporting of the status of those facts.

Hypothesis Generation

The clinician generates hypotheses for testing based upon the patient's subjective report of distress. The hypotheses should correspond to observed behaviors that are consistent with diagnostic categories. The formulation of these hypotheses within diagnostic categories leads directly to treatment options.

The forensic evaluator generates hypotheses for testing based upon specific psycholegal criteria presented to him or her by the court or attorneys. These hypotheses are directly tied to answering the psycholegal questions to be adjudicated. They often do *not* lead to diagnosis or treatment interventions. They should lead to the accumulation of facts directly related to answering the psycholegal questions posed by the court or attorney.

How Information Is Used

The clinician accepts information from the patient with little, if any, concern for collaterally supported facts. The patient's reality is the focus of the therapist's work. The clinician seldom seeks outside corroboration of the patient's story, choosing instead to work with the gestalt presented within the therapy office.

For the forensic evaluator, the perspective of the litigant is somewhat secondary to the larger concern of determining the reality of that perspective. The forensic examiner accepts information from the litigant as well as supplementary sources, referred to as collateral sources. In the case of child custody evaluations, forensic examiners seek information from other primary child caretakers, teachers, pediatricians, community agencies, the Department of Social Services, former and concurrent therapists, and so on. The forensic specialist *always* seeks independent confirmation of litigant-presented facts. These collateral sources of information are scrutinized by the evaluator, the attorneys, and the court.

Who Structures and Controls the Relationship?

The clinician and the patient work together to create a therapeutic structure conducive to change. The patient often directs the content, and the therapist directs the structure of therapy. The patient and therapist together decide how many sessions will be needed to reach therapeutic goals. The patient is free to end therapy when he or she wants.

The forensic evaluator provides the structure of the evaluation. Specific steps are taken that are intended to gather a similar set of data on each litigant in a custody dispute. Although the content of the evaluation sessions may vary from litigant to litigant, the fundamental structure is controlled by the examiner. There are often a minimal number of sessions that may be enlarged if the litigant and examiner see the need for more data gathering. The examiner is in charge of when the evaluation ends.

Character of the Relationship

The clinician's posture regarding the patient is based upon a helping relationship. It is understanding, curative, empathic, nonjudgmental, and nonadversarial. When the clinician confronts a patient over discrepancies in behavior, attitudes, or feelings, it is for the purpose of facilitating change.

The forensic examiner's posture regarding the litigant is based on an evaluative relationship. Its purpose is to gather facts, make judgments, confront discrepancies, and, when necessary, be adversarial. When the examiner confronts the litigant over discrepancies, it is for the purpose of discovering the true facts.

Goal of the Professional

The primary goal of the clinician is to assist the patient in the relief of distress or improving the quality of life. Another is to cure the patient of a mental disease. In either case, the professional is dedicated to working within the therapeutic relationship to benefit the patient.

The primary goal of a forensic evaluator is to discover facts and form opinions about specific psycholegal questions that are then presented to the court. The examiner advocates for the data, inferences, and conclusions drawn from an examination. The work product is to benefit the trier of fact with a better understanding of the issues before the court.

Role of Critical Judgment

The patient-therapist relationship is predicated upon the strength of the therapeutic alliance between helper and helpee. It is focused on helping to facilitate patient change through the establishment of a confidential, non-judgmental environment that encourages exploration, growth, and mutual trust. Critical evaluation and judgment often cause harm to the therapeutic alliance.

The evaluator-litigant relationship is based upon evaluation and judgment. It is predicated on the belief that the evaluator is able to determine facts based upon a thorough assessment of litigant claims and collateral information. It is a fact-gathering, judgment-producing endeavor in which critical judgment is unlikely to cause serious emotional harm.

Ethics and the Law

The American Psychological Association has been consistent in its concern for maintaining a separation between clinical and forensic roles. For example, the "Ethical Principles of Psychologists and Code of Conduct" of the American Psychological Association (1992) states that "in most circumstances, psychologists avoid performing multiple and potentially conflicting roles in forensic matters" (p. 1610).

Similarly, the Specialty Guidelines discourage engaging in dual professional roles.

Forensic psychologists recognize potential conflicts of interest in dual relationships with parties to a legal proceedings, and they work to minimize their effects. . . . Forensic psychologists avoid providing professional services to parties in a legal proceeding with whom they have personal or professional relationships that are inconsistent with the anticipated relationship. (Committee on Ethical Guidelines, 1991, p. 659)

Other professions have also encouraged their members to avoid dual role relationships between clinician and forensic examiner. Two such organizations are the American Academy of Child and Adolescent Psychiatry and the Association of Family and Conciliation Courts.

However, the line between dual role relationships can sometimes be unclear. For example, if you have completed a forensic custody examination and are asked by the court to coordinate treatment programs with cooperating therapists, does this constitute a role conflict? If the court orders you to perform therapy after completion of an evaluation, what do you do? If the court appoints you after completion of your evaluation to reevaluate the family after 2 years, is that a dual role? If the court asks you to develop more specific parenting plans in order to implement your custodial recommendation, is that a dual role?

There are no clear rules. These situations require judgment as well as consultation with other colleagues and possibly with your state association ethics chairperson.

Turning to case law provides little guidance. As a general statement, there are no judicial decisions to date about dual role concerns when the forensic specialist takes on the role of a therapist or when therapists assume the role of evaluator. In my experience, it is not uncommon for a judge to accept testimony from a treating therapist and then ask for a custody opinion. Worse, therapists are often too willing to offer such opinions.

The result is that mental health professionals sometimes offer testimony to the court that oversteps ethical boundaries. Such testimony is not illegal. Judges probably will view the testimony in terms of its weight or credibility. Although such testimony may be admissible in particular courts, it is likely that such testimony constitutes a breach of ethical conduct.

Professional Practice Among Experienced Evaluators

More than a decade ago, Keilin and Bloom (1986) reported on the practical aspects of the evaluation process practiced by experienced examiners. They found that custody evaluators prefer to be appointed by the court or serve as an impartial evaluator. However, in actual practice, the examiner is retained as an impartial evaluator only about half the time.

TABLE 2.2 **Comparison of 1986 and 1996 Evaluator Practices**

	Keilin and Bloom (1986)	Ackerman and Ackerman (1996)
Average hours per evaluation		
Total hours per evaluation	18.8	26.4
Adult individual interview	2.0	4.7
Child individual interview	1.5	2.7
Percentage administering psychological tests		
Adult administrations	75	98
Child administrations	75	92
Tests most frequently used in adult evaluations		
MMPI-2	70.7%	91.5%
Rorschach	41.5%	47.8%
WAIS-R	29.3%	42.8%
MCMI	—	34.4%
Tests most frequently used in child evaluations		
Intelligence testing	45.1%	58.2%
CAT	38.0%	36.8%
Bricklin Scales (BPS)	—	34.8%
Sentence Completion	12.2%	29.4%
Costs for evaluation services		
Total cost of evaluation (average)	$1,700	$2,650
Average cost per in-office hour	$90	$121
Average cost per court time hour	$115	$155

In a replication of the Keilin and Bloom study, Ackerman and Ackerman (1996, 1997) reported changes in current practice. Table 2.2 summarizes some results of the two studies. In the 1996 sample, 84.6% reported that they preferred to be appointed by the courts or a *guardian ad litem*. There was an increase in the number of hours spent on evaluations, from 19 hours in 1986 to more than 26 hours in 1996. It appears that today's evaluators are spending more time reviewing materials and more than twice as much time writing reports as they did 10 years ago.

Children are evaluated today using a variety of techniques; the most frequently used are intelligence tests, CAT, the Bricklin Scales, a Sentence Completion Test, achievement tests, Rorschach, and projective drawings. Adult litigants were most often administered the MMPI or MMPI-2, Rorschach, WAIS-R, MCMI-II or MCMI-III, TAT, Sentence Completion Test, and the ASPECT.

Approximately 31% of the sample used both a version of the MMPI and the MCMI. Four of the top nine tests reported to be widely used in the 1996 sample were not available in 1986.

Fees were higher in the 1996 sample. The average hourly fee was about $121, with court appearance fees averaging $155. The range for a complete evaluation was $650 to $15,000, with the average cost about $2,650.

A full retainer was required prior to testing by more than 50% of respondents. Only 5.1% required no retainer before testing. When the evaluator needed to testify in court, 83% required full payment prior to testimony. A more complete discussion of the Ackerman and Ackerman (1996, 1997) study results is presented in Chapter 11.

THREE

Expert Testimony
and Presentation of
Scientific Evidence

What I have learned is that for some potential expert witnesses, the prospect of ever testifying in court is frightening.
. . . For still other expert witnesses, testifying is a time of professional mastery, occasionally elation, a chance to explain
and defend their knowledge in a public forum. . . . At its best,
testifying in court is a time of exhilaration at meeting this intellectual and professional challenge.

Stanley L. Brodsky (1991, p. xi)

"Is it your testimony, doctor, that you are suggesting primary custody— both
physical and legal—to the mother?"
"Yes."
"Is it your testimony that the father should have limited visitation?"
"Yes."
"Tell the court how you came to these conclusions, Dr. Dowling."
"The psychological tests I administered to each parent reveal conclusively
that Mrs. Kaye is psychologically healthy. There is nothing on her MMPI-2
profile to suggest she would be a poor parent or present a risk to her child.
Further, results from the Rorschach test supported my conclusion that Mrs.
Kaye would be a good parent because her personality attributes are healthy.
She is fundamentally an emotionally sound person and a good parent."
"And Mr. Kaye, Doctor?"
"Mr. Kaye's test results show him to be highly defensive, very suspicious
of others around him, suspicious of authority, and angry over having to fol-
low social rules. His Rorschach responses also show him to be an emotionally
unhealthy individual who would not be as good of a parent to Justine as Mrs.
Kaye."

"Dr. Dowling, you have drawn your conclusions based upon the results of these psychological tests. Is that correct?"

"Yes."

"What data can you provide to the court that shows how use of the MMPI-2 can predict parenting capacity?"

"Excuse me?"

"I said, how do you know the MMPI-2 can predict how well a person can parent?"

"Mr. Gaspari, I have fifteen years of clinical experience to back up my conclusions. Whenever a patient scores as highly on the K-scale—that is, whenever someone is as defensive as Mr. Kaye was in taking the test—it is a clear sign that something is wrong. When I looked further, the elevation on two basic scales—Pd and Pa—just jumped out at me. They were above the cutoff for statistical significance. Each was around a T score of 70. That means that the scores were substantially different than the normal population."

"Dr. Dowling, are you familiar with the forensic use of the MMPI-2 in court?"

"I have studied the use of the MMPI-2. When I was in graduate school, I studied the MMPI in two courses on personality assessment."

"Did those courses address the forensic use of the MMPI?"

"No, the forensic use of a test is no different than the clinical use of a test. Results are results."

"Would you be surprised to learn that common forensic practice is to expect high K-scale scores when conducting an evaluation for the court?"

"Mr. Gaspari, these results were above the level of significance . . ."

"Doctor, the fact is that you don't know how to use the MMPI-2 in a forensic setting. You have never studied the application of the MMPI-2 in child custody evaluations and you do not know the literature cautioning professionals about the lack of validity in using such tests in a forensic context."

"Mr. Gaspari, the MMPI is a valid test. It has been researched for years and is probably the most widely used personality test in the world."

"Dr. Dowling, that all may be true. But the test was not developed for use in a forensic context, was it?"

"No, I don't believe so."

"The test has little data about its validity with custody litigants, isn't that true, too?"

"I don't know."

"I beg your pardon? You don't know. Doctor, you have based at least part of your opinion about Mr. and Mrs. Kaye's parenting capacity on the results of this test and you now tell the court you are not sure if the test is valid for use with this population."

"I guess I am agreeing with you, Mr. Gaspari."

"To the best of your knowledge, does the MMPI-2 predict parenting capacity?"

"Mr. Gaspari, I believe it does."

"Have you ever read any research supporting your unsubstantiated belief?"

"No."

"Now, let's move on the your use of the Rorschach. Dr. Dowling, you draw conclusions from the Rorschach about Mr. Kaye's parenting capacity. What evidence is there that the inferences drawn from the Rorschach tell us anything about parenting?"

* * * * *

One important forensic role is to provide testimony that may assist the court in determining what is in the child's best interest. This is referred to as *expert witness testimony*. There are specific rules governing expert witness testimony drawn from the Federal Rules of Evidence (FRE), case law, as well as state laws and rules of evidence. The box below summarizes different types of evidence.

Types of Evidence

- Relevant evidence: Federal Rule of Evidence 401
- Probative evidence: Federal Rule of Evidence 403
- Prejudicial evidence: Federal Rule of Evidence 403
- Substantive evidence
- Rehabilitative evidence

Federal Rule of Evidence 401 defines relevant evidence as "evidence having any tendency to make the existence of any fact that is of consequence to the determination of the action more probable or less probable than it would be without evidence" (Meyer, 1993, p. 9). The evidence provided by an expert witness must provide some fact or set of facts that the court does not possess. The role of the expert witness is to provide information or opinions not generally known to the average person or judge. It is expert precisely because it is not general knowledge.

Probative Versus Prejudicial Evidence

Federal Rule of Evidence 403 addresses the probative versus prejudicial value of the testimony. Probative value is evidence that supports an issue. Prejudicial value is evidence that leans toward one side of a cause based upon outside influence or for some reason other than a conviction of its justice (Greenberg, 1996).

Federal Rule of Evidence 403 serves a gatekeeping function. It allows into the record information that provides proof or contributes to the establishment of proof. It prohibits testimony that may have a prejudicial effect on the trier of fact.

Federal Rules of Evidence 401 and 403 are concerned with the evidence. An expert witness needs to have a fundamental knowledge of what testimony is admissible and what is not. There needs to be a logical association between your expert testimony and the facts of the case. Experts are not expected to be authorities on the Rules of Evidence. However, it is critical that experts enter a courtroom with a basic knowledge of what will and will not be considered admissible testimony. This may vary from state to state. It is imperative that you know the particular rules of evidence in the jurisdiction in which you are testifying.

Types of Evidence

Substantive Evidence

There are two types of evidence that can be offered in court: substantive evidence and rehabilitation testimony. Substantive evidence proves or supports facts. Information offered in court to prove that a parent acts in the best interest of the child is considered substantive evidence. For example, substantive evidence might consist of the parent's positive attachment to a child, quality of communication, impulsiveness, personality dysfunction, or interparental conflict. Substantive evidence might also be a pediatrician's medical records showing signs of physical abuse, teacher reports of academic achievement, or day care workers' observations.

Substantive evidence from an evaluator may take several forms. You may offer testimony about your *opinion* regarding a number of custody-related issues. You may offer *diagnostic* information, although providing a diagnosis is often irrelevant in custody evaluations unless there is concern about the impact of psychopathological behavior on parenting capacity. Expert witnesses may present *specialized knowledge*. For example, expert witness testimony might take the form of educating the court in theoretical concepts of child development or research on child adjustment to separation and divorce. Experts may also provide testimony about behaviors associated with parent alienation, issues about repressed memory and sexual abuse, and a variety of other relevant concerns. Whatever the nature of the information provided to the court, if it provides the trier of fact with specialized knowledge, it is considered substantive evidence (Myers, 1996).

Addressing the Ultimate Issue

There is considerable controversy over whether evaluators should provide testimony about the ultimate issue. Evaluators provide information, observations, inferences, conclusions, prognoses, and hypotheses to be used by the court in making a decision. Evaluators are not, in my judgment, empowered by professional practice standards or ethical guidelines to make direct comment on the ultimate issue. Evaluators serve the court through the provision of expert mental health testimony. The ultimate issue may include important psychological factors about which we are competent to testify. However, it often includes legal, financial, medical, and other areas of expertise that are outside the professional competencies of most examiners.

Our role is not to usurp the decision-making power of the judge. We are experts, not judges. Judges make judgments. Experts offer informed opinions.

This is only one side of the issue. Those who advocate addressing the ultimate issue feel a sincere sense of responsibility to the court and argue that the end product of an evaluation should be a clear decision addressing the ultimate issue about custody. However, any time an opinion about an ultimate issue is offered, it needs to be framed *only* within the context of the psychological variables assessed.

In practice, addressing the ultimate issue varies from jurisdiction to jurisdiction. Some judges insist that only they will answer the ultimate issue. Other judges expect the expert to provide the court with an answer to the ultimate issue. There are few more humiliating times in court then when a judge turns to you and says, "You were paid to offer the court an opinion, so what is your opinion about who should have custody?"

Experience informs that you have to know your particular jurisdiction and the judges for whom you are crafting your report. The evaluator who steadfastly stands on the ethical notion that the ultimate issue should never be addressed might be acting consistently with the Specialty Guidelines. At the same time, in many jurisdictions, that same evaluator may never see another case from that judge again. Balancing these often-conflicting needs may require the mental health professional to guide the court and attorneys toward a better understanding of the ethical limitations of expert mental health testimony.

Rehabilitation Testimony

Testimony that is offered for the limited purpose of rehabilitating the credibility of another witness *after* he or she is examined by the defense attorney is referred to as *rehabilitation testimony*. Rehabilitation testimony is a balancing mechanism. According to Myers (1996), "Courts generally hold that expert rehabilitation testimony is not subject to the special rule governing scientific principles" (p. 333).

Types of Witnesses

There are two kinds of witnesses allowed to provide testimony in court: lay or fact witnesses and expert witnesses. Box 3.2 displays the types of witnesses and the Rules of Evidence that support them.

Types of Witnesses

- Fact witness: Federal Rule of Evidence 701
- Expert witness: Federal Rule of Evidence 702

Fact Witnesses

A fact witness is allowed to testify to facts about which he or she has direct observational knowledge. The fact witness is not allowed to provide opinion testimony. Federal Rule of Evidence 701 states that witness testimony is "limited to those opinions or inferences which are (a) rationally based on the perception of the witness and (b) helpful to a clear understanding of his testimony or the determination of a fact in issue."

This is an important issue for treating therapists to consider. Typically, treating therapists are admitted to testify as fact witnesses. Such testimony should be limited to observations of the therapeutic treatment. This limits testimony from the treating therapist to what he or she observed, to facts only. The treating therapist cannot provide a diagnosis, prognosis, or opinion about the effectiveness of therapy. These are all opinions and, by definition, are allowed into testimony only by those admitted as experts.

My recommendation is that when you are called upon to testify as a treating therapist, be qualified as an expert in your field of specialization. In this way, you will be on solid ground when testifying about opinions that go beyond your observations of the treatment.

However, there is a trap that you must avoid. When qualified as an expert in your role as a treating therapist, do not overstep your role and respond to questions about parenting capacity, custody determination, or visitation arrangements. Unless you have performed an objective, neutral evaluation, you should provide no information to the court when asked for an opinion about the child's best psychological interests. Although you may understand the child better than the evaluator, you have not completed an independent, comprehensive evaluation. Thus, addressing what is in the best psychological interests of the child may reach beyond the data you have as a treating therapist. Furthermore, there is great concern that in their enthusiasm to help either the court or the child, treating therapists who testify about the child's best psychological interests or custodial placement may be answerable to a state ethics probe. One possible way to offer opinions about observed parent-child interactions drawn from a treatment intervention rather than a forensic evaluation is to identify clearly to the court that the information offered is not intended as scientific testimony but is based upon your experience as a practicing mental health professional. As summarized by Gindes and Otto (1997), mental health professionals "should not offer opinions about non-psychological matters for which they have no specialized knowledge but which may, at the same time, be relevant to the custody decision" (p. 356).

Expert Witnesses

Federal Rule of Evidence 702 provides the framework for expert testimony.

> If scientific, technical, or other specialized knowledge will assist the trier of fact to understand the evidence or to determine a fact in issue, a witness qualified as an expert by knowledge, skill, experience, training, or education may otherwise testify thereto in the form of an opinion or otherwise.

Expertness is a judgment made by the trier of fact based upon the presentation of your knowledge, skill, experience, training, or education. You may have specialized skill or knowledge. You may consider yourself an expert in a field of study. However, the determination of who is an expert in a court of law is made by the judge.

Designation as an expert is not based solely upon the academic degree you hold. It may turn on the degree and quality of your experience. For example, in Massachusetts (*Commonwealth v. Monico,* 1986), the court held that the qualifications of a psychologist as an expert witness testifying about criminal responsibility is related more to his or her actual experience than to his or her academic degrees. Similarly, being board certified is not necessary to qualify as an expert in any state (*Campbell v. Pommier,* 1985).

Different states may have different rules governing expert witness admissibility. For example, in *People v. McDarrah* (1988), the State of Illinois ruled that a master's-level psychologist not registered in the state as a clinical psychologist was not qualified to testify as an expert. On the other hand, the State of North Dakota found that disqualification of a psychologist as an expert witness based solely upon not having a state psychology license was an abuse of judicial discretion (*Oberlander v. Oberlander*, 1990).

The seminal case that opened the door for psychologists to provide expert witness testimony was *Jenkins v. U.S.* (1962). Three important decisions were handed down in *Jenkins*. First, psychologists were judged to be qualified as experts in the area of mental disorders if doing so aided the trier of fact. The court ruled, "We hold only that the lack of a medical degree and the lesser degree of responsibility for patient care which mental hospitals usually assign to psychologists are not automatic disqualifications."

The second finding of the court was that qualifying depends on the nature and extent of the knowledge base and not upon the title of the professional. The *Jenkins* court ruled, "Anyone who is shown to have special knowledge and skill in diagnosing and treating human elements is qualified to testify as an expert, if his learning and training should show that he is qualified to give an opinion on the particular question at issue."

A logical conclusion drawn from the above statement is that the qualification of *who* is an expert is a decision made by the judge, not a quality embodied by the witness. The *Jenkins* court decided that it was fitting to admit testimony based, in part, upon accounts of others that are not in evidence, but that the expert habitually relies upon in the exercise of his or her profession. To sanction the use of expert testimony, two elements are required. First, the subject of the inference must be so distinctively connected to some science, profession, business, or occupation as to be beyond the ken of the average person. Second, the witness must have skill, knowledge, or experience in that area of expertise, leading the trier to fact to believe that he or she will probably be aided in his or her search for truth.

Most case law decisions have supported the use of psychologists and/or mental health professionals as expert witnesses (*Childs v. Williams*, 1992; *Commonwealth v. Monico*, 1986; *Horne v. Goodson*, 1986; *Marriage of Woffinden*, 1982). However, when we testify, we must use language that is understandable to the court (*Illinois Psychological Assn. v. Falk*, 1986/1987; *State v. Lafferty*, 1988).

There have been some decisions against the use of psychologists as expert witnesses (*GIW S Valve Co v. Smith*, 1985). In general, though, psychologists are viewed as valuable contributors of evidence (*Howle v. PYA/Monarch, Inc.*, 1986). Of course, there is nothing that says a trial court judge needs to accept our expert testimony (*McFadden v. United States*, 1987; *State v. Perkins*, 1986). Some judges may assign limited weight to our testimony. There is also some case law suggesting that the testimony of a psychiatrist may be given more weight than the testimony of other mental health professionals, such as a psychologist (*State v. Perry*, 1985).

QUICK REFERENCE　**Potential Conflict in
Expert Witness Role**

- Experts step outside their role and provide moral advocacy.
- Experts place undue weight on personal opinions presented as science.
- Experts are seldom qualified in specific areas of forensic expertise.
- Tension exists between scientific and judicial methodologies.
- Experts have few protections.
- Experts are viewed as whores of the courtroom.

Potential Conflict in the Roles of the Expert Witness

There is some controversy over the varying roles played by an expert witness in psychology and mental health. Golding (1994) suggests six areas of potential contention.

Experts Step Outside of Their Role and Provide Moral Advocacy

Some authors have argued that the role of an expert witness is limited. Experts typically step outside their limited role of providing expert testimony to the court and become advocates for social, political, or moral views. However, the message of social, political, or moral conformity is couched within the language of inferences extrapolated from empirically derived data, making the distinction between science and moral perspective difficult to ascertain.

The Specialty Guidelines (Committee on Ethical Guidelines, 1991) address this issue in a number of ways. First, within the area of professional competence, we are advised that "forensic psychologists recognize that their own personal values, moral beliefs, or personal and professional relationship . . . may interfere with their ability to practice competently" (p. 658). Second, within the area of public and professional communications, "forensic psychologists make reasonable efforts to ensure that the products of their services, as well as their own public statements and professional testimony, are communicated in ways that will promote understanding and avoid deception" (p. 663). Third, and still with the area of public and professional communications, when testifying, forensic psychologists have an obligation to all parties to a legal proceeding to present their findings, conclusions, evidence or other professional products in a fair manner. . . . Forensic psychologists do not, by either commission or omission, participate in a misrepresentation of their evidence. (p. 664)

Experts Place Undue Weight on Personal Opinions Presented as Science

Experts have often been criticized for overstepping the bounds of their expertise, providing opinions of a personal nature couched in the aura of empirical science. It is not uncommon for an attorney to lead the expert into statements that go beyond the data, resulting in placing undue weight on the obfuscated personal opinions of a witness offered within the guise of scientifically based opinion.

The Specialty Guidelines address concerns for prejudicial testimony under the area of competence. Competent "forensic psychologists are responsible for a fundamental and reasonable level of knowledge and understanding of the legal and professional standards that govern their participation as experts in legal proceedings" (p. 658). Evaluators have a responsibility to understand the limits and boundaries of their forensic work product, of which testimony is but one element. Therefore, knowing about Federal Rule of Evidence 403 governing prejudicial and probative evidence is a basic building block when entering the legal system.

Experts Are Seldom Qualified in Specific Areas of Forensic Expertise

The process of qualifying as an expert is often based upon a cursory review of academic credentials within the field of expertise in general, rather than the specific area of study (e.g., expert in psychology vs. expert in the psychology of children's adjustment after divorce). Too often, we are qualified as experts in child custody evaluations based upon how many evaluations have been done rather than an examination of the various skills that comprise a competent evaluator, such as child development, adult development, family functioning, psychological tests and measures, and so on.

The Specialty Guidelines provide a clear statement about our need to present clear and precise evidence to the trier of fact during qualifying.

Forensic psychologists have an obligation to present to the court, regarding the specific matters to which they will testify, the boundaries of their competence, the factual bases (knowledge, skill, experience, training, and education) for their qualification as an expert, and the relevance of those factual bases to their qualification as an expert on the specific matter at issue. (p. 658)

This is a particularly important concern. Research indicates that when a mock jury is presented with testimony from a layperson compared with testimony from an expert, the mock jurors tend to weight the expert witness testimony more heavily than the other testimony. Thus, we need to take great care that the testimony we provide to the court is an honest and accurate representation of the science. When opinions beyond the data are requested, our responsibility is to provide such opinions within the framework of working hypotheses. We offer the court our prevailing hypothesis, testifying to its usefulness as well as its shortcomings. We also have an obligation to provide alternative, competing hypotheses with their proper argument and limitations. As noted in the Specialty Guidelines, "the forensic psychologist maintains professional integrity by examining the issue at hand from all reasonable perspectives, actively seeking information which will differentially test plausible rival hypotheses" (p. 661).

Tension Exists Between Scientific and Judicial Methodologies

This is almost self-evident. The philosophy of science is based upon the idea that we continually discover different ways of examining a phenomenon. Science is about discovery, *not* truth. Law is about the discovery of truth. The language of science is the language of probability, significance levels, alternative hypotheses, and inferences drawn from data. The language of law is the language of facts and fact patterns (data) and conclusions (inferences). There is seldom room for the generation of alternative hypotheses based upon inferences. The law appears content to show how a particular fact pattern logically leads to a certain conclusion.

The fundamental epistemologies of psychology and law are often incompatible (Melton et al., 1987). Thus, "evidence production in an adversarial system is seen as incompatible with the basic tenets of scientific methods of evidence appraisal" (Golding, 1994, p. 18).

Experts Have Few Protections

Defense counsel's responsibility is to find holes in your testimony. This is done in a number of ways. The attorney may attack your methods, conclusions, premise, discipline, and/or data. It is his or her job to *zealously* advocate for the client, and if you or your testimony happens to be in the way of winning the case, his or her ethical responsibility is to do what he or she can to discredit your testimony.

The expert witness is often forced into statements about his or her work that may be self-incriminating. For example, you have offered as evidence interpretive data from the MMPI-2 and made statements about its relationship to behavioral correlates. You are unaware of the limited amount of research data on the behavioral correlates of the MMPI-2. You made the assumption that the results from the MMPI-2 were similar to the MMPI regarding behavioral correlates. Your testimony is based upon this mistaken assumption. The defense attorney has read Ziskin (1995) and has prepared a headache of a cross-examination for you. He or she accurately identifies your mistaken interpretation of the MMPI-2 and now aggressively questions your credibility in *all* aspects of your work.

There is no effective assistance of counsel, no effective representation at critical stages of the cross-examination, and no rehabilitative testimony. When you make a mistake, you are compelled to discuss it and take public responsibility for your choices. The cross-examination may border on personal indictments as defense counsel continues to remind the judge that if you made one mistake, then certainly you have made many, many more. When the questioning stops, you slink away from the witness stand and hide somewhere in a corner, hoping it was all a bad dream and that the evil defense attorney was simply a psychic representation of last night's spicy tacos.

Experts Are Viewed as Whores of the Courtroom

The final area of concern is the perception that expert witnesses are hired guns. There are some forensic specialists who may travel from courtroom to courtroom, selling their wares to the highest bidder, giving testimony that will support the side that pays the most (Hagen, 1997). However, most forensic specialists take their responsibility to the court and society very seriously. Nothing would dissuade these honorable practitioners from the appropriate use of their skill and knowledge. Yet it takes just one unscrupulous witness to poison the public's perception of our value. This is why we need to take our relationship and responsibility to the court very seriously. Our charge is to "make a reasonable effort to ensure that [our] services and the products of [our] services are used in a forthright and responsible manner" (Committee on Ethical Guidelines, 1991, pp. 657-658).

Evaluators are obligated to all parties in a legal proceeding to accurately and fairly present their

findings, conclusions, evidence, or other professional products. . . . This principle does not preclude forceful representation of the data and reasoning upon which a conclusion or professional product is based. It does, however, preclude an attempt, whether active or passive, to engage in partisan distortion or misrepresentation. (Committee on Ethical Guidelines, 1991, p. 664)

During a recent deposition in which my role was as a consultant to the father's attorney, the attorney for the defense asked how many parental competency evaluations I had conducted. I told him I had completed somewhere in the neighborhood of 50 such evaluations.

His eyes narrowed, and he called me a "hired gun." He stated, "No self-respecting, ethical evaluator would ever work for only one side in a custody dispute!"

I asked why. He told me that any time he had hired an expert to do an evaluation for one side, the results always favored his client. "That's what I pay them to do!" he exclaimed.

I explained that the majority of one-sided cases on which I have worked have yielded a positive finding for the attorney who hired me about 20% of the time. I said, "My role is to call the data clearly and accurately. If you think that I would compromise my professional integrity and commitment to professional standards, you are dead wrong. My professional obligation is to provide information to the court regardless of who hires me." Incidentally, I have also found that many family law attorneys genuinely are interested in knowing about their client's parenting capacity, even though that information may never make it into a court of law.

It is possible to work for one side or the other and still do an honest, responsible, competent, and ethical job. As long as you remember that the court is your client—no matter who hires you and who pays you—and that your fundamental concern is the best psychological interests of the child, you can work for one side. Objectivity, neutrality, fairness, and impartiality are qualities you carry with you no matter where you work. You decide not to compromise on maintaining these standards regardless of who pays the bill.

However, there is a genuine concern about the perception that the court may have of a one-sided evaluation. In a recent case in which I was hired by the attorney for the mother, I requested through the attorney to invite the other side to participate. Under the unusual circumstances of this case, my request was brought before the judge. The judge felt it unfair to order the other side to participate, and the attorney for the other side declined, too. When the case was completed, I spoke with the judge about feedback regarding my work product (a standard inquiry on my part to those judges who will provide the feedback). The judge stated that the report had a different "feel" to it. She stated that previous reports that incorporated both sides had a more balanced feel. This report felt like I was "a hired gun" (the judge's words). I asked how, then, could I have presented the data in a manner that did not convey the impression that I was a hired gun. The judge's response was sobering. She stated that there may be nothing I could have done to avoid the appearance of a hired gun. She commented that she was aware of my request to evaluate both sides and was also aware the opposing attorney refused to participate. She stated, however, that any one-sided evaluation is looked upon more cautiously than one in which both sides are evaluated. She also stated that she saw no way out of the dilemma.

The conclusion drawn from this judge's candid assessment is that one-sided evaluations may be perceived as bias whether or not bias exists within the body of the report. Thus, when conducting one-sided evaluations, it may be even more important to demonstrate fair and objective data-gathering procedures and the way in which the conclusions are logically and directly drawn from the data.

Presenting Scientific Evidence

We have discussed the definition of evidence; different types of evidence, such as prejudicial and probative evidence; and how to be qualified as an expert. We have also discussed common pitfalls in expert witness testimony. Now, we turn our attention to the types of evidence most commonly associated with expert psychological and mental health testimony: scientific evidence.

Evaluators are expected to follow scientific procedures when conducting an investigation. We often explore a parent's general mental health and psychological well-being through the use of standardized tests, interviews, projective techniques, and other data-gathering tools. We take these separate sources of data and form inferences about their meaning as it relates to mental health.

We often use scientifically crafted data-gathering tools, such as standardized tests. We organize our data and form inferences based on theoretically developed models of human behavior that guide our conclusions. We are, in most aspects of our work, scientists struggling to fit our observations of individual and familial behavior into models of behavior that can inform the court about what is in the child's best psychological interests.

We should not delude ourselves, however. Our techniques and models are only in their infancy. Our tests are often not validated on forensic populations, let alone the specific populations of those undergoing custody evaluations. Our interview protocols often are home-grown, with little, if any, reliability data available concerning test-retest or internal consistency. Our recommendations are based not on empirically driven conclusions but on best-guess strategies.

For example, no empirical work has been done in which a matched set of children with similar test and interview data is placed randomly into different custodial arrangements to examine the overall effectiveness of one placement over another. Such an experiment would be blatantly unethical and inhumane. We cannot manipulate families to serve our science. Yet we often provide testimony to the court about custodial arrangements with the arrogance of "true" science implied. We are but sophisticated guides for the trier of fact through a confusing array of psychological technology, a technology never intended for use in custodial assessment. Through our learned and judicious use of psychological theories, methods, and data gathering, we determine our best guesses possible. Our tools are often not valid for custodial assessment. Our models are often rationally, not empirically, derived. And our opinions are more educated guesses than truth. We need to be careful in how we present our data and opinions to the court so as not to mislead.

The *Frye* Standard

The landmark decision permitting scientific testimony was *Frye v. United States* (1923). The Supreme Court held that expert testimony based on novel scientific principles is admissible only when the principle reaches "general acceptance in the field in which it belongs" (p. 1014). Simply put, the *Frye* standard asks the question, "Is this generally accepted within the field?"

The fuzzy question is, How does the court determine when a principle has gained "general acceptance"? Under the *Frye* standard, most courts admit scientific testimony when the principles or discoveries have been published in a peer-reviewed journal. This is not universally adhered to, but it is true more often than not. It is also a useful rule of thumb to follow because it helps guide our scientific evidence testimony to conform to the Specialty Guidelines as well as the ethical principles guiding our respective professions.

When scientific evidence testimony is allowed, be prepared to discuss the scientific or general acceptance of your methods, procedures, and instrumentation. The focus should be to show how your investigative steps are consistent with generally accepted standards within your field (e.g., *Kropinski v. World Plan Exec Council,* 1988). You should also be "prepared to explain the relationship between [your] expert testimony and the legal issues and facts of an instance case" (Committee on Ethical Guidelines, 1991, p. 665). You may be asked to demonstrate to the court how your testimony is related to the psycholegal issues before the court (e.g., *United States v. Shorter,* 1985). For example, when presenting data on the use of the MMPI, you can present testimony to the court that the MMPI is a well-researched test, has thousands of published articles in referred journals, is commonly used in custody evaluations to formulate hypotheses about the psychological well-being of a parent, and has published reliability and validity data available on a number of populations. However, you may also inform the court about limitations of the MMPI in forensic settings, citing, for example, how MMPI results should be used only as a hypothesis-generating rather than a confirmatory tool.

An interesting aside is that when courts refer to a test or technique's reliability, the issue being addressed is what psychologists commonly refer to as

---

QUICK REFERENCE   **The *Frye* Standard of**
                  General Acceptance

Just when a scientific principle or discovery crosses the line between the experimental and demonstrable stages is difficult to define. Somewhere in this twilight zone the evidential force of the principle must be recognized, and while courts will go a long way in admitting expert testimony deduced from a well-recognized scientific principle or discovery, the thing from which the deduction is made must be sufficiently established to have gained general acceptance in the particular field to which it belongs.

---

validity. This distinction is important as we discuss the next evolutionary step of expert scientific testimony: The *Daubert* standard.

Changes in the Frye Standard

The *Frye* standard of General Acceptance came under increasing attack in some courts. The concern was that scientific evidence testimony based solely on general acceptance had the effect of excluding certain types of scientific or clinical information that could assist a judge or jury.

The first significant change in the *Frye* standard appears to be a 1991 ruling by the Arkansas Supreme Court (*Prater v. Arkansas,* 1991). The court ruled that the admission of expert scientific testimony developed from novel scientific techniques must follow a three-part test. The court must evaluate (a) the reliability of the process used to produce the evidence, (b) the possibility of confusing or misleading the jury, and (c) whether the evidence would assist the judge in resolving a contested issue. In defining how to determine reliability of scientific evidence, the Arkansas court held that the trier of fact should consider (a) specialized literature, (b) the qualifications of the expert, (c) the frequency of erroneous results generated by the scientific techniques at issue (how often is it wrong?), and (d) the type of error that could occur (Type I and Type II errors).

The *Daubert* Standard

In 1993, a unanimous U.S. Supreme Court ruled that the *Frye* standard was superseded by the Federal Rules of Evidence, specifically Rule 702 (*Daubert v. Merrell Dow Pharmaceuticals,* 1993). The ruling appears to suggest that the trial judge is responsible for ensuring that an expert's testimony is based upon reliable (read: valid) methods, procedures, and/or instruments *and* is relevant to the present legal issue. The ruling changed the focus from an expert's testimony being allowed because it is generally accepted within the field to giving the judge primary responsibility to review the reliability and validity of scientific evidence.

The rationale was that a judge may determine "if scientific, technical, or other specialized knowledge will assist the trier of fact to understand the evidence or to determine a face in issue" (FRE 702). The ruling goes on to state that the focus must be on the principles and methodology used by the expert rather than the conclusions offered into evidence (Goodman-Delahunty, 1997).

A major concern was that the *Frye* standard may have excluded scientific information if it was not found in peer-reviewed journals or if it had not entered the mainstream of one's discipline. The Court wrote:

> Another pertinent consideration is whether the theory or technique has been subjected to peer review and publication. Publication (which is but one element of peer review) is not a *sine qua non* of admissibility; it does not necessarily correlate with reliability, . . . and in some instances well-grounded but innovative theories will not have been published. . . . Some propositions, moreover, are too particular, too new, or of too limited interest to be published. But submission to the scrutiny of the scientific community is a component of "good science," in part because it increases the likelihood that substantial flaws in methodology will be detected. . . . The fact of publication (or lack thereof) in a peer-reviewed journal thus will be a relevant, though not dispositive, consideration in assessing the scientific validity of a particular technique or methodology on which an opinion is premised. (p. 2797)

The intent of the court appears to be to modify the *Frye* standard so that new, unconventional, or unpublished scientific principles and methods might be considered as the basis of expert testimony if their reliability and validity could be demonstrated. Many scholars consider that the *Daubert* standard lowers the threshold of scientific testimony, whereas others view it as placing a greater burden of proof on establishing the scientific usefulness of the technology (Goodman-Delahunty, 1997).

The *Daubert* standard appears to suggest that expert witness testimony using scientific principles or methods can be qualified under any one of the aforementioned criteria. Evaluators may need to be prepared to offer testimony to the court about the reliability and validity of the tools, techniques, and tests used in custody examinations. Evaluators may also be required to provide data about the error rates associated with custodial determinations and parenting plans. Because there is a paucity of quality research covering most of the topics in custody determination, it is possible that such testimony will be ruled as inadmissible scientific evidence because of the lack of reliable and valid data.

QUICK REFERENCE **Primary Concerns of the *Daubert* Standard (adapted from Golding, 1994)**

- Has the validity and reliability of the "evidence" been subject to scientific scrutiny? That is, can the proposed scientific testimony be tested?
- Has the evidence been subject to peer review and commentary?
- Has the evidence been subject to sufficient scrutiny to permit estimation of rate of error, and is that rate of error justified in the context of application?
- Does the evidence have a sufficient *degree* of scientific acceptance?

There is no doubt that a skilled custody evaluation provides valuable data to the court about children, parents, and their custodial placement. However, it is equally true that much of what we base our conclusions upon is drawn from a poorly developed empirical basis.

> Psychological research that can be considered both relevant and useful to the problems of custody adjudication is minimal. . . . Similarly, judgements based upon psychological tests of either the parents or the child are not likely to be well founded, since there is little evidence that such test results have any implication in terms of the person's actual behavior. (Ellsworth & Levy, 1969, p. 198)

There are good reasons why psychological expert witness testimony should be allowed in court. The first is that social science is finally beginning to amass significant contributions to child custody law. There are empirical studies of the short- and long-term effects of separation and divorce on children's adjustment. There is a growing awareness and refinement of the clinical and forensic methodologies needed to conduct custody evaluations. There are aspirational professional practice objectives that guide evaluator behavior (e.g., the American Psychological Association and the Association of Family and Conciliation Courts). There have been improvements in the quality and focus of interventions aimed at helping families in transition cope with the effects of divorce. There is an emerging literature on custodial parent-child relationships, nonresidential parent-child relationships, gender issues, child-temperament factors, and other important aspects of custodial decision making. Finally, there has been a wealth of continuing education programs presenting models for custodial assessment, custodial evaluation instruments and techniques, case law, and ethics.

Since psychological hypotheses are sufficiently elastic to be pressed into the service of virtually any opinion or prediction, psychological testimony could easily be used to justify questionable custody awards, functioning as the cover under which unacceptable decisional factors gain expression. (Okpaku, 1976, pp. 1144-1145)

The continued growth of research into factors concerning child custody suggests that evaluators will increasingly have at their disposal an arsenal of empirically derived information that can help the trier of fact in making better decisions for children.

Second, the use of social science data and techniques helps to define the concept of the best interest of the child within the domain of mental health. However, it does not define the legal aspects, nor does it pretend to address the full range of custodial concerns considered by the trier of fact. Social science data are useful when they are presented within the context of their advantages and limitations. It is up to the judge to determine the probative weight given to the testimony.

We are skilled observers and arguably provide a unique perspective within the custody context. Unlike judges, we are probably better accustomed to making person-oriented judgments and predictions that are typically prospective in character and involve individual, dyadic, familial, and other relevant social relationships (Rohman et al., 1987).

A final note on *Daubert* is that the decision applies to federal courts, specifically federal civil courts. Some state courts have adopted statutes similar to the *Daubert* standard (Goodman-Delahunty, 1997). Once again, a good rule of thumb is to get to know your local courts and the standards used for the admission of scientific testimony.

Summary

The *Daubert* standard urges judges to consider a number of factors in determining the admissibility of scientific testimony. The first is whether the proposed scientific testimony can be tested to determine its reliability and validity. The second factor is how often the principle or method yields accurate results. This has been interpreted to mean a knowledge of base rate information, specifically Type I and Type II error rates. The third factor is whether the principle or method has been standardized. This has been interpreted to reveal whether there is a right way and a wrong way to conduct the investigation using said principle or method. The fourth factor is whether the testimony is based on subjective or objective analyses. The assumption is that subjective expert witness testimony is often less reliable and less valid because the subjective decision-making process follows no standardized format. The greater the reliance on subjective analysis, the greater the degree of error. The final factor is whether the principle or method has been published in a peer-

---

QUICK REFERENCE   **Federal Rule of Evidence 703:**
                            Admissibility of Scientific Evidence

The facts or data in the particular case upon which an expert bases an opinion or inference may be those perceived by or made known to him at or before the hearing. If of a type reasonably relied upon by experts in the particular field in forming opinions and inferences upon the subject, the facts or data need not be admissible in evidence.

---

reviewed journal. This has been interpreted as indicating a general acceptance of the principle or method in the spirit of the *Frye* standard.

Opinion Testimony by Experts

Expert witnesses are allowed to proffer their opinion to the court. Federal Rule of Evidence 703 speaks to the basis of the opinion testimony. The distinction between relevance (FRE 702) and basis (FRE 703) is important. Rule 702 addresses the question of when expert testimony in the form of "scientific, technical or other specialized knowledge . . . [will] assist the trier of fact to understand the evidence or to determine a fact in issue." Rule 703 examines whether the methods, assessment procedures, and data that form the basis of the opinion (FRE 702) are reliable and valid measures of the constructs and nomological relationships. For example, use of the MCMI-III in assessing psychological well-being may be qualified under Rule 702. The expert may be unable to demonstrate to the court the empirical basis for any statement tying MCMI-III results to behavioral prediction. If the expert attempts to extrapolate from the MCMI-III data statements about prediction of behavior, the testimony might be inadmissible because, to date, there is little empirical research examining the behavioral correlates of the MCMI-III. Thus, the basis of the inference is not "of a type reasonably relied upon by experts in the particular field" (FRE 703).

Federal Rule of Evidence 704 addresses the admissibility of testimony about the ultimate issue. "Testimony in the form of an opinion or inference otherwise admissible is not objectionable because it embraces an ultimate issue to be decided by the trier of fact."

This rule was amended in 1984 to include the following:

No expert witness testifying with respect to the mental state or condition of a defendant in a criminal case may state an opinion or inference as to whether the defendant did or did not have the mental state or condition constituting an element of the crime charged or of a defense thereto. Such ultimate issues are matters for the trier of fact alone.

Finally, Federal Rule of Evidence 705 focuses on experts needing to disclose, upon request, any and all facts underlying their expert opinion. Thus, when testifying in court, mental health professionals need to be prepared to reveal the data upon which their opinion is based.

Admissible Opinion Testimony

Opinion or inference testimony must meet two conditions to be admissible. The first condition is that the subject of the opinion must be beyond the knowledge of the average person *and* related to some science or profession in which the witness has been qualified. The second condition is that the witness must have sufficient skill, knowledge, education, training, or experience in that science or profession to make it appear likely that the proffered opinion or inference will assist the trier of fact in his or her search for the truth.

Expert witnesses are also allowed to offer testimony about hypothetical situations. Typically, a hypothetical situation will involve aspects of the present case changed sufficiently to make a point not discussed in your testimony. It may serve as a way to refute your testimony or to build upon it. No matter how the "hypothetical" is presented, the best attitude to take is to be open to answering the question honestly. Should the situation be convoluted or an intentional distortion of the meaning of your testimony, you can always indicate how the hypothetical is different from the fact pattern about which you have testified. Saying something akin to "Your Honor, I would be happy to address this hypothetical situation, which presents a fact pattern different from that to which I have testified. The limitations of extrapolating from the facts to the hypothetical are as follows . . . " Then, you describe the ways in which the hypothetical changes the facts of the current assessment and would reflect a completely different set of data. Only then do you answer the hypothetical question.

> As long as supposed experts in psychology are required to articulate the basis for their judgement, we are confident that judges . . . can be relied upon to distinguish between those psychological opinions that are well buttressed by the underlying facts of the case and the force of logic, and those psychological opinions which have no more weight behind them than the expert's titles. (Litwack, Gerber, & Fenster, 1979-1980, p. 269)

It is critical when providing opinion testimony that your opinions are formulated within professional and not personal beliefs. The opinion must show that you have considered rival hypotheses. The best way to demonstrate consideration of rival hypotheses is to present each different perspective to the court. The presentation should be to formulate rival ideas in the very best light you can and offer convincing data and opinion about why your opinion should be weighed more heavily than any other hypothesis.

An area of testimony to be avoided is providing an opinion about someone you have not evaluated. This is also discouraged in the Specialty Guidelines. The same argument should be used when asked to comment upon custodial arrangements that you did not consider during your evaluation. For example, at a recent custody trial, a young evaluator had completed a custody evaluation. At the trial, the mother's attorney stated that the mother intended to move to another state. The witness was asked to render an opinion about the effect of the move on the child. This factor had never been an aspect of the custody evaluation, and the expert indicated she had not considered move away factors during her assessment. The judge pressed her, explaining that her role was to provide the court with her "valuable opinion about the best interests of the child." She hesitated, thought for a moment, and offered an opinion. Based on the trial judge's ruling, he weighed heavily the evaluator's comments.

This is where we often overstep the ethical limits of appropriate expert testimony. We serve the court in our capacity as evaluators. But no matter what a judge asks, if you are not prepared to offer testimony on an issue, have not conducted the type of evaluation that would allow for testimony about an issue or the facts presented at trial, or do not have a sufficient basis to offer an empirically based opinion, *you should respectfully explain your ethical responsibility to limit comments to what has been assessed.* If you feel compelled to answer with an opinion not derived from the evaluation data, then clearly state to the court that the information upon which you are basing your opinion is *not* based upon scientific evidence gathered during the assessment, and *is* based upon clinical judgment, admissible under Federal Rule of Evidence 701.

There are situations when new information may be presented during trial that you did not know at the time of your evaluation. If you are provided with such information—and conclude that it appears valid—be honest with the court. Explain that you did not have the information at the time. Tell the court that your report is based upon the facts as you knew them at the time. When asked if the new information changes your opinion, you may consider acknowledging that the new information would change your opinion and further assessment might be warranted. If you do not have expertise in a specific area, explain that your opinion would be outside your area of professional competence. Never provide an opinion to the court about which you have no professional proficiency.

A final word on opinion testimony. Before you testify, always ask the attorney if there are any facts, issues, or laws that you need to be aware of that would lead you *not* to talk in open court. Once you provide testimony, there is no way of erasing its effect. Different states have different rules governing admissible testimony by an expert. Be sure to know those rules before you testify in court.

Testimony to Avoid

There is expert testimony that is expressly *not* allowed. Testimony about the guilt, innocence, truthfulness, or credibility of a witness or litigant is forbidden. The U.S. Supreme Court unequivocally made clear its ruling that in the courtroom, the jury is the lie detector.

> We have said this before, and we will say it again, but this time with emphasis—we really mean it—*no psychotherapist may render an opinion on whether a witness is credible in any trial conducted in this state.* The assessment of credibility is for the trier of fact and not for psychotherapists. (*State v. Milbrandt,* 1988, p. 624)

The Specialty Guidelines also inform us about areas of testimony not permissible under ethical constraints.

> Unless otherwise stipulated by the parties, forensic psychologists are aware that no statements made by a defendant, in the course of any [forensic] examination, no testimony by the expert based upon such statements, nor any other fruits of the statements can be admitted into evidence against the defendant in any criminal proceeding, except on an issue respecting mental condition on which the defendant has introduced testimony. (Committee on Ethical Guidelines, 1991, pp. 662-663)

There is also concern about providing testimony to the court based upon hearsay or otherwise inadmissible testimony. "When hearsay or otherwise inadmissible evidence forms the basis of their opinion, evidence, or professional product, [forensic psychologists] seek to minimize sole reliance upon such evidence" (Committee on Ethical Guidelines, 1991, p. 662).

In closing, recall the statement in the Specialty Guidelines about competent presentation of testimony to the court:

> Forensic psychologists have an obligation to present to the court, regarding the specific matters to which they will testify, the boundaries of their competence, the factual bases (knowledge, skill, experience, training, and education) for their qualifications as an expert, and the relevance of those factual bases to their qualifications as an expert on the specific matters at issue. (Committee on Ethical Guidelines, 1991, p. 658)

QUICK REFERENCE **Common Complaints**
About Expert Witnesses

- Evaluators use a lot of jargon.
- Evaluators answer questions that were not asked.
- Evaluators fail to address questions that need to be answered.
- Evaluators provide written reports and testimony with conclusions that do not follow logically from the data.
- Evaluators overstep their proper role.
- Evaluators answer the ultimate question.
- Evaluators do not answer the ultimate question.
- Evaluators are afraid of making the hard decisions about custodial determination.

Common Complaints Voiced by Attorneys About Mental Health Experts

The final section of this chapter addresses common complaints that attorneys and judges have about mental health professionals and their reports and verbal testimony. As a way of easing the anticipated pain of these concerns, let me remind you of the strong need for all professions to develop a strong sense of affiliation with professional concepts and language. It is not unusual for a practicing mental health professional to become so comfortable and conversant in the language of diagnosis, psychological concepts, tests and measures, and other professionally related content that we forget that people outside our profession hold simpler, less sophisticated ideas about mental health concepts.

Complaints are common about expert witnesses. The first is that mental health professionals use a lot of jargon. Often, when we phrase our ideas using the language of human behavior, attorneys and judges go numb. They may not understand what we are talking about yet are so confused (or bored) that they do not ask for a translation.

Three simple ideas to help avoid jargon overkill are (a) remember your audience, (b) distinguish between clinical information and forensic information, and (c) omit unnecessary information not relevant to answering the psycholegal question (Gindes & Otto, 1997).

The second complaint is that mental health professionals often answer questions that were not asked (Gindes & Otto, 1997). The easiest solution is to identify the psycholegal questions serving to guide your report and make sure that your data and conclusions directly address answers to the psycho-legal questions.

The third complaint is a close cousin to the above, suggesting that mental health professionals often fail to address questions that were asked. The same solution is offered. Clear questions at the beginning of an evaluation will help to determine clear answers.

The fourth complaint is that mental health professionals provide written reports and testimony with conclusions that have no clear relationship to the data. Too often, experts offer custodial determinations that do not reflect the trend or weight of the data. These reports often do not provide clear, logical analyses leading the reader from the data to the conclusions. Gindes and Otto (1997) suggest a data analysis method in which the report describes the data, then the inferences drawn from the data, and finally the conclusions determined from the inferences that are based on the data. This is classic scientific method and reflects the focus of this book. Furthermore, specific examples drawn from the data are helpful illustrators that guide the reader toward an integration of the data with the conclusions.

The fifth complaint has two parts. Part 1 is that evaluators overstep their proper role and answer the ultimate legal issue. Part 2 is that evaluators are too timid to offer the court their opinions about the ultimate issue. This is a debatable concept in the professional literature. However, what is clear is that when clear psycholegal questions are posed, it is the responsibility of the expert to gather data and provide interpretations of that data that assist the trier of fact to answer the questions before the court. If you provide an answer to the ultimate issue, first talk with your professional association as well as your local bar to help determine local rules and expectations. Second, be prepared to defend your position with a well-reasoned, literature-based argument about your decision to address the ultimate issue.

Conversely, when asked to assist the court in its decision, mental health professionals may determine after an evaluation that further evaluative services are necessary. However, this should not be a fall-back position because one is fearful of making a strong recommendation. The role of the expert is often to make a recommendation and to frame the recommendation within the context of the limitations of the data, methods, and procedures.

In summary, there are a number of concerns about mental health professionals' interaction with the legal system. Each of the complaints cited above is easily modified to serve the court better. It is useful to examine your behavior and seek others' comments about your work product so that you may better meet the expectations of the court and frame your work product in a manner most helpful to the court and its servants.

FOUR

Developing a
Conceptual Model for
Custodial Assessment

Psychology is a most dangerous science to apply to practical affairs.

Lord Chancellor of England (about 1920)

An Example

Conclusions and Custody Recommendations: Ms. Jefferson and her children were seen, both individually and together, in this evaluator's office for a total of 4 hours on December 3, 1996 for the purpose of conducting a comprehensive custody evaluation. Ms. Jefferson and her fiancé, Mr. King, were interviewed and evaluated over a 3-hour period on December 6, 1996. In addition to detailed clinical interviews, the Abrams Sentence Completion Test was administered to the mother, fiancé, and the 11-year-old son as a means of determining the presence or absence of abnormal or psychopathological behavior. The 5-year-old daughter was administered selected subtests from the Wechsler Pre-School and Primary Scale of Intelligence—Revised, along with the Abrams Sentence Completion Test for Kindergarten. The son was also given a House-Tree-Person Test and Kinetic Family Drawing to determine his custodial preference. Observational data were very revealing regarding the mother and children during the 1-hour observational session and proved conclusively that the children have a superior relationship with the mother. Similarly, the observational session between the mother and fiancé revealed an unquestionably healthy, sensitive, and child-focused relationship. The concerns about Mr. King's lack of experience with children of his own was discussed with the couple. Their firm and unequivocal assurances about the quality and direction of parenting leads me to conclude that they will be wonderful parents to these two children. I therefore have no reservations in

49

recommending primary custody to the mother. The mother's intended move to California should in no way interfere with the biological father's partial custody rights. I believe in the credibility of Ms. Jefferson's position that her life will be significantly enhanced by the move. Furthermore, I believe that the move will enable Ms. Jefferson to spend more time with her children. Thus, it is this evaluator's recommendation, within a reasonable degree of scientific and professional certainty, that the minor children should be allowed to relocate with their mother and that Ms. Jefferson be awarded primary physical and legal custody.[1]

* * * * *

Custodial determinations are intended to be scientific examinations of important psycholegal questions. Too often, custody reports read like fiction—some good, some bad, but fiction nevertheless. The evaluator conducts interviews, interprets psychological tests, and conducts collateral interviews and record reviews. When it comes to putting the data together in some meaningful manner, the evaluator provides little, if any, organization around the data. As indicated in the previous chapter, a significant frustration for attorneys and judges is when experts' conclusions and recommendations appear as if they have been pulled out of a hat. Conclusions should be built on inferences, that are built on data.

Often, custody reports allegedly provide information about the best psychological interests of the child without ever defining which variables need to be examined. Interpretations and conclusions are based upon the evaluator's idiosyncratic, implicit conceptual model of the best psychological interests rather than a more objectively determined conceptual model. The interpretation and results sections become the fiction of the evaluator's intuition, experience, and bias, but they are not results organized around variables drawn from behavioral science research. Too often, these conclusions do not answer the questions before the court because the evaluator has not requested a clearly expressed, written definition of the psycholegal question to be addressed by the examination.

The development of a conceptual model that stresses scientific procedures and reliance upon behavioral science literature in conducting custodial determinations is a relatively new concept. Three important books are cited as representative of the movement toward scientifically crafted custodial examinations.

Evaluating Parental Competencies

Among the first books to marry scientific and psycholegal aspects of evaluations is Thomas Grisso's seminal work, *Competency to Stand Trial Evaluations: A Manual for Practice* (Grisso, 1988). Grisso argues that a custody

---

QUICK REFERENCE **Objectives of Assessing Parental Competencies**

- Examine the functional abilities of each parent.
- Identify areas of strengths and weaknesses in parental competencies.
- Explore the relationship between observed parenting strengths and weaknesses and specific parenting demands.
- Assess goodness of fit between each parent's observed competencies in relationship to each specific child.
- Recommend remedial or dispositional options.

---

evaluation is, in large part, an evaluation of parenting *competencies*. Grisso's model of competency evaluation guides the evaluator in developing a framework for gathering data, generating inferences, making decisions, and developing recommendations that is both useful and reflective of important professional practice standards. "If we wish to assist legal decision-makers, then our evaluations must be guided by *legal* concerns, not simply *clinical* concerns. . . . In place of [clinical] questions we must ask, 'What is it that the law wants to know?'" (Grisso, 1988, p. 1).

Grisso describes two "underlying values" of competency evaluations for the courts. The first is to maintain the *fairness* of the trial process. "The rationality of an adversarial trial system requires that the accused must have a fair opportunity to mount any reasonable, available defense" (Grisso, 1988, p. 2). The second value is to "promote the accuracy of the trial's results" (p. 2). Evaluators who conduct impartial, comprehensive, neutral examinations provide evidence that helps toward these ends.

Grisso's Objectives of Competency Evaluations

Grisso outlines several objectives for competency evaluations. The first factor examines a litigant's strengths and deficits in the specific abilities defined by the legal standard. These are called the *functional abilities* of the litigant. Functional ability explores what the individual actually does. It is an evaluation of observed behaviors.

The second objective examines the causes of any deficits in competency abilities that have been observed. The evaluator examines the litigant within a specific context or role. The third objective assesses how the specific deficits affect behaviors of concern to the primary legal question. The evaluator is concerned with identifying and describing the causes of observed deficiencies related to the psycholegal questions guiding the assessment.

Assessment of a child's developmental needs becomes an assessment of the functional competencies of each child. Once accomplished, then a comparison of the goodness of fit between a parent's observed functional competencies and those of the child is critical.

A final objective is providing information to the court about "matters of remediation or other dispositional options" (Grisso, 1988, p. 21). Although a custodial evaluation may include suggestions for psychological or family treatment, the judge does not make a custodial determination under the assumption that some identified parenting deficit will be remediated in the near future. The judge may call for a follow-up evaluation at some future time to reassess a change in parenting skill or attitude, but the custody determination is not usually put off. It is made based upon the facts of the evaluation as represented to the court.

Choosing Evaluation Methods

Many custody evaluators choose a standard battery of tests, techniques, interview protocols, and self-report measures. The argument for using a standard format is that everyone is evaluated using the same methods. Using a standard format allows the data to be collected in the same way, increasing their reliability (Rogers, 1995).

The argument against using a standard format is that every case is different and requires different tools (Skidmore, 1994). Each custodial assessment could pose different variables to be measured. Using a standard battery of tests and other assessment techniques may overlook important variables specific to a particular case. Most evaluators appear to use a standard battery of tests (Ackerman & Ackerman, 1996, 1997; Keilin & Bloom, 1986).

Grisso's (1988) model posits that a

> data collection method is "standardized" when its procedure is sufficiently clear to allow various examiners to collect their data in the same way: that is, with the same questions, response formats, ways of evaluating the examinee's responses, and other matters of procedure. (p. 25)

Grisso suggests that examiners use a standard battery to reduce individual differences between evaluators. Each examiner is forced to collect data in the same way, resulting in a decreased probability of examiner error imposing itself on the data-gathering phase of the assessment. Another benefit of using a standard battery is that it ensures a consistent set of behavioral observations from case to case.

Because custody evaluations are limited in the number of psychometrically sound tools available for use in custodial determinations, the evaluator is almost forced to use nonstandardized data-gathering techniques at some point during the evaluation. However, using standardized *formats* (in contrast to standardized tests) whenever possible will greatly reduce the introduction and size of evaluator error. Standard interview protocols increase the reliability of the data (Rogers, 1995).

Issues Surrounding Reliability and Validity

Most sophisticated examiners are well schooled in theories of reliability and validity. Therefore, the recurrent message in this book to beware of the limited validity of many of our tests as applied in forensic settings should not be a surprise. However, it is possible (and preferable) that the tools we use have some information about reliability.

Validity is the area in which custody examiners have the most difficulty justifying their choice and use of a test or a set of tests. A valid instrument may generate data useful in determining behaviors and abilities that are of relevance to the legal questions before the court. However, we are limited in identifying valid instruments developed for use with a divorcing population. This is why custodial assessment is as much art as it is science. "Tests are important for many reasons, but often they do not provide the breadth, depth, or flexibility needed by the examiner to explore certain types of information relatively unique to an individual case" (Grisso, 1988, p. 26).

The best way to approach validity in a forensic context is to use many different methods of data collection on a particular variable. It is also wise to examine a number of variables within the original conceptual domain, looking for consistency of response. Using this multitrait-multimethod paradigm reduces error and poor reliability by requiring that behavioral observations are supported by at least two sources.

Organizing the Evaluation Around Behavioral Science Literature

The second book addressing the need for evaluators to formulate their observational data, inferences, and conclusions within a behavioral science framework was Schutz, Dixon, Lindeberger, and Ruther's book, *Solomon's Sword* (1989). Schutz et al. saw two limitations in the use of behavioral science research with custody evaluations. The first concern was that aggregate data may inform us of trends and probabilities, yet "in the courtroom, it is the destiny of the individual that is in question, not that of the group" (Schutz et al., 1989, p. 89). Aggregate data do not inform about the specific behavior of an individual. Test results and other forms of data gathering from inferential and descriptive techniques need to be viewed as hypotheses to be examined within the specific context of a particular custodial concern. As Schutz et al. conclude, "We can never accumulate enough group data to tell us how one single life will or should turn out" (p. 90).

The second limitation cited by Schutz et al. (1988) is the need to use a multitrait- multimethod paradigm in gathering data. Students of test and measurement theory may recognize the concept as similar to Campbell and Fiske's (1959) multitrait-multimethod matrix model of validity.

> We have argued that the content of a child custody evaluation should be anchored to the behavioral sciences literature on parent-child interactions. Likewise, we believe that the analysis of the data should be informed by the literature that has accumulated on postdivorce adaption of children. (Schutz et al., 1989, p. 89)

Campbell and Fiske (1959) suggested that any test is really a trait method unit. A specific test measures a given trait by a given method. When different traits are studied, or the same trait is studied using different methods, different results might be obtained. Therefore, when researchers want to isolate the separate and unique contributions of trait factors from method factors, more than one trait and one method must be studied simultaneously. The result is a matrix that provides information about convergent and discriminant validity. Convergent validity examines the correlations among the same traits measured by different measures. Discriminant validity examines the correlations among different traits measured by the same method.

The logic is similar in a forensic setting. Because there are few well-validated instruments specifically designed for custodial assessment, there is a larger error component to conventional tests used for custodial assessment. Therefore, the evaluator is wise to use many different perspectives on the psycholegal questions to be assessed. This provides a means of taking reasonable safeguards to ensure the usefulness of the tests and techniques used in drawing meaning from the behaviors observed in custodial evaluations. For example, when concerned about the potential effect of a parent's alleged abnormal behavior on parenting, the examiner might use two or three psychological tests, extensive collateral data interviews, multiple clinical/forensic interviews, self-report measures, and direct observation. Although there is always the possibility that our interpretation of the data is incorrect (i.e., a false positive), the use of multiple methods to measure a particular (target) behavior may decrease the chances of making a wrong decision.

Similarly, the importance of examining multiple variables that are directly related to the question at hand is also critical. The best psychological interest of the child is not a unitary variable. It is multidimensional. To assume that the best psychological interests of the child can be assessed without first defining the variables of legal relevance abrogates our responsibility to the court. Recall the defining features of the rules of evidence about relevance and basis. Our testimony to the court needs to be based upon an underlying theory of science, not guesses. The behavioral science literature has defined a theoretical framework and specific variables about children, adults, and their interactions. To gloss over these complex sets of factors and look only at the broadest concept—the best psychological interest—is similar to the researcher looking only for a statistically significant number with no concern for results pertaining to each main effect, the direction of the main effect, the relevance of the first- and second-order interaction effects, or the importance of moderator and confounding variables.

The challenge for the evaluator is to define the relevant variables to be examined based upon the legal questions before the court. This is where our skill as observers and interpreters of human behavior is paramount.

A first step is to request a list of specific psycholegal questions to be addressed in this particular evaluation (see boxes below). Once we understand the psychological relevance of the psycholegal questions, then the examiner operationally defines the variables to be measured.

Formulating Psycholegal Questions: The Court's Order

1. Is the plaintiff a fit and proper person to have the care and custody of the minor children?
2. Is the defendant a fit and proper person to have the care and custody of the minor children?
3. What recommendations does the psychologist make to the court with respect to the issues of custody and visitation between these parents and the minor children?

Reframing the Questions of the Court Into Specific Psycholegal Questions

- What is the ability of Mrs. Litigant to parent her two children effectively and safely?
- What are the parental competencies of Mr. and Mrs. Litigant?
- What are the behavior management strategies used in parental discipline of children?
- What are the risks of possible abusive behavior upon the minor children by Mr. and Mrs. Litigant?
- What concerns exist regarding the capability of Mr. and Mrs. Litigant to parent a 7-year-old and a 13-year-old child?
- Are the children afraid of Mr. Litigant? If yes, why?

We are not soothsayers. We do not predict the future. Predictive validity is not the province of the custody evaluator. Instead, as Schutz et al. (1988) suggest, the evaluator's primary focus in examining relative strengths and weaknesses of each parent is on discriminant validity. Examiners are concerned about discovering the degree of difference between parents on legally relevant psychological dimensions. In exploring the similarities between parents, the evaluator's search is for convergent validity.

This is a very difficult task, indeed. The behavioral science literature is good at helping us to determine the extremes of good versus bad parenting. We know that an actively substance-abusing parent generally presents more of a risk to his or her children than does a parent who does not use drugs. We know that a depressed, actively suicidal parent is often more neglectful of parenting responsibilities than is one who is neither depressed nor suicidal. Making the call between the extremes of parenting capabilities is often not difficult. However, these comprise few of the custodial cases that will tug on our skills.

The problem group is the majority. These are parents who are good parents. Each has strengths and weaknesses. Each provides for the best psychological interests of his or her children in unique ways. Within the context of a marriage, one parent's strengths balanced the other's weaknesses. The divorce has forced a separation of the dynamic combination of factors each contributed to make a balanced parenting environment. Now, the court wants to know which of these two good, responsible parents is *relatively* better at providing for their children's best psychological interests. Every evaluator knows that the real question in the majority of custodial determinations is one of *relative* contributions to the children's lives. We also know that each parent feels the court's decision to be a statement of absolute determination regarding who is the better parent. From the parents' point of view, there is no second place in custodial decisions—only winners and losers. The adversarial process tends to destroy the last remaining hope that divorcing couples will be able to talk with each other in the near future (Kelly, 1994).

In most jurisdictions, custodial evaluation is the last of a long series of attempts to solve the custodial dispute. Divorcing parents often have attempted out-of-court settlements, counseling, mediation, and other remedies. None has worked if they have progressed to the point of a custody evaluation. Our work is often the last resort for these parents. It is the end of the line in a long series of legal decisions, false hopes, and financial hardship endured by each parent.

Context and Incongruence

Schutz et al. (1989) supported the notion that custody evaluations could be viewed as measures of parental competencies, examining the litigant within the context of a specific competency *within a specific environment*. The litigant's parenting capacity (or capacities) is examined along a number of variables that measure the best psychological interests standard.

Another important issue is that an evaluation can reveal a degree of incongruence between the litigant's capacity and the best psychological interests standard. When this occurs, our reports may form the foundation for a judge to consider the incongruence between the observed competencies and the legal standard sufficient to "warrant a finding of legal incompetency and activate the state's authority for action on the basis of such a finding" (Schutz et al., 1989, p. 29).

The overwhelming conclusion is that our work has the potential— through the judge's interpretation of our work product—to exert significant influence over the fate of these families. It is a responsibility to be taken seriously and treated with great respect.

Integrating Behavioral Science and Psychometrics

Among the newest additions to the child custody literature is Marc J. Ackerman's (1995) book, *Clinician's Guide to Child Custody Evaluations*. Ackerman's approach to custodial assessment is unique because of its focus on organizing questions drawn from the behavioral science literature as well as the use of cutoff scores on different psychological tests and techniques.

Based upon the Ackerman-Schoendorf Scale for Parent Evaluation of Custody (ASPECT; Ackerman & Schoendorf, 1992), the book provides a conceptual framework imposed upon traditional data gathered in custodial assessments. The data are formatted into ASPECT scores, which then yield a Parent Custody Index (PCI). The PCI is a weighted average of scores drawn from three scales: Observational, Social, and Cognitive-Emotional.

As further discussed in Chapter 13, the ASPECT provides an overall index of parenting effectiveness. It has been and continues to be subject to empirical investigations providing information about the psychometric integrity of the scales. Ackerman (1995; Ackerman & Schoendorf, 1992) reports some reliability and validity data on the ASPECT. He describes data concerning content validity, construct validity, and predictive validity. Information is also presented about the interrater reliability and internal consistency of the scales. Recently, Melton et al. (1997) provided a useful critique of the ASPECT.

Evolution of the Best Interests Standard

No presentation of a conceptual model guiding custody evaluations is complete without a discussion of the ideas that underlie the best interests standard. The historical context of custody evaluations begins with Roman law and the presumption of paternal preference. Children were viewed as the property of their father. A father had absolute power over his children. He was allowed to place his children into slave labor or sell them for profit. The child's mother had no legal rights.

English common law also provided for absolute paternal power. Fathers had the legal responsibility to protect, support, and educate their children. Fathers had custodial rights based upon the presumption that paternal investment provided children with power, status, and wealth. Mothers had restricted access to their children after divorce.

The British Act of 1939 fundamentally changed how courts viewed children and the parental responsibility toward their care. British barrister Justice Thomas Noon Talfound conceived of the idea that young children needed the direct care of their mother until the age of 7. From age 7 on, the custodial responsibility of the children would revert back to the father. This became known as the tender years doctrine, and it was the first legal challenge to the historical paternal preference.

During the 17th and 18th centuries, American law often paralleled English common law. There was a presumption of paternal preference based on the transmission of social and legal legitimacy, power, and status from the father to his children. By the 19th century, American law began to apply paternal preference less pervasively than British common law. Several states developed laws that granted to both parents equal rights of custody responsibility of their children.

During the mid-1800s, the Industrial Revolution began to have an effect on legal solutions to divorce. There became an increasing concern for the welfare of children, especially as fathers worked outside the home and frequently beyond the farm or village. Mothers remained at home and cared for their children as their primary caretakers. This was the first time in history that family responsibilities were clearly divided into the role of "provider-wage earner" for the father and "child caretaker-nurturer" for the mother.

Maternal Preference

Paralleling changes in familial and workplace organization were changes in the legal status of women. Gradually, the paternal preference was replaced by a maternal preference in custodial care. By the 1920s, the concept of maternal preference was the presumptive direction of most American courts in determination of custodial responsibility.

The importance of the maternal preference was given a boost by the development and popularization of psychoanalysis. Sigmund Freud's theory of child development placed heavy weight upon the mother's role as primary and unique caretaker in a child's life. Subsequent theories of attachment, such as the work of Bowlby (1969, 1980), added much-needed scientific backing to the importance of infant-mother attachment. The focus on infant-mother attachment implied that infant-father attachment was somehow less important to the child's development. Thus, scientific theories of psychoanalysis and attachment theory appeared to lend scientific credibility to the legal standard of maternal preference. Current research has demonstrated that infants form meaningful attachments to both parents by the middle of their first year; however, it has only been recently that such research has affected—ever so slowly—the court's view of the tender years doctrine and maternal preference (Bray, 1991).

In the 1960s, a number of factors were brought together to pressure the courts to reexamine the maternal preference in custody determination. There was a rising number of fathers enduring divorce who wanted some legally acknowledged role in the postdivorce relationship with their children. Legal challenges to maternal preference were raised regarding sex discrimination in custody determinations, constitutional protection for equal rights, the feminist movement, and the entry of large numbers of women into the workforce (Kelly, 1994).

In 1971, the National Conference of Commissioners for Uniform State Laws developed a set of standards known as the Uniform Marriage and Divorce Act, which provided for a straight best interests standard. The tide had turned from a focus on paternal or maternal preference or rights to a measure of what was best for the child. Simultaneously, psychology offered a revolutionary idea. The concept of the psychological rather than the biological parent was developed (Bray, 1991).

The Psychological Parent

A psychological parent has been defined as one who, "on a continuing day to day basis through interplay, and mutuality, fulfills the child's psychological needs for a parent, as well as the child's physical needs" (Goldstein, Freud, & Solnit, 1979, p. 98). The idea of one psychological parent or a primary parent took hold in legal circles and was readily embraced by evaluators (Bray, 1991). The psychological parent holds great intuitive appeal and serves well as a way to understand a child's perception of the world. Further discussion of the psychological parent is presented in Chapter 7.

Best Interest Is Poorly Defined

When the best interests standard entered the public domain, there was no agreed-upon single definition. As in many other areas of the law, the best interests standard developed from individual case to individual case.

Mental health professionals are accustomed to working with operational definitions, nomological nets, and empirically crafted theoretical constructs. The defining criteria of the best interests standard appeared logically rather than empirically derived. The factors defined in many legal definitions of the best interests of the child appeared drawn partly from experience, intuition, cultural expectations, and preconceived notions of what was good for children's healthy development.

Among the variables considered in the emerging legal definition of the best interests standard were concepts such as the child's need for consistency in parenting and the importance of each parent's relative contribution to the child's well-being. There was an increasing recognition as well as pressure placed on the courts to expedite custody determination for the good of the child. The notion that children were well served by safety, security, and consistency provided the impetus for courts to make faster custodial decisions.

Another shift toward the best interests criteria was the consideration of children's feelings and desires about with whom they wanted to live. There developed a recognition on the part of many judges that children's own wishes might be appropriately considered if they were deemed to be of sufficient age to form an intelligent opinion.

Joint Custody Considerations

Beginning in the 1970s, the concept of *joint custody* was forwarded by a combination of forces that included the newly developed fathers' rights movement. The fathers' rights movement objected strongly to the reduction in fathers' parental rights simply because they had become divorced. Researchers increasingly were reporting hitherto unnoticed contributions of fathers to children's welfare and development. A belief began to develop that continuity in the father-child relationship after divorce would provide for healthier postdivorce family systems. Finally, the academic world began to take notice of positive father contributions in family systems and began to argue the advantages of joint custody awards.

Joint custody was seen as a panacea because the parental rights, status, and responsibilities of both parents were being preserved. The field of child development began to study a father's contribution to family welfare beyond that of provider. It began to look at attachment, child-rearing practices, communication skills, and a host of other important factors in father-child relations. Studies also began to appear that documented divorced men's sadness, alienation, depression, and loneliness resulting from reduced contact with their children. The proliferation of joint custody statutes throughout the United States has had the effect of promoting increasingly more positive attitudes toward greater paternal involvement after divorce among parents, lawyers, mental health professionals, and judges (Kelly, 1994).

QUICK REFERENCE **The Michigan Child Custody Act of 1970**

The Michigan Act identified 10 factors to be considered when making a custodial determination:

- The love, affection, and other emotional ties existing between the competing parties and the child
- The capacity and disposition of the competing parties to provide love, affection, guidance, continuation of education, and continued religious education, if the latter be deemed necessary
- The capacity and disposition of the competing parties to provide the children with what is regarded as "remedial care," that is, clothing and medical care (also refers to provision of other material needs)
- The length of time that a child has lived in a stable, satisfactory environment and the desirability of maintaining continuity of that environment
- The permanence of the family unit of the existing or proposed custodial home
- The moral fitness of the competing parties (note—there is no mention of fitness as a parent)
- The mental and physical health of the competing parties
- The home, school, and community records of the child
- The reasonable preference of the child if the court deems the child to be of sufficient age to express a preference
- Any other issues considered by the court to be relevant to a particular child custody suit

---

State of Michigan's Best Interest Standard

More than 25 years ago, a milestone in custody law was enacted. The Michigan Child Custody Act of 1970 has served as a model for outlining the basic tenets of the "best interests of the child" doctrine. The Act has served as the guiding light for defining the minimum standards for determining what is in the child's best interests. There are, of course, no guidelines available defining "love," "affection," "other emotional ties," "moral fitness," and other important ideas expressed in the Michigan Act. Definition of these ideas is assessed through the skill, experience, and wisdom provided by expert evaluators and other mental health professionals affiliated with the courts.

A critical reading of the Michigan Act shows a concern for the emotional, physical, educational, moral, and religious growth and development provided to a child. It also highlights a need for a stable and satisfactory living environment within which ancillary ("remedial") needs are also provided.

Another factor is how the child feels about living with each parent. Finally, the Act is interested in the overall physical and psychological welfare and stability of the parents.

Limitations of the Michigan Standards

Of the 10 Michigan standards, 3 appear to have minimal empirical support. The first concern is the focus on the permanency of the home. With the increasing number of move away cases, the concept of the permanence of a home is being challenged successfully in many jurisdictions (see discussion on move away cases in Chapter 8).

The empirical data addressing the relationship between a parent's moral behavior and its impact on child development are virtually nonexistent. This is due in part to the lack of common definition of the term. There is no empirical evidence that lifestyle issues (i.e., sexual preference of a parent) influence a child's development. Similarly, there is little, if any, published research on the relationship between sexually promiscuous adult behavior and its effect on child development. Rohman et al. (1987) concluded, "To the best of our knowledge, no social science research has systemically investigated the effect of a custodian's religious or moral behavior upon the well-being of a child" (p. 80).

There is little doubt that certain types of antisocial behavior on the part of a parent have been found to correlate significantly with delinquency of children (Glueck & Glueck, 1950). Although the law traditionally has emphasized the moral character of the disputing parties by presuming that the best moral or religious interests of the child are served by placing the child with the custodian who shows the higher moral character, social science has no empirical research in support of such a decision.

The final area in the Michigan standard for which there is equivocal empirical support is the variable of the child's wishes. As discussed more fully in chapters discussing children's adjustment to separation and divorce and the results of the recent Ackerman and Ackerman (1996, 1997) study, inquiring about a child's wishes is not a simple, clear measure. Evaluators, attorneys, and judges need to be aware of the child's developmental level, social influence factors that may affect the child, susceptibility to influence, motivation and underlying reasoning, as well as a number of other variables.

What Is the Best Interest Standard?

The Michigan Act has become an important standard against which to measure custody determinations. Attempting to codify its essential features and make the "best interests" criteria consistent across the states, the Uniform

> **QUICK REFERENCE   The Uniform Marriage and**
> **Divorce Act of 1979, Sec. 402**
>
> The U.S. Congress identified five factors to be considered when making custody determinations:
>
> - The wishes of the child's parent or parents as to his or her custody
> - The wishes of the child as to his or her custodian
> - The interaction and interrelationship of the child with the parent or parents, siblings, and any other person who may significantly affect the child's best interest
> - The child's adjustment to home, school, and community
> - The mental and physical health of all individuals involved

Marriage and Divorce Act was developed by the National Conference of Commissioners for Uniform State Laws. This Act identified five basic factors to be considered when making custody determinations.

The Act made it very clear that adult behavior directly affecting parenting was the focus of the best interests criteria. The court was not interested in behaviors that did not influence a child's health and well-being. "The court shall not consider conduct of a present or proposed custodian that does not affect his relationship to the child" (Uniform Marriage and Divorce Act, 1971). This has been interpreted to mean that a parent may have a mental condition, but if the condition does not affect parenting skills or competencies, it is not a factor to consider in determining the child's best interests (Weithorn, 1987).

There is no clear consensus among attorneys, judges, and mental health professionals in defining the dimensions to be evaluated in determining the child's best psychological interests in custody determinations. There are advantages and disadvantages to using the best psychological interests criteria. As an evaluator, you need to consider the philosophical and practical aspects of the best psychological interests criteria. You must have carefully considered why you are choosing to use the best psychological interests criteria, its pros and cons, and its meaning within the limits of your evaluation. As the Specialty Guidelines remind us,

> In offering expert evidence [forensic psychologists] are aware that their own professional observations, inferences, and conclusions must be distinguished from legal facts, opinions, and conclusions. Forensic psychologists are prepared to explain the relationship between their expert testimony and the legal issues and facts of an instant case. (Committee on Ethical Guidelines, 1991, p. 665)

When we determine the factors to be evaluated in a custody evaluation, we must be prepared to provide to the court an underlying logic and theory of science that ties the factors to the specific issues of concern in the case before us. We also need to be prepared to explain how our choice of which factors to assess is related to the relevant psycholegal questions before the court.

Our responsibility is to measure behavioral dimensions and interpret their meaning within the framework of this particular family. In this way, we provide the court with information useful in making its decision regarding custody. The determination of the best psychological interests of the child relies most extensively upon the child's developmental and psychological needs. It does not consider parental needs, legal tradition, or cultural expectations. The discussion may include examination of these variables with regard to their effect on the child, but they are not determinative.

Consensus Factors in the Best Interest Standard

Schutz et al. (1989) reported a review of the laws in all 50 states that address custodial determination. However, they point out that each statute on the subject of child custody cautioned that "other relevant factors, whether listed in the statute or not, may be considered by the court in making its decision" (p. 10).

The elements described in the Quick Reference (p. 65) are not comprehensive. They are important factors to consider in approaching a definition of the best psychological interests of the child. Most jurisdictions approach custody determination on a case-by-case basis, and so should we. Different states have different statutes governing the best interests of the child. Some provide authority to the court to make a custody determination. Other statutes order the court to act in the best interests of the child. Some statutes prohibit certain types of testimony or custody decisions based on sex.

Identifying Good Parenting

All child custody assessments must evaluate parenting. An important question is, What dimensions of parenting are relevant to providing for the best psychological interests of a child? The answer is that there is no definitive answer. More research is needed that examines both process and outcome variables.

Existing psychological research on parenting is, if you will pardon the pun, still in its infancy. There is little consistent information about the impact of different parenting activities on child development. For example, we do not know the short- or long-term effects of exposing a child to, say, art museums or pornography on later development. Each of us may hold beliefs about

---

QUICK REFERENCE   **Consensus Factors in the Best Interest Standard (Schutz et al., 1989)**

- Any instance of child or spousal abuse
- Ages and sex of the children
- Adjustment of the children to their environment
- Length of time in their present environment
- Child's need for special emotional or physical care
- Economic position of the parties (although few states would allow a decision grounded only on economics)
- Child's wishes, if of a sufficient age
- Parent's desires
- Educational needs of the child
- Agreements between the parents
- Separation of the siblings
- Mental and physical health of the parents
- Prior custody determinations
- Hostility levels between parents
- Flexibility on the part of either parent
- General parenting skills
- Substance abuse by either parent
- Religious concerns
- Caretaking arrangements prior to and after separation
- Likelihood that custodial parent will remove children from jurisdiction or alienate the affections of the children for the other parent.

---

which is better for children, which provides more intellectually, morally, and culturally relevant experiences, but there is little or no empirical research to support such beliefs.

Below is a summary of ideas and models drawn from the research and clinical publications that address minimal characteristics defining "good parenting."

Involved and Caring

Good parenting appears to include the parent's active and positive involvement in the child's life. A good parent understands and plans for the inclusion of the child in appropriate functions and encourages the sharing of

QUICK REFERENCE **Good Parenting Behaviors**

- Involved and caring
- Two-way communications: parent to child and parent to parent
- Clear emotional and physical boundaries
- Clear priorities
- Good supervisor of children's behavior
- Nurtures self-esteem in children
- Knows children's strengths and weaknesses
- Good role model
- Good disciplinarian
- Encourages relationship with other parent
- Good moral reasoning

mutually satisfying activities. Good parenting helps the child feel involved and a part of the greater family. The child feels special and wanted in his or her relationship with each parent (Derdeyn et al., 1982).

Two-Way Communications

Good parenting appears to include direct, open, and cooperative dialogues between parent and child. Communications in good parenting are characterized by a two-way exchange of feelings of closeness, warmth, interest, and care (Fisher & Fisher, 1986).

Good parenting also includes cooperative communications with the other parent. Each parent needs to understand and be aware of each child's needs, interests, and wants. Each parent needs to communicate his or her experience with the children to the other parent to provide for continuity of children's needs across homes.

Clear Boundaries

Good parenting appears to include flexibility in behaviors. Parents take responsibility for the setting of appropriate limits between themselves and their children as well as among children.

Good parenting appears to include appropriate modulation of intimacy. Good parenting avoids the extremes of psychological closeness and distance. It is characterized by the development and maintenance of interpersonal closeness that feels comfortable to both parent and child and is experienced consistently.

A good parent also sets clear boundaries between the child and the environment. When deemed necessary, a good parent acts as a buffer between the child and environmental challenges with which the child is unprepared to deal (Derdeyn et al., 1982; Schutz et al., 1989).

Clear Priorities

Good parenting appears to include the ability to identify and understand the child's needs. When appropriate, good parents are able to place their children's needs before their own (Ackerman & Schoendorf, 1992; Rohman et al., 1987; Schutz et al., 1989).

Good Supervisor of Behavior

Good parenting appears to include the ability to observe accurately the *behaviors* of the child as well as the parents' own. It is also characterized by the ability to interpret accurately the *feelings* of the child as well as the parents' own. Good parents are able to communicate these observations to their children in an empathic, sensitive, and understanding manner (Ackerman & Schoendorf, 1992; Bray, 1991; Fisher & Fisher, 1986).

Nurturing Positive Self-Esteem

Good parenting appears to include the development and nurturing of independence, individuality, social responsibility, and self-confidence. Positive self-esteem is encouraged when parents direct their children toward alternative forms of action and when their children feel a degree of freedom when making these choices.

Good parenting inspires positive self-esteem when parents set firm, clear, and consistent standards of behavior. Children develop positive self-esteem when they are expected to behave in mature and respectful ways. Positive self-esteem is also bolstered when the rights of both parents and children are recognized (Ackerman, 1995; Maccoby & Mnookin, 1992; Schutz et al., 1989).

Knowing Strengths and Weaknesses

Good parenting appears to include knowledge of the child's strengths and weaknesses. Each child in a family is different from his or her siblings. A good parent knows these differences, respects them, and supports them for each child (Ackerman, 1995; Ackerman & Schoendorf, 1992; Rohman et al., 1987).

Good Role Model

Good parenting appears to include the child's perception of the parent as a positive role model. A good role model teaches the child about limit setting, rule following, and respect of self and others (Schetky & Benedek, 1980).

Good Disciplinarian

Good parenting appears to include the parent's ability to sanction appropriately when necessary. Discipline is a necessary part of all development. Parental discipline takes many different forms and is often dictated by prevailing cultural expectations. A good disciplinarian sets appropriate limits, enforces consequences of transgressions, and provides guidance about the inappropriateness of the current behavior and how it may be changed (Ackerman, 1995; Bray, 1991; Derdeyn et al., 1982; Schutz et al., 1989; Stahl, 1994).

Healthy Family Functioning

Good parenting appears to include the custodial parent's awareness and encouragement of the legitimate need of the child to spend time with the noncustodial parent (Schutz et al., 1989). A good parent understands and encourages the child's need to participate in social groups and other extrafamilial activities that encourage social development.

Moral Reasoning

Good parenting appears to include the teaching of socially appropriate behavior and respect for rules governing society. Teaching social rules and respect for social norms helps teach children about moral behavior within our society.

Most courts are not interested in making judgments about particular moral philosophies, providing these philosophies do not place the child at risk. However, courts are standard bearers for social propriety and proper behavior. Most courts believe parents have a responsibility to teach their children about proper social behavior. Parents also have a responsibility to be role models for their children along these dimensions (Rohman et al., 1987).

QUICK REFERENCE **Deficit Parenting Behaviors**

- Substance use and abuse
- Alcohol abuse
- Physical abuse
- Emotional abuse
- Sexual abuse
- Verbal abuse
- Neglect

Summary

A good parent needs to understand the developmental needs of the child. The parent needs to provide for these developmental challenges, such as dealing appropriately with bodily functions, language acquisition, social development, and any special needs the child may have.

There are a number of relevant psychological factors identified as directly related to being a good parent. However, there is no *simple* way to measure these factors. Evaluators have been busy developing ways to measure these diverse and complex behaviors.

Identifying Deficient Parenting

Identification of deficient parenting typically is confined to behaviors that our society considers dangerous, unlawful, or harmful. Anything that is judged to place a child at risk may be concerned a deficit parenting competency. These deficiencies generally focus on abusive, addictive, or emotionally dysfunctional behaviors. Some deficient behaviors target inappropriate social behaviors and attitudes, such as racially motivated hate speech.

Adults who fit into these groups tend to be viewed as being at high risk for rearing children with significant emotional, psychological, social, and educational problems. There is also an increased probability of these children having a greater than normal frequency of physical problems.

Substance- and Alcohol-Using/Abusing Parents

Children of substance- or alcohol-abusing parents tend to grow up in highly dysfunctional families. When these children grow to adulthood, they tend to repeat many of the same dysfunctional patterns within their families.

There is some research supporting the notion that substance-abusing and alcoholic families are characterized by chaotic organization; inconsistent parental behavior; poor communication; inconsistent discipline and attention to children's needs; below-average school performance by the children; and an increased probability of violence and neglect, both toward the child by the parent as well as by the child toward other children.

Other issues that cloud easy decisions about substance and alcohol abuse concern the level and frequency of use. There are many occasional and recreational drug and alcohol users. At what level of use there is a significant impairment in parental functioning is unclear.

There is also the current cultural and political climate, which is sensitized to any parental behaviors that may be interpreted to indicate signs of abuse. The prevailing social beliefs are that any signs of abusive behavior by a parent are bad for the child. Intuitively, each of us probably agrees with this idea. However, the psychological research has been unable to establish a direct link between level and/or frequency of drug or alcohol use and parental impairment. We know that a parent who is always intoxicated or who beats his or her child every day is a danger to that child. We do not know if a parent who occasionally drinks to intoxication influences the child's development. We do not know if a parent who uses strict punishment in the form of paddling is significantly influencing his or her child's development, either in the long or short term. Most of us believe that such behaviors are wrong and have an influence on a child's long-term development. But the fact is, psychological and sociological research have not adequately researched these behaviors and their short- and long-term effects on child development (Ackerman, 1995; Ackerman & Schoendorf, 1992; Rohman et al., 1987; Schutz et al., 1989).

Emotionally/Physically/Sexually Abusive Parents

There is a significant body of literature examining the parameters of child maltreatment. Among the categories of maltreatment are emotional abuse, physical abuse, and sexual abuse. Each of these may result in a parent losing custody of a child.

There is research characterizing abusive parents. These parents show an increased likelihood of depression, low self-esteem, and dependency. They have been found to behave in less age-appropriate ways and to take fewer age-appropriate responsibilities as parents. Abusive parents have been found to be more likely to use anxiety- and guilt-inducing techniques with their children as motivators. They have been reported to be inconsistent in their application of discipline techniques, make unrealistic demands of their children, and generally to possess poor child management skills.

Abusive parents display a higher level of impulsive behavior. They show poor frustration tolerance, resulting in higher than normal levels of emotional distress, with which they are poorly prepared to deal.

Abusive parents also have been reported to be more emotionally unavailable to their children. Evidence suggests that they are also physically unavailable. Such parents tend to display an immature need for love and affection. They demand that their children fulfill needs normally filled by adult relationships, or else the children are expected to be a caretaker to the parent.

Abusive parents have been found to be lacking in awareness of their children's needs, their own needs, and how to place their children's needs ahead of their own (Gaines, Sandgrund, Green, & Power, 1978; Garbino & Gilliam, 1980).

Although each custody situation must be viewed on its own merits, most courts view evidence of current substance abuse, alcohol abuse, and other forms of abuse as important factors weighing against custody placement. However, it is unclear how a parent's history of abusive behaviors may be viewed when there is evidence of rehabilitation and long-standing recovery.

Most judges attempt to balance the parent's rehabilitation and recovery from abuse with two important factors. The first factor is the probability of relapse. The court is attempting to make decisions about the child's welfare and best interests. It is in no one's best interest to place a child with a parent who is at high risk for substance, alcohol, or physical abuse relapse.

The second factor is quality and extent of recovery from abuse. A parent who has completed a rehabilitation program and has remained free of drugs for 3 years while also providing evidence of job stability would probably be given a greater chance for custody than a parent who is 6 weeks out of a rehabilitation program with no established history of sustained abstinence.

Most states have legislation or case law that argues strongly *against* using a person's substance abuse history against them in custody determination when there is evidence that the abuse is part of the person's history and not their current lifestyle.

What We Can Measure Consistently

Of the 10 criteria outlined in the Michigan Act (1970), half can be measured consistently. Evaluators are often able to identify which parent is better able to provide the children with "remedial care" (Criterion 3). The evaluator can gather information about each parent's resources and availability of time and interest in providing material needs.

Evaluators are able to make relatively accurate judgments about the length of time a child has lived in a stable environment and the desirability of maintaining continuity of the child in that environment (Criterion 4).

Effectively assessing the permanence of a family unit of an existing custodial home is usually a simple task (Criterion 5). Evaluators are often better at identifying the probability of short-term stability permanence. The farther into the future we aim our predictions, the greater the chance that other factors will influence family permanence, resulting in lower accuracy of our prediction.

Evaluators are skilled and have the proper tools available to assess the mental and physical health of the competing parties (Criterion 7). They are also able to request and review the child's records from school and the community with little difficulty (Criterion 8).

Finally, when children get to a certain age, they are often able to make judgments for themselves about where they want to live (Criterion 9). Evaluators are skilled at discussing such decisions with children and figuring out whether they are being placed under undue pressure by one parent or the other. The evaluator is also able to identify the reasoning behind the child's decision and to help the court decide about the appropriateness of the child's reasoning concerning where to live.

More Difficult to Measure

There is no easy way to assess the remaining criteria identified by the Michigan Act (1970) as important in the assessment of the best psychological interests of the child. These criteria ask for judgments about qualities and feelings that reside deep inside each of us.

There is no way to measure accurately "love, affection and other emotional ties" or its "capacity." It is almost as difficult to judge the "moral fitness of the competing parties," because evaluators are privy to only a small view of each parent's full life. Finally, an evaluator is unable to anticipate "other issues considered by the Court to be relevant to a particular child custody suit," because the evaluator seldom, if ever, has direct contact with the judge prior to appearing in court.

Despite these limitations, it is precisely these factors of love, affection, morality, and capability to provide that constitute the lion's share of relevant information in a custody evaluation.

Developing Resources

A concluding word about the best interests standard is to become familiar with state and local statutes and conventions governing child custody evaluations within the jurisdictions in which you provide services. A useful approach is to develop a relationship with an attorney who can help you keep up with changes in laws, statutes, and conventions. In the thoughtful words of Schutz et al. (1989),

These laws set forth the minimum boundaries of an examination. As long as the evaluator has considered and can comment on the factors outlined in the statute, the evaluator will not be subject to attack on the grounds that it [the evaluation] does not comply with state law. (p. 12)

Another practical resource is your state professional association. For example, in North Carolina, there are custody evaluation guidelines published by the state psychological association. However, in states such as Pennsylvania, the state psychological association abandoned its efforts to develop state-specific guidelines and now uses those adopted by the American Psychological Association (1994). Another helpful resource is to maintain contact with other forensic specialists in your area(s) of competence. Explore whether there are local meetings, on-line forensic bulletin boards or chatrooms, or a group of forensic examiners that get together for mutual case review. In many communities, there are multidisciplinary task forces that focus on different aspects of domestic law, custodial concerns, and many other factors related to our work as forensic child custody evaluators.

Note

1. This is a modified version of a report submitted to the court in Delaware County, Pennsylvania. The evaluator was a licensed, doctoral-level psychologist who interviewed only the mother, children, and fiancé. She used only projective techniques in making determinations of emotional functioning and general psychological well-being. She conducted one collateral interview with a 20-year-old baby-sitter. There was no contact with other collateral sources, such as day care workers, school personnel, neighbors, the pediatrician, or other community resources. There were no interviews with the father or his fiancée, nor was there observation of the children with the father. There was no observation of the children with either future spouse. Yet the psychologist testified to a custody recommendation, citing many of the father's alleged limitations, which had been drawn from interview data gathered from the mother.

FIVE

The Forensic Interview
of the Parents

Evaluators must make a deliberate and systematic effort to compare the parents' behavior with those that have been found, through research, to have positive or negative effects on child development. . . . There is simply no substitute for as much empirical anchoring as possible.

Schutz et al. (1989, p. 16)

The evaluator directed the judge to pay particular attention to the father's interview data. It was highly credible, she testified. The father had been living with his 17-year-old son for about a year. Each had a history of relationship difficulties with the mother. The father wanted to end the mother's parental rights. She had no right to see her children after what she had done, he thought.

The 17-year-old, the oldest of three children, had not gotten along with his mother for the past 2 years. Bernie believed that his mother was at fault for the break-up of his relationship with his girlfriend and refused to entertain the idea that the young woman may have decided on her own to end the relationship. Bernie clung to the idea that his mother had intentionally sabotaged his relationship.

The evaluator interviewed the father and son over 3 days. She concluded that the father and son had an accurate view of the mother. Their opinions were judged to be credible and consistent. Based solely upon the information drawn from the father's and son's interviews, the evaluator concluded that the mother was abusive and therefore a threat to her children. Custody of all three boys was recommended to the father.

When the mother was interviewed, the evaluator began by complimenting her son and former husband for teaching her so much about their family life. She followed this statement with asking the mother, "How long have you

74

been abusing your children?" In the body of the report, the evaluator commented that as the interview with the mother continued, the mother appeared to become increasingly defensive and unwilling to provide detailed answers. The evaluator never saw how her opening comments frightened the mother, creating a cognitive set of caution and distrust.

Based on the mother's defensive responses, the evaluator concluded that the child's credibility was firmly established. The evaluator wrote in her final report to the court, "The child was found to be very credible as he described an hysterical mother out of control with anger, and using threats of suicide and homicide to control her children. It is strongly suggested that the Judge talk with the child; that the Court's decision could only benefit from his input."

When I became involved and gained access to collateral information, it became clear that the younger children's teachers, coaches, youth minister, therapist, and neighborhood parents described mother-child interactions as above average. These same sources described the father-child and father-mother interactions as significantly problematic. The father was a weekend alcoholic who often became violent and verbally abusive. Police records showed three arrests for DWI and one court appearance for disorderly conduct. The 17-year-old son had also been drinking for about 18 months and developed a style of verbal abuse similar to his father's. He had his license suspended until he was 21 for drinking while under the influence. Father and son often drank together during the evenings.

Furthermore, the MMPI and MCMI data revealed a father whose scores were significantly elevated on a number of scales suggestive of severe psychopathology. Elevation on each scale was tied directly to collateral data supportive of the father's substance abuse, disregard for rules, and highly suspicious beliefs. The mother's scores, with the exception of the MMPI K and the MCMI Y, showed no significant elevations.

Finally, interview data from the younger children revealed children who were afraid of their father, particularly when he was drinking. In separate interviews, they reported that their older brother often hit them and verbally abused them while the father was in the kitchen observing their interactions, sipping a beer and doing nothing to intervene.

Theoretical Frameworks
Guiding Interview Protocols

Custody evaluators need to be cognizant of the importance of conducting their investigations within an established, empirically derived theory of science. If the *Daubert* standard continues to define standards for expert witness testimony at the federal level, it will surely find its way to the state level

(Goodman-Delahunty, 1997). Custody evaluators will then be asked to formulate their methods, procedures, interpretations, and recommendations within an established theory of human behavior. This is a useful conceptual framework toward which custody evaluations should aspire today.

Systems Theory

One established theoretical model of human behavior is systems theory and may be used to guide a custody evaluation. The concept of a system is defined as a group of people who interact as a functional whole (McGoldrick & Gerson, 1985). The behavior of each member of a family is inextricably interconnected with each person within the family system.

From the point of view of the child, the family system is the most powerful system to which he or she will ever belong. The family is the basis for the child's construction of reality and his or her experience of stability, consistency, safety, comfort, predictability, and love. From the child's point of view, the family is defined as the entire kinship network. Disruption to any part of the system reverberates throughout the entire system and significantly affects each child, often in different ways and over long periods of time.

Families Are Highly Interconnected

The physical, emotional, and social interconnectedness of family members is "profoundly interdependent" (McGoldrick & Gerson, 1985, p. 5). Systems theory predicts that "family interactions and relationships tend to be highly reciprocal, patterned and repetitive. It is this redundancy of pattern that allows" the evaluator to formulate hypotheses about family functioning, individual functioning within family systems, and historical factors that may influence current family functioning (McGoldrick & Gerson, 1985, p. 5).

Families Operate on Different Levels

Families operate on many different levels. They operate on intragenerational (i.e., sibling systems), intergenerational (i.e., parent-child systems), transgenerational (i.e., grandparent-parent-child systems), intrapsychic; interpersonal, biological, social, educational, cultural, community, legal, and economic levels.

Individual Level

People are organized within family structures according to generation, gender, and age, among many other factors. How an individual fits into a family structure, the roles that are ascribed and assumed, and how others within the family system react to this fit are among critical variables to assess.

Intra- and Intergenerational Levels

Examination of behaviors within and across generations provides a rich source of hypotheses about possible family functioning. It also provides a framework to examine predictions about current and future conduct.

*Intra*generational examination incorporates horizontal views of family functioning. The evaluator may look for the degree of emotional, social, or intellectual connectedness between or among family members. For example, the examiner wants to note various subsystems, such as siblings, triangles, and complementary and symmetrically reciprocal relationships. Other systems to explore are the influence of community, courts, schools, church, social groups, and broader sociocultural and ethnic influences.

*Inter*generational examination incorporates vertical views of family functioning. The evaluator may look at the historical variables and place them within the context of the currently evolving family system. The evaluator should explore themes, myths, rules, stories, rituals, and traditions that have been passed down through the generations. Of particular importance within a custody context are the family's values about divorce, marriage, sex role responsibilities, social and cultural expectations around child rearing, and career development. The notion of family legacy and its transgenerational strength is also critical to understand.

Patterns Repeat Themselves

Family patterns repeat themselves. The interpersonal interaction patterns that existed in one generation are often repeated in subsequent generations. Relationship patterns in previous generations are thought to provide implicit models of individual, familial, and social functioning from generation to generation.

Disequilibrated Family Systems

Concurrent events in different parts of the system occur for a reason. There is an underlying homeostasis that characterizes family systems. Life transitions such as divorce plunge the family system into a state of disequilibrium. The resultant confusion often leads to maladaptive behaviors as the system struggles to find its previous balance.

Divorce is, by definition, an unsteady state of familial connectedness in which previous levels of equilibrium no longer exist. The structure that defined balance for a particular family is redefined. The family system takes time to adjust to a new homeostasis—one that may be in the process of development

QUICK REFERENCE   **Levels of Analyses Within**
                   Systems Theory (Partial Listing)

- Community system
- Family system
- Transgenerational system
- Intergenerational system
- Intragenerational system
- Social system
- Peer group system
- Dyadic/relationship system
- Sibling system
- Parental system
- Parent-child system
- Grandparent-parent system
- Grandparent-child system
- Maternal family of origin—paternal family of origin
- Individual system
- Biological system
- Intrapsychic system

as the divorced family system takes shape. Therefore, any impressions drawn
from family functioning when the system is disequilibrated must be viewed
within the context of a dynamic, unstable, unreliable, and unpredictable set
of intragenerational and intergenerational boundaries. The evaluators need
to remember that observations drawn from a disequilibrated family system
may not provide a reliable or valid understanding of how this particular family functions *when it is not under stress.*

Using a systems framework, it becomes easy to structure an interview protocol that reflects the multilevel variables that need to be assessed within systems theory.

Systems Theory Guides Evaluative
Decisions About Relevant Variables

A custody evaluator needs to assess many different levels of functioning
within a divorcing family. Systems theory provides a conceptual framework
from which to identify areas of investigation.

Community System

One level is assessment of the *community system.* These collateral contacts may include school performance and behavior, social activities, recreational activities and the degree of involvement, religious participation, career/job performance, child care outside the home, and medical and mental health status.

Another factor is whether the children and residential parent will need to move from their predivorce residence. Divorce often results in the custodial parent moving from a larger home to a smaller home that may entail changing schools or communities. When this occurs, children lose another primary source of stability and comfort—their friendship groups. Such concerns are imperative to explore.

Family System

Among the most important dimensions is the *family level.* The family system needs to be assessed. How did the previously intact family function? The evaluator needs to gather information about family roles, expectations, legacies, and traditions. The evaluator also needs to explore how the family in transition is operating. What family-of-origin factors are important, and how they might influence current behavior?

Intragenerational factors, such as the quality of sibling relationships and the nature of sibling dynamics, provide useful data about postdivorce family functioning. Intergenerational factors, such as triangulated relationships and parent-child alliances, are also relevant data.

Another intergenerational issue is the relationship among child, parent, and grandparent. Children often lose contact with the nonresidential parent's parents. Also, the custodial parent's parents may assume larger child care responsibilities. Addressing how these changes influence children's adjustment and overall best psychological interests is critical.

Social and Relationship Systems

Social and interpersonal relationships provide valuable information about relationship skills; communicative competence; and the development, maintenance, and regulation of emotional intimacy. Among the types of relationships to examine are friendship patterns, intimacy relationship patterns, parent-child patterns, sibling relationship patterns, and grandparent-parent patterns. An important focus is the goodness of fit between each parent and each child along different developmentally relevant variables.

Individual Systems

The *individual's behavior and functioning* are also important dimensions to evaluate. Systems theory suggests evaluation of the cognitive, social, and emotional aspects of each person. Focus should also be on gathering information about *developmental status* as well as identification of *personality variables* that may be related to adjustment problems (i.e., personality disorders in adults and temperamentally difficult children). Evaluation of intrapsychic factors may also be important.

Assessment of Different Levels

Each of these systems levels—community, family, social, interpersonal, and individual—may be assessed using conventional techniques of measurement. The community levels may be evaluated through the use of traditional collateral information-gathering procedures. These include, but are not limited to, direct or phone interviews and document review. Data about family-of-origin factors may be gathered using a technique such as a genogram. Social behavior and interpersonal relationships may be measured through direct observation, clinical interviews, and self-reports as well as collateral data. Personality functioning may be assessed using standardized personality tests and inventories as well as projective techniques. Thus, a systems framework allows for the evaluation of family and individual functioning within a scientifically accepted conceptual framework, of which many components have been subjected to empirical investigation and theoretical discussion in refereed journals. Table 5.1 suggests techniques to use in the assessment of different systems levels.

Interview Provides Hypotheses to Be Verified by Other Sources

There are few tools as important in data gathering as the forensic interview. The interview is where hypotheses generated from other forms of data are examined in direct, face-to-face exchange. The purpose of the forensic interview is to gather information, confirm or disconfirm hypotheses drawn from other data sources, and listen with your finely crafted ear.

The forensic examiner directly challenges discrepancies in the data. His or her responsibility is to discover and confirm psychological facts. Confronting discrepancies and seeking confirmation from other data sources is essential when interviewing either children or adults.

TABLE 5.1 Assessment of Different Systems Levels

Systems Level	Method of Assessment
Community system	Collateral contacts
Family system	Collateral contacts Direct observations Psychometric assessment Self-report Forensic interviews
Social and dyadic relationships	Collateral contacts Direct observations Psychometric assessment Self-report Forensic interviews
Individual system	Collateral contacts Direct observation Psychometric assessment Self-report Forensic interviews

The Forensic Adult Interview

The forensic interview of a parent should follow a uniform structure for several reasons. First, a standard protocol allows another interviewer to replicate your interview format and data-gathering procedure. This should allow for the accumulation of the same or similar data about an individual. The second reason is that a standard interview protocol ensures that each parent interviewed is evaluated along a similar set of criteria. A third reason is that a standard interview protocol serves an important organizing function. The data may be arranged into clear and somewhat discrete categories.

Systems Theory Guides
Choice of Interview Variables

Conceptualizing the variables to be assessed in a child custody evaluation within an accepted and empirically examined theory of human behavior provides a framework within which to define interview variables. Using systems theory as a guide, the questions that guide a child custody interview almost write themselves. The principal grouping of systemic family functioning includes at least six primary categories for assessment. Four of these categories are summarized in Table 5.2.

This listing of interview areas is not exhaustive. Instead, it is a beacon that points to areas of individual, family, and extrafamily functioning from which relevant information may be gathered.

Building the Interview Framework

Data need to be organized and analyzed along two dimensions: structure and content. A structural analysis examines the fundamental rules that guide the individual's information processing. It may include an assessment of the cognitive complexity of the adult's presentation of the information. Adults differ along dimensions of concrete versus abstract thinking; intelligence; problem solving; social perspective taking; moral judgment; and a variety of other cognitive, emotional, and social dimensions. Each of these dimensions may be categorized in terms of the sophistication and degree of cognitive complexity each adult brings to his or her view of the custodial dispute.

Content analysis examines the concrete information that the parent reports. This is a content-related focus because the parent is providing verbal data from which we draw meaning.

Structure

Each level provides important information about the individual, his or her parenting, and his or her ability to conceptualize and anticipate short- and long-term variables that may influence the child or parenting of the child. The structural components of a parent's current functioning provide useful information about personality development and possible concerns about psychopathology. They also provides a framework within which to understand the parent's view of the child, the other parent, and the multitude of factors that affect the custodial arrangements. For example, a concrete-thinking parent with an IQ of 95 may view the strengths and weaknesses of his or her child differently from an abstract-thinking parent with an IQ of 125. Similarly, a parent with predominant narcissistic features may view the child's needs and his or her ability to meet those needs in a qualitatively different manner from a parent with no personality disorder.

In a recent evaluation, a father's MCMI-II profile showed a base rate (BR) score of 95 on the Narcissistic scale. During the interviews, I also hypothesized the father to be a narcissistic personality, although I was uncertain about the degree to which his narcissism affected his parenting. After completing appropriate data collection, my conclusion was that he was a well-skilled parent with narcissistic tendencies that did not significantly influence his parent-

TABLE 5.2 **Systems Variables Within Family Functioning**

Individual Behavior	*Social/Dyadic*	*Extended Family*	*Community*
Cognitive	Friendship history	Paternal	School
Social	and dymanics	grandparents	Recreational
Emotional	Workplace	Maternal	Religious
Personality	Group involve-	grandparents	Legal
organization	ment	Aunts and uncles	Community
Object relations	Parent-child	Cousins	Medical
Empathy	Parent-parent	In-laws	After-school care
Social role taking	Child-child	Family	Youth ministers
Personal	Social boundaries	boundaries	Coaches
boundaries	Family behavior		Counselors/
Values and	before divorce		mental health
attitudes	Family behavior		
Separation/	after divorce		
individuation			
Reality testing			
Nurturing behaviors			

ing. This father was able to view his children's concerns and his former wife's requests with openness and fairness. The moral of this example is, do not jump to conclusions that the clinical conceptualization of the litigant necessarily is also a statement about his or her parenting capacity.

Content

The content of the interview is important because it helps to place into perspective the parent's experience with the child, the former spouse, the community resources, collateral information sources, and other relevant factors. It also provides insight into how the interviewee perceives each parent's adjustment to the new family arrangement as well as how the children's adjustment is viewed.

In the example above, I was concerned about the degree to which the father would be able to anticipate and understand the differing needs of his young adolescent girls, whose worldview was substantially different from his. The content of his discussions revealed a genuine empathy and appreciation for the role of a parent to be flexible and open to alternative views of life. Discussions about his former wife revealed little ability to see another's perspective.

Structural Considerations
in the Forensic Adult Interview

Science in general, and behavioral science in particular, continuously rede-
fines and reinvents itself. The conceptual notions that address structure are
drawn from the current zeitgeist and literature. Systems theory is one of the
currently accepted models of family functioning. The principles upon which
systems theory is based may eventually be discovered to be too broad, too
limited, or just plain wrong as our empirical science continues examination of
these variables. The evaluator needs to stay apprised of the evolving nature of
empirical research and conceptual modifications in any theory guiding custody evaluation. With these limitations in mind, some of the structural variables used to guide the interview process outlined above will be discussed
further.

Parent's Implicit Model of the World

Individuals develop models of reality based upon previous learning experiences and the ways in which the individual needs to construe present reality
to help maintain the current view of self. The family-of-origin assessment
described above may also provide information about how a parent has developed implicit models of parenting, couples and family communications, conflict resolution, problem solving, and decision making for intrapersonal and
interpersonal interactions.

Recognizing the rules governing each of these implicit models is critical in
understanding how the adult operates within a variety of family systems. For
example, the evaluator needs to construct a view of the adult's belief system
about parenting attitudes, values, and behaviors. A common assessment
request is for the litigant to describe his or her parenting philosophy and to
provide five events that exemplify this philosophy. Similarly, recognizing the
implicit model of behavior management or discipline is valuable. For example, if the mother was hit with a belt as a child, the evaluator may want to
know what discipline strategies the mother uses when faced with a child's
transgression. It is not enough to discuss the parent's initial strategy. The
examination needs to go beyond the initial response and explore the second,
third, and fourth step a parent would take to discipline a child. Too often,
adults from an abusive background recognize a need to change their discipline strategy. However, they often develop few alternatives beyond sending
the child into a time-out area before they turn to the lessons learned from
their family of origin and take out a belt.

A thorough evaluation of how each parent's implicit models differ may
provide useful information. It is somewhat common for marital distress and
the resultant divorce to be motivated by significant differences in the implicit

models about parenting, discipline, communication, and intimacy held by each parent. An evaluator who accurately assesses the fundamental differences in rules and behavior that guide each parent's behavior may be better able to create a parenting plan that suits the specific needs of the family, rather than some generic scheme.

Personality Functioning

Personality organization needs to be assessed. Not only is the identification of psychopathology important, but understanding personality organization within a systems framework allows for the conceptualization of goodness of fit between parental personality types and the ability to meet the child's needs. For example, it is possible to extrapolate from personality typology hypotheses regarding how the parent interacts with the child, how the parent interacts with the other parent, and where future communication obstacles may lie in light of these personality factors.

A useful tool in this regard is the Millon Clinical Multiaxial Inventory (Millon, 1987). As discussed in Chapter 10, the Millon is purported to be the best inventory available to measure the degree to which a parent may fit an empirically derived personality prototype. Each personality type may be characterized through its unique way of interacting with its environment. Each personality type may also be examined for its particular way of coping with other prototype behaviors. The result is that the evaluator should be able to predict two critical elements with a reasonable degree of accuracy. The first is the specific behavior and coping strategies on the part of a parent. The second is the ways in which one parent's personality type may fit with that of the other parent. A similar level of analysis of personality prototype characteristics and behaviors may be explored between parent and child prototypes.

Cognitive Development

Cognitive development covers a wide range of behavior. The evaluator should make judgments about intellectual and cognitive developmental functioning as it affects parenting. Level of parental cognitive functioning may be a relevant variable. It may affect how the parent makes personal and social judgments. It may affect the number or complexity of alternative options when problem solving. Intellectual functioning may also help to determine social role-taking ability and communicative competencies.

Most of the time, evaluation of cognitive developmental variables in adults is conducted through embedded measures, clinical observation, and collateral data. The evaluator should be able to make gross judgments about intellectual ability based upon the parent's interview data. One may observe vocabulary usage, syntax structure, verbal abstract abilities, social role-taking perspective, simple versus complex formulation of life events, reasoning ability, and dyadic-dialogue exchanges to infer a general level of intellectual functioning. The evaluator may use specific subscales of the WAIS-III or other similar tests to examine components of cognitive functioning. For example, a quick measure of social judgment and reasoning may be the Comprehension subtest of the WAIS-III.

Formal Intellectual Assessment

Ackerman (1995; Ackerman & Schoendorf, 1992) recommend using intellectual assessment in every evaluation. H. D. Kirkpatrick (personal communication, May 9, 1997) argues that the use of the WAIS-III should be a cornerstone in forensic evaluation for two reasons. First, psychologists' greatest strengths are in the development and application of empirically derived tests and measures. Thus, a well-developed test should be the foundation around which all other data-gathering tools are organized. Second, the WAIS-III provides a wealth of information about the litigant along a number of relevant dimensions. It has been used in many different forensic settings, has a long history of case law supporting its admissibility, is continually researched and updated, and is among the most psychometrically sound tests available. I believe that using tests such as the WAIS-III provides a potent overview of a variety of intellectual skills and reasoning abilities useful in understanding the match between parent and child.

Social Role-Taking Ability

How a parent is able to step outside of his or her view of the world and appreciate events from the view of the child is a critical factor in creating empathy and understanding. Social role-taking ability (Flavell, 1975) is the ability to step outside one's personal perspective and understand how others may view a similar event from another perspective. Role taking also includes understanding the effect of one's behavior on others. In the case of parenting, it is the ability of the parent to understand alternative perspectives about reality that do not reflect those of the parent. For example, a mother is able to recognize and understand the intense emotional struggles confronting her former husband as he attempts to reestablish a postdivorce relationship with his son. It is also understanding how a parent's behavior may affect his or her children. For example, a mother may recognize that telling a child about an upcoming date with a new man may cause significant distress for the child, who is still reeling from living in a divided family.

During the custody process, it is common that a parent's social role-taking abilities may be less well displayed than if you met him or her before or after the custodial dispute is complete. This, in part, is because the stress of the custodial dispute often compels a more rigid, either-or conceptual set about areas of life related to parenting—or at least related to the other parent. Often, one parent appears unable to recognize and understand the emotional obstacles confronting the other parent. Parents who, in other aspects of their lives, may function at extremely high levels of cognitive complexity find themselves arguing with their former spouses over the adult version of the childhood argument, "If you don't play by my rules, then I won't play with you anymore."

The challenges to an otherwise competent adult's social role-taking ability within a custodial dispute are enormous. Many find themselves unable to see the other parent's point of view. Some are unable to see their children's perspective as different from their own, despite a predivorce history of knowing and respecting their children's emotional and intellectual boundaries.

Some parents in custody disputes often lose sight of their children's needs and requirements. There is something about the passionate intensity of a custody dispute that turns well-intentioned, thinking people into intellectually rigid, emotionally constricted adolescents who are locked in a competitive battle with their former spouses.

When the evaluator has identified that the parent is functioning in a cognitively *simple* way along one or more dimensions, it is imperative to seek out collateral sources who knew the litigant prior to the marital dissolution. The collateral sources often will indicate that the parent is viewed as high functioning, verbally abstract, and sensitive to the needs and views of others, and has a multiyear history of being empathic, compassionate, and a stellar problem solver and team player. Yet when you interview the parent, he is a rigid, dualistic, concrete thinker who sees only manipulation from his former wife and plans nothing but revenge against her.

Adjustment to divorce may take many forms. One is to react to a former spouse in a manner not congruent with one's history or functioning in other parts of life. When the evaluator gathers information that demonstrates such discrepant behaviors, it is useful to explore the differences with the litigant.

Most current adjustment-to-divorce literature suggests that there is a gradual return to premarital separation levels of functioning within 2 years postdivorce. The evaluator must be careful not to overinterpret the meaning of behavior observed during the early stages of family realignment. One might hypothesize that the observed behavior may be a reaction specific to the divorce process rather than any significant factor that may influence parenting. This, in turn, may lead to fruitful discussions and a greater understanding of the pressures and contextual factors that the parent feels influences his or her behavior.

Overlooking the powerful influence of contextual variables on cognitive functioning related to one's adjustment to divorce may lead to a misunderstanding of the person as an individual, as a divorced spouse, and as a single parent. For example, in a recent case, an evaluator recommended against custodianship for the mother because she was perceived as emotionally incompetent to deal with the pain of her recent divorce. The evaluator apparently did not understand the profound effects of early postdivorce adjustment on cognitive functioning. He wrote:

> The mother is a very angry and bitter woman who tends to project blame on others for things she needs to take responsibility for herself. . . . She presents as "stuck" in her life needing psychotherapy to help her examine how this the divorce happened. . . . At age 45, she is furious at being left and being forced to be more independent than she would wish. . . . Her choice of Real Estate as a career is worrisome . . . and not conducive as a career change or a way to make a good living in the midst of a custody dispute when she is requesting primary custody of her children. . . . She needs to get on top of her depression . . . and also her anger. She needs to work and move from dependency to autonomy and independence. She needs to be able to make a living.

This evaluator did not conduct any collateral interviews, administer any standardized psychological tests to explore his hypothesis of depression, administer any self-report measures, use a standard interview format, or talk with the children or former spouse about overall caretaking within the family. If the evaluator had conducted a proper evaluation, he would have discovered that *all* extrafamilial collateral sources interviewed cited numerous examples of the mother being the primary caregiver. If the evaluator had talked with the children about their perception of each parent, he would have discovered that the children felt strongly about each parent, recognizing that their mother had more responsibility in their care and daily routines than did their father. If the evaluator had talked with the mother's therapist, he would have learned that the mother had been significantly depressed 6 months ago but was presently functioning at a healthy level of emotional stability.

Family-of-Origin Factors

The historical influence of each parent's childhood experiences and family structure need to be examined. The models of interpersonal interaction learned within the family system may provide important data about how the parent currently conceptualizes family dynamics, motivations, and conflict resolution. Family-of-origin factors provide data about deficit parenting variables such as history of alcohol or substance abuse, physical abuse, sexual abuse, emotional abuse, and marital or family dysfunction, among others.

The most frequently used method of data gathering for family-of-origin variables is the genogram. "A genogram is a format for drawing a family tree that records information about family members and their relationships over at least three generations" (McGoldrick & Gerson, 1985, p. 1). Gendgrams are tangible and graphic representations of a family. Use of the McGoldrick and Gerson model provides a standard means for gathering family history data. The use of a standard family history data-gathering format provides a means of replication.

There is no one way to approach family history data gathering. There is no universally agreed-upon set of family history variables that defines the direction of a custodial evaluation. Which specific variables need to be evaluated is dependent upon the psycholegal questions posed by the court order.

Examination of behaviors within and across generations is critical to understanding adult behavior. Family systems are assumed to repeat themselves from generation to generation. Therefore, developing a framework of familial functioning within and across generational boundaries becomes critical in the evaluator's emerging understanding of systemic operation.

The evaluator needs to explore how the parent connects with each member of the family. Each subsystem, such as siblings, triangles, and complementary and symmetrically reciprocal relationships, needs to be assessed along dimensions of emotional closeness-distance, regulation of intimacy, rigidity-flexibility, authoritarian-permissive, and active-passive, among other relevant factors.

Intergenerational examination incorporates vertical views of family functioning. The evaluator may look at the historical variables and place them within the context of the currently evolving family system. The evaluator should explore themes, myths, rules, stories, rituals, and traditions that have been passed down through the generations. Of particular importance within a custody context are family values about divorce, marriage, sex role responsibilities, social and cultural expectations around child rearing, and career development. The notion of family legacy and its transgenerational strength is also critical to understand.

Collateral Interviews

Forensic evaluators seek collateral data sources to help determine the facts of the psycholegal questions posed by the court. Collateral data provide two important dimensions in a forensic report. The first is to support the contention of one party in a litigation. The use of collateral data helps to remove the apparent conflict of interest inherent in asking the litigant for his or her point of view. The second reason is that litigants may, intentionally or unintentionally, distort data in a manner that serves their legal argument. Therefore, collateral data provide a means for controlling potential effects of deception and malingering.

There is near-universal agreement among published texts that collateral interview data and record reviews are critical components of a comprehensive forensic child custody evaluation (e.g., Schutz et al., 1989; Skafte, 1985; Stahl, 1994). The training arm of the American Academy of Forensic Psychology also stresses the need for collateral interview data in conducting forensic child custody evaluations (Greenberg, 1996; Greenberg & Moreland, 1996; Skidmore, 1994; Weissman, 1996).

According to Shapiro (1984),

> Disastrous results can ensue if a psychologist enters court merely on the basis of his therapeutic interaction with a patient, and tries to render valid opinions in a particular case on this therapeutic insight, without doing the investigative work necessary in any forensic case. . . . Clinical interview is *never* sufficient; interview must be supplemented by careful review of records, history taking and interviews with family, friends, or employees. (p. 131)

Who to Interview as a Collateral?

Collateral sources may take at least three different forms. A collateral source may provide information about the child. This group may include pediatricians, teachers, coaches, and other caretakers. A second group is individuals who have direct observational knowledge of the parent-child interaction. This group may include neighbors, coaches, teachers, family members, relatives, and friends. The primary contribution of this group's members is their view of how the parent and child behaved with each other. The third group is the child's primary caretakers who are not the parents. This usually applies to day care workers, after-school supervisors, therapists, tutors, and baby-sitters. These people often do not observe the parent and child interacting, but they can provide valuable information about the child's development, adjustment, and concerns.

According to Weissman (1991a), the decision to interview collateral sources should be "based upon criteria of relevancy, reliability and necessity" (p. 473). A general rule of thumb is that a more valued collateral source is one who is not related to either parent and has no vested interest in the outcome of the evaluation. Collateral information from other professionals is more likely to provide balanced, disciplined information than is information from friends, significant partners, or relatives (Weissman, 1991a).

There are a number of pitfalls to avoid when conducting collateral interviews. The most important is to maintain consistency with the role of custody evaluator. Some evaluators conducting collateral interviews focus on determining the truth of facts rather than simply gathering the data and reporting it to the court. Another common mistake is weighing the probative value of a collateral source. The evaluator's role is to gather data and interpret the data within psychological science; it is not to become a judge. Collateral information should be used to confirm or disconfirm hypotheses generated from other sources of data. Thus, collateral data may be granted a significantly more important role in a particular evaluation if the data speak directly to the parent-child relationship.

In a recent evaluation, observation of the parent-child interaction with each parent revealed caring, involved parents. Collateral information showed that the mother attended every school meeting, drove the children to all their activities, and was continuously involved in each child's school experience. The father was reported to ignore school meetings, and he abdicated responsibility for chauffeuring his children to his former spouse. Collateral sources submitted by the father, such as neighbors and teachers, described numerous direct observational incidents in which the father was seen driving intoxicated with children in the car. In this case, the collateral data provided overwhelming support for the mother's contentions about the father's behavior.

How to Interview Collateral Sources

The collateral interview contains at least three critical components. The most obvious is developing a list of appropriate collateral contacts. The litigant should compose the list. Once composed, it may be discussed with the evaluator. Useful information to have prior to the collateral contact includes who each person is and what information will be discussed. I usually ask the litigant to characterize the nature of the relationship between the collateral and the examinee. I also want to know how the collateral source knows the interaction between the parent and child. I verify phone numbers and explain the structure of the interview.

I request that the litigant complete a form called the "Collateral Data Form" (see Form 5.1). The parent is asked to indicate at least five collateral contact persons. The form asks that each person call the evaluator's office to schedule a telephone or in-person interview. There is a statement on the form advising that each person contacted by the litigant as a collateral source needs to be told in advance the basic reason for their interview with the evaluator. The form specifies that the litigant will be charged for the time reserved even if the collateral fails to call at the scheduled appointment time. It also indicates that a typical interview will last about 30 minutes. The form advises that each collateral source should also be forewarned that the interview is not confidential, and they may be asked to testify about the information they provide to the evaluator.

Two issues are important to review before continuing with the interviews. Collateral sources need to be informed that nothing will be held confidential. The second is a clear understanding that *their* statements to you may result in *their* being asked (subpoenaed) to testify.

FORM 5.1 **Collateral Data Form (Adapted from Greenberg, 1996)**

Indicate at least five people with whom I may talk about their observation of your parenting. *Please have them call our office* to schedule a telephone or in-person interview. These persons may be friends, family, neighbors, co-workers, teachers, ministers, youth counselors, employers, or anyone else you think might have observed you and your children. Please explain to your collateral sources why their participation is important. Advise them that I will reserve 30 minutes for an interview and you will be charged for that time whether they call or not. Advise each collateral source that the interview is not confidential and may result in them having to testify in court. Include at least two people who are not close friends or family members.

Your Name:

Your Phone Number:

Name of Collateral   Relationship to You   Phone Number

_____

_____

_____

_____

_____

I understand and agree that I am granting a full and unconditional release of information for Dr. Gould to discuss any aspect of this legal/forensic matter with each of the above listed persons. I do so knowing that I can not anticipate nor control what information will be exchanged in these consultations.

Signed: _____ Date: _____

The collateral interview should be structured around a set of questions determined by the evaluator prior to the interview. Generally, questions focus on what the collateral source has observed about the parent-child interaction.

Most individuals interviewed for such purposes find it difficult to place their observations into behavioral language. Interview data are usually filled with inferences and conclusions such as "She is a very loving parent" or "He cares deeply about his children." Such statements provide little information about what has been observed.

It is often useful to review with the person how to present behaviorally descriptive statements. A typical example is to use the phrase "loving parent." You may explain to the person that "loving parent" may mean different things to different people, but talking about seeing the parent hug his child while kissing and stroking her hair provides a clearer sense of the behaviors observed.

Collateral Example From Report

Mrs. Smith was asked to submit a list of names of individuals who were familiar with her and/or had direct observational knowledge of her parenting. She submitted a list of 33 names. I chose to contact 5 persons who appeared to have had significant contact with Mrs. Smith over the years and were not blood relatives. The phone interviews lasted in total approximately 4 hours and took place on Sunday evening, August 24, 1996.

Each collateral interviewee was provided with informed consent. Each was informed that the interview was not confidential and that they might be asked to testify in court about the contents of their interview. The interview continued when a participant provided a verbal statement that they voluntarily agreed to proceed. One participant declined to participate and the interview was immediately stopped.

Each collateral source was asked at least the following questions: (1) How would you characterize your relationship with Mrs. Smith? (2) Please described what you have observed of Mrs. Smith's parenting. (3) What do you view as Mrs. Smith's greatest strength as a parent? (4) What do you view as Mrs. Smith's greatest weakness as a parent? (5) Have you ever observed Mrs. Smith to discipline her children? If yes, please describe. (6) Do you have any concerns about Mrs. Smith's parenting skills? (7) Is there anything you would like to share with me about Mrs. Smith as a parent that I have not asked? If yes, please describe.

The following descriptions are summaries of these collateral contacts. At the end of each phone call, I read back to the interviewee the substance of their comments. What follows are comments that have been reviewed with the interviewee to ensure accuracy.

Factors That May Influence the Interview

Parties involved in a child custody dispute are highly motivated to convince the examiner of their ability to be the best parent. There is a strong probability that some distorted information will be presented to the examiner, either intentionally or unintentionally. The examiner must take precautions to evaluate the degree and type of deception or malingering (Rogers, 1988, 1995) or other types of response style (Heilbrun, 1995).

Standardized psychological tests often have measures of response bias built into the test. For example, the MMPI-2 has seven validity scales, the MCMI-II and III have three validity scales, and the 16 PF has two such scales. Such objectively obtained data may prove helpful in formulating ideas about how each interviewee may attempt to influence the data or the evaluator.

Some evaluators are becoming increasingly aware of the need to measure deception and malingering. Rogers (1988) worries that all data gathered in a forensic interview may be contaminated, intentionally or not, by the litigant. Understanding how to interpret standard psychological tests for potential malingering or deception is an important skill in any forensic examination.

Interview questions exploring parenting behaviors from both parents' points of view also may provide insight into response bias. For example, in a recent evaluation, the mother provided two pages of information about her role in the current custody conflict. Her husband indicated on the form three paragraphs about his former wife's culpability and nothing about himself. When asked during the interview to describe his role in the conflict, he maintained that it was entirely his former wife's fault. Later, when the father's sister was interviewed as a collateral information source, the sister indicated that after knowing the mother for almost 20 years, she had never observed the woman to do anything positive for the father or the children. "The only thing I can tell you is that one year she made pretty Halloween costumes."

The father's MCMI-II profile indicated a BR of 92 with the Narcissistic Personality type. After other collateral interviews and record reviews, my conclusion was that the paternal family of origin could be characterized as familial narcissism in which the mother would never been seen by anyone in the paternal family as having anything positive to provide the children. This was factored into the final custody decision regarding the father's ability to support and encourage the children's relationship with their mother.

As a final word on factors that may influence litigant behavior during an interview, the evaluator needs to be aware that the parent is motivated to make some kind of positive impression. It is not always clear exactly what agenda the parent brings into the interview, but the examiner needs to be cognizant of the multiple contextual factors that may alter a litigant's behavior during an interview. Some of these factors may be intentional attempts to manipulate the evaluator. Other behaviors may result from the litigant responding to nonquestion-related concerns, such as the anxiety associated with the evaluation process.

A recent custody case demonstrates the need for the evaluator to take exceptional care in understanding the contextual factors to which a parent may be responding during an interview *and* our relative lack of awareness of the powerful influence of these variables.

When Mrs. Smith was in my office with her son, she was able to relate to him in a positive manner. However, she appeared to be somewhat tentative in her approach. She did not want him to engage in certain behaviors. She asked that he stop the behavior, and she appeared to be anxious about her son doing anything that he was not supposed to do in my office. She appeared to be somewhat hesitant in how to work with him, although she talked as if she had a good grasp of this.

I was asked to reexamine the mother and child for a parenting competency evaluation. I observed that the child, who at the time of the initial interview was 18 months old, was a typical toddler who wanted to touch, lift, and play with everything in my office. The mother explained that she became anxious about her son damaging or breaking objects in my office. She was certain that her little boy's typical toddler behavior would be viewed as evidence of her having no control over her child. Therefore, she spent her time attempting to control his every move. I took the mother and child into a playroom where nothing could be broken, and the mother's anxiety left the room immediately. When I visited the mother and son at their home, I also observed an appropriately interactive, appropriately directive parenting style, a style presumably not observed by the first evaluator during the single-hour, in-office, parent-child interview.

Furthermore, the mother was a ninth-grade dropout who had never been involved in a custody dispute, never been evaluated by psychologists, and was convinced that the judge was going to place her child in foster care to punish the two young parents for having a baby out of wedlock. The young mother's beliefs about the interview process and results significantly influenced her behavior during the first evaluation and during her initial meeting with me. However, the first evaluator did not talk with the mother about the beliefs, attitudes, and other contextual variables that may have been exerting a powerful, though invisible, pressure on her behavior.

The moral: Understand the parent in order to understand his or her behaviors.

SIX

The Forensic Interview
of the Child

> My whole world is my parents. I wake up with them. I come
> home to them. I talk to them. They have always told us that a
> family is a team. My team broke up. I have nowhere to go. No
> one to talk to. My life is ruined. How could they do this to me?
>
> *Angela, age 14*

"I'm glad you were able to come in today with your mommy. Do you know why you are here today?"

"I dunno." Suzie looked ahead blankly. Her 8-year-old body was shoved up against the corner of the couch, her hands were strapped in front of her mouth, and her eyes were cast downward.

"Suzie, our talk today is very important. Your mommy and daddy spoke to a judge last week. Did you know that?"

Suzie shakes her head feebly up and down.

"Do you know what the judge said?"

She looked at the carpet, refusing to look up at me. "The judge was angry with my mommy and daddy. They fight too much."

"What do they fight about?"

"Me."

"They fight about you? Why do they fight about you?"

"Because I made them get a divorce."

"How did you make them get a divorce?"

"Because the judge wants to punish me. He's going to take me away from my mommy because I was bad."

"Suzie, that's not what the judge told me. The judge said he wants me to talk with you and each of your parents. Then, he wants me to write a letter to him explaining what I learned. In the letter, I will tell the judge my opinion of who you might feel better living with."

96

"You're the one who is going to take me away?"

"In a way, yes. I will talk to many people and then try to figure out what is best for you."

"Then, I won't say anything else. I don't want to choose. I love both of my parents!"

* * * * *

The Forensic Interview of the Child

Historically, evaluators were trained in graduate programs that taught clinical interviewing techniques. These techniques often provided training and experience in face-to-face interviewing and history taking. The data gathered from such interviewing techniques focused on intrapsychic, interpersonal, and social arenas. The inferences drawn from such data usually focused on concepts such as differential diagnosis, personality organization (Axis II), and reactions to life situations (Axis I). Those with an educational background would draw inferences about intellectual functioning and psychoeducational achievement. Those with a social work background explored the fit of the individual in the grander social systems in which he or she lived.

Clinical child interviewers often relied on their subjective judgments about what to do, where to take the interview, what was important and what was not, and how to make decisions. Their techniques tended to be based on a combination of discipline-specific training, personal experience, and professional seasoning. The presenting problem often guided the direction of the interview, helping more and more to narrow down the child's verbal reports and focus on a particular set of concerns (or events).

The forensic child interview is different because the interviewer is in control of the direction of the interview. The interview follows a standard protocol, providing uniformity in data gathering. The interview *should* explore areas of family functioning that reflect current behavioral science literature about relevant factors to assess in child custody evaluations. It *should* also explore the child's perceptions and feelings about family functioning, specifically aimed at understanding the child's relationship with each family member and how each contributes to the child's growth and development (best psychological interests). A primary quest of the forensic interview of the child is to gather information useful in understanding the goodness of fit between each child and each parent.

Standard Interview Format

Uniformity is important in all aspects of child custody evaluations. First, using a standard protocol allows another evaluator to repeat the interview steps you followed should the need arise for a second or follow-up evaluation. By using a standard protocol, it is hoped that a similar data set would be gathered by anyone conducting an evaluation.

The second reason that using a standard interview protocol is important is to ensure that each child interviewed is evaluated along a similar set of criteria. In this way, the relevant factors identified as a concern in a particular evaluation will be explored with each child, as appropriate. Too often, evaluators using nonstandard interview formats follow the emotional currents of the interview and discuss factors important to the child's emotional experience of divorce or current feelings about each parent, but they may not cover relevant factors such as who is perceived as the primary versus secondary caretaker, who is perceived as the psychological parent(s), preseparation adjustment, postdivorce adjustment, school performance, friendship groups, social skills, and so on.

A third reason to use a standard interview protocol is to allow for collateral confirmation of issues brought up during the interview(s). When a standard set of questions guides the forensic interview, it provides a useful organizing framework, allowing the examiner to pursue external confirmation of a defined set of criteria such as school performance, medical history, peer group behavior, and participation.

Finally, using collateral interviews to substantiate data gathered during a child interview is important. Many mental health practitioners were raised with the belief that children do not lie. The concept of "believe the child" has often meant "that children's demonstrations, assertions, and affirmations in interviews . . . should be taken at face value" (Faller, 1996, p. 84). Research has demonstrated that children's statements are *not* always reliable or valid. A child's assertions about a parent may depend heavily upon the context in which they were discussed. For example, a child may state a desire to live with her mother when she is brought to the interview by the mother, yet state a desire to live with the father when she is brought by the father. A child's reliability may be associated with her chronological age or developmental level. The evaluator's perception of a child's emotional connection to a parent may also depend upon the child's mood, most recent experience with the parent, or some other set of influencing factors. In fact, one of the most useful questions to ask during a child interview is, "What is it that your mother (father) wanted you to tell me?" A variation is, "What did your father (mother) say to remember to tell me?"

Children are easily influenced by parents as well as by the interview context. It is important that the evaluator is able to identify how each parent may

---

QUICK REFERENCE **Advantages of Standard Interview Protocol in Child Forensic Interviews**

- Allows for replication of data-gathering steps
- Provides for uniform assessment along similar criteria
- Organizes data around relevant psycholegal and behavioral dimensions
- Increases reliability and validity of collected data

---

have influenced—or is perceived to have influenced—each child's understanding of what to discuss during the interview.

These issues are particularly important for children caught in the middle of moderate- to high-conflict divorces. There is a precarious balancing act to perform. On one hand, care must be taken to approach a child's verbal report in a manner consistent with approaches used with adult self-report. Children's allegations need to be supported by external sources. On the other hand, a child's stories need to be embraced, explored, and understood from the child's point of view.

One way to seek confirmation of a child's story is through collateral interviewing. Another way is to ask each parent to bring each child for an interview. The hope is that whatever influence one parent has over a child will be balanced (or at least more visible to the evaluator) when the same child is brought in by the other parent. In fact, Schutz et al. (1989) recommend counterbalancing the interview structure. For example, after a mother has had a weekend with a child, the child is brought to the interview that Monday morning by the mother. After the child has had a weekend with her father, the child is brought to the interview before being placed back into the custodial care of the mother.

Limitations of Data Gathering

Gathering useful information about a child's perspective within a family in transition often relies on effective interviewing, which in turn rests on careful consideration and identification of salient factors drawn from the child development literature. For many years, Piagetian theory guided research and thinking about cognitive development and memory abilities. The belief was that children's thinking develops through a fixed sequence of stages, evolving from less to more complex. Neo-Piagetian theories have reported that even at specific stages, children's abilities vary (Fischer, 1980).

There is a growing acceptance that children's performance is enhanced when tasks are grounded in significant life events—experiences that are personally meaningful or emotionally powerful for them (Steward, Bussey, Goodman, & Saywitz, 1993). For example, young children have been reported to be well-structured, accurate, and logical in their recollection of simple events that have meaning for their lives. Compared with the richer detail provided by adults, children present simplified versions of events, yet they can recall both familiar and one-time events of a meaningful personal nature in a relatively accurate manner (Ceci & Bruck, 1995).

A good rule of thumb is that as events become more complex, younger children will have increasing difficulty discriminating and distinguishing among complex relationships. They may be able to describe individual events, but integrating complex events into a coherent gestalt may be beyond their intellectual abilities. The older the child, the better the accuracy. However, when complex events are broken down into simple, more manageable units that correspond to the child's level of development, children's accounts of complex events may be expected to improve (Steward et al., 1993). In general, the more peripheral the detail, the less likely a younger child will report the memory. The more emotionally meaningful the event, the more likely it is that the child will recall it accurately (Ceci & Bruck, 1995).

Use of Context and Cues

Children often rely on context and cues to facilitate memory of events. Younger children need more concrete and readily available cues than do older children. They may also need reminders. Questions may serve as external cues as well as exposure to different physical environments, props, stories, or pictures.

Younger children have difficulty with concepts of time, space, size, and permanence. They may have difficulty specifying the timing of events and certain features of people important in their lives.

Children have been reported to be quite accurate in their "free recall" of events (Steward et al., 1993). Only a small percentage of young children recall fantasy rather than the actual event. Each of us who has interviewed children knows how younger children describe events that appear, at first, to make little sense in the adult world. For example, a 4-year-old girl reported that she heard grandma's voice coming from the ceiling; she did not know that the phone was placed on "speaker phone." Distinguishing errors of communication from errors of confabulation is paramount in the forensic interview.

The type of questioning used in child interviews is the focus of much research (Ceci & Bruck, 1995). Can children be influenced through leading

---

QUICK REFERENCE **Cautious Questioning Techniques**

- Directive questions: Answers often consistent with the direction of the question rather than the child's true answer
- Complex questions: Several sophisticated skills for effective answer. Complex questions require linguistic competence, logical thinking, verbal reasoning, and memory functioning
- Yes-No questions: Provides needed structure for younger child. Price is child often guesses at "right" answer or provides response set of his or her own, independent of meaning of question
- Leading questions: Guides child to what evaluator wants to hear but may not reflect child's true experience

---

questions to provide inaccurate information? Yes. The use of suggestive questioning may lead to errors in children's reports; however, some types of errors are more likely than others (Steward et al., 1993). It may be easier to influence a child about the color of someone's hair or shirt, but more difficulty to influence his or her memory of a personally meaningful event such as a visit with a parent, going to a playground or being spanked. The work of Ceci and his colleagues is important to consult in this context (Ceci & Bruck, 1993, 1995). Other work to review is that focused on the use of open-ended, leading, direct and hypothetical questions in forensic child interviews (Brainerd, Reyna, & Brandse, 1995; Steward et al., 1993).

Communicative Competence and Type of Interview Questions

The child's communicative competence is an important variable to understand. Children aged 10 months to 13 months initially speak in single-word sentences, but their receptive vocabulary may be significantly more complex. Most 18- to 22-month-old children have about 50 single words in their vocabulary and begin to put 2 words together. Toddlers are using 2- to 3-word sentences, usually nouns and verbs.

Preschoolers are able to construct multisentence ideas that are often based in the here and now. The concept of time is vaguely understood, with a 4-year-old asking upon waking up in the morning, "Is it tomorrow yet?" Preschool children are able to recall past events with accuracy, yet their time frame will be faulty. "Thus, interviewers must either avoid questions about calendar dates with complicated past tense verb phrases (e.g., might have been) or interpret children's responses carefully" (Steward et al., 1993, p. 28).

Rule 1

Enhancement of Children's Diclosure (Steward et al., 1993)

Children report events and create narratives that are often quite accurate, though spotty. Children are more likely to make errors of omission than commission. Interviewers can help children retrieve information with minimal compromise of accuracy in a number of ways. One way is carefully offering support such as external cues and props. Another way is through different forms of questioning; specifically, direct forms of questioning. A final suggestion is to provide affective cues that signal to the children that they can feel free to recount an event or resist suggestions.

Children aged 5 to 10 are increasingly able to understand and use longer sentences, multisyllabic words, past and future tenses, more complex grammatical constructions, and implicit rules of conversation. First graders are able to tell a story containing concrete elements of a past event. Their word choice is critical because their understanding of the world is based on concrete constructions of reality.

When yes/no questions are used, follow-up questions are imperative. When a preschooler is asked a yes/no question, the child's answer may or may not be responsive to the question. Follow-up questions, such as "Tell me more" or "Tell me how you know that," will help identify how and what the child knows. Children often are not able to consistently answer "who," "what," "where," and "why" questions until ages 5 or 6 (Ceci & Bruck, 1995).

Children's language develops, like other areas of growth, unevenly over many different domains. A child may master an aspect of language in one context but be unable to use language at a similar level of complexity in another. Thus, the interviewer must be mindful of not overestimating a child's language capacity and making assumptions about the meaning of a message without thoroughly exploring its significance. Children often become increasingly more comfortable during an interview. For some children, increased comfort produces positive changes in their use of language and their ability to express themselves more clearly and in more complex words. The interviewer needs to remember that the interview context is a dynamic environment that may contribute to the quality of the child's performance.

Rule 2

Maximizing Children's Communication
(Steward et al., 1993)

The evaluator should listen to the child's narrative report, examining it for two variables: The content and the child's spontaneous use of language. The examiner should then match his or her own sentence length and complexity to that of the child. Younger children need shorter, less complex sentences.

The forensic interviewer also needs to remember to avoid long, complex sentences, such as "After you visited your father and he took you out for lunch you came back and took a nap. After your nap, when your father was talking on the phone, tell me what happened to you." Instead, use several short sentences that allow the child to respond to each. Use the sentences as building blocks upon which a solid foundation may lead to the formulation of a sophisticated concept. For example, "Where did you have lunch? . . . McDonalds. . . . Who took you? My daddy. . . . After lunch, what did you do?. . . . A nap. What did you do when you woke up from your nap? . . . Yelling. . . . Who was yelling? My daddy."

Other important rules are that you should avoid pronouns, always use the name of the person when asking a question, be direct, and avoid hypothetical constructions.

Children need emotionally supportive environments for optimal performance. Intimidation will lead children to withdraw from talking, respond less often to questions, and provide less data when they *do* answer. Intimidation may also increase the chances that children will be susceptible to influence by others or try to provide information consistent with what they think the evaluator wants to hear. Children's performance is enhanced when the questions asked or tasks performed are simple and the interview environment is supportive.

Rule 3

Increasing the Accuracy of Children's Communications
(Steward et al., 1993)

The younger the child, the more likely the child's use of language is idiosyncratic to either the child or the context. Evaluators need to ask the child to define each term used before using it or making the assumption that the child has used the concept properly. As Steward et al. (1993) point out, "If you ask 'Do you know what allegations are?' the child is likely to say 'Yes,' but be thinking of alligators" (p. 33).

A final word about enhancement of the forensic interview with children. Saywitz (1992) proposed the use of the Cognitive Interview modified for use with children. She reported that "the Cognitive Interview improves the quantity of useful information gained from children 7 to 12 years of age without creating heightened inaccuracy" (p. 10). Although originally developed for use with abused children, the Cognitive Interview may be a useful tool to help children elaborate upon memories that are somewhat more difficult to recall without assistance *and* that minimizes interviewer-related influence.

There are other enhancement-focused ideas in the literature. Whether you choose to use them is not as important as becoming familiar with their use. An informed decision not to use a technique will serve you better than being unaware of it.

Deciding When Further Assessment Is Necessary

Most forensic interviewers will have access to a variety of collateral data about each child. There may be school records, pediatrician records, and other reports of the child's behavior. For some children, previously conducted evaluations are included in the school or physician reports.

There are times when the interviewer may need to consult such records to determine the need for special services or further evaluation. The question that arises is, When does the custody examiner decide a comprehensive psychoeducational or personality assessment of the child is necessary *within the scope of a child custody evaluation?*

Rule 4
Increasing Children's Participation (Steward et al., 1993)

Children participating in child custody evaluations often have no conceptual framework about how the legal system works. They are vaguely aware that the evaluator is performing some function for a judge, but they are less clear about how the information will be used. Children's understanding of the legal system develops, like all other concepts, from simple to complex. Younger children often have naive or incorrect ideas about the legal system. Older children may have a greater grasp of the outcome of the legal process but no understanding of the process of law. Evaluators may wish to prepare a list of legal words and concepts, and a description of people who will be participating in the evaluation process. They may also wish to talk about the jobs of the evaluator, the attorney, and the judge.

In rare instances, the evaluator may wish to conduct his own psychological, psychosocial, psychoeducational, or personality assessment. Most information about a child's daily functioning is available from collateral resources. This is particularly true when a child has been in school for a number of years.

It is both inappropriate and an unnecessary expense to complete a formal assessment battery on each child without having solid reasons to suspect that the collateral data are insufficient for the purposes of the evaluation. It is inappropriate because there may be little information added from a formal evaluation that is not already available through some other source. The evaluator must remember that the children being evaluated have been under significant stress over many months. More stress will be added through their participation in the evaluation process. Choosing to conduct a formal personality assessment will add more time to the child's participation as well as more stress. Unless absolutely necessary, formal personality evaluations are discouraged.

However, use of specific psychoeducational tests may prove useful in helping to identify the fit between parent and child. For example, Ackerman and Schoendorf (1992) recommend using intelligence tests. They suggest that identification of the intellectual fit between parent and child is one of a number of important factors in determining custodial placement.

Ackerman and Ackerman (1996, 1997) reported that intelligence testing is the most frequently used psychological test in the assessment of children participating in custody evaluations. A general rule is that intelligence testing should be considered if there are questions about the child's cognitive or intellectual functioning that could affect a recommendation for placement or if there is suspicion that a significant intelligence difference exists either between each parent or between parent and child.

Rule 5

Feedback to Children About Their Interview (Steward et al., 1993)

Children often feel competent about their efforts when they are able to see results. The results of an evaluation may be presented to a child in terms of the information the evaluator learns from the child. This discussion allows the child not only to gain immediate feedback about the information he or she shared but also gives him or her an opportunity to change what was said to conform better to what was meant.

When you believe that there is a need for more formal evaluation along intellectual/cognitive or emotional/personality dimensions, list the concerns and the data upon which the concerns are based. Next, examine the parent and child self-report data, the collateral data, and your interview data. You may wish to discuss the data and your questions about conducting a more formal psychoeducational or personality battery with a colleague versed in child custody evaluations. You may also choose to talk with the child's therapist, the child's school counselor, parents, or other collateral resources who know the child. Then, ask yourself, Is there enough information based upon these other data sources to justify the time, expense, and effort required by a formal psychoeducational, psychosocial, or personality assessment? The custody evaluation process is long, stressful, and intrusive. Adding another assessment dimension may provide more data about the child. The critical question is, Will it add anything that can be used in making a custodial or parental competency recommendation?

The Forensic Child Interview

Gindes (1995) suggests that a child custody evaluation be viewed as a "psychological evaluation of individuals at different developmental stages within the context of a separating family" (p. 42). Such a family systems approach is consistent with the developmental family systems approach of Hetherington and Clingempeel (1992), as well as the focus of this book. Bray (1991) and Baris and Garrity (1988) have provided guidance about developmental factors within a family systems framework. Young children's responses to their parents' separation are mediated by their limited cognitive and social abilities, their dependence upon their caretakers, and their attachment to their homes. Older children face different challenges, making the choice of relevant factors to assess in child custody determinations different for older children than for younger children. Thus, there is some professional consensus to cast the focus of a child custody evaluation as a developmental continuum both for each child and for the family system as a whole.

Similar to the forensic interview of the adult, there are two levels of data that are important in any forensic interview of a child. One is assessing the conceptual complexity of the child's response within age-appropriate norms. This is a structure-related focus because the child is providing information about his emotional, intellectual, social, or linguistic level of development.

The second is providing an accurate description of what the child reports. This is a content-related focus because the child is providing verbal data from which we draw meaning.

Each of these levels is important for the examiner to assess. The structure is important because it helps to frame the child's response to transitional factors into a developmental context that may have significant implications in terms of the recommendations to provide to the court. A child's structural response is also important because it guides how and at what level of complexity the evaluation is conducted. The content is important because it helps to place into perspective the child's experience of living within a family in transition.

The remainder of this chapter explores the child interview from two complementary views. The first is a four-factor model of assessment that focuses on *structural* aspects of development. The second provides a description of different *content* aspects to be assessed within the child custody context.

Structural Factors in Custody and Visitation Determinations

Exploration of the structural developmental components of child development may be assessed using different theoretical models. One such model of assessment is drawn from a clinical model of assessment developed by Trad (1990). Trad suggests a four-factor model of assessment: Locus of Control, Aggressiveness, Cognitive Development, and Play Behavior.

Locus of Control

Locus of control refers to the individual's perception of control over the environment. Internal locus of control refers to the child's belief that he or she feels in control of the majority of events that occur in his or her life. An external locus of control refers to the child's perception that there is little that is within his or her control.

The development of self is directly related to how well the child is able to regulate and adapt to the surrounding environment. Control is a precarious balancing act between the child adjusting to the environment and the environment being molded to the needs of the child. Healthy adaptation may be defined as knowing how and when to apply each form of adaptation (assimilation vs. accommodation).

Children who are at risk for maladaptive behaviors often struggle with one of two possible experiences. These children may fail in their attempts to gain control over their internal environment, that is, they find themselves unable to control and direct their impulses and emotions. The other group at risk are children who fail to achieve a feeling of control over their external environment. A useful resource is Seligman's (1955) work about the development of optimism.

Thus, children of divorce may be assessed for the degree to which they feel in control of both their internal and their external environments. The trauma of divorce should be experienced by most children as negatively affecting their sense of control over both dimensions. However, the degree to which each dimension has been affected and the ways in which children reveal their ability to cope with challenges to their perceived control is critical information to gather.

Aggressiveness

Very little will happen in the way of personality development if a child is cut off from his emotions and unable to assert him- or herself in the pursuit of these emotions (Trad, 1990). Children who fail at controlling with adaptive responses to the environment may become too passive or too aggressive.

There are gender differences in the demonstration of aggressive play. Boys typically are more physical and aggressive in their play than are girls. However, the question for the custody evaluator is, Within the context of normal development, where does a particular child's demonstrated behavior fall along the developmental dimension of passive to aggressive behavior?

Children of divorce may display an increased frequency of aggressive behaviors. They may also show an increased frequency of passive or withdrawn behaviors. The evaluator needs to examine multiple factors in determining the degree of normalcy of the child's response.

Another question to consider is, When is the child being assessed relative to the separation? It may be expected that evaluations conducted closer to the separation may reveal more atypical behavior than will evaluations conducted after the family turmoil has settled down.

Another important factor is how a particular child fares along the passive-aggressive dimension when there is no familial stress. That is, what was the child's baseline behavior prior to the separation? Although the evaluator is unable to observe directly such historical behavior, the use of collateral data is paramount in establishing the child's preseparation behavior.

A third factor is the manner in which the child is expressing an increase in aggressive behavior. A child may display nondestructive aggressive behavior aimed at mastering the many challenges that arise throughout development. Or, a child may show hostile, destructive aggressive behavior.

Hostile, destructive aggressive behavior is not always inappropriate. The evaluator needs to explore *how* the aggressive behavior is being directed as well as upon *what* the aggressive behavior is focused.

There are some children, particularly young children with insufficiently developed linguistic competencies, who express their insecurity, fear, anger, or confusion through destructive behavior. The use of a play therapy paradigm may assist the examiner in understanding and evaluating the purpose, function, and intention of the aggressive behavior. Trad (1990) has a useful chapter on the diagnostic and evaluative uses of play behavior.

Cognitive Development

Cognitive development refers to the child's increasing ability to form mental representations of self and others. In the case of aggressive behavior, the degree to which a child can understand the impact of his or her behavior upon others is directly related to the ability to inhibit such aggressive behavior.

Empathy is defined as the accurate perception of the intent of others. It has been found that empathy may be the single greatest inhibitor of aggressive behavior. The presence of an adult mediator to explain the intention of others also contributes to a child's development of empathy. Such adult mediator contact is often disrupted and/or greatly reduced during divorce.

Cognitive development involves the progressive ability to make distinctions between appearance and reality. Children learn to make distinctions between physically different objects. They make distinctions about the actions of others as well as others' intention and meaning.

Inaccurate perceptions of the motives of others often lead to the development of false assumptions about the motives underlying their behavior. They may also lead to inaccurate understanding of the causes of behavior.

In a divorce situation, children are forced to deal with at least two, often more, versions of reality. There is the mother's story about the divorce. There is the father's version of the divorce. There is the court's version. How children learn to accept one or more versions of reality helps the evaluator to understand their internal representation of reality.

Younger children have a more difficult time understanding multiple views of reality than older children. Conflicting views of the same event may result in a child feeling confused, unsafe, uncertain, or angry. It may also result in a child having to take sides in an effort to reduce the perceived discrepancy of information in their world. A 3-year-old may actively align with the mother's view of reality because the mother has been the primary caretaker; thus, the child is more dependent upon the mother for providing a sense of environmental safety, security, consistency, and predictability. Any challenge to that safety may result in the child becoming highly anxious. Thus, in an effort to reduce the dissonance in his or her world, the child simplifies his or her reality by choosing the mother as the good parent and the father as the bad parent.

Play Behavior

Play is a critical part of child development. It is the primary means through which a young child is first able to make and coordinate distinctions between appearance and reality (Trad, 1990). Children's play often has at least three critical purposes. Play helps the child in the expression of wishes and fantasies. Play also assists children in creating make-believe scenarios that allow otherwise impossible wishes and fantasies to come true. A third purpose of play is to help children learn the difference between reality and fantasy.

It is through play that children progressively learn to direct their initial emphasis on hedonistic, impulsive pleasure seeking to living within the constraints of society. Play is both active and reactive. It is active when the child is able to explore his or her environment. It is reactive when the child escapes from the demands of the environment into the safety of fantasy and wishes.

Play provides children with opportunities to act out and practice behaviors that have yet to be mastered in real life. Play allows children to gain some emotional and intellectual distance from their environment and gain the benefit of a different perspective.

> Every play situation that the child represents internally must be reconciled with the physical environment in which the child wishes to express these roles and to make them both credible and acceptable. In this way, the child's play and the resultant appearance-reality distinctions created in the play scenario are the outcome of a synthesizing process in which internal states are reconciled with external "reality." (Trad, 1990, p. 106)

The structure of children's play becomes a useful evaluative tool when used to explore the developmental appropriateness of a child's social, emotional, intellectual, and intrapsychic processes. The analysis of play behaviors allows the evaluator to explore how children may reveal aspects of themselves without the potential limitations of language. Play provides a vehicle through which useful hypotheses about adjustment and reaction to familial change may be explored with little additional stress on the child.

Content-Related Dimensions of Custody and Visitation Determination

The American Psychological Association's (1994) custody guidelines provide a reasonable framework from which to approach custodial evaluations. Three criteria are defined.

> The primary purpose of the evaluation is to assess the best psychological interests of the child. The primary consideration . . . is to assess the individual and family factors that affect the best psychological interests of the child. . . . The child's interests and well being are paramount. . . . This involves . . . an assessment of the psychological functioning and developmental needs of each child and the wishes of each child where appropriate. (APA, 1994, pp. 677-678)

Specific content-related factors of psychological functioning and developmental needs are not defined.

The Uniform Marriage and Divorce Act of 1979 (discussed more fully in Chapter 4) also points to the child's adjustment to home, school, and community. Like the APA custody guidelines, it provides no guidance about which content-related dimensions to measure.

A number of state associations have recommended specific content areas to evaluate. For example, the North Carolina Psychological Association (Kirkpatrick et al., 1994) has published a suggested list of developmental factors to consider in conducting child custody evaluations.

Below are some of the relevant content-related variables to consider when conducting a comprehensive child interview.

Child's Presentation

An important general factor is the child's *presentation*. Generally stated, the evaluator wants to assess how the child comes across during the interview. What is the nature, quality, and age appropriateness of verbalizations? What is the predominant affect presented? Are you able to describe the emotional qualities associated with the child's behavior and verbalizations? How does the child connect with you during the interview? Do you observe a difference in presentation when the child is with different parents? With different children?

Child's View of Each Parent and Home

A second general factor is gathering data about the child's *perception* of each parent and home. One way to partially assess the child's perception is to ask for a description of each parent. For example, does the child perceive each parent as helpful, supportive, easy to talk to, responsive to emotional needs, helpful with homework, safe, and consistent?

Among the areas of relevant data gathering are descriptions about the amount of time and quality of contacts with each parent. For example, what activities do they share? How do they engage in different activities? How does the child participate in each parent's activities? How does each parent participate in each child's activities?

The careful evaluator not only records the child's verbal response to each of these questions but also monitors the child's emotional and behavioral responses. When the child describes events or activities with each parent, is the affect congruent with the story? If a discrepancy is noted, the evaluator may wish to explore the child's feelings more extensively. It may be important to discuss with each parent, at some later date, the discrepancy between story and affect that you observed during the child's interview.

The child's description of the parent's home provides useful information. The evaluator should explore questions about the child's level of comfort at each parent's home. Does the child feel physically comfortable? Does the child feel emotionally comfortable? Does the child feel socially comfortable?

Other important information involves who lives at the home and the nature and type of relationship the child has with each person in the home. What are the physical living arrangements when the child stays at the home?

Who sets the rules and consequences in each home? How are they enforced? When rules need to be changed, how are they changed? Who participates in rule changes? How? When there are legitimate challenges to current rules, how are these challenges handled? By whom? How are they resolved? What is the fairness and clarity of rules and consequences? Who is the enforcer? Who negotiates? Who does the child seek out when the rules are unclear? Who does the child seek out when the rules are perceived as unfair?

Child's Expressed Wishes

A third general factor is the child's expressed *wishes* or *preferences* for either parent. There are many cautions about how much weight to give to a child's wishes. However, exploring with the child the reasoning behind his or her choice may provide a rich source of information about the child's perception of each parent.

Child's Susceptibility to Influence

Another dimension is the degree to which a child may be *influenced,* or is perceived to be influenced, to view one parent negatively. Much has been written about Richard Gardner's concept of Parent Alienation Syndrome (PAS), which occurs when one parent encourages a child to reject the other parent (Gardner, 1986, 1992, 1997).

Despite the legal and academic argument over the use of the PAS label, there is no doubt that some parents attempt to influence their children to view the other parent in negative ways. Some parents actively encourage rejection of the other parent, whereas other parents more passively and insidiously influence the underlying fabric of the child's positive belief in the other parent. Therefore, examination of the child's perception of each parent's support for the child's relationship with the other parent is paramount.

Psychological Functioning of the Child

A fifth general factor is the *psychological functioning* of the child. Questions about the child's ability to adjust to change are important to explore.

Historical and current adjustment to home and family changes are relevant for examination. For example, how well did the child handle day care, school, other children, neighborhood, community, and other common events that introduce change?

What data can be gathered about the child's ability to form and maintain attachments? To whom is the child attached, and how, within the immediate family? Within the extended family? What is the relationship between the child and each grandparent?

The extensive literature on adjustment factors in separation and divorce will be discussed in Chapter 7. Of the many factors to be described, among the most important questions are, Which adjustment factors appear to be causing difficulty for this child? Which factors appear to be navigated with little concern? How does the child's adjustment speak to larger issues of his or her present and future overall well-being?

Exploring how the child adjusts to significant family transitions also provides information about the child's strengths and weaknesses. It also provides a picture of the nature and quality of the child's coping skills and may point to areas for therapeutic or remedial assistance.

Finally, judgments about adjustment lead to an evaluation of the child's self-concept, self-esteem, anxieties and fears, anger, and overall temperament. Although not generally necessary for a custodial determination, when significant behavior problems are noted, they need to be described, and a diagnosis may be appropriate along with a recommendation for therapeutic intervention.

Mood and Temperament

An important measure of the child's well-being and *emotional adjustment* to the divorce is his or her mood. From the first time you meet the child, you want to be observing the child's mood. You want to note how he or she came into the office, the ways in which the child displayed mood in the waiting area, and how the mood evolved during the interview. You also want to critically examine how the child's mood is affected when in the presence of one parent compared with the other parent.

Of course, it is important that you do not draw quick conclusions from your observations of a child's mood. It is possible that the sadness you observe when the child is with the mother is a reflection of how constrained he or she feels when with the father. There are some parent-child relationships in which the child is so constrained about displaying feelings that the only time one can observe the child's moods is when he or she is in the company of the other parent. The observation that the child shows signs of depression is valuable data. How to interpret its meaning without first conducting a comprehensive assessment is the tricky part.

In determining the child's mood, the evaluator uses any behavioral references available. These behavioral references include, but are not limited to, verbal behavior; social interactions; facial expressions; body movement and positions; voice tone and quality; eye contact; speech clarity and organization; syntax structure; conceptual organization and clarity; logical analysis skills; and attitude to self, others, and the future.

Evidence of Abuse and/or Neglect

The final general factor to be discussed is among the most difficult to handle within a custody evaluation: *evidence of abuse*. The substantial issues involved in this area will be discussed more extensively in Chapter 8. The evaluator needs to note the child's physical condition when brought by each parent. The evaluator takes note of the child's clothing, cleanliness, and general wellness. Similarly, awareness of the child's emotional condition when brought by each parent is important. The evaluator should note the child's emotional comfort and be aware of signs or symptoms of fear or distress.

Be careful not to overreact. Children may show signs of fear and distress simply because they have been inappropriately prepared for the evaluation session. A child may be highly anxious about being interviewed or the anticipated prospect of having to choose with which parent to live, and thus may display signs of cautiousness, suspicion, or anger. The lesson is for the examiner not to jump to conclusions when a child presents in an emotionally charged manner. Explore with the child the underlying concerns as well as what the child was told about the purpose of the evaluation.

Other behaviors to observe are those categorized as sexualized and/or eroticized. Again, be wary not to conclude such behaviors are definitive signs of sexual abuse. Explore thoroughly the history and meaning of such behaviors before considering the hypothesis that abuse occurred.

Summary

There is no one way to conduct child custody interviews. There is a generally accepted structure that includes multiple sources of data, hypothesis generation, and formulations centered around behavioral science literature. However, which factors need to be measured for a particular assessment is determined by the nature of the court order, the unique character of the family system being examined, and the current state of empirical and conceptual knowledge.

SEVEN

Psychological Variables to Consider in Custody Determinations

Divorce is not a one time event but a continuous process.

Garrity and Baris (1994, p. 12)

A perusal of current literature suggests that the definition of the best interests of the child is often a moving target. There is no *one* definition that clarifies which variables to assess. As Schutz et al. (1989) suggest, "Almost any variable in a child's life can be used to help determine whether a parent has acted in the 'best interests of the child.' Very few variables have been explicitly ruled out or given specific weighting" (p. 25). There is, however, some professional consensus about factors that have been demonstrated to be important in understanding the general adjustment and well-being of children of divorce. Although the factors reviewed here do not exhaust the domain of relevant variables in child, adult, or parent-child interactions, they represent either *core constructs* (i.e., attachment) or critical *adjustment variables* (i.e., age and sex of the child) for which there is empirical literature.

For the mental health professional, the evaluation question becomes, "Which parent is a better match for having primary responsibility for raising the child?" . . . The court . . . is more likely to ask "Which parent is the better adult?," using relatively apparent and verifiable indices of competence such as health, financial status, and reputation in the community. In order to be persuasive, the mental health professional must take the time, in testimony or written report, to convince the court that the qualities of the relationship have greater impact on the child's well-being than the qualities of the adults as individuals, that the welfare of the child is inextricably imbedded in the combined parent-child interaction. This may require "educating" the court about the needs of the child, given the child's age and pattern of abilities or deficits, and

115

> **QUICK REFERENCE**   **Custody Evaluation Factors (American Psychological Association, 1994)**
>
> • An assessment of the adult's capacities for parenting
> • An assessment of the psychological functioning and developmental needs of the child and the wishes of the child where appropriate
> • An assessment of the functional ability of each parent to meet these needs

about the style in relating to the child that will be most beneficial to the child's current adjustment and future development. (Lowery, 1984, p. 379)

Our task, then, is to summarize the results of our evaluation in terms of three important factors: the qualities of each child, the qualities of each parent, and the dynamic interactions between parent and child. We present to the court judgments about the degree of congruence between the child's developmental needs and the parent's abilities (competencies) to adequately meet those needs. In the words of Schutz et al. (1989), "The heart of our evaluation is the degree of congruence between a parent's functional abilities on these dimensions [of goodness of fit between a parent] and the individual needs of the children" (p. 29).

Children's Reaction to Separation and Divorce

A number of factors influence immediate adjustment to separation and divorce. The first is that the children are forced to adjust to *change,* the most dramatic and challenging being living within a restructured home. The children may need to learn to accommodate to a new home, new school, and new people. They may mourn the loss not only of their father living outside the house, but the loss of everything that is familiar—friends, surroundings, routine, security, safety, and predictability. They may react with noncompliance and aggression to their parents' conflict. They may react to the family disorganization by becoming confused, apprehensive, or withdrawn.

There is no boilerplate to measure a child's reactions to separation and divorce. Different children react in different ways. Some children show remarkable resiliency and actually are helped by having to cope with these transitional challenges. Some children find that the divorce provides them with life in a conflict-free environment in which their safety and security are not threatened (Block, Block, & Gjerde, 1988).

Other children suffer sustained developmental delays. They fail school, lose friends, fall into drug use, and get in trouble with the law. Still others appear to adapt well to the changes in the early stages of family reorganization and then slowly show changes 6 months or 1 year later that affect important areas of life functioning, such as school performance, peer relationships, or personal identity.

The literature review that follows addresses factors associated with the child's adjustment to divorce. This review provides a conceptual overview of important factors but does not pretend to be exhaustive. Overall, the recent research on children's adjustment to separation and divorce indicates that children's reactions vary widely across different ages (Hetherington & Camera, 1984; Kelly, 1994; Wallerstein & Kelly, 1980). Divorce is not necessarily worse for children at certain ages. Children at various ages tend to have different reactions and symptom patterns. Longitudinal studies of divorce suggest that it is important to consider separately short-term and long-term adjustment issues and their implications for custodial arrangements (Kelly, 1994). The age of the child is important because of the developmental changes and issues that arise at different chronological periods (Bray, 1991). In light of the emergence of predictable developmental differences and issues, visitation and access may need to vary depending on the (developmental and/or chronological) age of the child (Clingempeel & Reppucci, 1982).

Age Interacts With Developmental Level

Children's developmental status refers to the social, emotional, and cognitive psychological functioning that is associated with their chronological age. These factors interact with age, but there are substantial individual differences among children, and children's adaptation to divorce varies with their developmental level (Hetherington, Cox, & Cox, 1982).

Some studies suggest that younger children and those who are developmentally less mature at the time of their parents' separation will exhibit more disruptive behaviors. Other studies do not support these assumptions. Hetherington et al. (1982) suggest that "it might be more accurate to say that the type of behavior problems and coping mechanisms differ for children of different ages" (p. 305).

Young children's responses to their parents' separation are mediated by their limited cognitive and social abilities, their dependence upon their parents, and their restriction to home (Bray, 1991). For example, during the period immediately after separation, preschool children may view the nonresidential father's movement to another home as an example of how the father does not love his child. Or, if the father is 15 minutes late for a visitation pick-up, the 4-year-old child may think that "Daddy is bad because he promised to pick me up at 6 and it is now 6:15. He lied to me." Preschool children think in preoperational terms and often make up wild, fantasylike explanations for the events in their lives. Fathers and mothers alike need to be sensitive to such developmental limitations and provide explanations to the child *at the child's level of understanding.*

Elementary school-age children often blame themselves for the separation. Although at a higher level of intellectual functioning than the 4-year-old, the 9-year-old may need concrete, clearly spelled-out explanations that are consistent over time. School-age children may misperceive their parents' emotions and, without being aware of the magnitude of their assumptions, base future behavior upon poorly understood, potentially false ideas about their current situation. Children of the elementary school-age crowd also spend time fantasizing about reconciliation and their role in bringing mom and dad back together.

These younger children's developmental limitations may also have a positive side. Wallerstein, Corbin, and Lewis (1988) reported that the cognitive immaturity that creates such confusion for the young child may assist the child in the long run. Because young children's memory organization is somewhat unstable, they may remember fewer aspects of the emotional trauma of the divorce when they are older. For example, 10 years after their parents' divorce, these children have fewer memories of either the parental conflict or their earlier fears and suffering. Typically, these children have a close relationship with the custodial parent. These same children appear to adjust well to most of life's demands 5 and 10 years later. About one third of the children show some depression and anger about not having more access to their noncustodial parent. Even these children tend to show relatively good adjustment 10 years after divorce providing no other significant disruptions occurred within the family system.

Older children have better developed cognitive and social skills. They may feel angry about their parents' separation, but they are better able to understand the meaning and reason for the divorce. They are also able to assign blame and resolve loyalty conflicts. The older child also has a support system that extends beyond the family home. Although some adolescents from separated families show a premature detachment from their families, most show increased responsibility and maturity in taking on greater responsibilities within the home.

Adolescent disengagement is a double-edged sword. First, judging the motivation for their disengagement is difficult. Developmentally appropriate behavior for this group is to continue disengagement from the family unit and reach out to peer and social group identities. The adolescent whose parents are divorcing may show behaviors appropriate to his or her age group that may be based upon emotional traumas to the divorce. On the other hand, identical behavior may be observed yet be motivated by factors unrelated to the divorce, such as appropriate developmental changes. The evaluator's job is very difficult in trying to tease out what is developmentally appropriate and what is related to the child's experience of divorce.

Adolescent children should be encouraged to turn to their friends, school attachments, and other constructive relationships outside the family. If, however, the child gravitates toward antisocial groups and activities or other children who tend to be depressed, unmotivated, and troubled, the outcomes can be catastrophic.

Age and Adjustment to Divorce

The age of a child at the time of separation and divorce has been implicated as a major factor determining the child's postdivorce adjustment and behavior (Kelly, 1996). The early years of a child's life, generally through the end of the toddler years, constitute a critical period during which permanent or frequent disruption of parent-child attachment bonds may interfere with the child's later social and emotional development (Rutter, 1971, 1987). Generally, the earlier a divorce occurs in a child's life beyond infancy, the more profound is its effect (Wallerstein & Blakeslee, 1989; Wallerstein & Kelly, 1980).

The negative relationship between age at time of divorce and incidence of emotional or psychological disturbance may result from children at different ages having qualitatively different skills to deal with the trauma of divorce. Divorce is probably equally traumatic for children at any age. The critical factors appear to be the differing levels of cognitive/emotional developmental status (Hetherington, 1991).

Attachment Behavior in Children

Separation and divorce affect children's attachment to at least one primary caretaker. Attachment is defined as a child's insistence on maintaining closeness to protective (parental) figures (Bowlby, 1969, 1980). It is thought that an attachment behavioral system in infants has primary and immediate responsibility for regulating infant safety and survival in the environment (Bowlby, 1969). Attachment systems are viewed as equally important to other primary regulatory systems such as feeding and reproduction (Main, 1996). Attachment theory predicts that infants continually monitor the availability of one or more "attachment figures" (usually parents) in an effort to seek safety and protection. Attachment theory also predicts that infants flee "attachment figures" in times of alarm (Main, 1996):

> Whereas attentional patterning is fluid in secure infants, infants whose parents have been insensitive but not directly frightening appear to have developed somewhat inflexible, albeit organized, attentional and behavioral

strategies for dealing with moderately stressful situations. Because the attached infant inevitably seeks the parent when alarmed, however, any parental behavior that directly alarms an infant places the infant in a behavioral paradox by activating simultaneous impulses to approach the parent as a haven of safety and to flee from the parent as a source of alarm. (p. 239)

The primary developmental task of infants is to develop a trusting relationship with the world. The toddler's primary focus is to learn to seek independence from the primary nurturing figure. Disruptions to safety and predictability that accompany separation and divorce may significantly affect a child's ability to negotiate these developmental priorities successfully. Thus, attachment theory may be important to consider in infant and childhood adjustment to separation and divorce.

Attachment Theory

First attachments are usually formed by 7 months. Attachments tend to be formed with few people, although infants and children are known to accept more than one primary attachment figure (Bray, 1991). Research has demonstrated that virtually all infants become attached (Main, 1996).

Four types of attachment appear to occur. The *secure* response pattern appears in most infants. These infants showed signs of missing their attachment figure during her absence. They greeted her actively upon return and then returned to their play (Ainsworth, Blehar, Waters, & Wall, 1978). The secure response infants were characterized by the attachment figure's "tender, careful holding, with contingent pacing of face-to-face interactions, and with sensitivity to infant signals in the first year of life" (Main, 1996, p. 238).

A number of insecure attachment behaviors have been reported. Ainsworth et al. (1978) reported infants who were (a) either *insecure-resistant* or *insecure-ambivalent,* and (b) *insecure-avoidant.* The insecure-ambivalent infants were observed to behave with either anger or passivity, were preoccupied with their mothers, failed to settle down upon return of the mother to the setting, and failed to return to play upon reunion (Ainsworth, 1979). The mothers were not rejecting. Instead, they were observed to be inept in holding their infants, noncontingent in face-to-face interaction, and unpredictable in their actions (Main, 1996).

Insecure-avoidant infants were observed to focus on their toys rather than people, failed to cry during separation from their mother, and actively avoided and ignored the attachment figure upon reunion (Ainsworth et al., 1978). The mothers appeared to reject attachment. They were reported to avoid touch.

Another infant attachment is the *insecure-disorganized-disoriented* (Main & Solomon, 1990). Infant attachment was characterized by infants "rocking on hands and knees with face averted after an abortive approach; freezing all movement, arms in air, with a trancelike expression, and rising to greet the parent then falling prone" (Main, 1996, p. 239).

Children who feel secure as infants with their attachment figures show greater ego strength as well as social and exploratory competence than do insecure children in preschool. "Security with father also contributes favorably with outcome and differences favoring children secure with mother in infancy remain observable to 15 years" (Main, 1996, p. 238).

Two crucial components emerge from this line of research. The first is to consider historical as well as present attachment behaviors in custody examinations. The research appears to show a positive relationship between secure attachment figures and positive child development. Categorizing the child's pre- and postdivorce attachment behavior may aid in developing parenting plans designed specifically for each child. Second is to characterize parental pre- and postdivorce attachment behavior.

Externalize Versus Internalize Problems

Children display a number of reactions and problems to the trauma of divorce. Among the most frequent are the externalizing or internalizing behaviors. Most children of divorce externalize their problems. Boys show more aggression, impulsiveness, and antisocial behavior than girls. Boys also have different peer relationships, are less conforming to authority, and display more behavior problems in school.

Children of divorce tend to deal with feelings by projecting them onto the outside world. This is what is meant by externalizing. They also tend to watch more television, are more absent from school, and spend less time on homework than do children in intact families.

Girls are more likely than boys to internalize problems of divorce through the display of anxiety, depression, and withdrawal. However, children of divorce internalize behavior far less often than they externalize it. This is true for both boys and girls.

It is interesting to note that self-esteem does not seem to vary greatly as a result of divorce. Children's self-esteem is influenced negatively during the initial stages of separatio, but when given time to adjust to their new situation, children of divorce do not differ from nondivorced children on measures of self-esteem. Studies have found a strong link between parental conflict and self-esteem. They have also found a link between parental conflict and depression. However, there is no relationship between lower self-esteem and living in a divorced family (Kelly, 1993).

Child's Temperament

Another factor influencing a child's adjustment to separation is *temperament*. Temperamentally difficult children have been found to be less adaptable to change and more vulnerable to conflict and adversity. They are apt to become a lightning rod and elicit anger from their parents (Rutter, 1987). They are likely to attract more angry responses from those around them and potentially be more of a target for parental frustration.

Temperamentally easy children tend to have well-developed support systems. They are better able to cope with the challenges of change and uncertainty and are less likely to be the recipients of criticism, displaced anger, and anxiety (Hetherington, Stanley-Hagan, & Anderson, 1989). They are often better able to adjust to the unanticipated needs of their environment.

There are differences in temperament that are related to sex. Infants and young boys generally are viewed as having the most difficult makeup and have a greater impact on family functioning (Abbott & Brody, 1985).

Level of activity and moodiness are common aspects of definitions of difficult temperament. School-age boys are viewed as less temperamentally difficult than are younger children. This is due in part to the change in parental perception that increased activity and moodiness are more gender appropriate for school-age boys.

Temperamentally difficult children may be less able to gain needed support in times of stress and less competent at knowing how to use the support when offered. A common parental response is to pay less attention to the temperamentally difficult child's requests and focus positive energies in directions other than toward the child. The result is that the child feels more alone, vulnerable, and frightened, leading to increased feelings of insecurity, anxiety, and moodiness. This increase in moodiness results in an increase of parental perception of the child being more temperamentally difficult. The cycle feeds on itself. The child suffers more.

In summary, children who display poor cognitive competence, behavior problems, or difficult temperament are likely to have these characteristics exacerbated or amplified by stress (Hetherington, 1991; Wallerstein et al., 1988).

Need for Continuity and Stability

Throughout their life cycle, children need some degree of continuity and stability in their lives (Santrock & Yussen, 1987). The dilemma for young children is the need for both of those things (Kelly, 1988). There is a need to balance continuity, which promotes attachment, with a stable environment for the child, which promotes security (Bray, 1991).

Children of divorce experience a variety of stressful events. Even when parents fight all the time, the vast majority of children have no idea their parents are preparing to separate. From the child's perspective, the level of conflict in the home is what they have always defined as normal. They have no external standard against which to compare healthy and unhealthy marriages. Thus, when parents separate, children are thrown into emotional crisis. Their sense of continuity and security is threatened. The most common reactions to parental separation include sadness and acute depression, intense anxiety about their future well-being and caretaking, increases in anger, difficulty concentrating at school, concern over loss of contact with one parent, loyalty conflicts, and preoccupation with fantasies about reconciliation (Wallerstein & Kelly, 1980).

Length of Adjustment Difficulties

The majority of empirical research examining children's emotional adjustment reveals that most reactions begin to subside relatively quickly. Children's acute reactions diminish within the first 6 months to 1 year after separation (Wallerstein & Kelly, 1980). Children adjust to their new life within 2 to 3 years if their new situation is not significantly affected by further adversity (Hetherington et al., 1989). The general rule of thumb is that a child's predivorce adjustment is a good predictor of how quickly he or she will adjust to the new family constellation. In general, children who have no significant personality, emotional, or adjustment problems prior to the divorce often find that their acute emotional responses to the separation end within 12 months. Children whose preseparation adjustment was difficult or problematic take longer.

Memory Capacity of Young Children

Young children have limited memory capacity and conceptualizations of time (Santrock & Yussen, 1987). Infants and toddlers have some memory capacity and an ability to recognize objects over a short period of time. However, as a general rule, children have very limited conscious memories until after age 3, as well as limited time perspectives (Ceci & Bruck, 1995; Pope & Brown, 1996). Children below the age of 3 rarely understand the concepts of tomorrow, next week, or yesterday. Older children can begin to understand a future orientation around time. However, it is probably not until a child reaches the age of 6 or 7—the onset of operational thought—that he or she can understand what a week or a month means (Bray, 1991).

Dualistic Thinking:
Good Versus Bad Parents

Children from ages 3 to 5 can discriminate between parents and usually have unique relationships with each parent (Santrock & Yussen, 1987).

During these ages, children usually tolerate separation from their parents and caregivers. Preschool-age children have a difficult time understanding that people can be both good and bad (Bray, 1991). They tend to split people into "all good" or "all bad." They also have limited perspective taking. Preschool children have difficulty understanding the impact of their behavior on others, understanding how others view their behavior, and stepping outside their frames of reference to view events from another perspective (Flavell, 1975; Piaget, 1965). This limitation in social perspective taking affects their capacity to understand inconsistencies in parental behavior.

Separation and Anxiety in Preschool-Age Children

Preschool children may experience separation anxiety if they have not properly attached to and/or separated from their primary caretaker(s). The degree to which children have successfully adjusted to earlier disruptions may predict later problems with separation anxiety. A key element is the child's temperament (Kelly, 1993).

Exposure to Parental Conflict

Children are strongly influenced by parental conflict at this age. Children who are exposed to high levels of ongoing interparental conflict often have more difficulty making the transition between parental homes and are at greater risk for behavioral disturbance (Johnston & Campbell, 1988). This factor is discussed at length in Chapter 12.

Suggested Preschool-Age Visitation Considerations

Overnight and longer visitations are usually tolerated and beneficial for preschool-age children. A regular schedule is useful for children so that they may develop appropriate expectations about visitation, feel a sense of security in knowing when they will see their other parent, and develop a sense of predictability about the transitions in their lives (Bray, 1991).

Physical/Material Needs

The physical needs of a child are considered relevant to determinations of custodial arrangement (Wallerstein & Kelly, 1980). Among the factors considered are the child's present physical health and each party's ability to provide material benefits, such as food, clothing, and medical and other remedial care (Rohman et al., 1987). The physical environment determined by the parent's socioeconomic status has been shown to have an effect upon child development and adjustment to divorce (Kelly & Wallerstein, 1976). Younger children usually express concern about physical necessities like food, clothing, having enough money, and maintaining a place to live, whereas older children are concerned about chances to attend college. However, research indicates that the more immediate impact of the material need question relates to the degree of fairness perceived by the child (Wallerstein & Kelly, 1980).

Boys Have More Difficulty
With Divorce

One of the most consistent research findings is that young boys appear more reactive to separation and divorce than do girls. Boys' postseparation behavior has frequently been characterized in terms of increased aggressiveness, impulsiveness, and acting-out behaviors. However, Block et al. (1988) reported that "long before divorce occurs in a family, sons tend to be impulsive and undercontrolled relative to boys in families that will remain intact" (p. 212).

Hetherington (1991) reported that at 6-year postdivorce follow-up, divorced, nonremarried mothers were still showing many of the same signs of conflict and tension with their sons as were evident earlier in the transition process. In particular, divorced mothers were found to be "ineffectual in their control attempts and gave many instructions with little follow through. They tended to nag, natter, and complain and more often were involved in angry, escalating coercive cycles with their sons" (p. 177).

Another factor of concern is that spontaneous fights were more than twice as likely between divorced mothers and their sons than with a comparable group of nondivorced mothers and sons. Boys typically were seen as attacking their mothers, often for no discernible reason. Divorced mothers tended to counterattack more often than their nondivorced counterparts.

> In spite of the conflict between custodial mothers and their early adolescent sons it might be best to view this relationship in early adolescence as intense and ambivalent rather than as purely hostile and rejecting, since there also were warm feelings expressed. (Hetherington, 1991, p. 177)

If elementary school-age and early adolescent boys in families that eventually divorce tend to be more aggressive and impulsive, it may explain why there is more conflict between parents and sons than parents and daughters (Block et al., 1988).

Evidence also suggests that the relationship between adolescent son and mother is more conflict prone and tense than is the adolescent daughter-mother relationship. Even in intact families, the mother-son relationship is more problematic than the mother-daughter relationship. When the relationship examined includes the father-mother-adolescent son, the harmony of the mother-son relationship improves. The father's presence acts as a moderating influence over the degree of conflict between mother and son in early adolescence.

Other research indicates that the mother-daughter relationship in separated and divorced families often is comfortable, warm, and egalitarian, in contrast to the mother-son relationship, which is filled with tension and conflict (Kelly, 1988). Whereas adjustment difficulties in girls living with their mothers tend to disappear within 2 years after divorce, there is some concern that problems may reemerge during adolescence. Adolescent girls may have conflict with their mothers over the nature of the parent-child relationship as well as disruptions in heterosexual relations (Hetherington, 1991).

This raises a profoundly interesting question of how single mothers can more effectively cope with the anticipated changes and increased tension in the mother-son relationship without the moderating influence of the child's father.

In summary, research suggests that boys have a tendency to be more seriously affected by divorce than do girls (Hetherington, 1991; Wallerstein & Kelly, 1980). There is substantial evidence that boys and girls often receive qualitatively different care from adults both before and after divorce (Hetherington, 1991). Custodial mothers have reported greater subjective stress in dealing with their sons than with their daughters (Hetherington, 1991; Kelly, 1994; Santrock, Warshak, & Elliott, 1982). These results have given rise to proposals for same-sex custody arrangements.

No Basis for Same-Sex Preference

If mother-son difficulties are related to some inherent qualities of the mother or unique aspects of her interactional qualities with her son, it may be in the son's best psychological interest for the father to have custodial responsibility for his son or, if feasible, joint custody to allow for increased contact time between father and son.

The data do not provide a sufficient basis for adopting a same-sex preference. Hetherington et al. (1982) reported that stress within the mother-son relationship after divorce usually peaked around the end of the first year and subsided over time as the mother acquired parenting skills appropriate to the task of parenting a son. Recent studies have failed to find the extended postdivorce relationship between opposite-sex parent-child to be any more stressful than custodial relationships between same-sex parent-child, nor did these researchers find that such relationships are detrimental to long-term adjustment and development (Rohman et al., 1987).

Affectional Ties

The affectional ties between a child and each parent are an important consideration in determining custodial arrangements. There is a central presumption—in law and psychology—that the best psychological interests of a child are served by placing care of that child with the adult with whom the strongly affectional ties exist (Rohman et al., 1987).

Psychological Parent

A psychological parent has been defined as one who, "on a continuing day to day basis through interplay, and mutuality, fulfills the child's psychological needs for a parent, as well as the child's physical needs" (Goldstein et al., 1979, p. 98). Exploring who the child perceives as the psychological parent may provide useful information about the parent-child relationship.

Criticism of the psychological parent concept has revolved around four issues. The first is that there is little, if any, empirical work showing the validity of the concept. It remains mainly a theoretical concept that may or may not reflect the realities of parent-child dynamics. Clingempeel and Reppucci (1982) and Lamb (1987) have demonstrated that the notion of a psychological parent has little empirical support.

There is no empirical research to help determine how to make custodial determinations when a child feels strong affectional ties to each parent, that is, when each parent is identified in the child's mind as a psychological parent. Another criticism involves the recommendation that the psychological parent be granted complete control over the noncustodial parent's future access to the child. Ongoing conflict between many divorced parents could lead to the usurping of power by the custodial parent in denying visitation to the noncustodial parent for reasons other than those reflecting the child's best interest.

A final criticism is that current research indicates that children appear to develop multiple attachments to caregivers (Ainsworth, 1979) and may have more than one psychological parent. "There is usually a hierarchy of attachment figures, each of whom may have qualitatively different types of relationships with the child, although children may prefer one attachment figure over another" (Bray, 1991, p. 423).

Primary Versus Secondary Caregiver Roles

There are differences in each parent's role vis-à-vis the child. Thompson and Walker (1989) reported that parental caregiver roles are divided into primary and secondary caregiver roles. Typically, the mother is the primary caregiver, providing basic needs such as safety, security, protection, and continuity, as well as being a partner in low-key play. The father often is more typically involved in less specific caregiving activities and more focused on vigorous, physically stimulating play. Each parent performs a unique and distinct role in the child's life. Studies of infants and toddlers have shown that when children are distressed or frightened, they will usually prefer the parent who has been the primary caregiver to the parent who functions in the secondary role (Thompson & Walker, 1989).

Primary Caregiver Preference

Many believe that the primary caregiver should be the preferred custodian. The reason is that divorce is a stressful event for children (Johnston, 1994, 1995; Kelly, 1988, 1993; Wallerstein & Blakeslee, 1989; Wallerstein & Kelly, 1980). Children prefer contact with their primary caregivers during times of general emotional distress (Thompson & Walker, 1989) and are predicted to fare better in the custody of their primary caregiver during the crisis of separation and divorce. Because child adjustment has been found to correlate strongly with the quality of custodial parent-child relations during a postdivorce period (Santrock & Warshak, 1987), the stronger custodial parent-child attachment based upon child-focused concerns of safety, security, consistency, stability, and predictability would be between the primary caregiver and the child (Kelly, 1994; Wallerstein & Kelly, 1980).

It may be particularly important to place young children with the primary caregiver for three reasons. First, the physical ministrations by the primary caregiver are perhaps the most salient social interactions a young child experiences (Thompson & Walker, 1989). Second, "substitution of even the child's secondary caregiver in the primary parenting role would 'require a more significant renegotiation of relational expectations' than would be required by placing the child with the primary caregiver" (Rohman et al., 1987, p. 73). Younger children, more than any other age group, have shown greater propensity toward readjustment or maladjustment resulting from the psychological or emotional stress caused by divorce. A preference that minimizes the environmental and relationship instability that children experience during divorce is highly desirable. This may not be true for older children (Thompson & Walker, 1989).

Child's Wishes

Almost every state allows a judge to consider the wishes of a child of any age concerning his or her own custody, depending upon the child's ability to express a reasoned and intelligent preference. Chronological age usually determines whether a judge will ask a child for his or her preference. Once elicited, the judge determines how much weight to give the child's preference.

When considering the wishes of a preschool child, a number of factors need to be explored. Most often, preschoolers are prevented from giving a preference by their own developmental limitations. A preschooler typically lacks the cognitive ability to understand what information the judge is attempting to elicit, the emotional maturity to formulate a preference, and the verbal ability to communicate a preference. The reliability and validity of a preschooler's self-report would need to be scrutinized for the possible confounding or influencing effects of a number of psychological and social influence factors on his or her custodial preference (Ceci & Bruck, 1995).

Summary

Parental separation generally precipitates a crisis for most children (Kelly, 1988). Most children do not expect their parents to divorce, even when they live in homes in which their parents are continually fighting. They are stunned and upset when their parents separate. Their whole world has been turned upside down, their security and safety have been seriously threatened, and they are afraid of the unknown—the future without two parents. The exception is children from high-conflict families, who may be relieved that the repeated, intense conflicts between their parents have mercifully been put to an end. Even these children have significant emotional reactions despite their relief that the fighting has stopped.

Emotional reactions to separation usually last between 6 months to 3 years (Hetherington et al., 1989; Wallerstein et al., 1988; Wallerstein & Kelly, 1980). Most children adapt to their new situation if their situation is not compounded by additional life changes.

Children show many different types of reactions. Most children externalize their concerns through increases in impulsivity, acting-out, and aggression. Children in divorced families have been reported to show more loneliness and boredom than have children in intact families.

There are also personality differences. Children who are characterized as temperamentally difficult tend to do more poorly than do temperamentally easy children. Temperamentally difficult children have been found to be less adaptable to change and more vulnerable to hardship.

There are gender differences as well. Boys typically have more difficulty than do girls in adjusting to separation. Boys tend to have more difficult relationships with their mothers, characterized by increased conflict and tension.

In general, poor predivorce parent-child relationships lead to more negative child behavior and difficulty adjusting to the single-parent family. Maintaining good relationships with children provides a means of reducing the effects of conflict and disruption thrust upon the children (Peterson & Zill, 1986).

Rohman et al. (1987) suggest that these data point to important implications. Preschool children appear to tolerate separation from the noncustodial parent with few, if any, negative effects if the quality of the relationship between noncustodial parent and child remains positive. It appears that quality, rather than time, is the critical factor.

Younger children appear to be better off with their primary caretaker. Primary caretakers are better able to maintain consistency and stability in the child's life. Children are most accustomed to seeking security and comfort from a primary caretaker compared to a secondary caretaker. Children's postdivorce adjustment is associated with the quality of the custodial parent-child relationship. Finally, the child's wishes need to be interpreted in light of his or her current developmental level and cognitive/emotional maturation (Wallerstein & Kelly, 1980).

Factors Affecting Parental Adjustment to Separation and Divorce

Children are sensitive to the ways in which their parents adjust to the postdivorce family. When the custodial parent has difficulty adjusting to the family transition, children often have similar difficulties. The symptoms may be different and their manifestations separate, but there is emotional symmetry in most families. The more difficulty a parent has with postdivorce adjustment, the more difficulty the children have (Kline, Johnston, & Tschann, 1991).

Do Separating Parents Place Their Children in the Middle?

Marital conflict does not automatically place children in the middle. In fact, a high-conflict postdivorce relationship does not appear to cause children to feel caught in the middle (Buchanan, Maccoby, & Dornbush, 1991); it is usually high-conflict marital discord in which each party uses the children (Garrity & Baris, 1994). Feeling caught in the middle is defined as asking a child to carry a message to the other parent or to ask intrusive questions about the other parent, which leads the child to feel a need to hide information or feelings about the other parent (Kelly, 1992).

When parents use problem-solving strategies that resolve conflict through cooperation and communication, children's adjustment to separation and divorce is more positive. In particular, cooperation between parents is related to less aggression by children (Kelly, 1993).

The need for divorcing parents to keep their children out of the middle is important for children's adjustment to their new life. Four-and-a-half years after initial separation, adolescents who had lived in high-conflict family situations were found to be more depressed and anxious, and they displayed a higher frequency of deviant behaviors.

It is interesting to note that where the children live does not contribute to them feeling caught in the middle. The amount of visiting is not related to feeling caught. It is the nature of the conflict and how parents react to it, rather than anything specific to separation and divorce.

Another strong predictor of postdivorce conflict and low cooperation between husband and wife is the frequency of *child-specific* conflict during the marriage and the degree of conflict in the initial stages of the separation.

Who Gets Separated?

A conventional belief is that life in a predivorce family is characterized by loud arguments, high conflict, intense emotional exchanges, chaos, poor communication, and lack of cooperation between parents (Emery, 1982). Recent research has shown that all types of marriages can end in divorce (Kelly, 1982). Two separate studies reported that about 50% of divorcing couples acknowledged frequent and intense conflict, and more than one fourth of the men and women reported either minimal or no substantial conflict in the 2 years prior to the separation (Kelly, 1982).

Divorcing parents appeared to report significantly *less* child-specific conflict than marital conflict. They also reported significantly better cooperation at separation over their children than over other areas of anticipated cooperation. Although the respondents indicated that six different types of marital communication were rated as poor by both men and women, they viewed the adequacy of their communication about their children as significantly better (Kelly, 1996). On the other hand, marital couples who reported significant predivorce conflict over child-specific compared to marital-specific problems were more likely to separate and divorce. In fact, the intensity of predivorce, child-specific conflict is directly related to how well children adjust to postdivorce family transitions (Kelly, 1993).

Conflict

Conflict is seen as an important variable in predicting separation and divorce. Intense or frequent *marital* conflict is associated with poor postdivorce adjustment. Children of divorce whose predivorce home was characterized by low conflict were found to be better adjusted than were nondivorce children living in high-conflict families (Garrity & Baris, 1994).

Parental distress is a critical variable in the prediction of children's adjustment to divorce as well as a predictor of who is likely to get divorced. Conflict, however, is not a unidimensional variable. Conflict by itself does not predict who will get divorced—it is also the way in which the conflict is handled, its focus, frequency, and intensity, among other factors.

Children from high-conflict marriages were found to have three times more psychological distress than were children from low- to moderate-conflict marriages (Peterson & Zill, 1986). Preseparation factors of marital conflict, a history of psychological problems of the child, and relationship with the mother tend to be more predictive of adjustment to divorce than do postdivorce factors such as conflict, loss of parent, and change.

High predivorce marital conflict is associated with decreases in emotional warmth, decreases in empathic relating between parent and child, and more rejection of the child. When fathers experience high conflict, they often withdraw from contact within the family. This leads to an increase in behavior problems among children.

High-conflict, postdivorce parental relationships are linked with children's somatic, psychosomatic, social, and behavior adjustment problems. Mothers who come from high-conflict marriages often continue their conflict with their spouse postdivorce. These mothers have been found to be more rejecting of their children and to use their children more for emotional support and expression of conflict (Kelly, 1993). This results in some children feeling inappropriate expectations of loyalty toward the mother in detriment to their feelings about their father.

The conclusion drawn from this research is that couples may fight about their marriage and their choice of partner, but when it comes to the children, many separating parents view their parenting function as distinct. They tend to be better at communicating and cooperating with each other over what is best for their children. A critical variable in predicting who will divorce is marital conflict. High levels of marital conflict are associated with significantly more adjustment problems for children. A more extensive discussion of the role of parental conflict in residential arrangements is provided in Chapter 12.

Parental Psychological Problems

Some parents have a history of adjustment problems predating the marital distress and divorce. These problems often impose themselves on parenting. If the psychological disturbance does not affect parenting, then children should have little difficulty other than that typically expected of other children of divorce. However, there are times when psychological disturbance interferes with parenting.

Stress and anxiety are two conditions that may exacerbate a previous psychological disturbance and influence parenting. Such parental disruptions may take the form of neglectful parenting, erratic behavior, minimal investment in parental responsibilities, or potentially dangerous behavior (Emery, 1982).

When adult psychological disturbance influences parenting, children are at risk for a variety of behavioral problems (Emery, 1982; Wallerstein & Kelly, 1980). An interesting group of studies looked at marital discord, parental psychopathology, and problems among children. In families in which there were individual adult personality psychopathology *and* marital discord, children tended to be more at risk for emotional and psychological problems. Marital conflict was related to increases in antisocial behavior among children of normal parents as well as among children of parents with a personality disorder. When there was no marital conflict, there was *no* increased antisocial behavior among children. There was a trend, however, toward "an even greater risk for antisocial problems when both discord and personality disturbance were present" (Rutter, 1971, p. 256). This suggests that parental psychological problems do not *by themselves* influence children negatively. It appears to be the combination of marital discord and personality psychopathology that influences children's behavior negatively.

Maternal adjustment to postdivorce life was related to her level of depression and anxiety at the beginning of the divorce process. It also was a good predictor of her children's adjustment 2 years later. Paternal self-reports of alcohol abuse were reported to be related to children's inattention in the classroom and inappropriate involvement with peers.

Fathers' mood, on the other hand, was not predictive of children's adjustment in maternal custody. The best paternal predictor of adjustment is reported to be the quality of the father-child relationship.

Relationship With Nonresidential Parent

Another concern is father absence, suggesting that it is a more significant factor the earlier it occurs in a child's life. More recent longitudinal data indicate that there are few differences between the children of father-absent families compared with intact families along dimensions of emotional adjustment (Kelly, 1993). However, this issue is hotly debated (Blankenhorn, 1995).

No matter how good a nonresidential parent's relationship was with the children before the divorce, "neither the quality nor the frequency of contact between the noncustodial parent and child can be predicted from the predivorce relationship" (Hetherington et al., 1989, p. 309). Some fathers with very good predivorce relationships find it too painful to continue frequent contact. Other fathers who had poor relationships with their children find divorce to be a motivator to improve their emotional connection with their children.

Although not often reflected in the decisions of the courts, psychological research has reported for many years that the traditional visitation schedule of every other weekend, with a maximum of four overnight stays per month with the father, creates "intense dissatisfaction among children, especially young boys" (Kelly, 1988, p. 127). Wallerstein and Kelly (1980) reported that young boys experienced reactive depressions and that divorced children, in general, reported feelings of deprivation, loss, and loneliness over the loss of daily contact with their father.

Children report that they have a less positive view of the nonresidential parent (Nastasi, 1988). They report less father support, less father control, and less father punishment (Amato, 1987).

When children of divorce have frequent and predictable contact with the nonresidential parent, they show signs of better adjustment to the single-parent family. This is particularly true for boys. Visit frequency and regularity is significantly related to father-child closeness. However, frequency, regularity, and consistency of father-child contact do not appear to influence children's self-esteem. In fact, there are some studies indicating that paternal visit regularity (but not frequency) is related to decreases in self-esteem of adolescent boys and girls (Kelly, 1993).

Girls whose fathers visited regularly have been reported to have fewer behavioral problems. For both children, when parental legal conflict increases, frequency of paternal contact tended to reduce the chances of inappropriate behavioral concerns.

Interestingly, Issacs (cited in Kelly, 1988) reported that the stability of the visit was more important in helping children to adjust to their new lives than was the frequency of contact. When the custodial mother approved of and supported father-child contact, children were found to evince better adjustment.

Children have difficulty with adjustment when the nonresidential parent is poorly adjusted or extremely immature. Other studies have found poor adjustment in children when visiting is infrequent and unpredictable. There is also a significant relationship between unpredictable father contact and each of the following: poor self-esteem, depression, and anger.

There is some confusion in the literature about the degree to which father contact is maintained over the course of family disruption. Furstenberg, Nord, Peterson, and Zill's (1983) initial report of marital disruption and parental contact concluded that most children have had no contact with the nonresidential parent during the past year. These results have not been supported by subsequent research. However, it is clear that father contact decreases over time.

Not surprisingly, children in maternal custody families are significantly more likely to experience a decrease in father contact than are children in joint custody arrangements (Kline et al., 1991).

There is some research suggesting that noncustodial mothers are more likely to maintain contact with their children than are noncustodial fathers. In the months immediately after divorce, noncustodial fathers have as much, if not more, time with their children. Over time, noncustodial fathers rapidly become less involved in the lives of their children. There is also a gender bias. Noncustodial fathers tend to maintain more contact with their sons than with their daughters.

Paternal acceptance of the son and rejection of the daughter can have serious negative effects on girls' self-esteem. Although research indicates that boys have a more difficult time adjusting to the absence of the father, girls appear to need father contact as much as boys. A girl's world needs the balancing influence of two genders to help her develop realistic models of same-sex and different-sex worldviews.

Parental Differences in Behavior Management of Children

Discipline is a frequent topic of conflict. Some research shows that there are changes in postdivorce discipline. Hetherington and Hagan (1986) found that divorced parents were more likely to make fewer maturity demands, have poor communication, be less affectionate, and be more inconsistent with their children. Divorced parents also reported their children to be less compliant with parental directions, especially boys. In another study, the authors found that boys were exposed to more ineffective discipline than were girls (Hetherington, Cox, & Cox, 1978).

A number of studies have reported that custodial mothers have considerable difficulty disciplining their children after divorce. In particular, custodial mothers report being less patient, more inconsistent, and less firm with their children than are mothers or fathers of children in two-parent families. Custodial mothers also report having more trouble with child discipline than do custodial fathers (Rohman et al., 1987).

There is an important cycle to be identified. Custodial mothers have been found to be more inconsistent in their discipline. Inconsistent discipline leads to increased aggression and conduct disturbances among children, especially boys. It may be that the conflict and tension between mother and son is related to the mother's inconsistent discipline style rather than anything specific about being a divorced mother.

Dimension of Parenting Styles (Baumrind, 1971)

Permissive . . . . Authoritative . . . . Authoritarian

Parenting Style

Parenting style may be characterized along a dimension from authoritarian to permissive. Authoritative parenting is characterized by responsiveness to children's needs, explanation and negotiation of discipline and decisions, and appropriate monitoring of children's behavior. Authoritative parenting is associated with positive outcomes for children. In contrast, more permissive parenting is characterized by a warm parent-child relationship but low parental monitoring and control. Finally, authoritarian parenting is distinguished by dogmatic, nonnegotiated decision making and punitive discipline. Both permissive and authoritarian styles are associated with more negative outcomes for children.

A period of disrupted parenting is often associated with the early stages of divorce. Custodial mothers tend to be less authoritative in their parenting during the initial stages of divorce. The parent may be preoccupied with the transition and personal problems, resulting in less attention to the children. Typical problems are decreases in parental control and monitoring of child activities. Parent discipline often is erratic, uncommunicative, nonsupportive, and inconsistent.

When custodial mothers have taken a hard line and used an authoritarian child-rearing style, their parenting behaviors were linked to a number of negative outcomes, particularly for boys. Permissive parenting style by custodial mothers was linked to negative outcomes for boys but not for girls. Overall, children in divorced families in which the authoritative style is used appear to make a quicker adjustment to divorce and to perform better in school and with friends.

Gender Differences

Custodial mothers may have a more difficult time with their sons than with their daughters because they discipline the former less. Parents typically are more involved with disciplining same-sex children than opposite-sex children (Baumrind, 1971). Within two-parent families, sons are disciplined about equally by both parents compared with daughters, who are disciplined more by their mothers. If these same-sex discipline patterns continue in divorced families, it suggests that mothers may continue to discipline their daughters and may overfocus discipline attention on them. They may discipline their sons less because they and their sons are accustomed to the father assuming the disciplinarian role with the son. Thus, the son is provided with less discipline and guidance from the parent with whom he has most contact and who sets the standards of behavior for the home in which the son spends most of his time.

Custodial Determination and Adjustment
to Separation and Divorce

A final factor is the relationship of postdivorce adjustment of children to type of custodial placement. Results indicate that children living with the same-sex parent adjusted better than did children living with the opposite-sex parent, showing social competence, maturity, cooperation, and higher levels of self-esteem. Girls residing with their custodial father wanted more contact with their mother than did boys. Boys residing with their custodial mother wanted more contact with their father than did girls (Warshak & Santrock, 1983). Girls living with their father who had a positive relationship with their mother were more socially competent among their peer group (Camera & Resnick, 1988).

The overall conclusions appear to be two. First, same-sex parent-children custody appears to have a more powerful effect on adjustment than does opposite-sex custody. Second, custody arrangements allowing children to have frequent and continuous access to both parents are beneficial for most children. The only factor that may influence these positive results is when parents continue to have high interparental conflict that intrudes upon the children's daily life.

EIGHT

Special Circumstances

No one suffers more or has more to lose from a divorce than the children involved.

Marc J. Ackerman (1995, book jacket copy)

Custody evaluators are often faced with unique variables to assess. There are times when a custody evaluation leads to previously accepted beliefs or behaviors being challenged. Many years ago, I evaluated a couple who had a Saturday morning ritual of permitting their two girls to join them in the master bed. The parents lay in bed trying to catch a few more moments of sleep while the girls watched cartoons. During the custody evaluation, the mother complained that the girls should never be allowed in the same bed as their father. I concluded that the weekend ritual of cartoon watching, hugging, and snuggling was consistent with what the girls had done with their parents during the marriage. I concluded there was no risk to the girls. After I completed my report and recommended joint custody, the mother filed charges with the local Department of Child Protective Services against her former husband, alleging child sexual abuse. She stated that the father was enticing their daughters into his bed. She eventually was awarded primary custody because of the judge's uncertainty of the motivation behind the father's weekend cartoon ritual.

There are a number of variables that cause great concern in divorcing families. Nine of them will be reviewed here: religious differences, move away concerns, nonresidential parent involvement, same-sex custodial placement considerations, racial and cultural issues, gay and lesbian issues, allegations of sexual abuse within custodial assessment, allegations of parental alienation, and domestic violence.

Religious Differences

Religious differences within two-parent families are worked out with little public fanfare. There are no rules about how religious differences are resolved in a family. The children may share the mother's religion, or they may share the father's religion, and sometimes, they are brought up with dual religious identities. There are families in which religious beliefs are an everyday observance and part of the daily life of the family. There are other families in which religious observance occurs only over holidays and is not part of day-to-day life. However, once a couple divorces, religious differences may become a significant factor in the parents' attempts to gain custody of their children.

The courts are required by constitutional provisions ensuring religious freedom to maintain an attitude of strict impartiality among religions. They also maintain an objective, neutral position regarding religious beliefs and atheistic beliefs. The religious beliefs, customs, and practices of a parent are important only in terms of their impact upon the minor child.

Determining the importance of religious variables in the context of custody assessment is difficult for evaluators. There is no behavioral science research that has systematically examined the effects of a parent's religious beliefs on the best psychological interests of the child (Rohman et al., 1987).

There are several guiding concepts about the role of religion as a factor in the best psychological interests standard. The first is that the "child's welfare will not be sacrificed to permit or enhance the expression of religious beliefs held either by a potential custodian or by the child, should he not be mature enough to embrace a particular faith" (Rohman et al., 1987, p. 80). Evaluators need to explore the religious beliefs of each potential custodian to determine how his or her religious beliefs, customs, and practices influence each child. Of particular concern are those beliefs, customs, or practices that potentially threaten the child's physical or psychological well-being.

The intention is not to regulate religious practice. Rather, courts want to ensure that the religious beliefs of a potential custodian will not interfere with or threaten the physical or emotional health of the child. Similarly, when examining a mature child, the court is concerned that the religious beliefs embraced by a child will not interfere with or threaten his or her physical or emotional health.

The courts have also been reluctant to change custody of a child to a custodian who does not afford opportunities to practice that faith. In those instances in which the child has not yet been initiated into a particular faith, the courts generally have awarded custody to those who will raise the child in the faith professed by the natural parents. When a child too young to be initiated into a particular faith comes from parents with differing faiths, the courts have tended to award custody without regard to religious considerations (Rohman et al., 1987).

As described earlier, courts tend to ask "Who is the better person?" whereas evaluators ask "Who is the better parent?" (Lowery, 1984). The issues surrounding religion display this bias. Courts typically will emphasize the moral character of competing parties. The assumption is that a child is better served by placing him or her with the parent of higher moral character. However, there is no empirical research that has examined the effects of a custodian's religious beliefs or moral character upon a child's welfare.

In a recent case in which I was involved, the mother lost custody of her 8-year-old daughter because the *guardian ad litem* judged that the mother's dating habits cast her as an immoral person. This led the guardian to the conclusion that the little girl was at risk for developing a low quality of moral character. The father was a minimally competent parent, with awkward parenting and poor communication skills. The little girl was uncomfortable with her stepmother and had alleged that she had been hit a number of times by the stepmother. She loved her father but found it difficult to talk with him, stating, "He always makes me talk with Mary because he doesn't know what to say to me."

When in the custody of her mother, the little girl performed well at school. She was perceived by those with whom she had contact as a healthy, normal, socially interactive girl who was happy all the time. Yet, despite the collateral data that the girl was healthy, successful at school, had a solid friendship group, and had a very close, loving relationship with her mother, the courts awarded custody to the father, judging the mother to be of low moral character.

In summary, there is little available research on the questions of religious and moral character factors in determining child custody. Conclusions based on such factors will be made less on science and more on beliefs, personal values, and prejudices specific to the evaluation. The evaluator would be wise to examine carefully with respect to their underlying science and research support any statements in which issues of religion or moral character are addressed.

Move Away Considerations

Reasons for seeking to relocate to a new community may vary widely and may include anticipated economic advantages and opportunities; desire to return to a supportive family and friends in one's childhood community; pursuit of educational opportunities for oneself; and pursuit of an improved physical, social, academic, or cultural environment for the child (Weissman, 1994).

QUICK REFERENCE **Three Types of Move Away Cases**

- Primary caregiver opportunistically seeks to move in order to consolidate power and control and to deprive noncustodial parent of access to the children
- Primary caregiver, usually an upper-middle-class, educated mother, seeks to escape the perceived humiliation of remaining in the "father community"
- Primary caregiver seeks to move away to enrich life for her child and return to her family of origin or childhood community

---

It is difficult for a primary caregiver to relocate with a child in disputed circumstances. Social policy, supported by behavioral science research and literature, clinical experience, and case law, emphasizes that children's best psychological interests are most suitably advanced and protected through joint custodial arrangements and through parenting plans that promote frequent and continuous contact with both parents (*Carlson v. Carlson*, 1991; *Gruber v. Gruber*, 1990).

Weissman (1994) suggests a three-pronged test for custody evaluators to follow in evaluating move away cases. These three areas of examination are drawn from the Gruber decision and represent a set of factors commonly assessed in move away cases.

Weissman (1994) interprets the *Gruber* (1990) court as adhering to the best interest standard as the general standard and the relocation issue as an element that would be considered within the context of the best interest standard. In this regard, the *Gruber* decision stated that the need to modify parenting plans "to account for geographic distances will not defeat a move which has been shown to offer real advantages to the custodial parent and the children" (Weissman, 1994, p. 178).

In contrast to Weissman (1994), a recent decision by the Supreme Court of California in *Burgess v. Burgess* (1996) appears to redefine the psychological criteria for evaluating move away cases. The *Burgess* decision states that

> a custodial parent seeking to relocate bears no burden of establishing that it is "necessary" to do so. Instead, he has the right to change the residence of the child, subject to the power of the court to restrain a removal that would prejudice the rights or welfare of the child. (p. 1)

Move away cases assess stress factors. As a function of age- and stage-developmental considerations, it would be expected that children would experience a relocation with varying degrees of distress. Change for children—as

QUICK REFERENCE   **Weissman's (1994) Three-Prong Test for Move Away Cases**

- What are the potential advantages and disadvantages of the proposed move and the likelihood that it would substantially improve the quality of life for the custodial parent and child?
- What is the genuineness of the motives for and against the move, providing that the move is not motivated to frustrate the visitation rights or development of a healthy relationship between the child and noncustodial parent?
- Does there exist a realistic, substitute visitation arrangement that will adequately foster an ongoing relationship between the child and the noncustodial parent?

for most people—is known to be stressful. Relocation concerns about leaving the nonresidential parent may be somewhat diminished in circumstances in which the primary caregiver and child already live a significant geographical distance from the noncustodial parent. Such preexisting conditions may have the effect of already teaching the child how to cope with the stresses related to separation from the noncustodial father. Therefore, further movement away may not be perceived as threatening or disruptive beyond that usually experienced by children in any other kind of move (Weissman, 1994).

It is important to note that stress does not necessarily mean distress, maladjustment, or difficulties with adjustment. Kelly's (1993) research has demonstrated that divorce-related stress is typically transient for most children. Psychological distress or impairment occurs in only a small percentage of cases. Weissman (1994) states that "similar outcomes would be predicted for children who relocate with a parent who otherwise competently serves their best interests and in situations where the *Gruber* elements are satisfied" (p. 179).

In a powerful essay arguing against recent move away decisions such as *Burgess,* Shear (1996) posits that the courts erred by not considering a number of significant factors. "If [state courts] follow the approach of these three major jurisdictions, the standards will reflect a flawed and obsolete frame of reference" (p. 440).

Shear (1996) believes that the "core fallacy" of these recent move away decisions "is the belief that the word 'custody' not only means something, but means the same thing" to each family (p. 440). Court decisions about move away issues look at the labels "custodial" and "noncustodial." The label tells little about what each family situation involves. In fact, Shear argues that the labels themselves are a shield that protect the court from exploring in a fuller, more meaningful way the particular factors of each family.

QUICK REFERENCE **Shear's (1996) Eight Move Away Variables**

- Every parenting plan is a hypothesis about what would be best for the child and the family, not a scientific prescription. Parenting plans are often constructed on relatively little data in a very brief time period. Maintaining the myth of their infallibility hurts children.

- The labels "custody," "sole custody," "joint custody," and "visitation" (or "access") obscure the reality as the parents' respective involvement (and time-shares) moves closer and closer together.

- Childhood and the lives of families consist of constantly changing circumstances that both discretely and cumulatively have an impact on custody issues as profoundly as does the occasional dramatic change.

- To sustain any kind of relationship with a parent who lives more than 20 minutes away, the rest of the child's life and activities must be fragmented and compromised to some degree. The greater the distance, the greater the disruption.

- Parents and children cannot sustain close relationships unless the parent is involved in all aspects of the child's life and care.

- Moves cannot be seen in isolation; one must look at them in the context of the child's entire experience and resilience.

- The impetus for most moves is almost always parental best interests, not the child's best interests.

- Families cannot look at the needs of any one of their members in isolation. The family always has to balance and harmonize the needs of its members, whether complementary or competing.

As evaluators, our responsibility is to look "at the mess and mystery of family life" (Shear, 1996, p. 440). We need to understand each family's unique story, rather than simply presume that the primary custodian's relationship with the child offers significantly more than does the noncustodian's involvement.

Evaluators need to be aware that a request to move is one factor in a long line of events, experiences, and changes that have happened to the child. A move must not be examined in isolation but as part of the larger story of a child's emerging life. How the child has coped with previous changes and the manner in which he or she adjusted to stressors and other change agents inform us of the tolerance each child may have to another significant change. The changed circumstances doctrine, which allows for move away considerations, needs to recognize that the original parenting plan was based upon

assumptions of custodial and noncustodial involvement that contributed to
the best psychological interests of the child. When one parent moves away,
the relative contribution of each parent to the child's life changes significantly. Without a thorough reexamination of the child's best psychological
interest vis-à-vis the proposed change, no meaningful statements can be made
about the viability or impact of the move on the child's health and
development.

Nonresidential Parental Involvement

Legislation enacted in the past 15 years has been designed to increase the participation of nonresidential parents in the lives of their children (Depner &
Bray, 1990). There is some evidence that parents are increasingly electing
joint legal custody, and that rates of nonresidential parent involvement are
also increasing. Although nonresidential parents often express a strong interest in playing an active role in the lives of their children, father involvement
may depend upon a variety of factors, such as emotional adjustment to divorce, perceived status as nonresidential parent, perceived unfairness of divorce proceedings, and conflicts with former spouse (Dudley, 1996).

Whenever an evaluator approaches a family in transition, it is wise to
remember that everyone in the family unit is undergoing significant change.
Some changes are more obvious than others. Some changes appeal to our
sense of humanity, whereas some offend us. The literature on men's reaction
to divorce suggests that evaluators need to be sensitive to changes in behavior, attitudes, and perceived values that are observed during the evaluation
process but are artifacts of the turmoil and uncertainty that come with marital dissolution and family separation (Arendell, 1995). The following is a partial overview of the complexities of men's reaction to divorce drawn from
current behavioral science literature.

Noncustodial Father's Experience of Divorce

The emotional experience of divorce for a single father is filled with painful, unpredictable emotions. Many men feel victimized by the divorce. They
feel that the courts as well as their former spouse have violated their rights as
a parent. There is a common belief among single fathers that no one has the
right to tell a biological father when he can or cannot see his children. The
state is viewed as interfering with a father's rights to autonomy and self-
determination. Fathers believe that the state should have no say in the determination of postdivorce parenting responsibilities for those fathers who want
to maintain active involvement. There is a belief that the state maintains a
maternal bias resulting in a poor understanding of the needs and wishes of

divorced fathers to play a more active daily role in their children's lives (Arendell, 1995).

A father's position in the family is significantly altered by divorce. Fathers are most often relegated to living apart from their children. Interestingly, despite the continued high divorce rate among parents with children, there is very little professional literature available to help fathers figure out how to be single fathers. Cherlin (1978) suggests that fatherhood after divorce is an "incomplete institution."

A majority of divorced fathers viewed the divorce as a "battle" in which there was a winner and a loser. The clearly identified enemy was the former wife. Many viewed the divorce process as an example of a "war between the sexes." They saw game playing to gain strategic advantage as the major weapon of their former spouse and her attorney (Arendell, 1995). This may be an important factor to consider during the evaluation process.

Typically, how men respond to divorce and their status as single parents is entwined with ideas they hold about being a man. Divorced men tended to revert to more traditional genderized roles as a way of coping with the loss of status, power, and self-esteem previously gained through their involvement with the family. Their identity as family men has been stripped away, yet they have no understanding of how to restore even a part of their identities as family men or as involved fathers. Single fathers feel lost, alone, directionless, and empty without the rudder of fatherhood to guide them. Too often, their rudder is found in the form of power and control games. Many single fathers withhold child support, alimony, or other forms of family contribution in an apparent attempt to use their power in game playing, which interferes with their former spouse's ability to get on with her life (Arendell, 1995).

It is interesting to note the number of single fathers who, under previous circumstances, would have placed the importance of their children or the preservation of family stability at the center of their concerns, but now are hellbent on reasserting their personal power through often inappropriate, questionable, or unnecessary challenges to the custodial parent's decision making.

Another way in which single fathers regain their emotional balance after divorce is to develop multiple superficial relationships. Postdivorce single fathers typically date many different people, as opposed to postdivorce single mothers, who tend toward finding one close, safe interpersonal relationship.

In summary, divorced single fathers experience a wide variety of emotional ups and downs during their separation from the family. Many believe that the legal system is unfair and unbalanced. They believe that there is a "maternal bias" that results in a poor understanding of the needs of fathers to be actively involved in the daily lives of their children.

Divorced men lose much of their personal power and status. Their self-esteem suffers. Often, divorced men regain their sense of personal power through a rejuvenation of their "maleness." They focus their energies on more stereotypical male behaviors that tend to further alienate them from their family.

Topology of Single Fathers

Not all divorced fathers respond the same way to divorce. There are *traditional* fathers, who are so angry with their former spouses that they cannot get beyond their anger to deal appropriately with their children (Arendell, 1995). In these relationships, the father's relationship with his children suffers greatly because there is little, if any, contact. These fathers often move great distances away from their children, either geographically or emotionally. This results in their children losing sight of their father as an everyday contributor to their lives. They also lose sight of the importance of fatherhood as a culturally important concept. When children grow up in families in which the father has become unnecessary, there is an increasing likelihood that these children will grow into adulthood believing that family functioning does not need a contributing father. Thus, the meaning of fatherhood becomes diminished and thought of as unnecessary (Blankenhorn, 1995).

There are also *neotraditional* fathers, who vacillate between the postmarital conflict with their former spouses and an occasional recognition of their responsibility to their children to be a good father (Arendell, 1995). This results in children experiencing their father as a sometimes contributor to their lives. His inconsistent participation may be experienced as a lack of responsibility and commitment to the role of father. Thus, children who grow into adulthood from such families view the role of father as inconsistent, not responsible for reliable participation, and therefore unnecessary.

Innovative fathers are able to work cooperatively with their former spouses in placing the health and well-being of their children at the center of their concerns (Arendell, 1995). These men are able to create a child-centered parenting relationship with their ex-wives in which their children can grow. Children from such families develop fatherhood models in which the father is viewed as consistent, responsible, and necessary for the development of a healthy family.

Divorce Changes a Father's Involvement With His Children

Wallerstein and Blakeslee (1989) reported that 10 years after divorce, children of divorce felt a decrease in perceived parental protection, caring, and comforting. Children in their study reported vivid, intense, and painful memories of their parents' separation. The authors also found that younger children, ages 5 to 8, intensely missed the presence of their fathers in their lives after divorce.

A father's predivorce relationship with his children does not predict his postdivorce relationship. Many divorced fathers found it difficult to continue

---

QUICK REFERENCE   **Typology of Divorced Fathers**

- Traditional father: This father appears unable to get beyond his marital conflict and appropriately focus on the well-being and care of his children. He is virtually unconcerned about his parental responsibilities and his parent-child relationships.

- Neotraditional father: This father is more like a traditional father than not, but he vacillates between active resistance to his former spouse and reluctant adjustment. This father appears to be able to get beyond his immediate differences with his former spouse but with no consistency. His relationship with his children is dependent upon the level of tension with his former wife. When tension is low, the father is able to focus on his children. When tension is high, the father focuses on the conflict with the mother to the exclusion of his relationship with his children.

- Innovative father: This father is focused on learning how to adapt his new life to the needs of his children. He creates alliances with his former spouse over creative ways to enhance his children's development. He develops parenting partnerships based upon input from each parent and focuses exclusively upon what is in his child's best psychological interests. Innovative fathers accounted for less than 15% of those studied.

---

a close, loving relationship with their children, especially if one or both parents remarried (Arendell, 1995; Wallerstein & Blakeslee, 1989). Yet as Horn (1995) summarizes, "Children tenaciously held onto an internal image, sometimes a fantasy image, of their absent or even visiting father" (p. 8).

Furstenberg and Cherlin (1991) reported that more than 50% of all children who do not live with their father have never been in their father's home. Lerman and Ooms (1993) found that fathers with younger children tended to visit more often than did fathers with older children. Fifty-seven percent of fathers with children younger than 2 years old visited their children more than once a week compared with only 23% visiting their children when the children are older than $2\frac{1}{2}$ years old.

The National Commission on Children (1991) found that only one child in six saw his or her father as often as once a week. Nearly one child in five had not seen his or her father for 5 years. As time goes on, fathers see their children less. Ten years after marital breakup, more than two thirds of the children have not seen their father for at least a year.

Fathers who maintain regular contact with their biological children find their relationships substantially altered (Furstenberg & Cherlin, 1991).

Fathers behave more like relatives than parents. Instead of helping with homework, noncustodial fathers are more likely to take their children shopping, to the movies, out to dinner, or some other form of entertainment. They do not provide much traditional fathering, such as guidance and steady advice, leaving those needs either unfulfilled or left to the mother.

The role of father—distinct from the cultural role of fatherhood—requires men to play significant roles in the day-to-day lives of their children, yet research suggests that many divorced fathers provide little traditional parenting.

Divorce Changes How Fathers Parent

There are a number of ways in which divorce changes how a father parents. These many be categorized as follows.

Fathers have poor communication with former spouse. Parents need to talk with each other about the emergent needs of their children. In a divorced family system, the former spouses are less likely to talk with each other about their children's needs. Fewer than one third of divorced parents discuss their children with each other over a 12-month period (Arendell, 1995). Only one fifth—20%!—talk with each other about their children's welfare on a weekly basis. Among those parents who talk weekly, the father's participation in decision making is limited.

Fathers are poor communicators with their children. Mothers appear to mediate the father-child relationship in two-parent families. Mom serves as a kind of linguistic translator, helping the father understand the context and meaning of his children's stories (Arendell, 1995). When divorce occurs, mother-as-mediator serves a smaller role. The father is left to his own devices to negotiate quality relationships with his children, yet he has been poorly prepared for this task because he has had a translator for many years.

Fathers learn about their children differently from mothers. Noncustodial fathers tend to spend less time with their children the longer they are divorced. About 40% of children in single-parent households haven't seen their fathers in at least a year. Of the remaining 60%, one fifth spend one night per month in their father's home. Only one child in six sees his or her father an average of once a week or more (Furstenberg & Cherlin, 1991).

There is a paradox involved in the evolution of the divorced family system. As divorced children desire greater contact with their father, the father's knowledge of his children and his ability to understand his children is altered. He is forced to develop a new way of communicating with his children during a period when he has less time with them to understand how to develop this new communications vehicle, less time to practice its use with his children, and an increasing chance that he will focus his energies on play rather than more substantial parenting communications. The result is that what contributes most to the child's psychological development—the quality of the parent-child relationship rather than the frequency of contact—is what suffers the most because there is little time and less support for its development (Wallerstein & Blakeslee, 1989).

Father's role is devalued. Divorced mothers often place little importance on a father's input. Only about half of divorced mothers place value on the divorced father's continued contact with his children (Horn, 1995). Twenty percent report no value in a divorced father's continued contact with his children (Wallerstein & Kelly, 1980). Almost three fourths of former spouses indicated they would have no contact with their former spouse if they did not have shared parenting responsibilities (Ahrons & Rodgers, 1987).

Mother's role is devalued. Divorced fathers often send clear as well as subtle messages to their children that their mother is, in some ways, deficient as a parent. These messages serve to lessen her perceived effectiveness as a parent in many of the same ways that the mother devalues the role of father and his perceived effectiveness as a father.

When a single father abuses his power and control with the intent of undermining the emotional stability of the mother or her perceived efficacy as a parent, children rapidly learn to devalue their mother. One reason that single mothers have so much difficulty with their male offspring is that the single fathers have spent years teaching through example how to disrespect and ignore the legitimate power of the mother. The result is a primary residence that is in turmoil and children who become at risk for increased school failure, inappropriate displays of aggression, substance abuse, early onset of sexual behavior, and other serious behavioral problems.

To regain parental authority, single mothers often take one of three paths. The first is to engage in struggles to regain appropriate control within the family. This results in continuous fighting and emotional estrangement between the mother and her children or the splitting of the household into alliances. Another path is for the divorced father to step in to fill the gap. In this way, the children have been able to successfully sabotage the need of the divorcing parents to separate effectively. Dad finds that his place as a father remains important, and his children do not have to get on with the awesome task of learning to live without their father in the home. The final option is for the mother to give up and turn her parental power over to her children. When this happens, undisciplined aggression rages, and the children develop into significant behavior problems both at school and with their friends, and they get to know the local law enforcement personnel rather well.

Divorce changes children and places them at risk. The effects of divorce on children are unclear. Wallerstein's seminal works appear to suggest that there are significant negative short- and long-term effects on healthy children (Wallerstein & Blakeslee, 1989; Wallerstein & Kelly, 1980), whereas Kelly's analyses of the same data suggest that children who are basically healthy prior to the divorce will return to predivorce levels of functioning within a few months after the initial traumatic separation (Kelly, 1996).

Although we may not be clear about how long our children feel the pains and anxieties associated with family transitions resulting from divorce, we know that when fathers leave, children suffer. When a father lives within the family home, children tend toward more prosocial behavior. Boys raised by traditional masculine fathers within two-parent families tend not to commit crimes. Fatherless boys are more likely to commit crimes and to show an increase in violence (Gottfredson & Hirschi, 1990). Compared with children in two-parent families children living apart from their fathers are at risk of being expelled or suspended from school, demonstrate emotional or behavioral problems, have difficulty establishing and sustaining relationships with peers, and get into trouble with the police.

Girls are not free from the hazards of fatherlessness. Blankenhorn (1995) suggests that the risk of childhood sexual abuse is directly linked to the decline of married fatherhood. Wallerstein and Blakeslee (1989) argue that much of a father's role within the family is to protect his children. When a father participates in the daily routine of parenting activities, such as personal grooming, discipline, nurturing, education, and moral direction, his involvement tends to minimize the likelihood of him expressing desire or excitement. Instead, fathers are focused on protection, socialization, and guidance.

Children come to expect a different parenting style from single parents than from two parents. When living with the mother, children often receive less mothering. The mother can be only a mother, and a household that has only one parent cannot provide what a household with two parents can provide. Thus, the children receive less from each parent—less from the father because he is not physically present, and less from the mother because she has to take care of all her children's needs rather than dividing that responsibility more evenly with her husband.

Divorce changes how children live. The economics of divorce are relatively clear. Fathers leave and often increase their standard of living. Mothers work harder with fewer resources and often experience a decrease in their standard of living. About 40% of divorcing women lose more than half their family income as a result of divorce, compared with about 17% of men (Duncan & Hoffman, 1985). Generally, a woman's income drops about 30% after divorce. Divorced men, on the other hand, experience an increase in income primarily attributable to the reduction in monies that go toward daily child and home care concerns (Furstenberg & Cherlin, 1991).

The economic hardships placed upon single mothers after divorce significantly influence children's well-being. Single mothers disproportionately carry the financial burden of child rearing and maintaining the home. Children living in single-parent homes are far more likely to be poorer than are children living in other situations (U.S. Bureau of the Census, 1992). Child support payments account for only 17% of the income for single-parent households, with the monthly child support payment averaging $277 (U.S. Bureau of the Census, 1982). Fewer than 15% of divorcing women are awarded spousal support or maintenance (Furstenberg & Cherlin, 1991). Slightly more than 10% of women awarded alimony or spousal support actually receive any payments (Furstenberg & Cherlin, 1991).

Father-Son, Mother-Daughter (Same Sex) Custodial Decisions

An interesting question is whether the postdivorce adjustment of children is related to the parent-child gender pairing of custodial determination. In those studies in which sole maternal custody was compared to sole paternal custody, results indicated that children living with the same-sex parent adjusted better than children living with the opposite parent. Children living with the same-sex parent were reported to show better social competence, maturity, cooperation, and higher levels of self-esteem.

Girls residing with their custodial father wanted more contact with their mother than did boys. Boys residing with their custodial mother wanted more contact with their father than did girls (Warshak & Santrock, 1983). Girls living with their father who had a positive relationship with their noncustodial mother were more socially competent among their peer group (Camera & Resnick, 1988).

The overall conclusions appear to be two. First, same-sex parent-child custody appears to have a more powerful effect on adjustment than does opposite-sex custody. Second, custody arrangements allowing children to have frequent and continuous access to both parents are beneficial for most children. The only factor that may influence these positive results is when parents continue to have high interparental conflict that intrudes upon the children's daily life.

One of the most consistent research findings is that young boys appear more reactive than do girls to separation and divorce. Boys' postseparation behavior frequently has been characterized in terms of increased aggressiveness, impulsiveness, and acting-out behaviors. However, Block et al. (1988) reported that "long before divorce occurs in a family, sons tend to be impulsive and undercontrolled relative to boys in families that will remain intact" (p. 212).

Hetherington (1991) reported that at 6-year postdivorce follow-up, divorced, nonremarried mothers were still showing many of the same signs of conflict and tension with their sons as were evident earlier in the transition process. In particular, divorced mothers were found to be "ineffectual in their control attempts and gave many instructions with little follow through. They tended to nag, natter, and complain and more often were involved in angry, escalating coercive cycles with their sons" (p. 177).

Another factor of concern is that spontaneous fights were more than twice as likely between divorced mothers and their sons than in a comparable group of nondivorced mothers and sons. Boys typically were seen as attacking their mothers, often for no discernible reason. Divorced mothers tended to counterattack more often than did their nondivorced counterparts.

Hetherington (1991) notes that these intense interactions should not be blown out of proportion:

> In spite of the conflict between custodial mothers and their early adolescent sons it might be best to view this relationship in early adolescence as intense and ambivalent rather than as purely hostile and rejecting, since there also were warm feelings expressed. (p. 177)

If elementary school-age and early adolescent boys in families that eventually divorce tend to be more aggressive and impulsive, it may explain why there is more conflict between mothers and sons than mothers and daughters (Block et al., 1988).

Evidence also suggests that the relationship between adolescent son and mother is more conflict prone and tense than the adolescent daughter-mother relationship. Even in intact families, the mother-son relationship is more problematic than the mother-daughter relationship. When the relationship examined includes the father-mother-adolescent son, the harmony of the mother-son relationship improves. Father presence acts as a moderating influence over the degree of conflict between mother and son in early adolescence.

Other research indicates that the mother-daughter relationship in separated and divorced families often is comfortable, warm, and egalitarian, in contrast to the mother-son relationship, which is filled with tension and conflict (Kelly, 1988). Although adjustment difficulties in girls living with their mothers tend to disappear within 2 years after divorce, there is some concern that problems may reemerge during adolescence. Adolescent girls may have conflict with their mothers over the nature of the parent-child relationship as well as disruptions in heterosexual relations (Hetherington, 1991).

If mother-son difficulties are related to some inherent qualities of the mother or unique aspects of her interactional qualities with her son, it may be in the son's best psychological interest to grant the father custodial responsibility for his son or, if feasible, joint custody to allow for increased contact time between father and son.

Some research shows that there are changes in postdivorce discipline. Hetherington et al. (1982) found that divorced parents were more likely to make fewer maturity demands, have poor communication, be less affectionate, and be more inconsistent with their children.

Divorced parents also reported their children to be less compliant with parental directions, especially boys. In another study, Hetherington et al. (1978) found that boys were exposed to more ineffective discipline than were girls.

A number of studies have reported that custodial mothers have considerable difficulty disciplining their children after divorce. In particular, custodial mothers report being less patient, more inconsistent, and less firm with their children than did mothers or fathers of children in two-parent families. Custodial mothers also report having more trouble with child discipline than do custodial fathers (Hetherington et al., 1982).

A period of disrupted parenting is often associated with the early stages of divorce. Custodial mothers tend to be less authoritative in their parenting during the initial stages of divorce. They may be preoccupied with the transition and personal problems, resulting in less attention to their children. Typical problems are decreases in parental control and monitoring of child activities. Parent discipline often is erratic, uncommunicative, nonsupportive, and inconsistent.

When custodial mothers attempted to take a hard line and use an authoritarian child-rearing style, their parenting behaviors were linked to a number of negative outcomes, particularly for boys. Permissive parenting style by custodial mothers was linked to negative outcomes for boys but not for girls. Overall, children in divorced families in which the authoritative style is used appear to make quicker adjustment to divorce and perform better in school and with friends.

It is possible that one reason why custodial mothers typically have a more difficult time with their sons than with their daughters is that they discipline the former less. Studies have shown that parents are more involved with disciplining same-sex children than opposite sex children (Baumrind, 1971). Within two-parent families, sons are disciplined about equally by both parents, compared with daughters, who are disciplined more by their mothers. However, if these same-sex discipline patterns continue in divorced families, it suggests that mothers continue to discipline their daughters and may overfocus discipline attention on them. At the same time, mothers may discipline their sons less because both they and their sons are accustomed to the father assuming the disciplinarian role with the son. Thus, the son is provided with less discipline and guidance from the parent with whom he has the most contact and who sets the standards of behavior for the home in which the son spends most of his time.

Parents in Short-Lived Relationships

A distinctive group of parents who may seek custodial determination is those individuals whose relationship was short lived (i.e., never-married parents). Although the evaluation techniques remain unchanged in the assessment of relevant variables, there may be some unique factors to consider when making decisions about custodial recommendations and parenting plans for those individual who never developed a bona fide relationship.

Parents from short-lived relationships may differ from married parents in a number of ways (Raisner, 1997). Never-married parents have not established a separate family unit. They may not know each other very well, particularly if the pregnancy occurred during a short-term relationship.

A second difference is that the child often has little or no contact with the nonresidential parent. Some of these children have been raised with a parent substitute. This often adds another important dimension. The parent substitute, or stepparent, may have been identified to the child as his or her biological father or taught that his or her biological father does not care and therefore has no legitimate right to visit.

Under such circumstances, visitation plans may need to provide for increased time for the child to learn about and adjust to the concept of his or her biological parent. Time may also be necessary for the child to become accustomed to the participation of the biological parent in his or her life. Similar concerns are focused on the child's need to adjust to new siblings (stepsiblings), stepmother, grandparents, and other extended family members.

Children may also have significant emotional reactions to the knowledge and understanding of the role of the biological father. There may be a need for some of these children to participate in counseling, family therapy, or some other form of intervention. The respective parents may need to attend counseling sessions or some type of mediation through which they can negotiate unresolved issues that may interfere with the establishment of a healthy father-child relationship.

Particularly with younger, unmarried parents, there may be a need to educate the parents about the purpose and focus of psychological or psychoeducational interventions. Never-married parents "have extra anger, resentment, suspicion, or fear if they are being forced—by a court—into renewing a relationship with the other parent" (Raisner, 1997, p. 92). The educational focus may be, in part, to assure them that they need not reconcile their former relationship, but focus on ways to develop a working relationship through which their child can enjoy the support of each parent in encouraging their relationship with the other.

Besides concerns about how the child can learn to incorporate a new parent and extended family into his or her life, there is also the concern that some never-married parents have had their child reared by other relatives.

Thus, the introduction of the biological father into the child's life may result in feelings of displacement on the part of those who raised the child. These people and their feelings also need to be addressed in some respectful way.

A final factor is unique to same-sex relationships. Gay and lesbian parents who never married but lived within a structured, committed relationship in which parental roles were defined may struggle with their parental roles after the love relationship dissolves. The nonbiological parent in a homosexual partnership has no legal status, though he or she may wish to maintain an ongoing relationship with the child.

A similar situation occurs when the never-married parent eventually marries and then divorces the stepfather after many years. The stepfather may have had significant influence in the child's life, and the continuing relationship with the stepfather may significantly affect the child's best psychological interests. However, the legal status of the stepfather was never clarified through formal adoption. At some point, the biological father reenters the picture. The evaluator may need to consider not only the visitation issues related to the biological father but also the child's need to maintain an ongoing relationship with the stepfather.

As a cursory overview of these issues suggests, there are a myriad of complexities and subtleties surrounding the concerns of custodial determination and parenting plans with never-married parents. Similarly, there are significant concerns about the proper (not necessarily legal, but proper in the sense of what is best for the child) role of a stepfather in the life of such children.

Useful parenting planning may include a focus on educational information about child development for the parent who has had little contact with the child. There is also a need to spend time helping the parents create a workable communications system. This may include a stepparent(s) or the primary caretaker, who may feel displaced. The intervention needs to focus more on problem-solving and conflict resolution skills than on exploration of feelings and introspection. "Teach parents how to make and respond to a request, how to structure a discussion, and how to use solution-based decision making techniques" (Raisner, 1997, p. 99).

Racial and Cultural Factors

The issue of racial and cultural factors in custodial determination occurs in one of two situations. In one situation, the parents are biracial, and the question is, Who serves the child's best psychological interests? In such cases, racial factors are examined. Race has been found to be a legitimate factor to consider under the best psychological interest standard when the child is the product of a biracial relationship and one potential custodian does not share the physical racial attributes of the child (Rohman et al., 1987). However, race is not considered a legitimate factor when, after custodial determination has been made and the child's best psychological interests are being served, a modification is filed based solely on the custodial parent's involvement in a biracial relationship. For example, in *Palmore v. Sidoti* (1984), consideration of race was viewed as abuse of judicial discretion in a suit by a noncustodial parent to alter existing custodial placement because the mother had entered into a biracial relationship.

Generally, courts have presumed that a biracial child's best psychological interests are served by placement with the custodian who most closely resembles the child's physical characteristics. However, others have argued that custodial determination should focus on the child's identification with a particular racial or cultural heritage. Courts may also explore the willingness of people who share that heritage to accept the child into their community as one of their own.

Many courts have adopted a middle-of-the-road position. Racial issues are necessary to consider in exploring the child's best psychological interests, but the relative weight given to racial factors may vary from case to case. As established more than 20 years ago in *Beazley v. Davis* (1976) and *Tucker v. Tucker* (1975), race may not be the sole basis of a custodial determination.

It is important to note that there is little research examining parental divorce and the effects of race within the child custody context. We do not yet know how children are affected within the context of a biracial divorce. We also do not know who, based solely on the factor of race, may better serve the child's best psychological interests. What we do know is that transracial adoption of nonwhite children by white families does not appear to significantly alter the child's racial awareness, identity, or attitude (Rohman et al., 1987). These studies do not address custodial arrangements when biological parents are living and want to be the child's primary custodian.

In summary, courts have allowed examination of racial and cultural concerns within the context of the larger custodial issue. Courts often do not accept custodial determinations based solely on the race of the child. Instead, the court looks at all of the factors that may influence the child's best psychological interests, including racial identity, cultural exposure, and community support for ethnic development.

Gay and Lesbian Considerations

Historically, gay and lesbian lifestyles were considered deviant. Gay and lesbian lifestyles were viewed by the courts as signs of poor moral character. Thus, the sexual preference of a potential custodian was viewed as particularly probative of that parent's general moral character and therefore a sign of the lack of parental fitness.

Until recently, the generally held social belief supported the judicial presumption that sexual behavior that deviated from middle-class social norms was, by definition, bad for the child.

According to this supposition, a custodian who personally participated in socially unacceptable sexual practices would be incapable of serving as a child's role model for socially acceptable behaviors of either a sexual or nonsexual nature (Rohman et al., 1987).

Many gays and lesbians marry heterosexual partners and have children (LAMBDA, 1994, 1996; Rohman et al., 1987). Negative attitudes toward homosexual parenting abilities are reflected in state court cases in which gay and lesbian parents frequently lose custody of their children.

> The open homosexual raises at least two fears in the court: fear that exposure to homosexuals will pose a threat to the sexual and moral development of the children and fear that the children will suffer embarrassment and indignation at the hands . . . of the community. (Brownstone, 1980, p. 217)

Gay fathers may be even less likely than lesbian mothers to be awarded custody. Although attitudes toward gays and lesbians are consistently negative, attitudes toward gay men are significantly more negative than toward lesbians. The assumption is that gay men will attempt to seduce young children (Morin & Garfinkle, 1978). Such assumptions have not been supported in the literature. Child molestation is not associated with any particular sexual orientation. However, gay parents may suffer double prejudices: gender and sexual orientation.

Psychological research on gay and lesbian parenting indicates that parental homosexuality does not contribute to gender identity confusion, inappropriate role behavior, psychopathology, or homosexual orientation in children (Gibbs, 1988). Homosexual and heterosexual mothers displayed more similarities than differences in maternal caregiving behaviors (Gibbs, 1988). Homosexual and heterosexual fathers were similar in many parental attitudes (Scallen, 1981). Differences were found in gay fathers' tendency to place greater emphasis on nurturing behaviors and heterosexual fathers' greater emphasis on economic providing. Gay and nongay fathers displayed few differences in their expression of intimacy toward their children (Bigner & Jacobson, 1989). The overwhelming conclusion is that there is no research support for the presumption that homosexual parents are worse parents than nonhomosexual parents.

However, case law precedent does not always take into account current behavioral science literature. Frequently, the court awards custody to the heterosexual partner under the assumption that gay and lesbian parents are incapable of bonding with their children. There is also the presumption that homosexual parents are mentally unstable, even when there is no evidence of emotional problems (Susoeff, 1985). Finally, judges are sensitive to community standards of social and moral behavior.

An important factor in custody determination for a homosexual parent is public attitudes toward raising children with homosexual parents (Brownstone, 1980). Courts continue to hold that the best psychological interests of the child are rooted in the traditional heterosexual family system. Thus, courts may fail to ask for evidence establishing a link between homosexuality and its effect on the child's best psychological interests (Miller, 1985).

For example, the Supreme Court of Virginia reversed a joint custody order when it was revealed that the father was living with a male lover (*Roe v. Roe,* 1985). No evidence was presented to show that the 9-year-old child was being influenced negatively. To the contrary, the record shows descriptions of the child as "well adjusted." The judgment, however, concluded that the father's "immoral and illicit homosexual relationship rendered him an unfit and improper custodian as a matter of law" (p. 694).

The job of the evaluator is to become aware of community standards of social and moral behavior within the context of how these variables may affect the child's best psychological interests. It may also be useful to discuss behavioral science research that reveals attitudinal bias in the court's decision making based on presumptions about homosexuality that are not consistent with the empirical literature. The forensic evaluator's role is to present scientific evidence to the trier of fact. One way to fulfill this function is to educate the court about the current literature about gay and lesbian parenting compared with heterosexual parenting.

Sexual Abuse Allegations
Within Custody Evaluations

Any exploration into the potentially explosive, dangerous, and uncertain area of child sexual abuse allegations within the context of ongoing custodial dispute must be approached with great caution, yet a critical component of today's child custody evaluations is the increasing frequency of allegations of child sexual abuse. In past years, a prevailing myth about children was that they never lie; thus, any statement by a child of alleged abuse was immediately viewed as a true report. Research has demonstrated that intentional lying is relatively rare, accounting for between 2% and 8% of cases. However, intentional lying increases with age, with adolescents reporting a higher frequency of intentional lies than do preschoolers.

Making matters more difficult is that false allegations of abuse appear to be an increasingly serious problem. Recent estimates are that false allegations of sexual abuse arise in 23% to 33% of cases (Gordon, 1996). The mental health community's ability to discriminate true from false allegations is still in its infancy. We have little reliable information about which behaviors consistently and accurately distinguish abused from nonabused children. We are unable to consistently and reliably distinguish allegations of abuse based upon analysis of a child's report. There is no current research support for the notion that sexual abusers (i.e., the alleged perpetrators) can be identified through profile analysis of objective psychological tests or behavioral indicators (Weissman, 1991b).

> The psycholegal literature [assumes] . . . there exists some form of valid, generally accepted profile of the child victim and of the child offender. There is none (*People v. Ruiz,* 1990, *State v. Rimmasch,* 1989). No reliable constellation of historical, demographic, personality, or other factors has been found that accurately characterizes either the child victim or the child offender. Neither is there any reliable psychological or physiological test or method for determining whether a child has been sexually abused or whether someone has committed an act of sexual abuse. (Weissmann, 1991b, p. 52)

> Despite current myths about children and sexual abuse, the behavioral science literature provides a shaky foundation upon which to make clear, consistent statements about our ability to identify who has been abused, who has done the abusing, and when the child has been abused. Reflecting this developing database, custody evaluators are often asked to make judgments about sexual abuse within the context of custodial determinations.

> The explosion of cases involving allegations of child sexual abuse exceeds the resources available to deal with the problem. Many clinicians lack specific training in this area, and the legal profession is often confronted with an array of self-identified experts who have emerged to fill the void. Unfortunately, these evaluators often use inadequate diagnostic techniques or fail to evaluate the child within the context of the family. If conclusions are drawn on the basis of inadequate or insufficient information, children may be harmed, parent-child relationships seriously damaged, and these cases contaminated to the point that courts and other professionals have great difficulty sorting out what did and did not occur. (American Academy of Child and Adolescent Psychiatry, 1988, p. 655)

The following section describes one way to proceed in the assessment of child abuse allegations within the context of a child custody evaluation.

Conceptual and Empirical Obstacles to Accurate Sexual Abuse Evaluations

There is some empirical support for the notion that professionals tend to believe that allegations occurring within a custody context are less likely to be true. Evaluators have been found to view abuse as more likely when there are multiple rather than single-episode reports. Reports in which there was a prior allegation were seen as more likely than were those with no prior report. Finally, reports occurring within 2 years of filing were seen as less likely than those in which filing occurred more than 2 years earlier (Thoennes & Ijaden, 1990).

Evaluator Bias

The first potential obstacle is, How did the allegation come to the attention of the evaluator? Some cases exist prior to the custody dispute and are, in fact, the basis for the marital dissolution. Other cases occur after the marital separation but before the custody dispute is transformed into a court battle. Still other cases occur during the custody evaluation process. Some cases arise after a parent remarries and the stepparent is alleged to have perpetrated the abuse.

Allegations of sexual abuse may involve a clear history of sexual abuse, complete with medical evidence, appropriate verbal reports, and witnesses. Other allegations—most that call for a decision from a custody evaluator—are much more subtle and elusive. A variety of factors may influence and complicate the determination of support for an allegation. Some of the child factors that may influence decision making are age, gender, social and cognitive development, emotional maturity, linguistic competence, memory development, and sexual knowledge. Some of the adult factors that may need our attention are intellectual functioning, job status, access to the child, and status of current adult relationships.

Many of these factors interact with one another, resulting in a very confused and unclear picture of the events in question. Further confounding the ability to identify and measure relevant factors accurately is the passage of time, the number of interviews during which the child repeats his or her story, and the changing developmental level of the child. Another relevant factor is whether the particular context within which a sexual abuse allegation arises influences professional decision making.

> Professional bias, whether it results from the psychological needs of the professional, the commercial sale of professional opinion as in some expert testimony, or other factors appears to be a significant problem in this field. . . . Our concern here is with the extent to which assumptions about the nature of abuse reports . . . may limit accuracy of professional judgements. (Berliner & Conte, 1993, p. 112)

Classification Systems

A second obstacle is the decision-making and classification systems used by the evaluator in determining the accuracy or inaccuracy of an allegation.

Overall, empirical studies have yet to establish stable reliability and validity data for any one kind of judgment aid.

The primary purpose of a sexual abuse evaluation is to provide a judgment within a reasonable degree of psychological certainty that an alleged act of abuse did or did not occur. One method is to develop a classification of behaviors that identifies abused from nonabused children. To date, there is no clear database that helps to make this distinction.

Another area of research is the identification of statements that are predictive of true versus false abuse claims. A specific line of research has explored defining characteristics of true versus false statements about abuse using Gardner's Sexual Abuse Legitimacy (SAL) scale (Gardner, 1989a). The scale purports to discriminate "bona fide" from "fabricated" cases by disclosing the presence or absence of a series of characteristics. However, there are no published reliability or validity data on the scale. Thus, use of this scale is not recommended in a forensic context.

For many years, it was believed that certain statements or behaviors identified abused versus nonabused children. Among the most popular was the display of age-inappropriate sexual knowledge. The assumption was that sexually abused children would possess developmentally advanced concepts about sexuality and sexual behavior as a result of their exposure to sexually exploitative or abuse behavior. Research has demonstrated that both abused and nonabused children display sexual behaviors, with sexually abused children revealing significantly higher frequency of sexual behaviors in certain categories (Friedrich et al., 1992). Making matters more difficult to distinguish, only a minority of sexually abused children appear to exhibit problem sexual behavior, whereas some children who have not been sexually abused act out sexually (Berliner & Conte, 1993; Ceci & Bruck, 1995).

Another commonly held belief not supported by research is that sexually abused children tend to be somewhat hesitant to talk about the experience of abuse. The assumption was that sexually abused children feel ashamed or will have been threatened or bribed not to disclose the abuse. However, it is just as likely that a child may tell adults who have been supportive and helpful, thus increasing the likelihood that the child will talk openly about the abuse (Berliner & Conte, 1993; Ceci & Bruck, 1995).

Other professionals have suggested that a "true" incident of abuse is characterized by a delayed, conflicted disclosure, often with a recantation. "False" incidents are often characterized by easy and apparently spontaneous disclosures. No empirical research supports these notions, either.

> Indeed, the empirical literature of effects of abuse in general does not support the idea that there are consistent psychological responses to sexual abuse. The research is notable for finding that there are no emotional or behavioral responses which are found even in a clear majority of cases. . . . Although common psychological characteristics may be present in many cases, there is no

evidence for the assertion they are contained in all or even the majority of true cases of child sexual abuse. (Berliner & Conte, 1993, p. 116)

Conceptual Model Guiding Sexual Abuse Assessment Within Child Custody Evaluations

There is no one right way to conduct an evaluation of alleged child sexual abuse within the context of a custody determination. There are different models that have different suggestions about which factors to assess and how. The most important idea for the evaluator is to develop an underlying theory of science that guides the evaluation process.

Among the most comprehensive models guiding the assessment of alleged sexual abuse is APSAC's (1990) *Guidelines for Psychosocial Evaluation of Suspected Sexual Abuse in Young Children.* Another useful approach to the evaluation of child sexual abuse is written by the American Academy of Child and Adolescent Psychiatry's (1988) "Guidelines for the Clinical Evaluation of Child and Adolescent Sexual Abuse." Currently, the American Psychological Association is completing a position paper outlining evaluation procedures for child maltreatment. A final resource is the suggestions of your state professional association (e.g., state social work association). Different states have different laws governing the reporting of child sexual abuse during a custody evaluation. It is wise to know your state laws and your ethical obligations under those laws.

Know the Literature

The evaluator must be familiar with the considerable behavioral science literature involving directly relevant aspects of investigating allegations of child sexual abuse. Among these areas is the extensive literature about the forensic interviewing of children alleged to be sexually abused (Ney, 1995). There is also an extensive literature about children's memory (Ceci & Bruck, 1993; Gordon, Schroeder, Ornstein, & Baker-Ward, 1995); children's testimony (Ceci & Bruck, 1995); and children's sexual development (Gordon et al., 1995). In addition, there is an extensive literature basis regarding techniques of sexual abuse assessment (e.g., recent reviews about the use of anatomically correct dolls; APSAC, 1995a). Finally, there are important writings about investigator confirmatory bias within the evaluation procedures (Borum et al., 1993; Vogeltanz & Drabman, 1995).

The Evaluation Process

There are different ways of conducting forensic interviews. One way to proceed in the investigation of alleged child sexual abuse is to gather as much background and collateral information as possible prior to interviewing the child. It has been argued that by doing so, the evaluator is better able to control the influence of confirmatory bias on the interview process.

QUICK REFERENCE **Don'ts of Interviewing Children in Sexual Abuse Evaluations**

- Do not schedule an interview after a physical examination or another interview.
- Do not present yourself as someone with whom to talk about bad things.
- Be careful about how you share your empathic responses; that is, differential reinforcement of child responses consistent with evaluator bias.
- Monitor the potential use of generalized scripts in the child's narrative of events.
- Do not remind the child of previous interviews.
- Do not remind the child of previous statements unless specifically intending to confront discrepancies.
- Do not remind the child of how he or she may have behaved in other situations.
- Never promise to keep a secret.

Once you have gathered information from different sources and had time to review and understand its meaning, it is time to interview the child. The child should be evaluated alone. The parents may be included in the initial few minutes of the interview as a means of helping the child become comfortable with the interviewer and the environment. Then, respectfully request that the parents wait outside the interview room. Prior to the parents leaving, be sure that each parent verbally states his or her desire that the child talk to the interviewer about everything the child knows. This type of parental permission to the child often helps the child feel comfortable talking about many different topics.

The primary hypothesis that guides your investigation is that it is as likely that abuse did not occur as it is likely that it did occur. Too often, evaluators' hypotheses are based on the belief that they are trying to prove that abuse did occur. This, of course, is the worst case of confirmatory bias.

Our conceptual model needs to be predicated upon the belief that we do not know whether an event happened or not. We gather data in the most scientifically neutral and objective manner possible and draw conclusions after—yes, after—all data gathering is completed.

Similarly, the interviewer must give the child permission to not remember everything. Permission must also be given to be confused, to describe events differently from those previously reported, and to describe memories that have never been told to anyone else. The most important point is for the child to feel comfortable saying anything to the evaluator that the child wants to talk about. The child needs to know that the expectation is to tell the truth, but the message must be that the child determines what the truth is.

There are a number of "don'ts" in the interviewing of children when concerns of sexual abuse arise. Do not schedule the child's interview after a physical examination or after another interview. You want to talk with the child in a way that produces an independent representation of his or her thoughts, emotions, and behaviors.

Also do not present yourself as one with whom children talk to about bad things. The child should believe that you are someone who talks to many different people about many different things. Some kids may come to talk about fun and exciting things. Other children might talk about scary or upsetting events. No matter what the topic, the child needs to feel it is OK to talk about any topic that may be of importance *to the child*.

Similarly, be careful how you share your empathic responses with the child. Statements such as "It must make you very upset when someone gives you a 'bad' touch" or "You must feel very angry that someone touched your private parts" may help to contaminate the interview process by subtly guiding the child toward providing responses that may reflect the interview's bias rather than the child's true feelings.

Generalized scripts develop when children develop conceptual frameworks that help guide them through predictable, regularly occurring events in their lives. When a child gets ready for school, there generally is a sequence of behaviors that is followed each day. When a unique event happens during school preparation time, the child's self-report may reflect elements of the generalized script as much as it reflects elements of the unique event itself. Thus, it becomes very difficult for the evaluator to distinguish between the child's story about a unique event and the child's story about a unique event as told through the eyes of the generalized script.

Generalized scripts are important to monitor when a child is telling a story about alleged abuse. If the child has been interviewed previously, it is possible that the story being repeated is contaminated in some way by the child's memory of the previous verbal account rather than the child's specific memory of the event in question.

Avoiding generalized scripts occurs, in part, through *not* reminding the child of previous interviews. It is also important to *not* remind the child of specific statements made in previous disclosures or reported by different interviewers. Similarly, avoid reminding the child of how he or she may have behaved in other situations.

Never make promises to a child to keep a secret. The child needs to know that your job is to report your findings to the judge. You may want to explain that part of your job is to make decisions about what to describe to a judge, but that you will not tell other people unless it is very important that they

---

QUICK REFERENCE **Four Competencies in Evaluating Allegations of Sexual Abuse**

- Provide an estimate of the child's overall psychological state and emotional status
- Provide an estimate of the child's intellectual level regarding accuracy and inaccuracy of alleged event
- Provide an estimate of the child's ability to distinguish between "truth" and "lie"
- Provide an estimate of child's linguistic competence and ability to communicate based upon personal knowledge of the facts

---

know. Do not lie to a child. Explain at a level commensurate with the child's developmental level the notion of lack of confidentiality and why the judge needs to know the important information that the child is going to tell you.

Evaluating Competencies

Grisso (1988) has argued strongly for the major focus of forensic evaluations to be the evaluation of competencies. In the area of sexual abuse evaluation, there are four competencies that may need to be assessed.

The first competency is an estimate of the child's overall psychological state and emotional status. Among the relevant dimensions to assess are social development, cognitive development, physical development, intellectual ability, self-esteem, suggestibility, depression, anxiety, and personality structure.

A second is the child's intellectual competency regarding the accuracy and inaccuracy of statements about the alleged events. When exploring the child's ability to provide an accurate description of the alleged events, it is important to ask the child open-ended questions that avoid—to the degree possible—interviewer confirmatory bias.

A third competency is the establishment of the child's ability to understand the difference between "the truth" and "a lie." The more complex the child's explanation, the more confidence one has that the child's verbal statement is an accurate portrait of what the child wants to report. It may be important to establish degrees of accuracy and inaccuracy rather than just the dichotomous categories of truth versus lie. For example, exploring the difference between a mistake and a lie might be useful. Similarly, having the child talk about the distinction between pretending and real life may provide helpful guidance. The evaluator may have the child produce examples of each category and discuss differences among them.

A final competency involves the child's ability to communicate based upon personal knowledge of the facts. For example, the child needs to describe a memory of an event and respond to simple questions about the occurrence.

Weissman's (1991b) article provides a useful conceptual framework for structuring an examination of sexual abuse allegations within the context of a child custody evaluation. However, there are several authorities who would encourage the forensic examiner to stop the custody evaluation until completion of a competent sexual abuse allegation by an independent examiner. There also are some state psychological associations that encourage using an independent examiner for allegations of child sexual abuse that arise during a child custody evaluation.

It is best to check with your state association as well as consult with forensic colleagues who have worked in this area. In this way, you may be able to determine whether—or the degree to which—the custodial evaluation you have undertaken may be more useful to the court. Furthermore, undertaking the evaluation of a child sexual abuse allegation may influence—or be perceived to influence—how you view the litigants in the custody evaluation. This factor alone may argue strongly for having an independent examiner appointed to conduct the sexual abuse evaluation.

> During this . . . period, multiple interviews, advice, questions, and examinations by well-intended but variably trained interested parties take place with law enforcement and social service personnel, physicians, mental health examiners and therapists, lawyers, teachers, and parents and other relatives. Satisfying the elements of legal standards can thus be compromised. It is well recognized that competency varies as a function of chronological age and developmental stage. It is equally recognized that the ascertainability of guilt, liability, or damages varies as a function of a) the amount of time that elapses, b) the number and nature of developmental and circumstantial events that transpire, c) the number and quality of examinations that occur, d) family dynamics and pathology, and e) psychosocial influences available to alter the child's recall of the alleged abuse. (Weissman, 1991b, p. 49)

As you consider the appropriateness of involvement in a child sexual abuse assessment *during* a child custody evaluation, remember the complexity of the task and the myriad of variables that need to be considered when an allegation is raised. The undertaking of a child sexual abuse examination while conducting a child custody evaluation may cloud the acuity needed in understanding the family dynamics vis-à-vis the best psychological interest standards.

Parental Alienation Syndrome

Parental Alienation Syndrome (PAS) was first defined by Gardner (1985) as a conscious or unconscious attempt by one parent to behave in such a way as to alienate the child or children from the other parent. Typically, the alienating parent is the custodial parent, most often the mother (Gardner, 1992). The parent toward whom the alienation is aimed is most often the noncustodial parent, usually the father. Garrity and Baris (1994) have termed this parent the "target" parent.

The purpose of PAS is to align the child with one parent by forcing the other parent out of the child's life. PAS includes, but is not limited to, conscious, intentional programming techniques, such as brainwashing. Over time, the alienating parent is able to influence the child to view the target parent as a dangerous, harmful, and bad parent. Eventually, the child adopts the malicious, intolerant, rejecting attitude of the alienating parent toward the target parent, resulting in a belief system in which the child views the target parent with hatred and fear (Gardner, 1992).

Richard Gardner (personal communication, September 25, 1997) states,

> It is very important to emphasize that the PAS term does not simply refer to brainwashing or programming of a child by a parent. It includes the child's own contributions to the campaign of denigration. It is the *combination* of the two contributions that warrants the term PAS.

Time is the alienating parent's most powerful ally. The longer the alienating parent has direct control over the child, the greater will be the alienating influence. Because the alienating parent is able to dominate the child's time, the target parent is unable to spend time with the child. The result is a widening of the gap between the child's strengthening alliance with the alienating parent and the child's weakening alliance with the target parent.

Systems Thinking and PAS

Ward and Harvey (1997) suggest that PAS needs to be examined from the view of the total family system. The evaluator needs to examine not just the alienating parent and his or her effect on the child. The evaluator needs to examine how the target parent may contribute to the dysfunctional family system. Other factors to evaluate are the contributions made to the alienating system by extended family members, treating therapist and attorneys who may encourage the polarized view of the family, as well as other extrafamilial influences.

Stahl (1997) and Sullivan (1997) offer a seven-factor model in the assessment of PAS. These factors are (a) child factors, (b) alienating parent psychological factors, (c) target parent psychological factors, (d) alienating parent-child relationship, (e) target parent-child relationship, (f) environmental and contextual factors, and (g) alienating-target parental relationship.

It is critical that evaluators explore the entire family system, with particular emphasis on how the experience of alienation affects the child's world.

The evaluator needs to understand how the child's world has been affected by the polarization in the family. The child's pain, loneliness, lack of connection to the target parent, and unbalanced view of reality are critical components to assess.

In family systems in which there are many children across a broad age range, there is often a sibling-generated conformity to the alienation. Children who have already bought into the alienating alignment encourage the alignment with their siblings. This often occurs with older children attempting to influence their younger siblings to buy into the belief system about the target parent.

Children who resist buying into the alienating alignment often are treated with great hostility within the family system, especially by the children who have already aligned with the alienating parent. If the nonaligned child continues to resist the alienating influence, there is some chance that there may be an alignment formed with the target parent. These children often feel rejected by their siblings as well as the alienating parent, increasing the chances that the unaligned child will develop emotional difficulties related to rejection, depression, and anxiety (Stahl, 1997; Sullivan, 1997).

Self-Concept and PAS

Arendell's (1995) research into a father's reaction to divorce shows that the relative importance of different self-concepts is related to the amount of activity related to that concept. Thus, a man often will view himself as a "worker" and therefore place the concept of "worker" high in his self-concept hierarchy, in part because it is an activity in which he engages every day. A man may also place the concept of "fatherhood" high within his self-concept hierarchy when he frequently engages in positive, rewarding fatherhood activities. The less often an activity occurs, the less likely it is to be placed higher in the man's self-concept hierarchy. Concepts that are placed lower in the self-concept hierarchy tend to have a lower frequency of occurrence. Thus, the less likely it becomes for the man to engage or want to engage in those less frequently occurring activities.

A divorced father's belief about the importance of fatherhood and the resulting time the father will devote to his fathering activities is directly related to the frequency of contact with the child. Thus, divorced men appear to want to be involved with their children and rate their association with the concept of fatherhood higher when they are in continuous contact with their child. PAS interrupts this needed relationship and may contribute to the reevaluation of the concept of fatherhood within the target parent's hierarchy of self-concept. The result may be a lessening of the importance of the role of father, leading to a reduction in the number of attempts to contact his child.

This reduction in contact attempts serves two purposes for the alienating parent. The first is that fewer attempts to reach out to the child helps to fortify the alienating parent's argument that the target parent is uncaring, selfish, and uninterested. The second purpose is that less contact results in less knowledge. When a target parent and a child finally spend time together after a long separation, the father is less familiar with the child. The child may have been influenced by the alienating parent to interpret the father's unfamiliarity as further signs of uncaring, selfishness, or disinterest. As the child becomes older, the influence appears more and more as though it is the child's reasoned decision about the target parent rather than a continuing of the original influence.

This is particularly important in cases in which the alienation continues for years and the father continues his battle to maintain a relationship with his child. A judge may be less influenced by the testimony of a 7- or 9-year-old child. But that same child brought before the same judge at age 13 or 15 may be perceived as providing a clearer, wiser, more fully integrated belief about what is in his or her best psychological interests. What is overlooked is how the powerful alienating influence that began when the child was 6 years old has now become a worldview for the 14-year-old child. In an unfortunate irony, the process designed to protect the child—the deliberate, slow nature of the court system—may contribute significantly to the sturdiness of the child's belief about the target parent.

Eight Characteristics of PAS

Gardner (1992) identifies eight characteristics of PAS. The first is a campaign of denigration, in which the child incessantly affirms hatred and fear of the target parent. Behaviorally, the child increasingly withdraws from contact with the target parent and refuses to visit, speak to the parent on the phone, or have any other contact. When the child is with the target parent, the child often speaks indirectly to the parent, speaking in third person: "You tell Daddy that I don't want to go to Disneyland because he will force me to have fun when all I want is to be home with my mother." The child also will reject presents and toys from the target parent.

Gardner (1992) suggests two reasons for the child's rejection of the target parent's gifts. One reason is that the child has been taught to reject everything the father provides because it is evil, harmful, or dangerous. In this way, the child avoids anything that may be "contaminated" by the target parent. Another reason may be that the child would be placed in a conflict between the alienating parent and the target parent. Thus, rejection of presents and toys from the target parent is an affirmation to the alienating parent that the child has chosen sides and will continue to gain the favors of the alienating parent.

A second characteristic is the display of inconsistent, illogical, weak, or absurd rationalizations given by the child for devaluing the target parent. As Goldwater (1991) points out, "The hostility of the alienating client just never seems to be reasonably linked to the seriousness of the incidents alleged" (p. 125).

Another window into the development of PAS is the child's use of phrases, terms, and scenarios that either do not reflect the child's experience or are concepts that are developmentally inappropriate for the child. The child tends to be exposed to and accept as true the alienating parent's stories and beliefs about the target parent.

A fourth characteristic of PAS is a lack of ambivalence toward either parent. The child often feels that the target parent is all bad and the alienating parent is all good. Although younger children tend to think dualistically, the child experiencing parental alienation tends to maintain a dualistic belief system about each parent. It is unknown whether the cognitive development of children in such family systems shows delays in the acquisition of more complex forms of thought as a result of living in an environment that encourages dualistic rather than relativistic thinking. This becomes an evaluation question.

Another aspect of PAS is the allegation on the part of the alienating parent that the decision to reject the target parent is the child's. But the child frequently invokes phrases and concepts about the target parent that are exact duplicates of the alienating parent's statements, thus revealing the degree of parental influence as well as the child's lack of awareness of such influence. Although it has yet to be integrated in the PAS literature, issues about children's suggestibility and memory functioning may be important factors to consider in assessing PAS.

The sixth and seventh components of the syndrome appear to be directly related to the splitting described previously. PAS children provided an unconditional, unquestioning support for the alienating parent. The alienating parent becomes idealized as one who can do no wrong, or as the weaker of the two parents who needs protecting from the fearful, bad target parent.

There is also a significant lack of guilt or feelings of loss about the target parent. Empathic responding is an important developmental factor. PAS children often demonstrate a lack of empathy toward the target parent. A question that needs to be addressed is the degree to which the lack of empathic response toward the target parent contributes to a delay or interference with the development of the child's empathy and/or social perspective taking.

Finally, the feelings and beliefs about the fearfulness and danger inherent in a relationship with the target parent become generalized to include the extended family and, sometimes, friends associated with the target parent (Gardner, 1992).

Gardner's Continuum of PAS Severity

- Mild PAS defined as relatively superficial signs of eight primary symptoms. Visitation with noncustodial parent reveals few signs of difficulty. Primary PAS motive is to maintain stronger, healthy psychological bond between alienating parent and child.

- Moderate PAS is most common. Defined by alienating parent's powerful programming against the target parent. All eight primary symptoms are evident. Alienating effect is most intense around time of transition to target parent. Child views alienating parent as all good and target parent as all bad. Child feels no guilt over negative feelings toward target parent. Primary PAS motive is to maintain stronger, healthy bond between alienating parent and child.

- Severe PAS defined by paranoid fantasies about target parent. All eight primary symptoms are strongly present. Children show panic, fear, and rage before, during, and after visits with target parent. Primary PAS motive is based upon pathological symptoms that serve to strengthen the pathological bond between alienating parent and child.

Allegations of Sexual Abuse Encourage PAS

PAS is an inappropriate label to use when abuse is real (Gardner, 1992, 1997). However, increasingly in custody disputes, there are false allegations of child abuse. Richard Gardner (personal communication, September 25, 1997) suggests that

> PAS alienators are claiming that the children's alienation is not being programmed by them but is the inevitable result of the rejected parent's bona fide abuse of them. Similarly, abusive parents are claiming that the children's denigration is being programmed . . . by the other parent.

Gardner is working to differentiate between these two types of accusations (Gardner, in press).

Once the allegation is lodged against the nonresidential parent, the court, in its wisdom, takes the necessary time to conduct an investigation. In this way, the child is protected from being placed at risk. However, in instances of false allegations, the time taken to complete the investigation often results in the child being shielded from the alleged perpetrator—in this case, the target parent. The conundrum is that as the investigation goes on, the alienating parent has more time to influence the child into believing that the target parent is fearful, bad, and a dangerously abusive person.

Virtual Allegations

Another concern is what Cartwright (1993) terms "virtual allegations."

> They refer to those cases in which the abuse is only hinted, its real purpose being to cast aspersions on the character of the noncustodial parent in a continuing program of denigration. For the alienator, virtual allegations avoid the need to fabricate incidents of alleged abuse with their attendant possibility of detection and probability of punishment of perjury. (pp. 208-209)

Allegations of "virtual allegations" are predicted to continue to rise because the subtlety of their nature plants insidious seeds of uncertainty in the minds of those concerned about the child. However, the allegations are difficult, if not impossible, to prove, yet the virtual allegations leave lingering doubts that may subtly shade decision making without the decision maker being aware of their influence, a concern similar to issues surrounding confirmatory bias factors discussed elsewhere in the book.

Challenges to PAS

Some colleagues have raised significant concerns about the use of the PAS concept in custody evaluations. There is significant professional agreement that some custodial parents negatively influence some children against the nonresidential parent. Similarly, some nonresidential parents also attempt to negatively influence the children against the custodial parents.

There is also professional agreement that there are some custodial parents who negatively influence their children in a manner consistent with that described as PAS.

Use of the concept of PAS within a clinical setting presents few problems for practitioners. Whether the clinician can definitively establish a "syndrome" or not is less important than the task of helping divorced families heal or establishing a fact pattern of systematic negative influence by one parent upon a child that interferes significantly with that child's ability to form a healthy bond with the other parent.

When the concept of PAS is presented in a court of law, one must ask, Upon what empirical foundation does the syndrome exist? The answer to date is that there is little, if any, research establishing the empirical foundation for the existence of PAS. Thus, use of the PAS concept may not be admissible scientific testimony because there is no underlying theory of science, its psychometric characteristics have yet to be demonstrated, there are no established protocols to follow when attempting to measure it, and it has yet to be shown to be falsifiable.

I am not suggesting that the concept of parental alienation does not show itself frequently in the context of custody determination. I believe it does. However, because the premise of this book is that the competent evaluator is able to present to the court a clear underlying theory of science, statistical properties of the tools being used, and evidence that its primary assumptions are testable (falsifiable), the term *Parental Alienation Syndrome* should be applied carefully. Until PAS has developed an established research base, it is wiser to describe the behaviors and their effect on a child rather than present the same data as indicative of a scientifically accepted, empirically established syndrome.

A useful way to discuss PAS within the context of current behavioral science literature is to link it to the memory literature addressing suggestibility. Ceci and Bruck (1995) describe a number of components of a suggestive interview. If parent-child verbal exchanges in alienating families can be construed as a form of suggestive interviewing, then the evaluator may attempt to identify how the parent has used specific suggestive interview techniques to alter the child's perception of his or her father or mother.

For example, the type of PAS may be established by exploring the alienating parent's use of leading and misleading questions about the other parent. Data may be gathered about the frequency and nature of repeated questions, stereotype induction, aggrandizement of adult caretaker status, and repeating misinformation across interviews. Court testimony would then be based upon a more empirical foundation.

Domestic Violence

Conventional ideas about domestic violence often are framed within the presumption of "inherent power and status discrepancies between men and women, which are legitimized by widespread socialization and institutional practices" (Johnston & Campbell, 1993, p. 282). Based on the battered woman syndrome proposed by Walker (1984), the "cycle of violence" is viewed as a three-stage repetitive sequence of events. Tension builds up in the battering male, resulting in explosive, acute battering incidents. The physical assault upon the woman is followed by the man's loving contrition and the couple's reconciliation. Women caught in this cycle often show signs of "learned helplessness." They show signs of depression, fearfulness, helplessness, and submissiveness, yet they stay within the relationship.

So powerful is Walker's (1984) concept of the cycle of violence that behavioral scientists have seldom looked beyond the stereotype to explore other patterns of domestic violence. Johnston and Campbell (1993) reported five basic types of interpersonal violence among divorcing families involved in custody disputes. Their typology also provides information about parent-child relationships within each domestic violence pattern.

Defining Domestic Violence

Johnston and Campbell (1993) define domestic violence as the use of physical restriction, force, coercion, or threat of force by one parent to force another parent to do something against his or her will. Among the violent behaviors are hitting, slapping, biting, choking, threating with a weapon, unlawful entry, destruction of property, physical injury, suicide, and murder. Domestic violence also includes psychological intimidation, such as threats, control, and inappropriate use of power tactics. Power tactics may include harassment, stalking, threats against children, or violence against pets or property.

Johnston and Campbell (1993) do not include a definition of emotional abuse but note that emotional abuse often precedes, accompanies, or follows the physically violent behaviors.

Typology of Domestic Violence During Divorce

The five basic types of domestic violence identified by Johnston and Campbell (1993) are ongoing or episodic male battering, female-initiated violence, male-controlling interactive violence, separation-engendered violence or postdivorce trauma, and psychotic and paranoid reactions. Each of these domestic violence categories will be discussed below along with information about how children are affected by each style.

Ongoing or Episodic Male Battering

The classic battering male/battered female syndrome is found among those categorized as ongoing and episodic batterers. It appears that the propensity for physical abuse and violence lies with the men in these relationships. Typically, these males demonstrated low frustration tolerance, poor impulse control, and a high need to dominate and control their female partners. They also showed signs of significant jealousy and possessiveness. These males displayed traditional chauvinistic attitudes and an exaggerated view of their masculinity. About half of males identified as ongoing or episodic batterers were also found to engage in the use of drugs or alcohol as a precipitant or contributor to violence (Johnston & Campbell, 1993).

Physical abuse often began early in the relationship and continued, either intermittently or continuously, over the duration of the marriage. Typically, physical attacks were terrifying and severe. It would not be unusual for a physical attack to be experienced as life threatening.

QUICK REFERENCE **Johnston and Campbell's (1993) Typology of Domestic Violence Within Custody Evaluations**

- Ongoing or episodic male battering
- Female-initiated violence
- Male-controlling interactive violence
- Separation-engendered violence or postdivorce trauma
- Psychotic and paranoid reactions leading to violence

Johnston and Campbell (1993) described these men as displaying little restraint when they acted out their internal rage and frustration. These men appeared to want to hurt their partners as much as control them. They also tended to deny or minimize their abuse, or they placed the blame for their violence on their wives.

When the women separated from the marriage, the episodic male batterers tended to become extremely dangerous. They would stalk their wives, terrorizing them with threats of, or actual attempts at, murder or suicide. Accompanying these violent actions were pleas for reconciliation and forgiveness characterized by promises to change. Johnston and Campbell (1993) reported that the possibility for violence often remained very high, lasting years after the separation.

The women in these relationships often reacted in one of two styles. Some women became fearful and depressed, and showed signs of helplessness. They developed (or had coming into the marriage) low self-esteem and an inadequate ability to protect themselves or their children.

The other style was one of assertiveness. These women took a stand against their husbands' physical abuse early in their marriage. Johnston and Campbell (1993) indicate that neither style of victim appeared to intentionally provoke or escalate the physical abuse they received. However, some became caught up in the violence and defended themselves or their children.

Parent-Child Relationships in Episodically Violent Divorcing Families

Female children under 8 years of age were typically very passive and constricted. They revealed a high degree of underlying fearfulness and insecurity in relation to both parents. These young girls felt unprotected by their mothers. They showed some difficulty in knowing how to separate from their mothers, reacting to separations with whiny, regressive behaviors. They often had repressed or intrusive memories of violent experiences. These memories were the foundation for realistic fears and avoidance of their fathers.

Interestingly, these young girls showed a "princesslike" relationship with their fathers. Their fathers often would intermittently lavish attention on their daughters while also being focused on their own needs. These girls were confused about the nature of their relationship with their father. They appeared to view him in two opposing ways. Father was viewed as a loving suitor as well as a dangerous man.

There were poor boundaries between these men and their daughters. The father-daughter relationship was characterized by mutual seductiveness and provocation of his aggressiveness. Johnston and Campbell (1993) reported that these men needed validation of their attractiveness and maleness, and they found ways to garner it from their young daughters, "who became watchful and oriented to managing their father's narcissistic equilibrium and anger" (p. 287).

Older girls (8 to 14 years of age) displayed more anger, rejection, and avoidance of their father, or they aligned with their mother as a way of taking a stand against their father's violence as well as protecting their mother. These older girls often felt responsible for protecting their mother. They also felt angry at their mother for tolerating their father's abuse, resulting in the girls targeting their irritation and anger upon the mother, too. The mothers tended to be too oppressed and depressed to be emotionally available to any of their children.

Younger boys (under 8 years of age) were found to be oppositional, difficult, and aggressive. They displayed manipulative and controlling behaviors, especially toward their mother. Similar to younger girls, these boys were often confused, anxious, and worried about their mother's safety, and they experienced intermittent memories of their father's violent experiences.

Older boys (8 to 14 years of age) showed signs of modeling their behavior on that of their father. They displayed explosive, rageful attacks upon their mother. The mother's typical response was to be passive, ineffective, and submissive. Johnston and Campbell (1993) speculate that these boys wanted a closer relationship with their mother but feared that becoming closer would result in becoming passive, weak, and victimized like their mother, all of which they equated with being feminine.

Younger and older boys tended to show fear and obedience in the presence of their father. The violent father was preoccupied with his own needs and inconsistently available to his son. These boys longed for their father's approval, were fearful of being shamed by him, and held significant amounts of anger and rage at their father. The father often provided mixed messages about aggressiveness. When boys displayed aggressiveness, the father would punish the aggressiveness in an abusive manner.

Boys and girls who had little or no contact with the violent father tended to repress their memories of the violence within the home. They tended to idealize their father, longed for contact with him, and blamed themselves or their mother for the father's absence.

In those instances in which the violent father had significant child care responsibilities, the father's low frustration tolerance, need to assert power and to control events, and his hypersensitivity to minor transgressions often resulted in episodic explosions. This display of violence toward his children resulted in a deterioration of the father-child relationship and increased the possibility of child abuse (Johnston & Campbell, 1993).

Female-Initiated Violence

There are some domestic violence situations in which the female initiates the aggression. Johnston and Campbell (1993) suggest that the violence within these women lies "primarily within their own intolerable internal states of tension" (p. 290). They are often characterized as histrionic, emotionally labile, dependent, and self-focused. They tend to display explosive temper outbursts when they believe their expectations or needs are not being properly met by their husbands. Alcohol also played a role in some of these households.

Unlike the episodic male batterer, these women often were able to admit their violent behavior.

These women were reported to throw objects, destroy possessions, attack their partner, hit, bite, kick, and use other physical assaults. These attacks might include threats to use weapons, especially when the security of the relationship was being threatened, such as during marital separation.

The husbands of these women often tried to prevent or contain the violence by passively fending off the attacks. They may also have attempted to restrain their wives from hurting family members. When the marriage ended, these men often ended their attempts to contain or placate their wives' aggressive reactions.

These men were characterized as passive, depressed, obsessive, and intellectualizing. They felt intimidated by their wives' aggressiveness and embarrassed when they were pulled into the fight. Johnston and Campbell (1993) describe the husbands' style as "passive-aggressive" (p. 291). Compared with the episodic male batterer, female-initiated violence tended to result in less severe damage and injury. The authors speculate that the lower level of destruction results from the husband being able to maintain his emotional control and frequently being able to "disarm his wife" (p. 291).

Parent-Child Relationships in Female-Initiated Violence in Divorcing Families

Children in these families had erratic and unpredictable relationships with their mothers. Mothers were described as intermittently loving and nurturing and unpredictably explosive, angry, and rejecting. Boys often took the brunt of their mother's attacks.

Young girls were reported to be intimidated, fearful, and recoiling from contact with their mother to avoid her wrath. Some girls assumed the role of caretaker to their mother during her emotional outbursts. These girls also were found to play the role of parent and manager of household tasks. Such parentified girls tended to be more protected from their mother's rage than were boys.

Girls tended to be supported by emotionally closer and more protective relationships with their father. These girls often were viewed by their father as the "good girl" in contrast to the "bad mother." However, as these girls developed, they tended to become more demanding, display temper outbursts, and enter into power struggles with both parents, suggesting identification with the aggressive female role model (Johnston & Campbell, 1993).

Boys in these female-initiated violent families displayed behaviors more similar to their father's. They were characterized as passive-aggressive and demonstrated sadness, behavioral inhibition, and depression. Boys were found to be overtly angry with their mothers, frequently entering into power struggles.

Younger boys appeared to have more ambivalent and confused relationships with their mother. They showed more difficulty in emotionally separating from her, thus interfering with their normal development progression toward autonomy. These boys needed their mother's nurturing but found that her intermittent, conditional acceptance and punitiveness interfered with their ability to develop a secure attachment with her. Furthermore, if their father was passive and intimidated by the mother, the boys were unable to be protected or rescued from their mother's rage. This resulted in the boys feeling very angry at their mother for her aggressiveness and rejection, as well as angry at their father for his inability to protect his children.

Male-Controlling Interactive Violence

Violence in this category appeared to arise out of increasing disagreements between the spouses. There appeared to be a trend of escalating aggression, from verbal insults to verbal abuse to physical violence. Johnston and Campbell (1993) reported that the most prominent aspect of this category was the male's overwhelming need to assert control over his wife. Men were observed to use physical force in their attempts to dominate and overpower their wives. This aggressive behavior did not, however, involve sadistic acts or brutal beatings. These men showed varying amounts of control over their behaviors, which was related to the amount of resistance put forth by their spouses.

Psychological characteristics of the male were traditional beliefs in authoritarian and dictatorial behavior as appropriate within the family. Physically violent behavior was an accepted way of resolving intrafamilial conflict. Such men often would become physically violent with their children, their siblings, and their parents. They also tended to display physically aggressive behaviors as a way of resolving interpersonal conflict outside the family.

Parents in this category of violent behavior tended to blame each other for the frequency and intensity of aggressiveness. As more stress was placed on the divorcing couple, there was a greater chance of violence. Once separated and no longer able to provoke each other, Johnston and Campbell (1993) reported that the violence between spouses often ended.

Parent-Child Relationships in Divorcing Families With Male-Controlling Interactive Violence

Somewhat unique to this category of violence is the co-occurrence of male-dominated violence with female violence. Both parents were poor role models for nonviolent conflict resolution, ego control, and anger management. Thus, children within these family systems observed each spouse to become violent with the other. Children of these families often displayed aggressiveness or passive-aggressiveness. Families were characterized by inconsistent family rules, contradictory messages, unreliable discipline, and high levels of tension. Children's alliances were found to change frequently within the family, aligning with one parent and then the other. Physical punishment as a primary discipline style was common, as well as physical fights between siblings.

Some girls living in male-controlled interactive violent families were observed to be assertive, strong-willed, and demanding. They appeared ready and prepared to fill the void of parental control abdicated by their warring parents. Other girls were reported to react with passive-aggressive behaviors, varying between passiveness and subtle defiance. Their behavior often revealed a cycle of passive to overtly aggressive responses.

Younger boys showed discipline and behavior control problems. They revealed a somewhat less well-developed ability to appropriately channel their excitement when faced with minor difficulties—that is, they overreacted. Older boys tended to be defiant of authority, belligerent, and outwardly disobedient to each parent. This was particularly true between older boys and their mothers.

Fathers appeared to have peerlike relationships with their sons, creating almost a "boys' club" type of atmosphere through which the boys developed a sense of identity and esteem. However, these boys also appeared more likely to use aggressive acting out and coercion in their attempts to get what they wanted, especially from their mothers and sisters. Fathers were reported to reward their sons' toughness and acting out, and some mothers also rewarded their sons' aggressiveness. Fathers were observed to be more controlling and punitive with their daughters compared with their sons, whereas mothers were reported to have difficulty managing both boys and girls.

Separation-Engendered Violence
or Postdivorce Trauma

Males and females identified as belonging to this category displayed acts of violence that were uncharacteristic of their everyday lives. Increased aggressiveness was associated with increased tension around the separation and divorce. Although, physical violence was absent during the marriage, either party might be observed to lash out in anger during times of acute stress or times of symbolic importance, such as their anniversary. The violence was unpredictable and infrequent. However, when it occurred, the violent behavior tended to cast a dark shadow of mistrust on the offending spouse precisely because it was unexpected. Johnston and Campbell (1993) reported that both men and women were able to acknowledge their aggression and expressed genuine shame over their loss of control. In general, the risk for further violence was small once the emotional and legal issues involved in the divorce were resolved.

Parent-Child Relationships in
Posttrauma Divorcing Families

Children from posttrauma violent families were observed to show behavioral signs similar to posttraumatic stress disorder (PTSD). They displayed anxiety, fear, difficulty in concentrating, and withdrawal of verbal exchange within the family. They also showed signs of behavioral inhibition and emotional constriction. Younger children tended to report intrusive memories, nightmares, headaches, and stomachaches. Several showed a temporary fear of the parent perceived to be violent.

Mothers were observed to be more emotionally supportive of their daughters and fathers of their sons in these cases of unpredictable, infrequent violence. Although the children were frightened by their witnessing of parental violence, the parents generally demonstrated good judgment, good ego control, and good anger management. The damage to the parent-child relationship appeared short lived, with rehabilitation to the parent-child relationship resolved through therapeutic treatment strategies.

Psychotic and Paranoid Reactions
Leading to Violence

A small number of divorcing parents engaging in violent family behavior were found to be experiencing significant psychopathology. The psychotic and paranoid reactions often were exacerbated by the stressors associated with the marital breakup. According to Johnston and Campbell (1993), "the marital separation often triggered an acute phase of danger wherein a disturbed spouse pieced together the rubble of their marriage and mentally rewrote history, perceiving their partner as having intentionally plotted to exploit them and cast them off" (p. 294). The disturbed spouse was likely to respond with some type of aggressiveness to perceived feelings of betrayal. His or her violent behavior may come in the form of a preemptive strike against the spouse. There may also be a series of aggressively provocative attacks that result from events that appear to have no clear trigger. The attacks upon the spouse often are perpetrated with a sense of righteous indignation and a belief that they are protecting either themselves or their children from the malicious intentions of their spouse.

The abnormal behavior ranged from fleeting, incoherent ideas that were coupled with unpredictable outbursts of verbal and physical aggression, to full-blown paranoid delusions. These delusional systems often were logically coherent beliefs that linked the perceived betrayal of the spouse to a conspiracy with others. In such situations, not only was the spouse found to be at risk but also those who were perceived to be part of the conspiracy. The victim spouses appeared to react in one of two ways. Either they understood the threat and were frightened by it, seeking to avoid or calm the aggressor, or else they appeared oblivious to the significant danger in which they found themselves.

Parent-Child Relationships in Divorcing Families With Psychotic or Paranoid Reactors

Johnston and Campbell (1993) reported that there were not enough children in their sample from which to make generalizations. They observed that children in these family systems either were a part of the aggressive-psychotic parent's delusional system or were emotionally separated from the disturbed parent. When observed to be part of the delusional system, the child was found to display psychoticlike behavior with "massive identification with the disturbed parent's affective state and reality distortion" (p. 295). When the child was able to maintain emotional distance from the disturbed parent, symptoms similar to acute or chronic trauma were observed. Johnston and Campbell (1993) reported that the trauma appeared similar to that observed in children with the separation trauma or battering categories.

Summary

Johnston and Campbell (1993) reported that boys' adjustment tended to be affected most significantly in the male batterer category. They were equally likely to be less disturbed in the male-controlling and female-initiated violence categories. Boys were equally likely to be *least* disturbed in the separation-trauma and nonviolent divorcing families.

Girls were found to be equally disturbed in male batterer and male-controlling violent families. They were less disturbed in female-initiated vio-

lence and separation-trauma families. They were least disturbed in nonviolent divorcing families.

Johnston and Campbell (1993) conclude,

> It is important to differentiate among the various profiles of domestic vio-
> lence when helping parents make postdivorce plans for custody of their chil-
> dren. . . . Parent-child relationships are likely to vary with the different
> patterns of violence, and children of different ages and gender are affected
> differently. (p. 296)

They recommend that consideration of sole or joint custody is inappropriate with a father who has engaged in ongoing or episodic battering. Similarly, any parent who is psychotic or has paranoid delusions should not be
awarded sole or joint custody. In fact, when the threat of violence is real, visitation may need to be supervised or suspended until the children's safety is
ensured. They also warn that spouses who left battering or psychotic relationships may have diminished capacity to parent children effectively as a
function of their victimization. They may need assistance in rehabilitating
their parenting competencies to a level of satisfaction.

A careful examination of the parenting capacity of a mother who is a
female initiator is needed before considering placement of children under her
care. It may be that the father is the more appropriate residential parent;
however, he may be too passive and unavailable to his children as a result of
his victimization.

Fathers who are male-controlling aggressors may need parenting skills to
manage their children assertively. Similarly, mothers may also need such
skills. Very clear, structured transition routines are needed to ensure the
safety of the children as well as effectively manage the potential for conflict
between the parents.

NINE

Beyond the
Court-Ordered Evaluation

From the earliest stage of legal activity, be certain to have
mastered the foundations of your knowledge and role.

Stanley L. Brodsky (1991, p. 99)

Dear Dr. Gould:

Thank you for speaking with me today regarding preparation for the temporary custody hearing and custody trial in this matter. We have decided to
use an Affidavit from you at the temporary custody hearing, rather than having you testify live.

The Affidavit simply should explain the empirical data and research
regarding the separation of a child 4 years old from his primary caretaker for
long periods of time. It would help if you include information supporting the
idea that it is not detrimental for a 4-year-old child to return to California
with his mother and primary caretaker until the time of the trial. It is understood that you cannot include specific opinions regarding the mother and
child in this Affidavit because you have not completed your evaluation
report. You may certainly explain that circumstance in your Affidavit.

For your expert report, we prefer for you to evaluate the mother and
child only. We understand your concern for fairness. We also understand that
the lack of paternal participation will result in no opinion about custody, only
an opinion about the mother's parenting competencies. We understand your
concerns about this arrangement, but have many reasons for our preference.
We have contacted the mother and asked her to get in touch with you within
the week.

If you have any questions, please call me. We look forward to receiving
your Affidavit. Thank you for your effort.

Sincerely,

Robert K. Smith, Esquire

* * * * *

Range of Services

There are a variety of different assessments that may be requested. An evaluator may be asked to assess parental competence by examining a parent and his or her children. The examiner may be asked to complete a follow-up evaluation to update the court on a case for which there is a previous evaluation. The evaluator may be asked to complete a psychological examination of the child or a psychoeducational assessment of the child.

There are times when a document, rather than an evaluation, is requested. These documents may take the form of a critique of a previous report or a review of relevant literature pertaining to a specific topic (e.g., move away literature, custodial issues in same-sex relationships). Some evaluators have been asked to write amicus curiae (friend of the court) documents that take a position on a particular issue.

There are a number of nonevaluation functions in which the custody specialist may engage. Private consulting to one side is a legitimate area of forensic work. For example, an evaluator may be asked to provide information and opinions to an attorney in preparation for a trial. Many custody experts are asked to prepare a work product in which examination and cross-examination questions are prepared and their answers discussed. Similarly, an evaluator may be asked to educate the court by providing expert testimony in open court about a particular area of behavioral science. Finally, a custody specialist may be asked to forgo the evaluation and become involved in the role of mediator, parent coordinator, or treating therapist.

> The scope may be limited to evaluating parental capacity of one parent. . . . Likewise, the scope may be limited to evaluating the child. Or a psychologist may be asked to critique the assumptions and methodology of the assessment of another mental health professional. A psychologist might also serve as an expert witness in the area of child development, providing expertise to the court without relating it specifically to the parties involved in a case. (American Psychological Association, 1994, p. 679)

Custody Evaluation Requested by Attorneys

Custody evaluators usually prefer conducting their examinations under the authority of the courts. More than 84% of evaluators say that they prefer working under a court order (Ackerman & Ackerman, 1996, 1997), even though only about half of all evaluations are so conducted (Keilin & Bloom, 1986). Requests for evaluation services may come from attorneys who agree to use your services as an impartial evaluator. A letter from the attorneys, cosigned by both counsel and litigants, may provide an appropriate referral for custodial evaluation services. When such a referral is forthcoming, it is always preferable to request a consent order despite the agreement of the attorneys. If the attorneys refuse to obtain a consent order, then there are certain steps you should take to ensure that your work product and efforts will be protected properly and used appropriately.

Among the steps you should take are specifying who the client is, what is expected from the evaluation, how the evaluation results will be used, with whom the evaluation results will be shared, who is responsible for payment, what the payment structure will be, how the payments will be made, who will make the payments (attorney or litigant), and on what schedule of payment. This is not an exhaustive list, but it should help guide your thinking about how to protect yourself when no court order or consent order is in effect.

Parental Competency Evaluations (One-Sided Evaluations)

There are times when the court is interested in the mental health and emotional well-being of an individual. Such examinations are *not* custody evaluations because the assessment includes neither the former spouse nor the children.

> Although comprehensive child custody evaluations generally require an evaluation of all parents or guardians and children, as well as observations of interactions between them, the scope of the assessment in a particular case may be limited to evaluating the parental capacity of one parent without attempting to compare the parents or to make recommendations. (American Psychological Association, 1994, p. 679)

The most common form of single-parent evaluation is to provide information about a litigant's mental health. Grisso's (1988) functional abilities analysis may be useful to follow in such cases. It is always helpful if the court or an attorney is able to more specifically identify what area or areas of concern they want assessed. Remember, the Grisso (1988) and Schutz et al. (1989) models focus on the identification of *specific* competencies within a defined *context*. The development of a set of psycholegal questions to guide the evaluation provides an invaluable framework.

There are at least two different types of single-parent evaluations in which you may become involved. The first is a court-ordered evaluation of parental competency. A court may be interested in having information about the overall psychological mental health or emotional well-being of a parent. For example, a parent may be examined to determine the degree and severity of his or her depression and its effects on parenting capacity. In this case, the examination may include a psychological evaluation of the parent as well as examination of the child and their interaction. Collateral interviews and record review are also important in assessing parental competency.

The court may also be interested in having information about a particular parenting competency. For example, a parent who previously worked full-time and is now becoming a full-time parent may need to demonstrate to the court various aspects of parental behaviors and competencies.

Another evaluation is for parental risk factors. The evaluator would be focused on potential areas of abuse or risk. One such area of concern, child maltreatment, will be discussed under a separate heading below.

One-Sided Evaluations

A one-sided assessment usually is composed of the forensic examination of one parent with his or her children to determine parenting capacity and parental competencies vis-à-vis the children. The examiner may be guided by methods similar to those used in a general custody evaluation. These methods may be obtaining collateral information, psychological test data, self-reports, behavioral observations, and other data gathering measures.

It is critical that mental health professionals consult their ethical guidelines governing one-sided evaluations. In the case of the American Psychological Association, the Specialty Guidelines (Committee on Ethical Guidelines, 1991) state:

> Forensic psychologists avoid giving written or oral evidence about the psychological characteristics of particular individuals when they have not had an opportunity to conduct an examination of the individual adequate to the scope of the statements, opinions or conclusions to be issued. Forensic psychologists make every reasonable effort to conduct such examinations. When it is not possible or feasible to do so, they make clear the impact of such limitations on the reliability and validity of their professional products, evidence or testimony. (p. 663)

Most mental health professionals may engage in such one-sided assessment. The information provided in such assessments may address issues on a parent's competencies, a child's (children's) well-being, the quality of interaction between the parent with each child, the quality of interaction among the parent with all children, collateral information about the parent and/or each child, direct behavioral observations of children with different caretakers, and other such data. The observations and measures of behavior are limited to the parent and the child (children). The examiner *may not* make comparative statements vis-à-vis the other parent. The examiner may not offer recommendations about custodial determination.

The opinion of the evaluator must be limited to discussions of one parent's strengths and weaknesses. The opinion may also address the strengths and weaknesses of each child or of the parent-child interactions. The opinions may discuss data gathered from collateral sources, such as pediatricians, school personnel, child care workers, community resources, and other primary or secondary caretakers (e.g., baby-sitters).

The examiner may not offer opinions about custody determination. The examiner also may not offer opinions about the strengths and weaknesses of a parent *in comparison* to the other parent, because only one parent has been assessed. The examiner may not offer opinions about with whom the child feels most comfortable, again because only one parent has been assessed.

There are times when collateral data may provide information about, for example, that the parent who was not assessed has a history of emotional instability. It is often tempting to conclude from the collateral sources that, indeed, there is some problem that may influence parenting capacity. Too often, the uninformed evaluator will include this data in a report and speculate as to its potential impact on the children's best psychological interests.

A fairer and more conservative approach would be to exclude the data from the report because the unassessed parent has had no opportunity to respond to the data either by giving his or her story or by providing a list of collateral sources who may counter the identified concerns.

A position that lies between the above extreems is to include the data in the report as well as a clear statement of the limitations of the data. This limitation may reflect the one-sided nature of the evaluation and the inherent bias involved in such evaluations. Another limitation may include a discussion of the data from alternative perspectives that do not support the litigant's point of view.

The Specialty Guidelines (Committee on Ethical Guidelines, 1991) provide a reasonable suggestion for approaching discussions of all data within a forensic evaluation. The guidelines are particularly useful when conducting a one-sided examination. The Specialty Guidelines state that "the forensic psychologist maintains professional integrity by examining the issue at hand from all reasonable perspectives, actively seeking information which will differentially test plausible rival hypotheses" (p. 661).

You should consult your state association's ethical code and guidelines for forensic activity before undertaking a one-sided evaluation.

Critique of a Colleague's Work Product

A common and acceptable arena for forensic expertise is to critique another forensic work product. However, our public role as experts to the court places upon forensic experts "a special responsibility for fairness and accuracy" (Committee on Ethical Guidelines, 1991, p. 664). Therefore, when providing a second opinion, the criticism needs to be focused on either the professional work product or the qualifications of another expert. Second-opinion criticism should be limited to evaluations of methodology, interpretation of data, and alternative conclusions drawn from such interpretations. They should never be personal attacks upon the examiner.

An important concept guiding professional forensic activity is to provide the court with reasonable rival hypotheses to test the data. This suggests that even a second opinion may include not only a reasonable second perspective but other plausible explanations that do not necessarily support your position.

Whether we are conducting an evaluation or offering second-opinion testimony, our role is to provide the court with scientific information, not just the scientific information that fits our argument. Forensic specialists

> do not, either by commission or omission, participate in a misrepresentation of their evidence, nor do they participate in partisan attempts to avoid, deny or subvert the presentation of evidence contrary to their own position. . . . [They] actively disclose all sources of information obtained . . . [and] actively disclose which information from which sources was used in formulating a particular written product or oral testimony. (Committee on Ethical Guidelines, 1991, pp. 664-665)

Taken literally, the above statement appears to suggest that our opinions need to be crafted around the specific data points from which our conclusions were drawn, *and such reasoning needs to be represented to the court.* That is, we need to inform the court of the data used in forming our opinions. When providing alternative opinions, we need to inform the court of our use of different data points or alternative interpretations of the same data. When offering opinion testimony, not only do we explain alternative rival hypotheses, but we describe these alternatives fairly and accurately. We can then explain to the court why the strengths and weaknesses of the rival hypotheses are less convincing in this particular circumstance than in the point of view we are presenting as more useful.

We can discuss our opinions in a forceful, open, and honest manner. We can provide cogent reasoning to support our beliefs that one explanation fits the data better than another. However, we should never intentionally exclude or misrepresent the meaning of a rival hypothesis nor the cogency of its logic. We can be forceful. We can attempt to convince the trier of fact of our conviction, but we should never attempt to deceive, withhold, distort, or ignore reasonable, cogent alternative arguments.

Consultant to an Attorney

Occasionally, a forensic examiner will be asked to consult with an attorney without seeing the litigant(s). Such consultation may take the form of a literature review and synthesis, discussion of psychological principles applied to the attorney's legal strategy, review of the psychological components of a legal brief, psychological analysis of the litigant's claims, review of the litigant's file, and discussion with other professional forensic specialists and synthesis of their opinions for the attorney's use. Experts are also asked to review a colleague's report and prepare cross-examination questions for the attorney.

When the forensic specialist is hired as a consultant, it is important that the attorney hires the expert directly. In this way, all work conducted for the attorney is covered under the attorney work-product privilege.

The relationship between attorney and forensic expert must be clearly defined in a letter that outlines the areas of professional involvement being requested by the attorney. These areas include, but are not limited to, the fee structure for requested professional services; current or historic activities, obligations, or relationships that might suggest a conflict of interest; identification of areas of competency as well as limits of those competencies; the known scientific foundation and limitations of the methods and procedures to be used; and the expert's qualifications to use such methods and procedures (Committee on Ethical Guidelines, 1991).

Forensic specialists need to be aware of the boundaries of their professional competencies; the limits of confidence and privilege that apply in such consulting relationships; and the need to maintain their objective, impartial, and fair approach to the data and the data's interpretation.

Even within the context of a consulting relationship with an attorney, the forensic examiner is responsible for the proper presentation of the data and its interpretation. Forensic mental health experts "take special care to avoid undue influence upon their methods, procedures and products, such as might emanate from the party to a legal proceeding by financial compensation or other gains" (Committee on Ethical Guidelines, 1991, p. 661).

Of course, how the attorney uses the expert's work product is often beyond our control. However, we need to take reasonable steps "to correct misuse or misrepresentation of [our] professional products" (Committee on Ethical Guidelines, 1991, p. 664).

We also need to be aware that our work product may (not necessarily will) be presented at some future time to the court. Therefore, our behavior must be guided from the outset by proper, ethical professional behavior. The duties and obligations of forensic specialists

> with respect to documentation of data that form the basis for their evidence apply from the moment they know or have a reasonable basis for knowing that their data and evidence derived from it are likely to enter into legally-relevant decisions. (Committee on Ethical Guidelines, 1991, p. 661)

Experts Educate the Court

Forensic experts are fundamentally experts to the court. Their primary role is to "assist the trier of fact to understand the evidence or to determine a fact in issue" (Committee on Ethical Guidelines, 1991, p. 665). The court may ask a forensic expert to comment about an area of child development, adult behavior and its impact on parenting capacity, or children's adjustment to divorce, to name just a few. There are many ways of educating the court, such as through the preparation of an Affidavit, a Declaration, a report, or open court testimony.

The rules that govern expert witness testimony presented within the role of educator to the court are the same that govern all forensic activities. The expert maintains fairness and accuracy in all public statements. The information being disseminated must be communicated in ways "that will promote understanding and avoid deception" (Committee on Ethical Guidelines, 1991, p. 663).

When providing information to the court that is intended to educate, the forensic specialist should present the conceptual models, data, or interpretation of data by examining their meaning from a variety of rival hypotheses. Although the expert may believe strongly in a particular model or interpretation of data, his or her responsibility is to educate through the presentation of alternative models that make reasonable arguments from the same data. It is up to the judge to determine what weight to give to the testimony. It is not up to the expert to arbitrarily decide which conceptual models should be presented and which should be avoided. If there are reasonable alternative explanations of the data, they should be presented to the court. You may wish to state your preference. You may want to provide the court with the best possible arguments *for each theoretical model or interpretation of data* and then explain to the court why your preference is the one that best serves the current issue. However, the judge is the trier of fact, not you.

Amicus Curiae Briefs

Amicus curiae literally means "friend of the court." In forensic practice, an amicus curiae brief allows for a person or organization to provide information to the court about a legal matter (Melton et al., 1987). There is some question about whether forensic experts should participate in writing amicus curiae briefs. Common practice is to forward an argument that advocates for a particular position. That is, the merits of a favored position and the inadequacies of the opposing position are argued.

The Specialty Guidelines (1991) charge the forensic specialist to be fair and advocate for the results rather than a particular legal position. Examiners do this by discussing their conclusions in light of their preferred hypotheses as well as those of competing views. Amicus curiae briefs that advocate for a position rather than for the data appear to be skirting ethical boundaries. The court needs to know that an evaluator consistently provides objective, neutral, and unbiased information to the court. Amicus curiae briefs that advocate single positions undermine such objectivity unless competing hypotheses are fairly addressed and competently discussed.

Nonevaluative Roles for the Forensic Specialist

There are a number of nonevaluative roles that may be assumed by an expert in child custody work, providing, of course, that one has the requisite training and experience. The forensic specialist may play the role of mediator, parent coordinator, or court-appointed therapist. In each case, once the mental health professional has assumed a role vis-à-vis the parents and child, that professional should never blur the role distinction and assume the role of evaluator. Once you assume one role, that is the role you play for this particular case.

Mediation

Mediation is the process of settling disputes outside of the court system with the aid of an impartial, objective third party. The first mediation models were applied to divorce mediation (Kelly, 1996). They were proposed as models to reduce conflict, improve communication and coparental cooperation, produce better agreements with less time and expense, enhance psychological adjustment for parents and children, and improve compliance with agreements. Compared with traditional court interventions, divorce mediation has been demonstrated to significantly help couples resolve differences over their marital dissolution more effficiently. The work of Joan Kelly has been paramount in revealing the powerful and conflict-reducing role played by divorce mediation.

Research has shown that parents who go through the custody evaluation process are more likely to destroy any remaining civility and joint communication they had previously attained. Through the use of divorce mediation, however, children are often left with two functioning parents and a method of intimate communication with them. Mediation promotes communication between the parents following divorce and facilitates ongoing communication between parent and child (Fisher, Ury, & Patton, 1991; Folberg & Taylor, 1984).

Mediation research indicates that parental agreement occurs about 50% to 85% of the time. This is true for both court-based and community-based mediation. However, there is no relationship between the number of mediation sessions and settlement rates (Kelly, 1996). Interestingly, higher rates of agreement have been reported in comprehensive divorce mediation than in custody-specific mediation. The idea is that agreement is more diffficult in single-issue compared with multi-issue disputes.

Emery (1994) reported that mediation-involved parents reached resolutions of their disputes more quickly than did parents in litigation. The parents in litigation took more than twice as long with more than twice the expense.

Mediated results appear to promote joint custody more often than the adversarial process (Emery, 1994). Kelly (1996) reported two studies that found no differences in child support amounts between mediated and litigated processes. However, fathers who completed the mediation process appeared to provide more extras for their children and were more likely to agree to provide for college expenses. Kelly (1996) states that "there is no empirical support for the claims . . . that mediation forces women to give away custody or primary care 'entitlements' or that women are disadvantaged financially by the strategic use of custody conflicts by men" (p. 377). This is also reflected in client satisfaction reports. No significant gender differences in mediation satisfaction have been found. Typically, mediation clients are significantly more satisfied with the process and outcome than are those in the adversarial system. This satisfaction included property agreements and support agreements.

It is important to recognize the unique skills developed by a sophisticated mediator. The therapist or forensic evaluator should never assume the role of mediator without first being trained in a mediation model. As is true with all other areas of psychological endeavor, one should never venture into an area of professional practice without first having reached a level of competency that has been earned through training and experience.

Parent Coordinator

Another role that the forensic expert may play is *parent coordinator.* The coordinator role is not that of an evaluator but is a critical part of the custodial dispute determination. Garrity and Baris (1994) suggest that 20% of parents who undergo custodial evaluations will maintain their conflict at least 2 years after separation. These couples tend to fight over a variety of issues within the family system, placing their children in the middle. Parental conflict has a significant effect on children, particularly when the conflict involves differences over parenting styles.

An assumption guiding the Garrity and Barris (1994) model is that this subgroup of parents brings with it psychological obstacles that are unfixable. These individuals appear unable to let go of the marital relationship and maintain inappropriately high levels of conflict that interfere with the effective implementation of parenting plans leading to healthy postdivorce family functioning.

Increasingly, jurisdictions around the country are developing protocols to protect the children in these families and assist the parents who are unable to disengage from the conflict. The parent coordinator is one such role. (Some jurisdictions use the term *special master.*)

There is a group of parents who find it difficult to implement the parenting plan recommended by the custody evaluation and ordered by the court. The parent coordinator assists the parties in promoting the minor children's best psychological interests and needs. The parent coordinator helps parents in implementing the parenting plan while containing or reducing conflict. Assistance is provided with the execution of residence and visitation plans specified in agreements or orders. Coordinators monitor the parenting plan and mediate disputes. They are called upon to teach communication skills, principles of child development, and children's issues in divorce. Coordinators ensure that both parents maintain ongoing relationships with the children and may act as temporary decision makers on any issue over which the parents reach an impasse until further court order.

The court is the client of the parent coordinator, and he or she is required to provide regular reports to the court, the parties, and their attorneys describing major issues and their resolutions as well as overall progress of the parties. Finally, a parent coordinator may file a motion requesting a modification to the custody/visitation order if fundamental changes in the parenting plan are recommended.

The parent coordinator has the authority to talk to the children and any individual involved in their development and care. All parties are ordered by the court to execute any releases necessary for the parent coordinator to have access to other necessary people or records that may assist in the transition to a healthy divorced family.

Parent coordinator is an exciting new role for a forensic specialist. It assists the court in guiding moderate- and high-conflict families toward healthy resolution with minimal court involvement. Although there is no empirical work available on the efficacy of the parent coordinator model, such research will undoubtedly be forthcoming as more communities attend to the concept.

Court-Ordered Therapist

A court-ordered therapist functions in much the same way as a treating therapist. The techniques, focus, and relational variables are identical to those of clinical work. The only significant difference is that the court is the client and may request information about the progress of therapy. When this occurs, the therapist must be very careful about what is communicated to the court, how it is communicated, and the form in which it is communicated.

Typically, a clinician accepts an appointment to conduct therapy. The order specifically identifies the name of the child and therapist and orders that therapy begin by a specified date. The parent contacts the therapist to begin work, and the therapist attempts to fit the client into treatment as quickly as possible.

In their haste, many court-appointed therapists neglect to specify several important preconditions of therapy. The most important is identifying who is the client. The assumption is that the child is the client, yet the order indicates that the therapist provide information to the judge. If the information is allowed to be communicated to the judge without the parent's permission, then it seems the court is the client. When the court is the client, a number of questions are raised. First, How is the nature of the therapeutic relationship changed? Second, What information can the therapist withhold from the court?

In a recent case on which I was consulted, a psychologist was ordered to work with the child. The court had concerns about the child's ability to cope effectively with the stressors placed on her by the parents. The order specified that the parents would participate based upon the judgment of the therapist. Slowly, the therapist determined that a major concern was the mother's aberrant behavior.

The therapist was under the impression that the court wanted any and all information that directly affected the child's best psychological interests. The therapist's belief in the potential risk posed by the mother appeared to be such information. Thus, the therapist felt a responsibility to communicate this concern to the court. The potential ambiguity was that the court order provided for the therapist to communicate only information about the child.

The mother, sensing the therapist was concerned about her behavior toward her daughter, refused to give permission for the therapist to talk to the judge, claiming that that privilege was held by the parent. The mother claimed that the judge did not specifically order the therapist to provide written communications to the court. Furthermore, the mother claimed that the court order did not specify that the therapist could provide information about all parties involved in therapy. The mother concluded that the therapist was ethically compelled to protect the information gained from sessions in which the mother participated.

The court's interest was with the child's welfare and any information that may affect the child's well-being, including potentially dangerous parental behavior. However, the issue of who was able to say what to the court took more than 6 months to resolve. It all could have been avoided had the original court order clearly specified who the client was, what was expected by the court, and how information was to be communicated to the court.

The lesson is to make sure *before you begin your work* that the court order specifies who the client is and how the information will be shared. Make sure the court orders *written* communications about the progress of therapy with all participants and any referrals (i.e., psychological evaluations, psychoeducational assessments) that occur as a result of the therapy. Finally, make sure the order allows for the release of information from any and all professional or lay collaterals.

Summary

There are a number of noncourt-ordered activities in which a forensic specialist may engage. Some continue the role of evaluator, others require the role of educator, and some require the role of behavior change agent. Each requires understanding the psychological, legal, and ethical responsibilities in that area of professional practice.

TEN

Use of Psychological Tests in Forensic Assessment

Mental health professionals are testifying in court cases more than ever before, creating a need for standards that ensure psychological assessment tools are utilized properly, ethically, and to their fullest potential.

McCann and Dyer (1996, book jacket copy)

Those of us who have been involved in expert witness testimony have become accustomed to attorneys' use of the ideas proposed by Ziskin (Ziskin & Faust, 1988), which often guide cross-examination. However, even outspoken critics of the presentation of psychological science in the courtroom acknowledge the relative usefulness of objective psychological testing in a forensic context. This is because a well-developed psychological test appears to meet many, if not all, of the psycholegal criteria for presenting scientific evidence in court.

Among the tests most commonly used in child custody evaluations that assess adult personality functioning are the MMPI and MMPI-2, WAIS-R, MCMI-II and MCMI-III, and the Rorschach (Ackerman & Ackerman, 1996, 1997). Each test has both an empirical and a case law foundation supporting its use in court. However, only two tests will be discussed in this chapter, the MCMI and the MMPI. These tests are especially well-suited for use in a forensic setting because of their emphasis on standardized format, use of unambiguous stimuli, standard administration and scoring procedures, and the availability of "quantitative analysis of test results" (McCann & Dyer, 1996, p. 1). Advocates of the WAIS-R and the Rorschach would put forth similar claims. Thus, the choice to review the MCMI and MMPI reflects my bias, not any consensus within the field of forensic evaluation.

An important aspect of the forensic use of psychological testing is that the test must be useful (read: valid) for the purpose for which it is being used.

This is not only an important professional practice and ethical issue, it is also case law. In the landmark case of *Griggs v. Duke Power* (1971), the U.S. Supreme Court held that psychological tests have to be valid and directly related to job performance. This ruling has been interpreted to mean that the tests we use must have been shown to have an empirical literature basis for their use in a particular type of situation. Similarly, when we offer opinions about test results, they must be framed within the appropriate interpretative context of that test. For example, the MacAndrews scale on the MMPI and MMPI-2 does not measure alcohol use or abuse but the propensity to be prone to use or abuse alcohol should the individual drink (*Adkerson v. MK-Ferguson Co.,* 1991).

This chapter does not presume that the Millon Inventories and MMPI-2 are the only tests to be used in a forensic context. There are several useful publications supporting the use of the Wechsler scales and the Rorschach, just to name two often-used tools. What this chapter endeavors is to provide a framework within which to organize information about a particular test in a manner consistent with some of the criteria of the *Daubert* standard.

It is anticipated that a *Daubert* examination will include discussion about a test's underlying theory of science; whether it has been published in a peer-reviewed journal; its status as a current standard among the psychological community; and psychometric data about its reliability, validity, base rate estimates, and falsifiability.

This chapter is not a review of case law in which any one particular psychological test has been subjected to a *Daubert* analysis during a trial. *Daubert* examinations are a recent addition to case law, and few, if any, have focused on custody cases. Instead, this chapter suggests particular dimensions important to the acceptance of psychological tests in a forensic context.

This chapter outlines the fundamentals of the Millon Inventories and the MMPI. Its purpose is to provide a conceptual framework for using these tests within a forensic child custody context. For further reading about use of the Millon in a forensic setting, see *Forensic Assessment With the Millon Inventories* (McCann & Dyer, 1996). Further reading about the use of the MMPI in a forensic setting is found in two current texts: *MMPI, MMPI-2 & MMPI-A in Court: A Practical Guide for Expert Witnesses and Attorneys* (Pope, Butcher, & Seelen, 1993) and *Forensic Applications of the MMPI-2* (Ben-Porath, Graham, Hall, Hirschman, & Zaragoza, 1995).

The Role of Psychological Testing in Forensic Assessment

The use of psychological test data in court should provide a genuinely empirical basis for an expert's opinion. Psychological testing has the potential of providing objective support to the expert's opinion. A properly developed standardized test should provide the expert with data grounded in objective, empirical research (Heilbrun, 1995). Furthermore, the use of psychological tests helps to balance the bias and potential errors inherent in clinical interview data with objective results (Ben-Porath et al., 1995; McCann & Dyer, 1996). However, it is critical that the evaluator understand that any test results provide *only* hypotheses that are subjected to verification from alternative data sources (Heilbrun, 1995).

> Although it is perfectly appropriate to place great weight on psychological tests as scientifically grounded methods for generating valuable assessment data, it is inappropriate—to the point of verging on malpractice—to place great weight on the psychological test as constituting the opinion as though the expert were merely a recorder and not an interpreter of test data. (McCann & Dyer, 1996, pp. 41-42)

The function of psychological testing in court is ancillary to the capacity of the expert. It is the expert witness who provides to the trier of fact the conceptual and psychometric characteristics of the test instrument forming the basis for opinions.

Psychological tests do not provide information about the ultimate legal issues (Heilbrun, 1992). The interpretation of test data provides answers *only* to psychological questions, *not* legal questions. Therefore, psychological experts provide testimony regarding issues of mental health, emotional well-being, intellectual functioning, and other psychologically related issues. Psychological tests do not answer questions about who is the better custodial parent, who is insane, or who is a perpetrator.

Another important reason that our testimony is always limited to psychological rather than legal questions focuses on practicing within professional competencies. Psychologists are not attorneys or judges. It is unethical for a psychologist to provide a legal opinion. Legal opinions are outside the realm of professional competency for mental health professionals.

> As self-evident as this may seem, it bears repeating that the test results on which experts rely simply provide data for a further process of inference in which connections are drawn between conditions diagnosed by the test and the particular facts of the case. These connections are most helpful to the trier of fact and most resistant to cross-examination when based on solid theoretical propositions. (McCann & Dyer, 1996, p. 39)

Case Law

The evidentiary admissibility of psychological tests and their interpretation is governed by the Federal Rules of Evidence in the federal courts. At the state level, admissibility of psychological tests is governed by the specific rules of evidence established in each state (Pope et al., 1993). Often, there is a direct correspondence between the Federal Rules and those developed by states.

Psychological tests have been a hallmark of expert witness testimony for some time. With more than 7,000 empirical studies published, the MMPI is the most frequently used psychological test in a forensic setting (Lees-Haley, 1992). In an interesting survey, Ben-Porath et al. (1995) examined the use of the MMPI in state cases in the United States and found that the MMPI is used most frequently in cases involving custody, child access, or parenting capacity.

Use of the MMPI and MCMI has been judged as consistent with the *Frye* standard, the *Kelly-Frye* standard and the *Daubert* standard (Ben-Porath et al., 1995; McCann & Dyer, 1996).

As summarized below, case law has provided a legal basis for the use of the MMPI and MCMI in court. Three cases are of particular importance in the history of the admissibility of the MMPI and MCMI: *Applied Innovations, Inc. v. Regents of the University of Minnesota* (1989), *Regents of the University of Minnesota v. Applied Innovations, Inc.* (1987) and *People v. Stoll* (1989).

Acceptability of MMPI Testimony

Two cases helped to pave the way for the use of the MMPI in court: *Applied Innovations, Inc. v. Regents of the University of Minnesota* (1989) and *Regents of the University of Minnesota v. Applied Innovations, Inc.* (1987).

The threshold issue in determining the admissibility of psychological test data into evidence in a particular case rests on whether the results are sufficiently trustworthy to warrant their acceptance (Pope et al., 1993). A federal court explored the origins and scientific foundation of the MMPI and upheld its usefulness as a tool in forensic evaluations. It explored aspects of the assumptions upon which the test was designed, test construction, item construction, administration, scoring, interpretation, and psychometrics. It concluded that the MMPI provided information in a standard, reliable manner when used correctly and applied appropriately.

Admissibility of MMPI and MCMI as Standard Bearers

In *People v. Stoll* (1989), the court's decision explicitly upholds the admissibility of the MCMI and the MMPI as standard bearers in the field of psychological assessment. The court's decision stated clearly that both tests have had widespread acceptance in the field of psychology and that each is part of a typical standard psychological test battery (*People v. Stoll,* 1989).

The MMPI and the MCMI were demonstrated to *not* be novel or new scientific techniques. The court said, "Contrary to the dissent's claim, expert reliance on the MMPI . . . for this particular purpose is not a 'revolutionary' development. . . . It would be anomalous to view the MMPI and similar tests as a 'new' technique at this late date" (*People v. Stoll,* 1989, p. 712).

Regarding the MCMI, the court held that it "was copyrighted in 1976, and had achieved widespread acceptance in the three or four years preceding trial" (*People v. Stoll,* 1989, p. 705). It was further stated that "diagnostic use of written personality inventories such as the MMPI and MCMI has been established for decades" (*People v. Stoll,* 1989, p. 711).

Regarding the MMPI, the court held that "qualified individuals routinely use raw material from the MMPI . . . as a basis for assessing personality, and drawing behavioral conclusions therefrom" (*People v. Stoll,* 1989, p. 709). It further opined that "the psychological testimony [of the standardized tests] raises none of the concerns addressed by *Kelly-Frye.* The methods employed are not new to psychology or the law, and they carry no misleading aura of scientific infallibility" (*People v. Stoll,* 1989, p. 711).

Use of the MMPI and MCMI in Custody Determinations

The correct use of these tests is critical to the proper, ethical, and competent performance of forensic functioning. This is of particular concern in applying psychological tests in custodial determinations. Because there are no data supporting the use of the MMPI or MCMI as tools that measure parenting capacity, the evaluator needs to be particularly careful in choosing a just and ethical application of these tests in custodial assessment.

The use of any standardized test must be examined with an eye toward two important questions. The first question is whether the admission of the test data would make some fact more probable or less probable than it would be without the evidence. Therefore, for the MCMI or MMPI to be admitted into evidence, the data from the testing must assist the trier of fact to determine whether some issue is true.

The second question is whether some matter related to mental state, personality, emotional stability, intellectual functioning, or other psychological characteristic is at issue. Therefore, for the MCMI or MMPI to be admitted into evidence, the data from the testing must address some issue about mental state, emotional or psychological functioning, or some other psychological characteristic relevant to the issue before the court.

Neither the MMPI nor the MCMI provide data about parenting capacity. Neither test provides data about who is a good parent or who is a bad parent. Each test provides data about aspects of psychological functioning. The evaluator infers from this and other data an opinion about parenting capacity.

In the legal case summarized below, the question asked is whether the psychologist appropriately used the proper test, drew reasonable conclusions, and performed in a manner consistent with the ethical use of psychological tests.

Tipton v. Marion County
Department of Public Welfare (1989)

There is no current empirical work directly linking MMPI or MCMI results to an individual's ability to care for a child. However, in a recent case, a trial court in Indiana terminated the parental rights of two men who were fathers of two children born to the same mother (*Tipton v. Marion County Department of Public Welfare*, 1994). The decision was based, in part, on results from the MMPI.

On appeal, the Indiana Court of Appeals ruled that the MMPI results for one man indicated that he was a less than optimal father but found no evidence that he posed a threat to his child.[1] Based in part on the results of the MMPI presented by the psychologist, the court overturned the lower court decision to terminate parental rights.

The second man's parental rights termination was affirmed. The court found that the MMPI indicated that he was unable to function adequately as a parent. "Results of Mr. Boster's depression, anxiety, poor judgement and impulse control and resentment of external demands all suggest an inability to function adequately as a parent" (*Tipton v. Marion County Department of Public Welfare*, 1994, p. 14).

It is critical that when evaluators provide written testimony for the court in the form of psychological reports, there is a clearly articulated understanding within the body of the report about what these particular test results mean as well as what they do not mean. In the above case, the court operated under the assumption that the MMPI data provided some useful information about parenting capacity or competencies. Thus, the appeals court rendered a decision about termination of parental rights, basing its finding, in part, on the evidence entered into the record by the psychologist about the MMPI results.

The point to remember is that we are accountable for our written as well as our verbal testimony. Our testimony may significantly affect people's lives in very direct ways. Judges and attorneys are not often skilled in the interpretation of psychological test data. Thus, our presentation of psychological test data within the context of our expert testimony must include the limitations as well as advantages of a particular test.

In re Marriage of Luckey (1994)

In another court case, a question was whether a father would be permitted to continue to have unsupervised visitation with his son (*In re Marriage of*

Luckey, 1994). A former stepdaughter alleged that the father had sexually abused her when she was younger. The psychologist administered the MMPI to the father. The psychologist stated that the father's "scaled scores matched the profiles of known child molesters" (*In re Marriage of Luckey,* 1994, p. 4). The trial court decided that the father would be allowed to see his son without supervised visits. The case was appealed. The court of appeals upheld the lower court decision, stating that the use of the MMPI to determine whether a father was a child molester was questionable (Ben-Porath et al., 1995).

Here is another case in which use of psychological test data was presented inappropriately to the court. There is a significant body of research that calls into question the scientific basis of profile analysis (Oglogg, 1995). In fact, in many jurisdictions, the offering of psychological profile testimony is prohibited. The reasoning is that there is no consensus in the literature that a particular profile, a particular set of profiles, or even individual subscale scores may be directly related to sexually abusive behavior or a propensity toward sexual abuse.[2]

In re Marriage of L.R. (1990)

In a case similar to *In re Marriage of Luckey,* the MCMI was used in exploring the termination of a father's visitation based upon a mother's allegations of child sexual abuse. The court held that the use of the MCMI to determine whether the father was a child sex abuser was questionable. Commenting upon the qualifications of the psychologist who administered the test, the court ruled that the psychologist lacked experience in administration and interpretation of the test and questioned the applicability of a clinical rather than forensic focus.

This is an important point often lost on mental health professionals who do not regularly perform forensic assessments. The use and interpretation of test results within a forensic context is a specialized field of endeavor. The conscientious evaluator should follow the literature on forensic issues regarding test use (Brodzinsky, 1993; Butcher & Pope, 1993), books written about specific tests within a forensic context,[3] as well as continuing education courses on the use of psychological tests in a forensic context.[4]

In re A.V. (1993)

Trial courts, however, have also viewed as appropriate the use of standardized tests within the context of a complete forensic evaluation. In *In re A.V.,* a mother petitioned the court to terminate a father's parental rights based on alleged sexual abuse of a child. Because the MCMI was used as part of an overall evaluation of the alleged perpetrator, the use of the MCMI was included in the report and admitted without objection.

It is important, however, when using standardized testing within a foren-sic assessment to recognize how the context of the evaluation may influence the respondent's scores. For example, an individual taking an MMPI within the context of a $5 million personal injury lawsuit may be motivated to pres-ent him- or herself differently on a test from someone who is attempting to demonstrate to the court that he or she is not a risk to their children. In the former, one may expect an overestimation or negative exaggeration of symp-toms. In the latter, one may expect an underestimation of symptom severity. The overall profile configuration may appear similar in each evaluation, but the degree of severity may differ markedly.[5]

Garibaldi v. Dietz (1988)

However, use of standardized tests may appropriately be applied when examining the degree of psychopathology. For example, in *Garibaldi v. Dietz* (1988), the question of termination of parental rights included an investiga-tion about a parent's psychological status. Specifically, the MCMI was used to help establish whether the parent's bipolar illness was being controlled.

The lesson taken from this brief review of case law is that psychologists need to be extraordinarily careful in using psychological tests in court. The trial court judge and the attorneys often do not know, nor do they under-stand, the profoundly important issues of proper test use. Based in part on the expert status of the witness, courts may admit data from psychological tests that should never have been administered in the first place. Further insulting the judicial process, the mental health practitioner's interpretation of the inappropriately administered test is admitted into evidence and contributes toward the ultimate ruling. On appeal, the appellate courts have only the trial court transcript and evidence. There is no additional evidence admitted upon appeal. Thus, the error of admissibility of incorrectly used psychological tests or their inappropriate interpretation that contributed to the ultimate decision may continue to play a role throughout the appeals process. The moral is simple: Know your tests and their proper use, and never overstep these boundaries!

Fisher v. Johnson (1993)

A final area of consideration is what information you may be required to disclose. Issues of disclosure may arise in any phase of forensic involvement. They may occur during the discovery phase or the trial. You may be asked to disclose psychological test data during direct or cross-examination. It is important to understand the ethical, professional practice as well as the case law concerns involved in the disclosure question.

In *Fisher v. Johnson* (1993), a psychologist was questioned during cross-examination to provide the answers to three specific items on the MMPI that the plaintiff had endorsed. The judge would not allow the questions. The defense attorney intended to use the information to discredit the testimony of the psychologist. Based upon the judge's refusal to allow the questions, the defendant's attorney made a motion for a new trial. The trial judge denied the motion. The case was appealed to the North Dakota Supreme Court.

The court affirmed the lower court's decision, stating that an expert may be required to disclose the underlying facts that lay the foundation for expert opinion. However, in this particular case, the psychologist relied *not* upon individual item endorsements but scale scores in forming her opinions. The court decided that although the plaintiff's responses to the items might be viewed as "prior inconsistent statements" that could be used to impeach the testimony of a witness, the individual item responses were not allowed because their prejudicial value would have outweighed their probative value against the plaintiff.

Thus, the lesson to be taken from *Fisher v. Johnson* is that when providing testimony about standardized tests in court, particularly the MMPI, statements should be confined to interpretation of scaled scores and not individual items. It is possible that this case law precedent may extend to other tests as well, such as the MCMI.

Summary

The conclusion drawn from these and other case law decisions is that standardized tests such as the MMPI and the MCMI are used routinely in civil forensic evaluations. However, the courts are somewhat inconsistent in their acceptance of test data when the underlying relationship to the issue at hand is unclear. The examiner would be wise to use psychological tests only when the test is relevant to the issue before the court and only when the test provides data directly related to questions of mental, emotional, psychological, or intellectual functioning. Furthermore, it is incumbent upon the examiner to inform the court about the test's limitations in the body of the written report as well as during trial.

The remainder of the chapter will describe the MCMI and MMPI as they are used in forensic evaluations. Aspects of the tests underlying science, psychometrics, and other aspects pertaining to admissibility under the Daubert Standard will be discussed.

The Millon Inventories

The Millon Inventories used most often in custodial evaluations are the Millon Clinical Multiaxial Inventory (MCMI) and the Millon Adolescent Clinical Inventory (MACI). This discussion will focus on the MCMI.

The Millon Inventories are in their third generation. The MCMI was copyrighted in 1976 (Millon, 1983). The revised version, the MCMI-II, was published in 1987 (Millon, 1987) and the most recent update was published in 1994 (Millon, 1994, 1997).

Each is built upon Millon's theory of personality (Millon, 1969, 1981). With each generation of the MCMI, there is an increasing correspondence between measured personality features and the diagnostic criteria presented in the most recent edition of the *Diagnostic and Statistical Manual of Mental Disorders* (American Psychiatric Association, 1994).

Underlying Theory of Science

The MCMI is based upon a theory of personality that postulates three basic polarities underlying human behavior: pain-pleasure, self-other, and active-passive. The assumption is that human beings are naturally driven to maximize pleasurable experiences and minimize unpleasant or painful events. Millon (1997) posits that personality development is part of a bioevolutionary process. Personality functioning is the manifestation of *how* individuals are able to adjust to their environment. The polarities represent the range within which an individual is able to function in an adaptive manner. When stress is introduced, the individual typically operates in a more narrowly defined arena defined by each polarity, but still within the parameters of the polarities that define the individual's normal adaptive functioning. Dysfunction occurs when the individual is unable to operate within the boundaries of his or her normal adaptive functioning and is compelled to adapt using strategies that are ego-alien or ego-dystonic.

Importance of Reinforcement

The acquiring of reinforcement is another important element of Millon's theory. Individuals actively engage in the pursuit of pleasurable and life-enhancing activities through their interaction with the environment. This interaction leads to activity that is reinforcing. Other people may passively engage their environment, waiting for pleasurable and life-enhancing activities to occur. These more passive individuals tend to accommodate to and follow the direction provided by external cues.

Millon theorizes 11 basic personality patterns derived from an examination of the active-passive personality types and their reliance on one of five sources of reinforcement.

Withdrawing From Pleasure

Individuals may become *detached* from seeking out pleasurable experiences. The active form of detaching from pleasure seeking may be seen in individuals who actively avoid interface with others and the environment.

This is similar to the *avoidant personality pattern*. The passive form of detaching from pleasure seeking is often expressed through behaviors categorized as depressed or schizoid. This is similar to the *dependent personality pattern* and the *schizoid personality pattern*.

Pain Becomes Pleasure

There are other individuals who find rewarding the experience of pain. Experiences that most people find rewarding, comfortable, and enjoyable are viewed as painful. Experiences that most people find painful are viewed as rewarding, comfortable, and enjoyable. Millon labels this personality style as *discordant*. The active version is the *aggressive or sadistic personality pattern*. The passive version is the *self-defeating personality pattern*.

Fulfillment Comes From Self-Focus

Some people develop a unique focus on themselves, seeking out rewarding experiences that are wholly dependent upon self-gratification and the fulfillment of their own needs and desires. Millon labels these personality types as *independent*. The active version is the *antisocial personality pattern*. The passive version is the *narcissistic personality pattern*.

Fulfillment Comes From Others

The polar opposite of the independent personality types are those who seek reward and satisfaction solely from others. Millon labels these personality types as *dependent*. The active version is the *histrionic personality pattern*. The passive version is the *dependent personality pattern*.

Uncertainty

The final type is a confusing mixture of each of the above. These individuals are uncertain whether to attend to and follow their needs or comply with and follow the direction of others. Millon labels these personality types as *ambivalent*. The active version is the *negativistic personality pattern*. The passive version is the *compulsive personality pattern*.

Pathological Personality Disorders

Normal personality patterns are distinguished from pathological personality patterns in several ways. The first is the degree of *flexibility*. Most people are able to use different personal characteristics to adapt to a variety of situations. For example, during a custodial battle, a mother who historically has behaved as quiet, shy, passive, and dependent is forced to act verbally assertive, independent, forceful, and with overt anger at her former husband.

Dysfunctional or pathological behavior occurs when personality patterns become rigid and inflexible. These patterns tend to become repetitive and disruptive. They are associated with erratic behavior, intense moods, or a disturbed self-image. Other characteristics of disturbed behavior may include confused thought processes, bizarre thought content, emotional instability, and extreme interpersonal difficulties.

Three severe personality disorders defined in the theoretical model are viewed as extensions of the 11 basic personality patterns. They are different in the amount of distortion but are not viewed as being qualitatively different personality organizations. Pathological personality functioning is conceptualized as a endpoint along a continuum of behavior ranging from normal to abnormal.

The *schizotypal personality pattern* is conceptualized as an extension of the detached personality types. It is characterized by vague, diffuse, and autistic thought processes, and withdrawal from social and interpersonal interactions. The schizotypal personality appears odd in behavior and appearance.

The *borderline personality pattern* is conceptualized as an extension of the dependent and ambivalent personality types. It is characterized by erratic and unstable interpersonal relationships, unstable moods, and self-destructive and impulsive behavior. The borderline personality demonstrates constantly changing, unpredictable feelings toward others. The single best word to describe the borderline is *unstable*.

The *paranoid personality pattern* is conceptualized as an extension of the independent and ambivalent personality types. It is characterized by intense suspiciousness and rigid defensiveness against the control and direction of others. The paranoid personality reads threat and mistrust to his or her autonomy from those around him or her.

Test Construction

The Millon Inventories were developed following a three-stage process. The *first stage* was the selection of items that were rationally and logically related to the theoretical constructs represented in Millon's theory. Item selection was based on prototypical theoretical descriptions drawn from the theory describing personality disorders, as well as the diagnostic criteria of the *DSM* (Millon, 1994).

The *second stage* involved the psychometric development of individual scales, focusing on the internal consistency of each scale. Information such as internal consistency of scales (alphas), item-to-total correlations, and item endorsement frequencies were derived. Thus, scales were developed that possessed high internal consistency correlations.

The *third stage* involved studies examining the external validity of each scale. Information such as external criterion measures with clinician ratings of psychopathology and scores from other standardized psychological tests were used. In this way, the internally consistent scales developed in Stage 2 were shown to be empirically related to meaningful diagnostic-related criteria.

Base Rate Scores

Another unique aspect of the Millon is the use of *base rate*, or BR, scores. The assumption underlying many statistical tools is that the phenomenon being studied is normally distributed in the population. For example, the MMPI and the MMPI-2 use *t*-scores to convert raw scores into distributions with a mean of 50 and a standard deviation of 10. Uniform *t*-scores provide a means of extracting percentile rank scores across different scales at the same *t*-score level (Weiner, 1995).

However, personality disorders are not equally distributed across the population (Millon, 1994). The use of base rate scores allows for the conversion of raw scores into a standard scale that reflects the specific distribution of a particular personality disorder within the population (Weiner, 1995).

The development of base rate scores is logically simple. First, the prevalence rate for each personality disorder and clinical syndrome is established in a normative sample for each particular scale. Next, a frequency distribution of raw scores is plotted for each scale. An arbitrary set of three anchor points is assigned at BR scores of 0, 60, and 115. A BR score of 0 corresponds to a raw score of 0. A BR score of 60 represents the median raw score for each scale. A BR of 115 indicates the maximum score possible on any scale.

Millon also describes two other important base rate scores. A BR of 75 corresponds to the percentage of people in the normative sample who were judged by collateral rating as demonstrating the *presence* of the personality trait, disorder, or clinical syndrome. A BR of 85 reflects the percentage of people in the normative sample who were judged by collateral ratings as *prominently displaying* the personality trait, disorder, or clinical syndrome (McCann & Dyer, 1996; Millon, 1994).

For the purposes of expert witness testimony, the Millon scales provide data useful in answering questions about base rate frequency. BR scores are calculated for each scale. This means it is possible to render an estimate of the degree of confidence you have in stating that the individual evaluated is, in fact, of a particular personality feature (Millon, 1994).

The Millon scales also provide information about whether the individual was identified as having the personality features (test positive), sensitivity, specificity, and hit rate information inferred from your test results. A discussion of these dimensions is found in the MCMI-III manual (Millon, 1994).

Malingering and Deception

Any forensic examiner needs to be acutely aware of the possibility of an intentional or unintentional misrepresentation displayed on standardized tests. The Millon provides four measures that are sensitive to the degree that individuals may attempt to misrepresent themselves.

The first is *Scale V.* This is a three-item scale on the MCMI-III, a four-item scale on the MCMI-II, and a three-item scale on the MCMI. It contains items that have bizarre content, such as "I flew across the Atlantic thirty times last year." It is designed to measure an individual's tendencies to respond with random, oppositional, or other response sets that may show a failure to read the test items accurately (McCann & Dyer, 1996; Millon, 1994).

Scale X is called the Disclosure index and is composed of the differentially weighted raw scores of the basic personality scales (Scales 1-8B). The Disclosure index purports to measure general openness to revealing personal aspects about oneself. A low score may reflect a tendency to be secretive and defensive. It may also suggest an unwillingness to reveal aspects of one's private life. A high score may suggest a tendency to use little discretion when making self-reports. A high score may also reflect a tendency to look to others for attention, sympathy, or support. High scorers tend to be overly revealing of personal difficulties (Millon, 1994).

Scale Y is called the Desirability index and is composed of items that purport to measure social desirability response bias. A social desirability response set occurs when an individual attempts to present him- or herself in a highly favorable light. High scores are interpreted to mean a tendency to present the self in a favorable light. There is a tendency to minimize personal faults and to hold unrealistically positive attitudes about one's stability and emotional well-being (McCann & Dyer, 1996; Millon, 1994).

Scale Z is called the Debasement index and is composed of items that purport to measure a tendency to magnify and overreport difficulties or personal faults. High scores are interpreted to mean a tendency to overreport problems or personal difficulties. An assumption is that high scores reflect a motivational set reflective of "malingering, psychological 'cries for help,' or other instances of unrealistic overreporting of problems" (McCann & Dyer, 1996, p. 15).

Use of the Millon Inventories in Child Custody Assessments

Generally, individuals who undergo custody evaluations are concerned about presenting a favorable picture of themselves and their ability to cope with the challenges before them. This kind of response set reflects the litigant's desire to present him- or herself in a favorable light while minimizing difficulties. Thus, one would predict that most individuals involved in custody evaluations would score higher on Scale Y than on Scale Z or Scale X.

In those rare instances in which a custody litigant does not score in a manner logically predicted by the circumstances described above, the evaluator needs to explore what is different about this individual or the circumstances. It is unusual for a custody litigant to overreport psychological symptoms when his or her agenda is to gain primary caretaker responsibilities for the child. Therefore, it is imperative that the examiner explore such discrepancies carefully. A useful place to start is performing an item analysis, examining each question as it relates to the individual's present functioning and its impact on parenting.

The MCMI provides a listing of critical responses under the heading "noteworthy responses." The item responses and their endorsed direction are reported. These responses afford a valuable opportunity to examine unusual or noteworthy responses within an interview setting.

The MCMI can generate valuable hypotheses about a parent's personality traits and possible psychopathology that may affect the parent-child relationship. Similarly, the MACI (Millon Adolescent Clinical Inventory; Millon, 1993) may provide useful hypotheses about psychological functioning and possible maladaptive indicators in adolescents who may be involved in the assessment process.

There is no single personality trait, group of traits, or profile that indicates that an individual is a good parent (McCann & Dyer, 1996). Similarly, there is no single personality trait, group of traits, or profile that indicates that an adolescent is a good child who is easily parented. Results from the Millon inventories must be placed within the broader context of a comprehensive child custody evaluation. The results of each test are potential hypotheses to be critically examined and supported by collateral interviews and other sources of data. The psychological test results are not, by themselves, definitive of anything in a forensic evaluation. Test scores are pieces of a larger puzzle that may, or may not, fit the present context accurately.

Historically, objective psychological tests have been criticized for their use in parental assessment within a comprehensive child custody evaluation (Brodzinsky, 1993). The concern has been based upon the degree to which the test's normative sample reflected individuals embroiled in custody disputes. The argument has been that because normative samples tended not to include couples in conflict, the results were not valid because they were being compared to an inappropriate normative group.

To account for this concern, the MCMI-II normative sample contains data from a significant number of high-conflict couples undergoing marital treatment (Millon, 1994). Because divorcing couples are married couples undergoing conflict, the applicability of the data in the normative sample to custodial evaluations is deemed appropriate (McCann & Dyer, 1996).

> Moreover, because child custody is a highly conflicted situation in which some form of personality disturbances or psychopathology is suspected or presumed, the Millon inventories provide a useful measure of psychopathology that must be considered in making child custody determinations. Therefore, we strongly advocate the use of the MCMI-II in child custody

evaluations. This particular use of the instrument is endorsed by Dr. Millon. (McCann & Dyer, 1996, p. 118)

The MCMI provides data about basic personality styles of parenting. It screens for areas of possible dysfunction that may have an impact on the quality of the environment that a particular parent may provide. It also provides a useful measure of the parent's response style and overall level of disclosure in the assessment process.

Minnesota Multiphasic Personality Inventory

The MMPI and MMPI-2 are the most widely used tests of personality in the world. Their combined empirical literature comprises more than 7,000 publications (Pope et al., 1993).

The MMPI was originally developed in the late 1930s and early 1940s as a screening instrument for the differential diagnosis of psychopathology. It included scales to identify the presence of hypochondriasis, depression, hysteria, paranoia, psychasthenia, schizophrenia, and hypomania (Ben-Porath et al., 1995; Pope et al., 1993).

The items for the MMPI were selected from a rational analysis of previous empirical work in combination with the authors' clinical experience. However, the test performed poorly in distinguishing among psychopathological conditions. The test was found to offer other applications. Various combinations of scale elevations were found to be helpful in identifying various symptoms of psychopathology. As research progressed, investigators were able to identify statistical correlates of MMPI scores and code types (Pope et al., 1993).

An important lesson from the early work was the "conviction that empirical research must guide clinical uses of the MMPI" (Ben-Porath et al., 1995, p. 1). The revised MMPI, the MMPI-2, builds on the conviction of the need for empirical research to guide uses of the test. "The MMPI-2's solid empirical scientific foundations allow forensic psychologists to rely on the test in a variety of evaluations" (Ben-Porath et al., 1995, p. 2).

Test Construction

Historically, there have been substantial difficulties with the original MMPI as an instrument that accurately reflects the demographic composition of the United States. The norms established in the 1930s were based entirely on a white sample of individuals who lived in a geographically limited area. The normative group included a group of visitors to the University of Minnesota hospital, airline workers, and members of the Civilian Conservation Corps. Their average profile was a 30-year-old with 8 years of formal education, residing in a rural area or small town, and employed as a skilled or semiskilled worker.

The MMPI-2 was developed to eliminate, or at least minimize, the difficulties inherent in the MMPI. Rather than revise the test using empirically contrasted groups, as was done with the MMPI, the MMPI-2 has been developed through content-based scales. The content-based approach to scale development emphasizes item content as a primary criterion for inclusion in scale membership. There are important advantages to a content-based approach to item selection. The items tend to be relatively homogeneous. For example, the set of content scales developed by Wiggins (1966) are more homogeneous in content and more internally consistent than are scales developed through empirical keying. The result is that scores on the Wiggins scales are interpreted to more directly measure differences along a symptom severity dimension than those drawn from the original clinical scales.

A content scale that purports to measure depression, contains items that rationally reflect depressive symptoms, has been statistically correlated with external measures of depression, and whose internal consistency is high will yield a more accurate measure of depressive symptomology than the empirically keyed depression scale found on the MMPI.

On the original MMPI, the clinical scales contained items that had no conceptual relationship to the construct intended to be measured. For example, the depression scale (Scale 2) contained items that had no conceptual relationship to depression. They were included, in part, because of inadequate validation procedures. They were also included because the authors' concept of pathology at the time reflected the prevailing belief that syndromes were inherently heterogeneous (Pope et al., 1993).

Today's conceptual framework guiding diagnosis and treatment of psychopathology is based on the premise that homogeneous symptoms exist. These symptoms can be diagnosed through accurate measurement. Once identified through accurate measurement, specific treatment strategies can be used to treat specific symptoms (i.e., cognitive-behavioral treatment of depression).

With the movement away from heterogeneous syndromes to homogeneous symptoms (i.e., from the diagnostic group of people suffering from major depression to the dimensional construct of depression), the heterogeneous nature of the clinical scales became a hindrance to their interpretation. This problem was overcome by reliance on code types that allowed for classification of individuals into potentially homogeneous classes based on their MMPI profile configuration. (Ben-Porath et al., 1995, p. 7)

The development of content-specific measures of clinical phenomena is useful in the forensic evaluation of parents. The evaluator needs to determine what, if any, psychopathology may exist. Once determined, then several critical questions need to be asked. The first is, How severe is the symptomology? That is, What is the relationship between an elevated scaled score and the degree of real-life impairment in the individual's life? Another critical question is, How does the apparent psychopathology influence or impair the individual's parenting? A third question to be asked is, In what ways is the child influenced by the parent's apparent psychopathology?

The distinction between the second and third questions is perspective. The former refers to the ways in which the *parent's behavior* may affect his or her ability to parent the child. Such information may be gained through observation, collateral data, and self-report. For example, a parent who scores highly on Scale 4, Scale 7, and Scale 8 might be found to demonstrate impulsive behaviors that create an unsafe, unpredictable environment for a child. Gathering collateral data from neighbors, school personnel, coaches, and other people who have observed the parent may help determine whether the elevated scores do, indeed, affect the individual's parenting.

The third question approaches these data from a different perspective. There may be times when a individual's parenting fits criteria for good parenting skills, yet its effect on the child is negative. Thus, the third question refers to the ways in which *the child* is affected by the parent's perceived unusual or abnormal behavior, yet is not a concern in terms of parenting. For example, collateral reports support the view of the individual as a competent, responsible parent with odd characteristics. Yet a child may feel embarrassed by certain behaviors that result in increased social alienation at school and from friendship groups, and an overall impairment to his or her social development. Further investigation would be warranted in such situations.

What Does the Test Measure?

The MMPI-2 is composed of 13 basic scales. Eight of these purport to measure psychopathology. Two measure important aspects of personality, and 3 provide information about test-taking attitude that may affect the test's validity (Ben-Porath et al., 1995; Pope et al., 1993).

The eight basic scales are called the clinical scales. They are hypochondriasis (Scale 1, *Hs*); depression (Scale 2, *D*); conversion hysteria (Scale 3, *Hy*); psychopathic deviate (Scale 4, *Pd*); paranoia (Scale 6, *Pa*); psychasthenia (Scale 7, *Pt*); schizophrenia (Scale 8, *Sc*); and hypomania (Scale 9, *Ma*).

The following brief scale descriptions are only summaries. They do not do justice to the complex and rich information each MMPI-2 scale may provide the evaluator. The reader is referred to Pope et al. (1995) for further discussion and a more extensive reference list.

Hypochondriasis appears to measure a variety of issues focused on preoc-cupation with bodily concerns. Depression purports to measure a variety of issues including depression, hopelessness, low self-esteem, and pessimism. The Hysteria scale examines how an individual reacts to stress and avoids responsibility through development of physical symptoms. The Psychopathic Deviant scale appears to explore antisocial behavior. The Paranoia scale pro-vides information about psychotic thinking, sensitivity to others, and feelings of mistrust. Psychasthenia purports to measure level of anxiety, tension, and worry. The Schizophrenia scale appears to measure psychotic behavior char-acterized by confusion, sense of social isolation, alienation, and feeling mis-understood by others. The Hypomania scale measures level of activity char-acterized by accelerated speech, among other indicators.

The two scales that measure more characterological aspects are Masculine-Feminine and Social Introversion-Extroversion. Scale 5, labeled Masculine-Feminine (Mf), appears to measure tendency toward things and action versus emotional awareness and sensitivity to feelings. The assumption is that things and action tendencies reflect more masculine attributes. Aware-ness and sensitivity to feelings reflect more feminine attributes. High scores reflect a more action-oriented tendency, lower scores reflect more focus on awareness of feelings.

Scale 0, labeled Social Introversion-Extroversion (Is), appears to measure the tendency toward shyness versus gregariousness. High scores reflect shy-ness, social sensitivity, and reluctance to be placed in the spotlight. Low scores reflect a need for social approval, social engagement, and the spotlight.

Malingering and Deception

Similar to the validity scales on the MCMI, the MMPI-2 provides a number of validity measures. These measures help to determine how the indi-vidual approached the test. Some individuals undergoing forensic evaluation may actively attempt to distort test results. The validity scales of the MMPI-2 may help to identify those individuals who respond randomly to items, those who intentionally exaggerate the presence of false symptoms, and those who present themselves in an unrealistically favorable light.

The L scale, called the lie scale, is purported to be a measure of the degree to which an individual is open and self-disclosing on the test as well as provid-ing negative self-views. High scores above 65 may suggest a perception of self-virtue not found among most people.

The K scale, called the Subtle Defensiveness scale, purports to measure test defensiveness. It is used as a statistical correction for the tendency for people to deny problems. The K-score correction is added to five MMPI-2 scales: Hs, Pd, Pt, Sc, and Ma. High K suggests high defensiveness. When interpreting the MMPI-2, it is important to examine the degree to which K-score corrections contribute to a scale's determination. For example, it is not unusual in custodial assessments for a parent to score somewhat high on the *Pd* scale, due more to a high level of defensiveness rather than overall mistrust. Thus, the examiner needs to critically examine the contribution K scores make to the overall clinical scale elevation.

The *F and F(B) scales* measure the *tendency to exaggerate symptoms* or the tendency to claim an excessive number of emotional difficulties. The F scale may also measure the tendency to answer questions in a random or unselective manner. The F scale items occur early in the test, before Item 370. Concerned that the subject's response set may change during the test, the F(B) or Back Side F scale was developed to measure possible unusual responding to items located toward the end of the test.

The VRIN or *Variable Response Inconsistency scale,* is a general *self-contradiction scale.* It is made up of pairs of patterns (i.e., true-true, true-false, false-true, false-false). It is intended to measure response inconsistency. In conjunction with a high F scale, a low to moderate VRIN rules out the likelihood that the F score indicates random responding (Pope et al., 1993).

The TRIN, or *True Response Inconsistency scale,* measures a *response set of responding with all true or all false answers.* Similar to the VRIN, it is a measure of self-contradiction. The scale is composed of true-true or false-false item pairs that are semantically inconsistent. For example, an individual might answer false to the item, "Most of the time I feel blue" and also endorse as false the item "I am happy most of the time."

In light of the massive amount of empirical research examining each of these variables, the reader is referred to the MMPI-2 manual for further readings and references.

Comparison of MMPI and MCMI
for Child Custody Evaluations

If the use of the MMPI-2 were to be subjected to a *Daubert* test, it appears that the MMPI-2 is presently less well-suited for forensic work because it does not have a clearly articulated underlying theory of science. Unlike the MCMI, the MMPI-2 does not have published data about base rates, specificity, sensitivity, and other relevant psychometric criteria that appear important in conforming to the *Daubert* standard.

However, there are many elements of the MMPI-2 that argue favorably for its use as an instrument in forensic evaluations. It has been and will continue to be well researched. The hypotheses drawn from its data are falsifiable—that is, they can be empirically tested. Each scale has published reliability and validity data. Work on refining the instrument continues, with greater focus on homogeneously developed content-related scales (Ben-Porath et al., 1995).

Advocates of the MMPI-2 would argue that the test provides information about Type I and Type II errors (Weiner, 1995). The revised MMPI-2 presents better developed and more adequate normative data than do most objective personality inventories. Because of its relatively recent publication, research examining the temporal stability of the MMPI-2 is scarce. There are also few studies available examining the test-retest reliability of the MMPI-2. Furthermore, there are little data about the predictive validity of the MMPI-2 (Weiner, 1995). Thus, the general consensus is to administer the better constructed MMPI-2, but have the test scored on MMPI norms. This may be accomplished through the use of a computer testing service. One such service, NCS, provides a means for scoring the MMPI-2 on both MMPI-2 and MMPI norms. It also provides a profile of corrected and uncorrected K scores. The report name is the NCS Extended Score Plus.

Advocates of the MCMI would argue that the MMPI-2 provides psychometric qualities that are inferior to the Millon. They would argue that because of the degree of heterogeneity inherent in the basic scales, the overall picture drawn of the individual is less clear than that drawn on the MCMI. They would also argue that some of the subscales have reliability data of limited value (McCann & Dyer, 1996).

Like any other standardized instrument used in a forensic context, the MMPI-2 should be viewed as an hypothesis-generating tool. When viewed in this manner, the MMPI-2 provides a wealth of data from which to generate hypotheses about each individual's personality structure, the manner in which parents may conflict or cooperate with each other, and how the parent may influence the child.

It is worth recalling that the MMPI-2 does not yield a measure of parental fitness or competence. It is not a test that provides a direct measure of parenting behavior. However, it does provide a wealth of information about possible behaviors, attitudes, and beliefs about self and others. How the evaluator chooses to learn about the litigant with such an extensive database depends upon competency in the forensic interpretation of the MMPI-2 and a knowledge of how to use the hypotheses as guides for further interviews.

One useful way is to use the Harris-Lingoes content-related scales as a framework to guide interviews. For example, an individual who scores high on Familial Discord (Pd1), Social Alienation (Sc1), and Amorality (Ma1) may be guided toward more in-depth discussions of family discord, examining both family-of-origin issues as well as current family issues. Similarly, a high score on Ma1 may lead to explorations of rule following and other attitudes and beliefs about socially appropriate rules and conventions. Another helpful technique is to explore the litigant's responses to the critical items section of the computer-generated report.

Greenberg and Moreland (1996) recommend the *Marks Adult Feedback and Treatment Report*[6] to guide feedback to the litigant. The *Marks Adult*

Feedback and Treatment Report translates results from the MMPI into simple, easy-to-understand statements descriptive of the litigant's responses. For example, in describing the test-taking attitude of a respondent, an individual whose validity indexes may have suggested defensiveness may be told the following: "The way you approached the test suggests that you were feeling vulnerable to being criticized and judged. You have very high standards, and so it is easy to feel vulnerable to some kind of moral review. Perhaps you felt that the test would expose you in some way and you approached it very cautiously."

The *Marks Adult Feedback and Treatment Report* provides a kinder and gentler way of introducing important information from which to base further investigative discussions.

Conclusions

The use of the MMPI-2 in child custody evaluations is indicated when a parent's personality or mental status is to be assessed. Similar to the MCMI, there is a paucity of research related to the MMPI-2 in determining parental competence. Similar to the argument set forth concerning the use of the MCMI in custodial determinations, the MMPI has several research studies involving couples undergoing marital therapy, experiencing marital problems, or undergoing divorce.

Little research has been published establishing a link between MMPI-2 scores and parental behaviors. There is no one profile or constellation of scores that is consistently associated with parenting characteristics related to negative impact on children. Furthermore, there is no clear, identifiable profile or code type that distinguishes a parent as an abuser or one who is associated with abuse.

The MMPI-2 may be able to help assess the emotional functioning and adjustment of parents. Inferences may be drawn about how these adjustment variables may affect child adjustment, among other factors. Yet the evaluator must use such indicators as hypotheses to be explored and further supported through collateral data.

Therefore, the MMPI-2 may help to establish and/or support the absence of alleged or suspected mental disorder. The test results may assist in establishing the extent to which such disorders may present difficulties to a child and his or her environment. The MMPI-2 may also provide useful ideas about prognosis, development of parenting plans, and treatment planning.

A double-edged sword is using the data from the MMPI-2 in helping the court to understand potentially negative attributes that the caretaker may display, and the caretaker's ability to establish positive or negative relationships with a child. Relative strengths of parents may go untapped by the MMPI-2 because it is designed to explore psychopathology. The wise evaluator seeks out collateral support for any inference drawn from the MMPI-2 associating some score with real-world behaviors. Too often, our colleagues draw erroneous conclusions about the meaning of a score or set of scores and its relationship to real-world behaviors.

> Because use of the MMPI/MMPI-2 in this manner presents the greatest potential for misuse of the instrument, and is probably the practice that forms the basis for much of the criticism leveled by mental health and legal commentators, examiners should make clear to the legal decision maker the inferences that they make when extrapolating from personality traits or behavioral styles suggested by the MMPI-2. When offering descriptions of the parents or potential caretakers in this way, the psychologist should be careful not to make assumptions about how particular behavior patterns, personality styles, or ways of responding may affect a child's development. . . . The psychologist should not begin to offer conjecture to the court about how such styles might positively or negatively affect the child, in the absence of any data supporting such claims. (Otto & Collins, 1995, pp. 237-238)

Summary

This chapter has reviewed the two most commonly employed standardized personality tests in forensic child custody determination used in assessing adult functioning. Each test examines aspects of emotional health, mental well-being, and personality structure. Neither test is based upon a research base that enables direct association between test scores and statements about parental competency, parental behavior, or parent-child interaction. Each test does provide a reasonable set of hypotheses to be drawn from results that, when used in conjunction with collateral data sources, clinical interviews, direct behavioral observations, and other self-report measures, help to paint a more complete picture of the individual's parenting competencies.

Notes

1. The reader is reminded that an appeals court does not take new testimony. Its role is to examine the evidence presented at the trial court level and make determinations about law. Therefore, the appeals court did not directly hear, nor did it question, the psychologist who conducted the testing.

2. Oglogg's excellent chapter in the Ben-Porath et al. book provides a more comprehensive discussion of the issue of MMPI profile testimony in criminal cases. The reader is referred to pages 31 to 36. Another resource for MMPI profile testimony is Chapter 2 of the Pope et al. text. For a discussion about concerns regarding MCMI profile testimony, see Chapters 3 and 4 in McCann and Dyer (1996). Specific attention may be directed to pages 51 to 54, 60 to 66, and 97 to 101.

3. Among the books that fall into this category are the McCann and Dyer book on the Millon inventories, Ben-Porath et al.'s book on the MMPI-2, and Pope et al.'s book on the use of the MMPI, MMPI-2 and MMPI-A in forensic context.

4. An excellent example is the workshop on "Civil Forensic Applications of the MMPI-2," offered by the American Academy of Forensic Psychology. For the MCMI, Frank Dyer's workshop, "Forensic Use of the Millon Inventories With Adults," is an excellent example of how to use the Millon in a forensic context. Dr. Dyer's workshop has been offered through NCS.

5. Drs. Greenberg and Moreland provided a vivid example of this conundrum in their MMPI-2 workshop on the civil forensic use of the MMPI-2, presented in Las Vegas, Nevada on April 19, 1996 by the AAFP. They presented five profiles of the same litigant who was involved in lengthy personal injury (PI) litigation (Profile Example #29). During the course of the personal injury litigation, the litigant's marriage ended and a custody evaluation was performed. The profile configurations displayed the overwhelming influence of context on test scores. The litigant's basic scale scores were significantly more elevated when being assessed for the PI case compared with the results completed for the custody case. The differences do not necessarily attest to attempts to lie or deceive. Rather, different testing circumstances often exert different influences to present oneself in different ways.

6. The *Marks Adult Feedback and Treatment Report* was developed by Philip Marks, PhD, Richard W. Lewak, PhD, and Gerald E. Nelson, PhD. It is published by Western Psychological Services (WPS).

ELEVEN

Custodial Determination

Winning is never more important than the well-being of your children.

Marc J. Ackerman (1997, p. 11)

For many years, I did not clearly distinguish between the need to make a custodial determination and the need to develop a parenting plan. The two concepts seemed so intertwined that their unique contributions were not clearly understood. There is, of course, an important distinction between deciding which parent provides for the best psychological interests of the child and a determination about the best residential arrangement. In this chapter, we discuss the question of how to make the determination of which parent provides for the best psychological interests of the children. In the next chapter, we take up the question of parenting plans, that is, how will the custodial determination translate into a workable residential arrangement?

Organizing Data About the Children

The primary question to address is, What are the developmental needs of the child? This is a broad area to explore. No examiner can assess all aspects of a child's development. However, when clearly formulated psycholegal questions are posed at the beginning of the examination, the evaluator is able to operationally define the most relevant areas into a set of testable hypotheses. For example, the first box on page 221 displays possible hypotheses regarding the examination of potential parental alienation. Once the hypotheses are formulated, it is a matter of collecting data from a variety of sources that will aid in determining the answer to these hypotheses. Hypotheses exploring different areas of concern would be formulated using a similar structure. The second box on this page shows a different set of hypotheses generated for the exploration of allegations of child sexual abuse.

Parental Alienation Hypotheses

Following Gardner (1997) and modified here to address concerns about the mother rather than the child, four hypotheses were posed to address the possible negative influence of the mother upon the child.

1. The mother is not creating an atmosphere that negatively affects the minor child's relationship with his or her father.
2. The mother is creating an atmosphere that mildly and negatively affects the minor child's relationship with his or her father.
3. The mother is creating an atmosphere that moderately and negatively affects the minor child's relationship with his or her father.
4. The mother is creating an atmosphere that severely and negatively affects the minor child's relationship with his or her father.

Sample Hypotheses Exploring Allegation of Child Sexual Abuse

Robin (1991) suggested five hypotheses to explore in examining allegations of child sex abuse:

1. The child is truthful, credible, and accurate about the child sexual abuse allegations.
2. The child is truthful, but has misperceived an ambiguous or innocent situation, or has misidentified an alleged suspect.
3. The child does not have the mental capacity because of age or disability to give a reliable account of the alleged event(s).
4. The child has been influenced inappropriately by a third party or parties to make a false allegation.
5. The child is intentionally fabricating an accusation as an act of anger or revenge or for some type of secondary gain.

Questions Organizing Children's Evaluation Data

There is no one grouping of factors that has been demonstrated to fully define the best psychological interest criteria. Each evaluator needs to consider

QUICK REFERENCE **Sample Organizing Questions for
the Forensic Interview of the Child**

1. Emotional well-being
2. Physical well-being
3. School performance
4. After-school activities
5. Recreational activities
6. Cognitive development
7. Social development
8. Social involvement (i.e., peer group involvement)
9. Religious identity
10. Sex-role identity and gender-related issues
11. Communication skills
12. Child's perception of primary and secondary caretaker
13. Child's perception of psychological parent
14. Sibling relationships
15. Child's perception of relationship with each parent
16. Child's perception of extended family involvement
17. Child's description of daily routine and parental involvement
18. Child's description of each parent's discipline and rules
19. Child's involvement with each parent (i.e., uniquely shared activities)
20. Child's custodial preference and exploration of why

the available behavioral science literature; the current personal, social, and cultural factors of the evaluation; and the psycholegal questions being posed by the court.

There is, however, some professional consensus about the psychological factors of children at different ages to consider in child custody evaluations (Baris & Garrity, 1988; Bray, 1991; Rohman et al., 1987; Schutz et al., 1989). What follows is *not* an exhaustive list. You may wish to create your own list of relevant factors and search out the behavioral science literature to support their importance in the custodial decision-making process. Another option is to use published questionnaire formats, such as those included in the ASPECT (Ackerman & Schoendorf, 1992), the Child Questionnaire developed by Schutz et al. (1989), or the child interview data forms of the Uniform Child Custody Evaluation System (UCCES) developed by Munsinger and Karlson (1994).

No matter which set of questions you decide to use, there are two important considerations to follow. The first is to use a similar set of questions for each child that will contribute to maintaining a more reliable data-gathering format (see discussion of the importance of using a standard format in Chapter 4). The second is to impose a theoretical structure on the content areas being assessed. In Chapter 4, I argued that organizing data around systems theory provided a useful conceptual model. However, there are other theoretical models around which data may be organized. Choose one and be consistent in its application across data-gathering techniques (i.e., organizing collateral data around factors drawn from the theoretical model).

The examiner can gather data from the child interview as well as from collateral sources, such as pediatrician, teachers, and coaches. Data may also be collected from standardized psychological testing, projective techniques, and direct observation of the child.

Organizing the Parents' Evaluation Data

A major task confronting a custody evaluator is the determination of a primary custodial parent. Among the factors to consider is, Which parent is better able to provide a safe, secure, stable, and predictable environment for the children? Another question to consider is, Which parent provides better for the children's physical, financial, material, religious, and cultural needs?

Questions Organizing Parents' Psychological Well-Being and Parenting Competencies

There is no one grouping of factors that has been demonstrated to fully define what makes a good parent. As discussed in Chapter 7, there is some professional consensus about deficit parenting behaviors (Ackerman, 1995; Ackerman & Ackerman, 1996, 1997; Rohman et al., 1987; Schutz et al., 1989). In general, each evaluator needs to consider the available behavioral science literature; the current personal, social, and cultural factors of the evaluation; and the psycholegal questions being posed by the court in determining which factors are relevant to measure and which provide enough incremental validity to justify their inclusion in the evaluation process.

There is some professional consensus about the psychological factors that parents need to provide for their children (Baris & Garrity, 1988; Rohman et al., 1987; Schutz et al., 1989). A sample list of such factors, although *not* exhaustive, is included here. As described above regarding the organization of children's data, evaluators are encouraged to use a standard format around

QUICK REFERENCE   **Sample Questions Exploring Parental Ability to Meet Child's Needs**

1. Which parent provides the children with
   a. a safe environment?
   b. a secure environment?
   c. a predictable environment?
   d. a consistent environment?
   e. a stable environment?

2. Which parent is better able to meet the children's
   a. physical needs?
   b. material needs?
   c. financial needs?

3. Which parent respects and encourages the children's religious heritage?

4. Which parent respects and encourages the children's cultural identity?

5. How does each parent perceive each child's understanding of who the child views as the psychological parent?

6. How does each parent perceive each child's understanding of who the child views as the primary (secondary) caretaker?

7. Which parent provides the most encouragement for the children's educational performance?

8. Which parent provides the most guidance and assistance for the children's educational performance?

9. Which parent is available to help the children with their homework on a consistent basis?

10. Which parent provides a more flexible schedule?

11. Which parent provides better supervision?

12. Which parent provides a more reliable schedule?

13. How does each parent participate in each child's daily life?

14. In what ways are the age-related issues for which each child needs the other parent's involvement being appropriately addressed?

15. What is each parent's understanding of how each child feels about the current (proposed) parenting plan?

which the data may be organized. This may include creating a list of relevant factors drawn from the behavioral science literature or use of published parent questionnaire formats.

The examiner may gather data from several sources, including, but not limited to, the adult forensic interview; self-report questionnaire(s) com-

---

QUICK REFERENCE **Sample Questions Exploring Inter- and Intraparental Well-Being**

1. The emotional well-being of each parent
2. The lifestyle stability of each parent (i.e., job changes, residential changes, number of marriages)
3. History of alcohol or substance use or abuse and a rating of its severity
4. Communication skills
5. Accurate perception of each child
6. Ability to set appropriate emotional and physical boundaries
7. Quality of attachment to each child
8. Reasonable expectations of each child
9. Level of parental conflict
10. Type of parental conflict
11. Measurable signs of abnormal or psychopathological behavior
12. History of criminal behavior
13. History of physical, sexual, or emotional abuse
    a. perpetrated upon the parent when young
    b. perpetrated upon parent by other parent
    c. perpetrated by parent upon child
14. Intellectual level of functioning
15. Social and moral judgment and reasoning

---

pleted by each parent; and collateral sources such as former and current employers, former spouse or significant other, teachers, and coaches. Data may also be collected from standardized psychological testing, projective techniques, and direct observation of each parent, both individually and with the children.

Assessing the Parent-Child Goodness of Fit

The toughest part of the custodial decision making occurs at this stage. Prior to this stage, most decision making has involved which questions to ask and which instrument or technique to use in gathering the data. Now, the question becomes how to integrate the data; assign weights to the relative meaning of each factor; and make a responsible, fact-based decision about the lives of each person within this changing family system.

QUICK REFERENCE **Sample Questions Exploring Parent-Child Goodness of Fit**

1. Which parent is better able to support the children in their academic pursuits?
2. Which parent is more available to assist with homework?
3. Which parent places a greater emphasis on academic performance?
4. Which parent has the more reliable schedule that allows for consistent participation in the children's school activities as well as supervision of their school projects?
5. Which parent is more likely to support a child's further educational aspirations?
6. Which parent's cognitive style is more similar to that of the child?
7. Which parent's emotional make-up is more similar to that of the child?
8. Which parent's temperament is more similar to that of the child?
9. Which parent's problem-solving style is more similar to that of the child?
10. Which parent's personality features are more similar to those of the child?

There are no rules to follow. Some have tried, and in Chapter 13, Ackerman's ASPECT (Ackerman & Schoendorf, 1992) and Bricklin's ACCESS (Bricklin, 1984, 1990) are discussed as the first empirically grounded attempts to develop measures of custodial placement.

Many of the questions posed in the preceding sections may need to be examined further by assessing each parent's relative contribution to his or her child's development. Suggestions are provided regarding questions used in examining parent-child goodness of fit. Any custodial determination is, after all, a judgment call. It is decision making applied to real life. It is precisely this unique aspect of forensic work—rendering a conclusion based upon inferences drawn from the myriad of data—about which many of our colleagues voice great concern.

Psychiatrists, psychologists, and other mental health professionals are often called upon by the courts to provide evaluation, consultation, and expert testimony in a wide variety of criminal and civil matters. However, some legal authorities and mental health professionals have criticized, on a variety of grounds, the scientific bases of expert testimony that these professionals offer.

They cite the limitations of clinical judgement as particularly problematic when considering introduction of expert mental health testimony into evidence. . . . The extant literature nonetheless suggests that a variety of factors can operate to limit the accuracy of clinical judgement, regardless of its context. . . . This is particularly important when conducting forensic evaluations, given the nature of the questions and the legal and professional requirements that apply. (Borum et al., 1993, pp. 35-37)

The temptation to provide a conceptual framework for how to make custodial decisions is great. If the behavioral science literature was able to inform us about which factors are most relevant to measure and how to determine their relative weight in each custodial decision, our task would be, if not easy, at least clearly defined. There is no consensus either about relevant factors or how to determine weights for each factor in forensic decision making. There is, however, a substantial literature about how people make decisions and factors that contribute as well as interfere with effective decision making (Borum et al., 1993).

Rather than speculate how custody evaluators make judgments about sole versus joint custody or guess at how child custody decision making may occur, this section will summarize factors discussed in the behavioral science literature as confounding, diminishing, or threatening the reliability and validity of forensic decision making and the data upon which such decisions are made. It is hoped that increased awareness of factors affecting forensic decision making will result in better, more accurate observation of data; inferences drawn from these data; and ultimately, more useful custodial recommendations.

Factors Affecting Forensic Decision Making

There is a substantial behavioral science literature exploring how people make decisions. Better understanding regarding clinical judgment and decision making in child custody evaluations may aid in the production of better quality reports to the courts. Better quality reports ultimately serve four important purposes. First, a better quality report should reflect a better underlying social science. Second, a better report should more easily conform to rules governing admissibility of scientific evidence. Third, a better quality report should be more useful for the trier of fact in determining wise custody determinations. Fourth, a better quality report should help the families enduring the custodial determination process.

This section will review some of the literature pertaining to clinical judgment and forensic decision making as they are applied to child custody evaluations. Decision-making literature cuts across disciplines. It may be found in the social sciences, such as psychology, medicine, and business, as

---

QUICK REFERENCE   **Suggested Variables to Consider in**
                   Child Custody Decision Making

- Do not rely on memory
- Document, document, document
- Observe, infer, then conclude
- Consider simple (linear) versus complex (configurational) decision making
- Formulate specific psycholegal questions
- Development of good questions leads to well-chosen measurement tools
- Understand behavioral prevalence and base rates
- Always be aware of possible confirmatory bias
- Recognize the contribution of covariation and illusory correlation
- Control for the effects of hindsight bias
- Beware of overconfidence concerning the reliability and validity of your data, conclusions, and recommendations
- Guard against the tendency to overinterpret the meaning of unique data
- Know your tests and how they may be correlated

---

well as mathematics. For those unfamiliar with this literature, a useful introductory article is Borum et al. (1993); some of their decision-making factors are summarized here.

Factor 1: Do Not Rely on Memory

Too often, evaluators depend upon their recollection of interview data rather than take copious, contemporaneous notes. Because human beings store memories in a constructive and often nonsequential manner (Borum et al., 1993), overreliance on memory may result in a decrease of accurate information as well as an increase in judgment bias.

The decrease of accurate information results from our natural tendencies to recall things that are unique or special rather than those that are mundane. Yet it is the daily routines and mundane reality that helps determine the factual basis of our reports. Research has shown that it is much easier to remember information that has been prompted by another or that confirms a hypothesis or conclusion being considered. Information that is more vivid and exciting tends to be recalled more readily than does information about behaviors that occur every day. Finally, overreliance on memory often leads to inflated estimates of covariation. That is, people often believe that something has occurred more (or less) often than it really occurred when there is a greater amount of information. Note that the information does not have to contribute to any significant increase in the predictability of outcome. When human beings are exposed to high volumes of information, they tend to see patterns of similarity (covariation) where none exists.

Factor 2: Document, Document, Document

In light of the great potential for memory biases—and our uncanny ability to be unaware of their influence on our work product—forensic examiners should take steps to document as accurately as possible. There are some professionals who suggest that we videotape all interviews. When videotaping is not possible, then audiotape or take contemporaneous notes. The least favored technique is to take notes immediately after the interview.

Factor 3: Observe, Infer, Then Conclude

Another important way in which to minimize memory bias is to use a data-gathering method that requires the listing of behavioral observations as distinct from the inferences drawn from those observations. After itemizing the behavioral observations, develop a list of reasonable inferences or meanings that may be drawn from each observation. The more possible meanings drawn from the observations, the greater the chances are that bias will be eliminated. Finally, based upon the various types of data accumulated, the evaluator should be in a position to credibly examine each inference and the body of evidence that confirms or does not confirm it. Once the different inferences are weighed and assigned a value that is within a reasonable degree of psychological certainty, then the evaluator is in a position to make a statement of conclusion about the question at hand.

Factor 4: Simple Versus Complex Decision Making

Some experts insist that forensic decision making is a complex task in which the interactional relationships among various scores and data points are integrated into a configuration from which a final recommendation is opined. There are other experts who insist that forensic decision making is complex but proceeds along a linear rather than configural pathway. This group views decision making as an equal-weighting rather than a variable-weighting system (Borum et al., 1993).

Academic as this argument may sound, it has important implications for custody evaluators. It is precisely the evaluator's unique and specialized skill at extrapolating meaningful recommendations from a decision-making strategy that combines data from a variety of different people, a variety of different data sources, along a variety of different behavioral dimensions into a coherent whole.

If there are no rules governing the systematic application of forensic decision making to custody decisions, the question becomes, What is the quality, reliability, and validity of the data we present to the legal system?

There is no clear-cut answer to this important question. However, it is important to consider your decision-making strategy and how you weigh each variable in making your recommendations to the court.

When exploring your decision-making strategy, be aware of the issue of incremental validity in gathering your data (Borum et al., 1993). More information is not necessarily better information, nor does it yield better results. The most important question you can ask yourself is, How will this information further help me to arrive at a more valid opinion? Another question is, What will this information teach me that I do not already know? Furthermore, if you already have data to support an opinion, the question becomes, Will this information provide me with the type of quality data that can be used to support or disconfirm my present opinion?

Research has demonstrated that judgment accuracy improves somewhat when additional information of proven validity is provided (Borum et al., 1993). However, accepting data of questionable validity or data that have a lower validity than the data already gathered may not increase but decrease the quality of the judgment to be made.

Too often, evaluators gather more information than they need because of their uncertainty about the focus of the psycholegal question they are being asked to address. The thinking is that by gathering as much data as possible from as many different sources as possible, it becomes virtually impossible to be unable to answer any question posed by an attorney. Yet more information is not always better. For example, in conducting an assessment for a modification of custody between a sanitation worker father with a history of marijuana abuse and a bookkeeper mother with a history of prescription drug abuse, it may be important to gather information about current drug and alcohol use. For the father who is required under law to submit to random and for-cause drug and alcohol testing at work, there is a multiyear history of clean drug and alcohol tests. In fact, work records indicate four recent random drug screens over the past 24 months and no for-cause testing. Therefore, it would not be necessary to request additional drug and alcohol testing. The father is under continuous scrutiny by the county's workplace rules.

For the mother, whose business is not governed by the workplace rules of the Drug Free Workplace Act or any similar legislation, it may be appropriate to require drug testing during the evaluation process.

When the mother provides the examiner with the names of three close friends, former participants in a residential drug treatment facility at which the parents originally met, who will tell you about the substantial and continuous on-the-job drug use of the father, the question becomes, Do you interview these collateral sources?

The most important question to ask is whether the information provided by the collateral sources will assist you in developing a more valid opinion. If you decide that the collateral sources provide valid data useful in the question of continued drug use, then interview the sources. However, be prepared to answer questions about the comparative validity of the collateral's self-report information versus a multiyear history of drug and alcohol screening performed by a NIDA-certified laboratory whose results are checked by a medical review officer. The point is worth repeating: Consider the issue of incremental validity when gathering data during an evaluation.

Factor 5: Formulate Specific Psycholegal Questions

Another reason that many evaluators gather too much data is that they are unclear about how the data will be used. That is, they are unclear about the psycholegal questions posed by the court. It is not unusual, for example, for the court to order psychological evaluations of the plaintiff and defendant and their minor children. This question is so broad that it begs for further definition and focus. Yet how often do evaluators undertake an evaluation without first gaining clarity about the court's primary concerns?

Without focus from the court, how does the examiner know which type of "psychological evaluation" to conduct? One may argue that the obvious question is to conduct a child custody evaluation. Then, I ask, given the broad and varied factors involved in defining the child's best psychological interests, which of the many factors do we choose to assess? Is the choice of which factors to assess left up to the evaluator? Or are there specific concerns about specific child, parental, or parental child care behaviors that need attention?

Do not grapple with these questions in the solitude of your office. Evaluations are time-consuming, stressful to the parties, and expensive. If you are uncertain about what the court wants you to evaluate, ask!

Another reason to seek clarity of the referral question has to do with the ability of examiners to make quality judgments. Borum et al. (1993) suggest that there may be limitations on the amount of information that can be effectively and properly analyzed and integrated by evaluators in their forensic decision making.

It is easy to ask the court or attorneys to define the psycholegal questions that guide the report. Write a letter to either the judge or the attorneys of record asking for clarification. The first time or two that you request such focus, you may receive some mild resistance—particularly if the attorneys need to meet with the judge. However, once it becomes known that you need clearly stated, well-focused evaluation questions, the judges and attorneys will begin to provide such increased focus in their court orders or referral requests.

Factor 6: Good Questions Lead to Well-Chosen Measurement Tools

Once the questions are formulated, the choice of data-gathering tools can be made. The focused nature of the psycholegal questions should lead to identifying those measurement techniques and tools that are most helpful in efficiently gathering the data. For example, if the court is concerned about possible antisocial and impulsive behavior on the part of the father, choosing standardized measures of adjustment or psychopathology may be indicated. For example, the MMPI-2 and the MCMI-II each may provide useful data where a measure of healthy personality functioning, such as the 16PF, may not.

After the data-gathering tools are chosen, the evaluator will have an easier time determining the amount, frequency, and quality of data needed to draw reasonable (testable) inferences. Using this research paradigm helps to alleviate many of the continuous concerns about accuracy and veracity of self-report and projective measures in forensic examinations. By using instruments with known validity measures or techniques specifically designed to assess the specific behaviors of concern, confidence in the accuracy and veracity of the data is increased. When one carefully chooses the data-gathering tools to reflect the psycholegal questions, a common result should be a reduction in the confounding effect of gathering more data of limited validity (Borum et al., 1993).

Factor 7: Behavioral Prevalence and Base Rates

Base rate refers to the prevalence of a specific characteristic in a population. Research suggests that individuals do not sufficiently use base rate information when making judgments. For example, how often does a report include a statement that one or both parents have been depressed since the divorce, resulting in a reduction in pleasurable activities, an increase in irritability, and overall lower energy?

When considering base rate information, an important first task is to identify the population to which the evaluee belongs. Then, identify the behavior of concern—in this case, depression. Within the population of those individuals undergoing divorce and custody evaluations, is depression a likely behavior to observe? The answer is yes, it is somewhat common for individuals whose marriage has ended and who are engaged in custody litigation to show signs of depression.

The idea behind base rate information is to provide some estimate of the reasonableness of the set of observed child or parent behaviors within the population to which they belong. Children whose parents have divorced may be predicted to demonstrate some behaviors of distress or confusion more often than may children in intact families. Knowing which behaviors are more likely to occur within a population of children of divorce—that is, knowing the base rate of these behaviors within that specific population—helps to put into perspective the uniqueness and relative meaning of observed behaviors.

For example, in a recent custody modification trial, one expert testified that a well-functioning 7-year-old child needed to remove herself from her parents' divorce conflict. She stated that "this little girl's exposure to her parents' conflict is disturbing. We must find a way to rid this child of these stressors. My recommendation is to switch custody to the mother in the hope that this will rid the child of this stress."

I testified that the parents' level of conflict appeared to correspond to Garrity and Baris's "moderate" level of conflict. I stated that when examined from the perspective of children from moderately high parental divorce conflict, the range of possible child reactions may range from little disruption of daily life to severe disruption. The data from all sources indicated that this little girl was functioning wonderfully in school, had a wonderful and stable friendship circle, a positive and close relationship with her father, and wanted to continue her present custodial arrangement. I made the point that within the population of children drawn from moderately high parental divorce conflict, this little girl appeared to belong to a group of children that is coping very effectively with the externally imposed stressors of their parents' conflict.

It is essential that forensic decision making be based upon an analysis of the unique characteristics of the individual who is the focus of the examination *in relationship to* the comparison group of which he or she shares membership.

Factor 8: Confirmatory Bias

Confirmatory bias refers to the tendency to look for data that support your expectations (Borum et al., 1993). For example, an evaluator recently completed a report on a father who was alleged to have a drinking problem. No data supported the mother's allegation of his drinking, yet the evaluator was suspicious of a smoking gun. In the report the evaluator said, "It was probably about 9:00 when I called him to arrange an appointment. The line was busy for about half an hour after which Mr. B . . . answered. During our brief discussion he talked more slowly than was usual and his words were slurred. . . . He sounded to me as if he had been drinking."

This is an example of confirmatory bias. The examiner was looking for examples of alcohol use. The usual behavior observed over the phone may have had multiple explanations. It could have been the reaction of someone awoken from a deep sleep, or someone using prescription or over-the-counter medication. He may have recently hit his head and was groggy, he may have been drinking alcohol, or many other possible explanations. The evaluator reported her bias as the only possible explanation. Even if she had considered other explanations of the data, the report represented to the judge only one possible explanation.

The initial error of being unaware of confirmatory bias and allowing only one explanation of the data to influence her interpretation is compounded by introducing that bias in the body of the report as the only possible explanation. The examiner's bias resulted in a data presentation that may have significantly influenced the judge to believe that the litigant may have been drunk. Thus, the examiner's confirmatory bias may have now been adopted by the judge.

Confirmatory bias is contagious. It is spread through subtle messages that appear on the surface to make sense. In a recent case, I was quite disturbed to run into a powerful bias I held about a mother I was evaluating. The court pleadings, as well as the woman's attorney, informed me that the mother had "abandoned her children two years ago, lived in a trailer, was a high school drop out, married her first cousin, and had numerous allegations of physical abuse and neglect against her and her husband investigated by DSS." Before I began the evaluation, I was aware of how negatively I felt toward the mother.

Following the suggestions of Borum et al. (1993), I listed as many alternative hypotheses as possible to my initial expectations of finding an incompetent mother. I also specifically searched for data that might disconfirm my initial hypothesis. Ceci and Bruck (1995) recommend deliberately seeking out data that will *not* support your bias. Finally, I sought a professional consultant who aided in double-checking my work to ensure that I was not allowing my initial bias to influence either my data collection or the interpretation of the data.

Confirmatory bias is insidious because we often do not know that we hold certain beliefs. Even when we effectively overcome the bias in the data-gathering phase, it is just as important to be vigilant of the bias tendency when interpreting or forming conclusions from the data.

Decision-making research has demonstrated that human beings have a tendency to underrevise initial hypotheses. In the words of Borum et al. (1993):

There is a tendency to not revise an opinion based on disconfirmatory evidence, and, when a revision is made, it is often not revised substantially enough, given the subsequent information. . . . In reevaluating [forensic] hypotheses the evaluator needs to be aware of the general tendency to be drawn to initially established hypotheses. (p. 49)

As evaluators, we are trained to be objective surveyors of human behaviors. However, we also fall prey to our personal and professional biases that may subtly affect our view of the data. It is incumbent upon each of us to be continuously aware of how issues of confirmatory bias may influence our reading of the data. It is also important to know how your awareness of your bias and attempts to limit or eliminate its effect may alter the data in the opposite direction (e.g., by paying less attention to relevant variables precisely because they support your initial expectations).

Factor 9: Covariation and Illusory Correlations

How do we know when a *true* relationship exists between two observed events? I observe that when Event A occurs, so does Event B. Is it genuinely related or coincidence?

For example, parents from the Smyth family have agreed upon a residential arrangement in which the children spend every weekend with their father and every weekday with their mother. On Friday evening, children from the Smyth family are picked up by their father for a weekend at the beach. Each weekend they are with their father, they spend time at their father's beach house. Lo and behold, the Smyth children discover an intriguing relation. When they visit their father, they do not attend school. Does that mean that if the Smyth children visited their father during a weekday, there would be no school, too?

Covariation refers to whether or not there is a true relationship between two or more factors or variables. In clinical decision making, examination of covariation often occurs in the context of determining whether observed behaviors do or do not fit a diagnostic category. A related issue involves the phenomenon of "illusory correlation."

Determination of covariation is concerned with whether movement in one factor is associated with movement in another. Individuals examined for their emotional reaction to separation may display signs that appear similar to a generalized anxiety reaction. However, upon further exploration, the phenomenon is found to be associated only with activities directly involved in contact with the former spouse.

Borum et al. (1993) provide a conceptual framework through which to evaluate covariation. They describe a 2 × 2 grid juxtaposing Sign/Symptom × Disorder/Condition. This yields the matrix shown in Figure 11.1.

	Disorder/Condition Present	Disorder/Condition Absent
Sign/Symptom Present	A	B
Sign/Symptom Absent	C	D

Figure 11.1. Conceptual Model to Analyze Covariation (Adapted from Borum et al., 1993)

The examples involve determining the covariation of behavioral signs or symptoms with the differential diagnosis of a disorder. In Cell A are those observations in which both signs and symptoms as well as the accurate diagnosis of the disorder are present. This is a true decision that the diagnosis exists.

Cell B represents those instances in which the signs and symptoms are present, but the diagnosis is not. That is, in Cell B are those cases in which the behaviors appear to fit the diagnostic criteria but are not, in fact, symptomatic of the diagnosis. This is commonly called a false positive.

Cell C are those instances in which the signs and symptoms are not present, yet the diagnosis is appropriate. Such instances often result in the misdiagnosis of the behavior because the signs and symptoms that are primary indicators of the diagnosis are not present. This is commonly called a false negative.

The final cell contains those cases in which there are no signs or symptoms as well as no diagnosis. This is a true decision that no diagnosis exists.

Borum et al. (1993) point out that individuals most often draw conclusions based only upon the data represented in Cell A. Again, it is incumbent upon forensic evaluators to understand the distribution of scores across all four cells. If the probability of an individual drawn from a particular population is 5% (Cell A), we may need to know that 80% fall into Cell D. Thus, our statements of confidence regarding our diagnostic accuracy may need to be framed within the unique distribution of this characteristic in the population. That is, we may need to make a statement about how unusual it is to find a true diagnosis of this particular behavior within a particular population.

A related concept is the *illusory correlation*. In the area of custody evaluation, the question may involve a child's reaction to parental transfer after a weekend visit. "Every time I drop off Jimmy at his mom's home after my weekend, he cries, he pleads with me not to go away and says he wants to live with me. This is why I decided to file for custody of my child."

What are the possible explanations for this child's behavior? One hypothesis is that the child genuinely wants to live with his father. Another is that the child is reacting to the stress associated with the transition from his father's weekend visit to residential placement with his mother. A third hypothesis is that no matter who the child is with, each transition from each parent results in a similar set of behaviors.

One way to examine these different hypotheses is to organize them into a hierarchy from most likely to least likely. Then, seek out information about each hypothesis. In this case, the child demonstrated identical behavior during transition from each parental home. Thus, the father's interpretation that the child's statements were associated only with movement from his home to the mother's was not supported by the data. The correlation was illusory, an artifact of the circumstances and not supported by the data.

In both covariation and illusory correlations, most errors come from an incomplete assessment of the relationship between the sign or symptom and its apparent outcome. Evaluators need to understand two important bits of information. First, they need to know the co-occurrence of the proper symptoms and proper diagnosis. They also need to know the co-occurrence of the proper diagnosis without the proper symptoms. Only when the occurrence of the symptoms is greater in the presence of the target behavior (or diagnosis) than in its absence do these observations have any diagnostic potential (Borum et al., 1993).

Illusory correlations are a version of confirmatory bias. They are a type of error that comes from the intuitive connection of events that "seem to go together" or relationships that "seem to make sense" (Borum et al., 1993, p. 52). To counter the temptation to use illusory correlation, the examiner needs to be well grounded in the empirical relationship between the observed and expected behavior. Thus, statements such as, "In my 20 years of clinical experience . . . " should never cross your lips when testifying as an evaluator in a custodial matter. You either know the empirical data, or you offer no opinion drawn from the behavioral science literature. If you are asked for an expert opinion about an issue that has no empirical grounding, it is critical that you state this to the court clearly, "Your Honor, I offer the court an opinion on this question. There is no empirical literature that addresses this issue. However, my expert opinion is . . . "

When asked to provide unscientific opinion testimony in the role of evaluator, I strongly encourage colleagues to offer such opinions with great care. The court must be fully informed when the offering of an opinion is based on scientific data that are admissible under Federal Rules of Evidence (FRE) 702, 703, and 705. Similarly, when testifying as an evaluator and offering opinion about nonscientific information, the evaluator needs to be particularly vigilant in advising the court of the quality of the data. Offering nonscientific opinion data in the role of an expert is permissible under FRE 702. Clearly distinguishing between scientific and nonscientific is important in assisting the trier of fact in assigning weights given to certain types of evidence.

The same recommendation is given when a treating therapist is providing testimony to the court. The clinician may be allowed to offer opinion testimony under FRE 701 that is not based on reasoning or theory but is rationally based on perceptions (Goodman-Delahunty, 1997). However, the witness should inform the court that the opinion is not based on scientific theory or data. In this way, opinion testimony can be presented to the court in a manner that accurately reflects the relative contributions of science and rationally derived opinion from everyday experience (Goodman-Delahunty, 1997).

Mental health professionals, in their role as evaluators for the court, only cautiously should offer opinions that have no basis in behavioral science literature. There is a growing research base of analogue studies demonstrating that mock juries recall and weigh more heavily the testimony of an expert than a lay witness. Although I am aware of no research on the topic, I suspect that judges may be prone to interpreting data in much the same way as laypeople. That is, judges may weigh more heavily the testimony of an expert simply because the "expert" designation may prepare the judge to accept testimony under the assumption that the expert has knowledge beyond that of the average layperson. If the evaluator's testimony is not based upon behavioral science literature, then one must ask, What scientific value does it provide to the court?

Ceci and Bruck (1995) suggest that a major part of the problem is the vagueness of the definition of "expert." They state:

> The Federal Rules of Evidence 702 states that if scientific, technical, or other specialized knowledge will assist a fact finder in understanding evidence, a witness may be regarded as an expert by virtue of his knowledge, skill, experience, training, or education. This rule construes expertise broadly enough to cover all fields, including emerging areas within fields, and is constrained by two other Federal Rules of Evidence (401 and 403), which specify that the expert testimony must be relevant. Together, these Federal Rules allow virtually anyone who possesses an advanced degree, or who has some clinical experience, to offer expert testimony . . . even though the expert may have scant knowledge of the current scientific findings. (p. 284)

Goodman-Delahunty (1997) suggests that the recent *Daubert* ruling will help redefine the ambiguities in deciding who and what is expert testimony. Golding (1992) states that most of the controversy in admitting expert testimony is knowing when specialized knowledge and/or scientific data are sufficiently reliable and valid to qualify as expertise. The *Daubert* standard appears to provide a framework for resolving such uncertainty.

> Many commentators believe that *Daubert* will result in a more rigorous standard for the admissibility of scientific evidence than that under *Frye*. . . . This viewpoint is premised on the notion that by abandoning the emphasis on consensus in the scientific community, the *Daubert* Court excluded methodolo-

gies that may be endorsed by large numbers of professionals in the field but which lack specific scientific characteristics. Per *Daubert,* scientific knowledge must be "grounded in fact" derived by way of the scientific method. The method must generate hypotheses that can be proven or disproven, and that may be refuted. (p. 132)

The *Daubert* standard appears to place greater scrutiny upon the expert's use of scientific theory, methods, and procedures. There may never be any control over how inferences drawn from such methods and procedures may be developed. However, the focus on expert scientific testimony needing to reveal an underlying theory of science as well as the use of scientific methods and procedures sets a higher standard for the admissibility of expert scientific evidence (Golding, 1992; Goodman-Delahunty, 1997).

Factor 10: Hindsight Bias

Everyone can make better judgments after the fact. Hindsight bias "refers to the fact that after an event has taken place, its occurrence seems so inevitable that one believes that it could have easily been predicted in advance" (Borum et al., 1993, p. 53).

In custody evaluations, there may be a temptation to examine parenting decisions retrospectively in an effort to determine whether a parent should have anticipated the outcome of his or her behavior or decision differently than its real-life outcome. Especially when evaluating parenting behavior occurring in a family in transition, it is often difficult to view the parent's decision in the same manner, within the same context, and feel the same emotional and environmental pressures. Thus, applying an examiner's dispassionate, objective analysis may result in weighing, indeed, seeing, different factors than the parent considered. The challenge is whether examining past parenting judgments is a fair and accurate way of examining parenting competence.

One solution is to generate and list the reasons for alternative behaviors under the conditions that occurred at the time. Engage the parent in a discussion of the different possible solutions, examining each solution for its underlying logic and parenting competence. There will be times when what appears to be an inappropriate parenting decision viewed through today's lens is a reasonable decision when viewed through yesterday's framework.

Factor 11: Overconfidence

There is considerable debate about the force with which we offer our opinions. Some colleagues argue that forensic experts express more confidence in their judgments than is justified by the data (Borum et al., 1993). Overconfidence is an important issue in forensic evaluations for two reasons.

First, an overzealous expert may affect the judge's interpretation of the data. An overconfident expert may lead the judge to conclude that the testimony is "true." Similarly, testimony that is offered in which the expert presents as uncertain may convey the message that the data upon which the conclusions are based are similarly uncertain.

The second reason is that overconfidence on the part of the expert may lead to overlooking critical evidence because it does not fit with the expressed judgment. As discussed earlier in the section on confirmatory bias, it is incumbent upon examiners to be aware of how our biases and zealous support of our position do not lead us to stop searching for disconfirming data.

What leads to overconfidence? Some examiners forget that our data are based upon tools of stated reliability and validity, not truth. The validity of an opinion is only as strong as its empirical foundation. Thus, strong opinions are based on strong empirical data, and weak opinions are based on weak empirical data. The statements we make about our confidence in the conclusions should reflect the validity of the data upon which we make our decisions.

Factor 12: Focus and Use of Unique Data

Frequently, custody reports will be submitted that contain stories depicting parental competencies/incompetencies. These stories often are drawn from unsubstantiated stories provided by one party or a collateral source close to one party. They often involve vignettes that, supposedly, are examples of overall parenting competencies. In the example below, a grandmother interviewed as a collateral source was attempting to show how, despite her daughter's illness, the children still came first.

> After Joe left, my Sarah had to take care of these two precious little children and work at the same time. Her life was miserable. She had no time to figure out what was happening to her life. Her life was her children and her work. I remember she got the flu just after Joe left. She called and begged him to help with the children. I know because I took her to the doctor! She was sick. Fever. Medicine. She had to take medicine from a doctor. That Joey, he didn't help when his children needed him the most!
>
> Sarah couldn't get out of bed. But, you know what that woman did? This will prove how good a mother she is. She still drove Mary and Rob to school and picked them up. She made them lunch. She checked over their homework. She took them to soccer practice and girl scouts and piano and still she didn't complain. What does that tell you, Mr. Doctor? My daughter is one good parent, isn't she?

Upon further exploration, the story was told differently by the father, physician, children's teachers, and neighbors. Sarah refused all help because she did not want to appear weak or demonstrate she could not take care of her children when she was ill. Thus, the apparently unique data were, in fact, a biased interpretation of the data as discovered through further collateral interviews.

Other types of unique data that may appear as important statements about parental competencies involve one-time experiences. These one-time experiences may appear to be useful metaphors for how the parent handles other, similar situations. However, a single incident does not make a trend. No matter how strong or compelling the unique example, evaluators need to determine trends. Predictions based on trends are typically more accurate because of the larger database than are predictions based on a single event.

Factor 13: Correlated Measures

Often, evaluators use different measures to examine a behavior. There are two situations where this may occur. Situation 1 is when test results are unclear. Typically, examiners select another test that purports to measure the same dimensions. As Borum et al. (1993) point out, the potential problem with this strategy is that the measures may be highly correlated. When a second test, highly correlated with the first, is administered, the results may tell us less about the behavior of concern and more about how different tests measure the same behavior. The similarity in results may result from "redundancy in measurement rather than incremental information about the examinee's ability or condition" (p. 63). The solution to this quandary is to select a second test that is positively correlated with the criterion but negatively correlated with the first instrument.

Situation 2 happens when the evaluator is attempting to measure the same criterion using a variety of different measures. The evaluator must explore whether the results are a function of true convergence upon the behavior or the result of the correlation between the different measures. The solution is to be knowledgeable about the concurrent validity of different measures. This information is usually found in the test manuals in the section addressing validity. Again, examine the convergent data with an eye toward measurement redundancy.

Summary

This section has reviewed some of the factors affecting forensic decision making. This review is not intended to be either exhaustive or comprehensive. Rather, it is intended to provide a conceptual overview of some of the salient decision-making factors that may influence how examiners make custody decisions.

There is an extensive literature pertaining to forensic and clinical decision making. It is incumbent upon the evaluator to maintain an active awareness of new research identifying confounding factors that introduce error into our decision-making process.

Research Examining How Evaluators Make Decisions About Parenting Plans

Among the most difficult tasks of a custody evaluator is the consistent application of a set of decision-making criteria that accurately reflects the relative weight of the variables assessed. There is no universal formula for decision making. In fact, there are few, if any, empirically examined decision-making models in the field of custody determination. However, there is some information about the *attitudes and beliefs* that evaluators hold regarding how they make decisions about custody determinations.

In Chapter 2, we discussed two studies that have explored the practice habits of mental health professionals involved in custodial determinations. Both the Keilin and Bloom (1986) and Ackerman and Ackerman (1996, 1997) studies attempted to determine attitudes held by examiners in the decision-making process. In this section, discussion will describe *how* custody evaluators think they make their decisions and the relative weight they assign different variables.

Custodial Preference

Do evaluators tend toward recommending sole or joint custodial arrangements? A review of the literature indicates that current thinking is that children need as much time with each parent as possible. Do evaluators' attitudes and practices support conventional wisdom?

The answer appears to be "yes." In the Ackerman and Ackerman (1996, 1997) study, respondents indicated that they prefered "joint custody with primary placement with one parent" almost half of the time (46.4%). The second most common practice was to award "single parent/sole custody with visitation" almost a third of the time (31.7%). The third most often endorsed custodial arrangement was reported to be "joint custody with shared placement," and it was recommended 17.5% of the time. The final category endorsed by practicing evaluators was "single parent/sole custody without visitation." This recommendation was preferred only 2.7% of the time.

Overall, evaluators tended to agree that joint custody was a better choice for children. When asked to endorse joint versus sole custody on a 5-point Likert-type scale, rating from 1 = *poor idea* to 5 = *very good idea,* joint custody arrangements rated a 4, compared with sole custody, which rated a 3.1. Seldom did evaluators recommend splitting placement of children between parents. This option was endorsed only 6.4% of the time. Foster placement was endorsed at an even lower rate, achieving only 2.9%. Mediation, which was discussed in Chapter 9, was recommended almost half of the time (48.5%).

Finally, a majority of practicing evaluators indicated that they should be allowed to testify to the ultimate issue (64.6%). About 20% believed they should not testify to the ultimate legal issue, whereas about 7% indicated they did not know, and 6% did not know what the "ultimate issue" meant.

Factors Contributing to Custodial Determination

Custody evaluators who made recommendations for sole custody cited five important factors that contributed to their decision making. Sole custody would most often be recommended when the parent was found "psychotic, mentally ill, or unable to function." Factors in which a parent was found to be unable to communicate, resolve conflicts, or unwilling to cooperate constituted the second category of reasons why sole custody would be recommended. A third category of factors that affected the decision to suggest sole custody was "evidence of physical or sexual abuse." These factors were followed in importance by concerns for "alcohol or other drug abuse" and "geographical distance between parents."

Sole custody determinations tended to be less likely when the evaluator observed that the child was attached and bonded to both parents as well as showed evidence of a positive relationship with each parent. A second factor that argued against sole custody was the ability of both parents to cooperate. The remaining factors, in order of their relative importance, were "sole custody excludes other parent," "both parents have equal skills," and "sole custody facilitates alienation."

Joint custody was endorsed most often as the preferred option when the evaluator observed good communication and cooperation between the parents as well as an absence of conflict. Joint custody was also suggested when the child was observed to have developed positive attachment to each parent. The final three factors that contributed to how evaluators made recommendations for joint custody, in order of importance, were "both parents psychologically healthy," "more parenting and child rearing for both parents," and "desires of parents."

Evaluators preferred not to recommend joint custody when they observed that the parents did not cooperate or communicate well. They also shied away from joint custody when parents demonstrated conflict or hostility toward each other. Geographical distance was the third factor that entered into the decision against joint custody. The final two factors, in order of importance, were "family/domestic violence history" and "children cannot adjust to transitions/too young."

Factors Affecting Sole
Custody Recommendations

When examining how custody evaluators make their decisions in the realm of sole custody, three options must be explored: Awarding custody to Parent A, who was the primary caretaker; awarding custody to Parent B, who was not the primary caretaker; and awarding custody to neither parent.

Parent A was chosen over Parent B when there was evidence that Parent B was an active alcoholic. Another factor was when Parent B attempted to alienate the child from the other parent by negatively interpreting the other parent's behavior. A third reason was when Parent A displayed better parenting skills than Parent B. A fourth factor was Parent A's active participation in the child's education.

Other relevant factors included predivorce history of Parent A as a primary caretaker, Parent B displaying significantly lower intelligence than Parent A, Parent A remaining in the predivorce school district while Parent B moved to another school district, and Parent A's economic stability.

Reasons arguing for placement of a child with Parent B included child having a closer emotional bond, the parent showing greater psychological stability, Parent A not being cooperative with previous court orders, Parent A threatening to move to another state with the child, Parent A showing more anger and bitterness about the divorce, and Parent A being less tolerant of the other parent's visitation.

Other relevant factors included awarding Parent B sole custody when Parent A used physical punishment, had a criminal record, had significantly worse MMPI results, or needed to place the child in day care when Parent B did not; Parent B had more extended family available; and predivorce history indicated that Parent B had primary responsibility for disciplining the child.

Factors that appeared not to be particularly important in the decision making about sole custody included physical or sexual abuse allegations against a parent, evidence of a parent being a recovering alcoholic, parental taking of prescribed psychiatric medication, a new partner living with a parent without marriage, involvement in a homosexual relationship, level of parental social activity, parent and child of the same sex, a parent's remarriage while the other parent remains single, or whether the parent was the mother or father.

Factors Affecting Joint
Custody Determinations

The ability of parents to separate their marital difficulties from their parenting decisions was endorsed as the factor most often associated with joint custodial recommendations. Another important factor is the quality of relationship that the child has with each parent. A third factor arguing for joint custodial placement is the psychological stability of each parent. Parental willingness to enter into a joint custody arrangement is also important.

Other factors related to joint custody decision making included parental problems with substance abuse, amount of anger and bitterness between the parents, a parent's problems with the law, differences in parental discipline style, flexibility in parents' work schedule, geographic proximity of parental homes, a child's school behavior, and age of the child.

Many other factors were cited, decreasing in frequency of weight in evaluator decision making.

Children's Wishes

An interesting note is that evaluators tended to weigh the wishes of a child when the child was over the age of 15 significantly more heavily than those of younger children. Evaluators considered the wishes of 10-year-olds to an extent, and they paid little attention to the wishes of 5-year-olds.

Summary

Results from the Ackerman and Ackerman study appear to suggest that among the factors most often identified as playing a significant role in sole custody recommendations are active substance abuse, parental alienation, parenting skills, psychological stability of the parent, and emotional bonding with the child. Joint custody arrangements appear to incorporate decisions such as ability to separate adult interpersonal difficulties from parenting decisions, quality of parent-child relationship, substance abuse problems, psychological stability of the parents, amount of anger and bitterness between parents, and the willingness of parents to enter into a joint custodial arrangement. Custody evaluators tend to make their determination based upon an examination and weighing of many variables. Evaluators are less likely to make a recommendation to the court based upon a single issue.

How to Use the Ackerman and Ackerman Results

The results of the Ackerman and Ackerman (1996, 1997) study provide a useful guide for practitioners in determining whether the standards and practitioner-reported decision-making factors used in an evaluation procedure are similar to those reported by a sample of current practitioners from across the United States. In their concluding section, Ackerman and Ackerman (1996) urge attorneys to explore the degree to which a particular evaluation follows convention. They state:

When a child custody evaluation is performed in a manner that is outside the ranges of responses, the attorney should use that information as part of cross-examination of the psychological expert. . . . When examining Tables 7 and 8, the attorney recognizes that psychologists give more weight to some issue areas and less weight to other issue areas. If a psychologist is ignoring an area that is near the top of the list, or putting too much weight [on one] that is near the bottom, the attorney should question these responses as part of determining the psychologist's rationale for these weightings. (pp. 585-586)

It is critically important that each evaluator explore his or her implicit decision-making model regarding custodial recommendations. Each of us needs to have a reasonably good explanation about why certain variables are more important in our decision-making scheme than others. It is best that such explanations are grounded in the behavioral science literature pertaining to custody evaluations, child development, adult development, and family systems.

Without a well-considered underlying logic driving custodial decision making, the evaluator leaves him- or herself open to an attorney's proper examination aimed at revealing the evaluator's lack of considered, empirically grounded, or logically derived explanations. For each psychological variable discussed in the report, the evaluator should be able to provide to the court a reasonable explanation as to why certain factors were included. The evaluator also should be able to discuss the weight assigned to each psychological variable in the final custodial determination. Finally, the evaluator should be able to discuss how the factors considered relevant in the report reflect the standards of professional practice within the field.

TWELVE

Developing Parenting Plans

> I need to touch my children. I need to see 'em smile. I need to hear their laugh, cries, hell, even their fights. There's nothing like living with your kids. Remember this, Doc, because for me, it's too late. Court told me once how important I am in their life. Ain't gonna tell me again. I'm gonna find a way to see my kids more. Bet on it.
>
> *Bruce, a 30-year-old father involved*
> *in a custody modification dispute*

Parenting plans are hypotheses. They are not facts. Evaluators develop best-guess scenarios about how certain children living under particular circumstances at transient developmental levels in a new family structure with parents whose lives have been turned upside down will fare in some novel arrangement of time with each parent in different geographical locations. Although this is a complex and awkward sentence, it is even more complex to understand and evaluate.

Parenting plans are experiments in social engineering guided by little, if any, empirical research. They are works in progress, needing to be continually reassessed for their usefulness with a particular family. This is not to say that families have to be continually reevaluated by a professional examiner. Rather, families change, and parenting plans—or at least the administrators and enforcers of those plans—need to be cognizant of and responsive to changing, dynamic family systems. A parenting plan that works with preschool children may be inadequate to meet the emerging needs of a preadolescent. A parenting plan established when parents lived within 10 minutes of each other may not adequately address the children's needs when one parent moves to another state. Similarly, a parenting plan developed for two single parents struggling with their new, separate households may need to be revised upon the remarriage of one or both parents.

Developing a Conceptual Model

Baris and Garrity (1988; Garrity & Baris, 1994) suggest that a well-balanced parenting plan takes into account the dynamic, continuously evolving nature of family systems. No one parenting plan fits every 5-year-old. Similarly, no one parenting plan fits every family with two children. There are individual differences within, between, and among the members of the divorcing family.

There are two critical components to a well-developed parenting plan: What the children need and what the parents are capable of providing. In what follows, the developmental needs of children across different ages will be discussed. It is assumed that for successful parenting plans to be implemented, parents engage in minimal or mild conflict over the children.

However, not all parents are able to overcome their strong feelings toward the other parent. When parental conflict becomes moderate or more severe, different ideas about parenting need to be explored. Accordingly, after discussion of parenting plans for children of different ages in minimal- to mild-conflict families, there will be a discussion of how to develop parenting plans for parents engaged in at least moderate levels of parental conflict.

Developmental Guidelines for Children From Infancy to 2½ Years

Infants are the most vulnerable to changes in their environment because of the challenges presented in developing attachment (Main, 1996) and basic trust (Baris & Garrity, 1988). Infants may build strong attachments to primary caretakers and, when separated from these caretakers, may experience a profound sense of loss, depression, and behavioral and emotional regression (Bowlby, 1969, 1980; Main, 1996). Included here are some developmental guidelines for the infant and toddler.

In those instances in which a separation or divorce results in a residential change, the infant may experience a sense of loss of familiarity and comfort (Baris & Garrity, 1988). Thus, it may be important to consider either (a) continuing placement in the familiar and comfort environment or (b) examining the degree to which the residential placement is similar to that of the marital home (Bray, 1991).

Examining the infant's attachment behavior may provide a useful set of data about present behavior and may also be predictive of later behavior. Another way to analyze infant attachment behavior is as a means of categorizing parental caretaking behavior (see Chapter 7). Finally, an infant's normal development will involve stranger anxiety, object constancy, and separation anxiety. Exploration of how each child is progressing through these developmental milestones yields valuable information.

QUICK REFERENCE **Developmental Guidelines From Infancy to 2½**

Primary developmental tasks
- Infants need to build trust and attachments.
- Toddlers need to balance opportunities for independence with security of caretaker presence.

Challenges to well-being
- Infants may experience a profound sense of loss, depression, or behavioral and emotional regression resulting from disruption in attachment to primary caregivers.
- Toddlers may experience similar reactions based upon loss of diminished contact with caretaker. Toddlers may also show confusion, cognitive and linguistic disorganization, and overall maladjustment. They may demonstrate difficulty in attachment (reunion).

Toddlers begin to venture into their environment and need opportunities to explore their newfound independence with the knowledge that their caretaker is near. Older toddlers show increasing signs of self-awareness, use of language, parallel play, and activity. Similar to infants' reactions, toddlers will feel a strong sense of loss with diminished contact with a primary caretaker. Disruption in attachment behaviors may lead to depression, confusion, cognitive and linguistic disorganization, and overall maladjustment.

Toddlers who are too long separated from primary caretakers may demonstrate difficulty with attachment (reunion), separation and the resultant need to independently explore the environment, and the development of healthy relationships in later stages of development (Baris & Garrity, 1988). How the toddler is progressing through the challenges of separation and individuation may be valuable information for the examiner.

Residential Arrangements

When parents live close to each other, the selection of a primary caretaker is based on caretaking history (Baris & Garrity, 1988). Because the primary developmental tasks of the infant are to create healthy attachments and build basic trust in his or her surroundings, there is some consensus suggesting that the primary caregiver during the marriage needs to be maintained as the primary caregiver during the divorce. The reasoning is that when the child feels tense, uncertain, or frightened, it is the primary caretaker to whom the child turns to regain a sense of security, safety, and comfort (Rohman et al., 1987). Another argument is that the primary caregiver has been established in the child's mind as the psychological parent. During a time when the child's world has been turned upside down because of the termination of the marriage, the young child is most in need of a safe, secure attachment figure with whom to regain a sense of protection (Goldstein et al., 1979; Rohman et al., 1987).

However, the notion of the primary caretaker has been challenged by Henry (1991) and Warshak (1992, 1993), and the concept of the psychological parent has been challenged as empirically unsupported (Rohman et al., 1987).

Because of the infant's as-yet-undeveloped sense of object permanence, he or she may profit from frequent and somewhat short-lived visits with the nonresidential parent (Bray, 1991) rather than the typical weekend visits often recommended by the courts. In those instances in which history supports the view of both parents being primary caretakers and psychological parents of the child, the infant may be best served by sharing caretaker duties in relatively equal time distribution. Baris and Garrity (1988) recommend sharing daytime caretaking yet establishing one nighttime caretaker. I do not know of any empirical literature that either supports or refutes their recommendation. I suggest exploring how the child copes with overnights at each primary caretaker's home. As Bray (1991) points out, children often have many primary caretakers and appear to demonstrate no ill effects from spending time with multiple caretakers.

When the parents live far apart, the challenge is to encourage the child's relationship with the nonresidential parent while also respecting the developmental limitations imposed on the child by memory functioning and other basic infant needs. There is some professional consensus that both parents need to travel to the other party's home. In the case of the custodial parent traveling to the nonresidential parent's home, the child is given an opportunity to visit in the nonresidential parent's home. In the case of the nonresidential parent visiting the custodial parent, the child is given the opportunity to visit with the other parent in the child's environment. In this way, the child invites the nonresidential parent into his or her world and involves the nonresidential parent in his or her daily routine.

Major concerns about dysfunctional reactions include withdrawal from social contact, depression, anger, regression, prolonged separation anxiety, and delay of critical developmental milestones (Baris & Garrity, 1988). Another concern is disorganized and disoriented interaction with the environment after loss of attachment figure (Main, 1996).

2½ to 5 Years Old

The preschool child is changing in wondrous and challenging ways. The preschooler is continuing the stretch toward individuality. At this age, chil-

---

QUICK REFERENCE **Developmental Guidelines for the Preschool Child**

Primary developmental tasks

- Preschool children are socially active, needing ritual and structure to guide their day.
- Significant verbal development includes expression of feelings, needs, and purpose.
- Memory capacity improves, allowing child to hold the memory of the absent parent in mind.
- There is a continued building of trust with the world, including social and familial relationships. Children are highly sensitive to having their basic needs met by their parents.

Challenges to well-being

- Magical thinking may result in the child believing that he or she is responsible for the divorce.
- The need for safety and continuity is directly threatened with increased visitation with each parent. The result is that the child does not handle transitions well.
- Age-appropriate awareness of abandonment and caretaking is accentuated by separate parental residences.

---

dren often need a ritual surrounding many activities. The structure that the ritual provides aids in the establishment of the preschooler's sense of safety, security, and predictability of his or her environment.

Verbal skills are exploding for the preschooler, as is an increasing awareness of the universe around him or her. Verbal skill development often involves expression of feelings, needs, and purpose. There is an increasing identification with the same-sex parent as gender identification becomes a prominent developmental milestone.

The memory functions of the preschooler change considerably from $2\frac{1}{2}$ through 5 years old. Most preschoolers, especially older preschoolers, develop the memory capacity to hold the absent parent in mind as a source of comfort for lonelier periods of time (Baris & Garrity, 1988). Thus, visitation may occur over longer periods of time, with weekend visits common.

Magical thinking is a common characteristic of this stage of development. Thus, a concern about the preschooler's adjustment to separation and divorce is the degree to which the child believes he or she is responsible for the marital dissolution. Children of this age are also concerned about having their basic needs met by their parents. Anxiety about feeding ("Who will feed me?"), residential placement ("Where will I live?"), and abandonment ("Will you leave me the way that Daddy left me?") are common and need to be openly discussed with each child.

The magical thinking of the preschooler is an important and powerful force in the child's life. The child may have frequent fantasies about the parents reuniting. The child may play games that involve an intact family or, alternatively, express anger through fantasy games in which one parent is killed off. The challenge for parents is to encourage the child's use of fantasy as an effective means of coping with anger and frustration, while at the same time not rewarding the fantasy play so that it takes on secondary reinforcing properties.

Finally, preschool children have a notoriously difficult time with transition from one parent to the other (Baris & Garrity, 1988). Bray (1991) provides some suggestions about how to explore the child's adaptation to residential transitions by examining how long the child takes to calm down after the transition.

Residential Arrangements

Preschool children are increasingly able to handle longer periods of time away from their primary caretaker. However, it is important to remember that the child needs the primary caretaker to aid in the maintenance of emotional as well as environmental safety and security. Thus, preschool children may spend 2 or 3 days away from their primary caretaker, but daily phone contact should be encouraged. As the child moves closer to age 5, visitations can move toward half- to full-week visits.

Initially, early-stage preschoolers should be moved gently into a single overnight with the nonresidential parent. As the child becomes increasingly accustomed to being away from the primary caretaker, and as the secondary caretaker begins to competently take on more primary caretaking responsibilities during overnights, the child may begin to comfortably expand his or her understanding of primary caretaker to include the nonresidential parent. Such a conceptual shift helps the child to feel a somewhat equivalent degree of safety, security, and comfort with both parents. When each parent actively seeks to encourage the child to maintain phone contact with the other parent during overnight visits, the child learns that each parent is no farther than a phone call away.

When parents live far apart, the preschooler may build toward a 2- to 3-day overnight with the other parent. However, as discussed above, these transitions must be introduced gradually. Parents need to be respectful of each child's pace of accommodation to the frequency and length of overnight visits. They also need to find ways to establish a sense of routine similarity across households. Preschoolers are best served by predictable routines. The more dissimilarity, the greater the chances that the overnight visit will entail increased anxiety, fear, and frustration.

When a preschooler travels to the other parent's home, the child's adjustment to the transition may be aided by having photographs of parents, siblings, grandparents, and other important people in the child's life. The child may also bring important transitional objects such as bears, blankets, toys, movies, and other such articles.

Major concerns about dysfunctional reactions include losing mastery of previously accomplished tasks and loss of opposite-sex parent as socializing agent or same-sex parent as identification model. Other concerns are frequent, almost obsessional worries about abandonment, protecting the custodial parent from hurt or despair, and carrying power struggles characteristic of this age into later development (Baris & Garrity, 1988).

6 to 8 Years Old

The early grade school child begins to change focus substantially, from parent focused to friend focused. Children often begin to develop peer and community relationships through involvement in scouting, recreational sports, and other after-school activities. There is a substantial focus on moral thinking and moral judgment, especially with the establishment and following of rules for games as well as social interactions. Children in this age group begin to develop a clear sense of empathy toward those around them. They also begin to focus their emerging self-concept on competency and mastery objectives (Baris & Garrity, 1988).

Six- to 8-year-old children are still profoundly tied into their relationship with their parents. There is continuing sex role identification as well as an increasing understanding and appreciation for sex role differences.

These children often react to separation and divorce with pervasive sadness. Some may show signs of increased distraction at school, increased irritability among family and friends, decreased interest in formerly enjoyable activities, and a sense of pessimism and hopelessness. They often directly express their anger and pain to their parents. Their fear and anger are often about not only losing the safety and security of having both parents living together, but also losing both parents. At a time when many children are exploring the meaning of death and dying, these children are faced with the real-life experience of the death of their family unit as they know it.

Such children often fault themselves for the marital breakup, taking responsibility for attempts to reunite their parents and blame when their attempts fail.

Residential Arrangements

Many 6- to 8-year-old children still require a predictable home base from which to explore their changing world (Baris & Garrity, 1988). Providing that the child's after-school routine and activities are maintained, the child often is emotionally and psychologically capable of alternating half weeks at

> **QUICK REFERENCE** **Developmental Guidelines**
> **for the Elementary School-Age**
> **Child, Ages 6 to 12**
>
> Primary developmental tasks
> - Focus on peer group and community relationships
> - Enhancement of moral thinking and judgment
> - Enforcement of rule-following behavior
> - Development of empathy and social perspective taking
> - Emergence of self-concept on competency and mastery
>
> Challenges to well-being
> - Increased sex role identification leads to increased mourning of lost parental relationship
> - Pervasive sadness about divorce demonstrated through disruptions in school, friendships, and other social experiences
> - May continue to blame self for marital breakup
> - Visitation arrangements may interfere with social, community, or recreational participation, thus disrupting normal social development

each parent's home. The child could have multiple overnights or spend a week with one parent and the next with the other parent.

The measure of success is the degree to which the child feels a sense of safety, security, and comfort with the alternating schedule. Many children who are capable of such split visitation arrangements request a single home base from which to visit the other parent. A frequent challenge is that these children know where they feel most comfortable and secure yet are reluctant to discuss their preference for fear of hurting one of their parent's feelings.

When parents live far apart, 6- to 8-year-old children are capable of multiweek visits. As discussed above, the visits must not seriously interfere with the child's ongoing community, peer group, school, and extracurricular activities (Baris & Garrity, 1988; Bray, 1991).

Frequent contact with the other parent is important. However, it is not unusual for a planned 4-week visit to be modified because a 6-year-old feels intensely homesick. The feeling of homesickness may involve the other parent. Often, it is as much missing the familiarity and predictability of the residential routine as it is missing the other parent.

Major concerns about dysfunctional reactions include difficulties at school, acting out, long-term depression, preoccupation with divorce, and attempts to play a role in the parents' reconciliation (Baris & Garrity, 1988).

9 to 12 Years Old

The late grade school child is often multiskilled as well as multi-involved. These children are involved in a variety of academic subjects, athletic leagues, community activities, and cultural- or humanities-oriented endeavors (e.g., music, dance, theater, or art lessons). They are very involved with their friends and very involved with their activities.

They increasingly become aware of their strengths and weaknesses, both from an absolute as well as a relative perspective. Often, these children are competitive, rule bound, and focused on fitting into their peer group social order. They also appear to bounce from acting like more mature teenagers to little more than first graders.

Children in this age group usually have developed a keen understanding of each parent's reaction to the divorce. Their feelings may vary from understanding each parent's point of view to blaming one or both parents for the breakup of the family. When there is conflict and the child is negatively influenced by one parent, children in this age group often take sides with intense loyalty to the parent whom they view as having been wronged.

Children at this level frequently demand a complete, adultlike explanation of events (Baris & Garrity, 1988). They want to explore why, who, when, where, and how. Yet they also want to examine these concerns on their own timetable. When the information they requested begins to stir feelings inside of them, they often will state that they have discussed all they are interested in and wish to end the conversation immediately.

These children are acutely aware of their sensitivity to both their own sense of rejection as well as their belief that their friends view them differently. Some children in this age group act embarrassed when news of the family breakup becomes public knowledge. They feel intense ambivalence about this public knowledge. On one hand, public knowledge brings the possibilities of a better, more diverse support system to aid the child in the transition. On the other hand, public knowledge may place a spotlight on a child who is struggling to not display feelings of vulnerability, sadness, anger, shame, or hurt. The result is that these children often behave erratically. Another result is that they may seek out the support of others in a similarly unpredictable manner. How parents cope with these inconsistencies may help determine how each child approaches and overcomes the challenges to the family's reorganization.

Residential Arrangements

Parenting plans may be highly flexible. Children in the 9- to 12-year-old age group may enjoy spending extended amounts of time with each parent. Cognitively and emotionally, most children in this age group are able to accommodate multiweek visits. However, these children are usually verbal and insistent upon any visits not infringing on their social, recreational, or after-school activities. For these children, missing a weekend party may be a significant event because of their apparent need to actively fit into their peer social network.

Parents need to understand and respect the child's intense feelings of social alliance with peer group activities. However, children in this age group are also capable of discussions surrounding the need to maintain consistent contact with each parent. Thus, it may be possible for parents to have constructive conversations with their children, focused on effective problem solving of the visitation versus peer activity participation challenges.

When parents live far apart, weekend visits may be appropriate. However, there is a strong possibility that weekend visits to a distant home will result in the child feeling angry or sad about missing important peer group activities.

It may be possible to explore similar activities in the nonresidential parent's home area. It may also be possible for the nonresidential parent to rotate weekend visits with the child, with one visit occurring at the residential parent's home and the next visit occurring at the nonresidential parent's home.

The nonresidential parent will need to take the initiative in involving him- or herself with the child's teachers, school conferences, and activities, as well as other important events. Cooperative parents will be continually exchanging information about the child's progress in school- and nonschool-related activities that will allow the nonresidential parent to be as current as possible with the child's daily life. In this way, the child will come to know and expect that the nonresidential parent is highly interested in the child's everyday stories.

Major concerns of dysfunctional reactions include academic difficulties, loss of motivation, loss of sense of belonging to peer group, possible lying or deception, loneliness, depression, and low self-esteem (Baris & Garrity, 1988). Other concerns include being vulnerable to the possibly alienating influence of one parent against another.

Teenagers

Teenage children continue their ongoing quest for freedom. They seek freedom from their parents. They seek freedom from the rules that society asks them to use in navigating their daily life. When they find their freedom, teenagers often seek the safety of parental rules. This wonderfully ambivalent relationship between chaos and order, between freedom to choose and dependency upon parents, is a challenge to parents, whether in intact or divorced family systems.

As children progress from early to late teens, some begin to mourn the loss of childhood, dependency upon parents, and protection from within the family (Baris & Garrity, 1988). They are struggling with feelings of their

---

QUICK REFERENCE **Developmental Guidelines for Teenagers**

Primary developmental tasks

- Increasing movement toward freedom and individuality
- Struggle between dependency of childhood and independence of adulthood
- Emerging sexuality
- Increasing identification with peer group and its influence
- Gender identification provides understanding of maleness and femaleness

Challenges to well-being

- Increasing concern about peer group influence regarding drugs, alcohol, promiscuous sex
- Confusion from divorce may lead to poor academic performance and subsequent academic failure
- Potential competition with single parent in areas of sexuality
- Concerns about intimacy development

---

emerging sexuality, attraction to the other sex, and their changing body image.

They are increasingly ruled by their peer group identification, yet seek to also be treated as an adult and abide by the rules and regulations of society. In all respects, it is a very confusing time for these children.

When they are also thrust into the turmoil of family transition and residential reorganization, these children may be among the most prone to maladaptive behavior. However, they also are the most skillful at hiding their feelings and reactions from those who might provide the most help.

Boys often seek out their fathers in an effort to understand their emerging sexuality. They may also seek out their fathers as a means of helping them figure out their evolving concept of maleness. Adolescent boys have been reported to have significantly more conflict and behavioral difficulties when living with their single mothers (Rohman et al., 1987).

Girls often seek out their mothers in an effort to understand their emerging sexuality. They may also seek out their mothers as a means of helping them figure out their evolving concept of femaleness. Adolescent girls have been reported to have significantly more behavioral difficulties when living with their single fathers (Rohman et al., 1987).

The argument for same-sex custodial placement has been discussed in Chapter 7. Although the research appears to support that same-sex custodial placements provide fewer behavioral problems for children, recent research seems to support the view that fathers are more interested in maintaining legal custody with a visitation role in their children's lives rather than being the primary custodial parent (Dudley, 1996).

Major concerns for behavioral dysfunction among teenagers include possible acting out, drug and alcohol use, promiscuous sex, and a vulnerability to cult groups through which the child may find a sense of belonging (Baris & Garrity, 1988). Other concerns may be uncertainty about relationship establishment and maintenance, intimacy development, trust, and abandonment.

Residential Arrangements

Developing parenting plans for adolescents needs to include the views and opinions of the children. Unlike children at younger stages of development, it is likely that adolescents will insist that they cannot be forced into a visitation schedule about which they had no involvement in developing (Baris & Garrity, 1988; All parents of teenagers, 5000 BC to present).

Teenagers often respond best when they actively participate in the creation of a routine that is dependable and consistent, yet flexible enough to accommodate their emerging and emergent social life. Parents need to maintain an appropriate level of respect for their child's interest in maintaining active involvement in school, peer group, extracurricular, community, and after-school activities.

There is no set recommended parenting plan when parents and child are able to develop a flexible residential arrangement. Baris and Garrity (1988) recommend identifying one home base, with specific, predictable (read: planned) evenings, weekends, and activities at the other parent's home. Most teenagers will plan their activities around their parent's scheduled activities once the visitation arrangement is implemented, considered fairly arrived at, and consistently followed.

When parents live far apart, weekend visits may be encouraged depending on distance, capacity to travel, and the degree of the child's involvement in local activities.

It may be possible to involve the child in similar activities in the nonresidential parent's home area. It may also be possible for the nonresidential parent to rotate weekend visits with the child, with one visit occurring at the residential parent's home and the next visit occurring at the nonresidential parent's home.

The nonresidential parent will need to take the initiative in involving him- or herself with the child's teachers, school conferences, and activities, as well as other important events. Although cooperative parents should be continually exchanging information about the child's progress in school- and nonschool-related activities, the teenage child is competent to maintain a dialogue with the nonresidential parent about such daily events.

> **QUICK REFERENCE** **Typology of Residential Arrangements for Parents in Conflict**
>
> - Minimal conflict
> - Mild conflict
> - Moderate conflict
> - Moderately severe conflict
> - Severe conflict

Residential Arrangements for Parents in Conflict

Many recommendations occur within an acrimonious custodial dispute. Divorcing couples are often in conflict. Parental conflict during divorce is probably the single most destructive experience for children of divorce. Recently, research examining parental conflict and children's reaction, and adjustment to different types of parental conflict has been available to custody evaluators. This section focuses on this literature on determination of residential arrangements.

Parenting Plans for Parents in Conflict

Garrity and Baris (1994) provide a conceptual framework for the development of parenting plans. They view parental conflict as a significant variable to be considered when developing residential arrangements. They suggest a continuum of parental conflict from minimal to severe.

Minimal Conflict

Minimal conflict is characterized by the parents' ability to cooperate on issues related to their children. These couples are able to show self-restraint and self-control, and to find effective means to resolve conflict.

Mild Conflict

Mild conflict is characterized by occasional events of acrimony. Most of the time, the parents are able to coparent. They may argue or berate each other in front of the children only occasionally. These couples only periodically disagree, and certain issues are often the trigger for their conflict. However, overall, their conflict is contained, seldom exposed, and infrequently involves the children.

Moderate Conflict

Moderate conflict involves individuals "who function effectively as parents on one level. Individually, they promote positive ideals for their children, but when they attempt to work together, power struggles and almost-constant conflict ensue" (Garrity & Baris, 1994, p. 47). Children from moderate conflict are frequently exposed to their parents' arguing, verbal abuse, insults, and threats of litigation.

This is the first level of the Garrity and Baris model in which it is predicted that the level and frequency of conflict do not significantly diminish over time. For some parents engaged in moderate conflict, the acrimony may intensify over time as each parent becomes increasingly convinced of the "rightness" of his or her parenting and the "wrongness" of the other parent's parenting.

Moderately Severe Conflict

Moderately severe conflicted parents "subsume all high conflict situations short of those that involve direct endangerment to a child through physical and sexual abuse" (Garrity & Baris, 1994, p. 48). This is a very violent environment in which children live. Often, parents threaten each other, physically and verbally abuse each other, and have no concern for display of such behaviors in front of their children.

It is not uncommon for parents to actively attempt to negatively influence their children against the other parent. Parents engaged in moderately severe conflict may attempt to alienate children from the other parent, demand loyalty to one parent at the exclusion of the other, and place children in the middle of the postmarital conflict with little regard for their children's welfare. For these parents, all factors concerning the children are filtered through one parent's personalized (pathologized) view of his or her parenting as being good for the children and the other parent's parenting as being bad for the children. For a more extensive exploration of these issues, see the discussion about Parental Alienation Syndrome in Chapter 8.

Severe Conflict

Severely conflicted parents represent

an immediate and direct threat to children's emotional and physical safety. Children in these families are at exceedingly high risk of damage from parental physical or sexual abuse, drug or alcohol abuse, and/or severe psychological pathology. Safeguards are essential to protect such children. (Garrity & Baris, 1994, p. 49)

In developing parenting plans, there are no rules about what kind of time distribution is appropriate. The acid test is what works best for each child. The evaluator needs to consider variables outlined in Chapter 7, such as the child's developmental level, adaptability, and temperament. Basic information such as school performance, after-school activity participation, and friendship group involvement may be among the plethora of factors used to aid in monitoring the goodness of fit between a recommended parenting plan and a particular family. The degree to which parents are able to coparent, rather than disengage, is also an important variable. It is currently believed that children are best served when parents coparent and coordinate the disciplinary and lifestyle rules between households. As parental conflict increases, the ability of parents to coordinate such parental responsibilities diminishes greatly.

In most custody evaluations, the examiner is asked to develop parenting plans and, by default, identify a residential and nonresidential parent. There are some circumstances in which shared residential placement may be considered, but the majority of recommendations will entail determining a primary placement. The norm, however, is placement with a residential parent and some allowance of time for the children with the nonresidential parent.

Traditional Residential Arrangements

Among the most frequently recommended arrangement is the 12/2 split. Children live with the residential parent for 12 contiguous days followed by 2 days with the nonresidential parent. The visitation schedule for the children is usually every other weekend with the nonresidential parent. Many nonresidential parents dislike this schedule because of the infrequency of contact with their children. Children often feel that they see the nonresidential parent too infrequently. The residential parent often feels overwhelmed by the amount of time needed to devote to the children in this arrangement, too.

Another variation is the 11/3 split. The nonresidential parent is provided an additional opportunity to visit with his or her children one day during the off week. This results in the children visiting with the nonresidential parent on alternate weekends and one day during the off week, resulting in 3 out of every 14 days. It is interesting to note that Wallerstein and Kelly (1980) reported that children dislike this frequently recommended visitation schedule.

The Ackerman Plan

Ackerman (1995, 1997) has proposed an extension of the traditional visitation schedule of alternating weekends. Children are provided opportunities to visit with the nonresidential parent from Thursday after school until Monday morning, when school begins. The increased time allows for greater possibilities in relationship building between the nonresidential parent and children. The nonresidential parent is also provided an additional contact day during the off week, resulting in 5 days of contact every 2 weeks. Thus, the designation 9/5 split.

During nonschool time, the nonresidential parent has contact with the children 10 out of 14 days. The residential parent has contact with the children from Friday until Monday morning. This is a 10/4 split and allows the residential parent additional time away from the children to engage in personal, adult time while providing the nonresidential parent a schedule of visits that significantly encourages the development of positive relationship patterns with the children over extended lengths of time.

Typically, the Ackerman plan provides for the residential parent's 9/5 split from September 1 through June 1, or the beginning of school through the end of school. The nonresidential parent's 10/4 split begins June 1 and extends through September 1, or from the end of school through the beginning of school (Ackerman, 1995). According to Ackerman (1997), using the 9/5 and 10/4 split provides roughly equal access for the children to each parent, resulting in only 20 days more per year for the residential parent.

However, as will be described below, there is some research indicating that increased visitation results in increased adjustment difficulties for some children (Johnston, 1994). Thus, the level and type of parental conflict becomes an increasingly important assessment variable when designing parenting plans.

Constructing the Plan

There are few rules to which most evaluators would agree when determining parenting plans. However, among those rules for which there is uniform consensus is that children need predictable, stable, and consistent structure and organization (Bray, 1991). Chapter 7 provided an overview of factors considered important in addressing children's adjustment to divorce. You may wish to review aspects of Chapter 7 as you prepare to write a parenting plan.

It is often helpful for the evaluator to construct a 4-week grid, mapping out days spent at mother's house and days spent at father's house in a visually graphic manner. Then, map onto the visitation schedule each child's activities and commitments, using different colored ink to represent those that are

required attendance (e.g., religious school), those that are voluntary attendance (e.g., music lessons), and those that are anticipated but not yet scheduled (e.g., yearly camping trip). It may also be helpful to indicate activities in
which joint parental participation is needed (e.g., school conferences, school
plays).

This helps the evaluator examine the flow of the proposed plan as well as
identify potential problem areas. It is often useful to include pick-up and
drop-off times in your proposed parenting plan. If the exchange of children
from one parent to the other is scheduled for 6 p.m. or later, the evaluator
may wish to anticipate potential conflict over who feeds the children on such
days. This is of particular concern with young children, for whom mealtime
decisions are often important concerns. Ackerman (1997) recommends that
the parent who has the children at 6 p.m. is responsible for feeding them.

Another variable to consider is the location of the exchange. For minimal-
and mild-conflict parents living within the same community, the children
may be dropped off at the other parent's home. It is often advisable *not* to
encourage the picking-up parent to go to the former spouse's home to pick
up the children. Too often, children are able to find ways to procrastinate in
getting ready for the transfer, resulting in the picking-up parent waiting
either in the driveway or in the house. This is uncomfortable for many divorced parents, yet may send the message to the children that they have some
power in helping their parents to reconcile. As one sixth grader said to me,
"Why should I hurry up and get ready? When I'm not ready, Mom comes into
the house and they begin to talk to each other while I'm upstairs pretending
to pack my clothes. Maybe they will start to like each other again."

Mild-conflict and some moderate-conflict parents may also drop off their
children at the other parent's home. However, there may need to be clearly
articulated rules surrounding the exchange to minimize parental contact,
which will minimize parental conflict. For example, moderate-conflict parents may decide that the children will be standing at the door waiting for their
pick-up 5 minutes before the scheduled transfer. When the children observe
the car pull into the driveway, the children hug and kiss the other parent
goodbye and walk themselves out to the car. In this way, no parental contact
occurs.

Another variation is for moderate-conflict parents to agree to limit their
conversation with each other to a set of agreed-upon topics from which they
do not vary. For example, most mild- and some moderate-conflict parents are
able to exchange information about the children's visit with the other parent.
For many moderate-conflict parents, however, this simple exchange of information is too difficult and may result in the expression of conflict in front of
the children.

For parents in conflict, the less direct contact, the better for everyone
concerned. Thus, one important question in designing parenting plans for

moderate-conflict parents is not only *when* or *where* the exchange will occur, it is also *who* will participate in the exchange.

Transitional Challenges

Children, particularly younger children, find the transition from one home to another among the most stressful components of their new family life. Children often resist moving from one parent's home or going to one parent's home because they dislike the upset brought about by transitioning from one home—a predictable set of rules and responsibilities, and a stable group of friends—to a different home. Of course, children usually adjust to the other parent's home quickly, reestablish themselves within the other parent's rules and responsibilities, and reconnect with their other set of friends. However, the transition itself is upsetting, and parents need to be aware of how their children may react.

When parents in conflict exchange children and their children display predictable, common transition reactions of resistance to the transfer, conflicting parents often blame the other parent for their children's upset. Moderate-conflict parents have been known to interpret their children's emotional distress during transitions as indicators of the children's wishes not to visit with the other parent. Some parents, upon observing their children's emotional reaction to the transfer, will interfere with visitation and refuse to allow the other parent to see the children, citing the children's emotional reactions as evidence of the unfitness of the other parent.

One way to anticipate such increased conflict among these conflicted parents is to arrange for the children's exchange to be conducted by a nonparent. For example, a parent's friend may drive the children to an agreed-upon drop-off point.

Some parents in conflict are unable to find people to assist in the exchange yet understand that contact during the exchange of children often results in conflict observed by the children. It is helpful for these mild- and moderate-conflict parents to develop a set of clear rules about the exchange. Typically, these exchange rules involve no verbal or physical contact.[1] Some parents find it helpful to participate in public exchanges that may serve to inhibit parental conflict. For example, parents may meet at a local shopping center parking lot. Each parent parks in his or her car on opposite sides of the store's front door. The children may be dropped off in front of the store and walk the few feet from one car to another.

Holidays

A parenting plan may include recommendations about how to distribute holiday time. One plan is to propose holiday placement on an alternating year schedule. Another is for holidays to be shared. When holidays are alternated every year, children often lose the opportunity to share time with each family. Instead, they are forced to spend time with one family per year for that holiday. The result is that children miss the chance to spend time with one parent as well as time with that parent's extended family (Ackerman, 1997).

Among the holidays to consider are Thanksgiving, Christmas, Easter, Fourth of July, Jewish holidays, religious events, Mother's Day, Father's Day, Memorial Day, Labor Day, and Martin Luther King's birthday. The last three holidays often take on increased importance in divorced families because they often result in 3-day, extended weekend visits. Parents' birthdays are often important to consider in a parenting plan.

Parenting Plans for Children of High Parental Conflict

The majority of divorcing couples battle continuously during the first year. Wallerstein and Blakeslee (1989) reported that by the third year postseparation, most parents have disengaged from conflict and begun the process of healing. This process of disengagement and emotional healing aids in the reduction of conflict.

Maccoby and Mnookin (1992) reported that about 25% of couples find ways to parent cooperatively. Fifty percent tend to disengage from each other and parent independently, and another 25% are in high conflict. For those couples in high conflict, children's adjustment is impaired significantly. Visitation arrangements often are areas of continuous challenge, resulting in children being uncertain when, where, and with whom they may be spending the weekend.

High-conflict divorces produce high-risk children. These children are less likely to learn to deal with the challenges of living in a divorced family system. Their parents' conflict is a constant reminder that their safety, security, and environmental consistency have been compromised. Their parents' conflict reminds them that "their right to be loved and cared for by both parents has been irretrievably compromised" (Garrity & Baris, 1994, p. 20).

Parents who develop cooperative parenting plans tend to influence their children more positively and provide a best-case scenario for their adjustment to divorce. Traditional visitation schedules such as those outlined above may be useful. However, parents who cannot cooperate may be unable to use traditional parenting plans. Traditional plans may be a poor choice for high-conflict parents because they provide numerous opportunities for parental conflict. Often, traditional parenting plans require at least a minimal level of communication between parents; a minimum degree of cooperation to facilitate conflict-free transitions (both pick-up and drop-off); and an ability to not frighten their children, either through an increased level of stress and tension or overt hostility toward the other parent.

A successful visitation plan satisfies three essential conditions. First and foremost, a plan will serve the best psychological interests of the children only if it is designed to minimize conflict. Second, it should maximize the time children spend with both parents as long as both parents (1) know and love the children, (2) are safe guardians for them, and (3) are willing to parent. Finally, the developmental needs of the children must be taken into account. (Garrity & Baris, 1994, p. 21)

Coparenting Patterns

Before discussing parenting arrangements for moderate- to severe-conflict parents, it may be useful to explore the research concerning parenting patterns. Maccoby and Mnookin (1992) provide a system for classifying postseparation parenting patterns. The three categories are cooperative coparenting, disengagement, and conflicted. The evaluator may find it useful to consider each family within the parameters of this taxonomy.

Divorce research is just beginning to address critical issues concerning how postmarital parental conflict affects children's adjustment. The discussion below is drawn from a study of 1,124 families with 1,875 children (Maccoby & Mnookin, 1992) taken from divorce filings in two counties. Participants were interviewed at the time of filing (T1), 1 year after filing (T2), and 3½ years after filing (T3).

Most of the families in the study were able to find solutions to their custodial disputes that avoided legal entrapments. Half of the custodial disputes were uncontested. One third of the cases were contested but resolved without the help of the court or related services. Twenty percent used formal conflict resolution procedures such as mandated mediation (11%), formal custody evaluation (5%), trial (2%), and judge's decision (1.5%).

Maccoby and Mnookin (1992) estimated that 10% of families experienced "substantial" legal conflict, and 15% experienced "intense" legal conflict. Thus, the majority of couples with children involved in divorce proceedings navigated the legal system without the involvement of the court or ancillary services. Those involved in high-conflict divorce, however, were found to display three types of coparenting patterns: cooperative, disengagement, and conflicted. Each coparenting pattern was assessed along dimensions of discord, frequency of communication attempts, and frequency of attempts to coordinate with the other parent.

Cooperative Parenting

Cooperative coparenting was defined as parents talking frequently with each other about their children; attempting to coordinate two sets of household rules; and each parent supporting ongoing, continuous contact between the children and the other parent (Maccoby & Mnookin, 1992, p. 235).

QUICK REFERENCE   **Coparenting Patterns**

Cooperative parenting
- Frequent parental exchanges about children
- Attempts to coordinate rules in two households
- Each parent supports other parent's continuous contact with children

Conflicted parenting
- Parents often argue
- Other parent viewed as undermining relationship between self and children

Disengaged parenting
- Contact with other parent avoided
- Parallel parenting, with each home having different parenting rules
- Little consistency in family rules across households

There was considerable stability in cooperative parenting over time. Parents who were characterized as cooperative 18 months after separation (T2) tended to display cooperative parenting 3½ years postseparation (T3). In their study, 26% of their sample displayed cooperative parenting at T2 and 29% at T3. Typically, cooperative parents tended to display high communication and low discord.

Conflicted Coparenting

Conflicted coparenting was defined as parents who often argued. They tended to perceive their ex-spouses as attempting to upset them when they disagreed. Conflicted parents reported their ex-spouses to have refused—or threatened to refuse—to allow visitation. Ex-spouses were viewed as undermining their parenting as well as creating logistical problems in managing visits with the children. Maccoby and Mnookin (1992) found that the percentage of couples reporting conflicted coparenting decreased from 34% at T2 to 26% at T3.

Disengaged Coparenting

Disengaged coparenting was defined as parents who avoided contact with each other. This resulted in parallel parenting in which each household carried its own set of rules and responsibilities. There was little, if any, coordination between parents regarding the establishment of consistent rules across households. Eighteen months after separation (T2), 29% of the sample

QUICK REFERENCE   **Questions About Coparenting Patterns**

The following questions may provide a useful framework in determining coparenting patterns.

1. What is the degree of discord between the parents? Provide self-report, observational, and collateral data for preseparation as well as postseparation functioning.

2. What is the degree of disengagement between the parents? Provide self-report, observational, and collateral data for preseparation as well as postseparation functioning.

3. What is the degree of cooperation between the parents? Provide self-report, observational, and collateral data for preseparation as well as postseparation functioning.

4. How do you characterize the quality of communication between the parents?

5. How does each parent characterize the quality of communication between themselves?

6. How does each parent characterize the quality of communication in the marriage prior to marital difficulties?

7. How does each parent characterize his or her amount of preseparation involvement with each child?

8. How does each parent characterize the other parent's amount of preseparation involvement with each child?

9. What are the observational and collateral data about how each parent has been involved with each child?

10. How does each parent characterize his or her ability to coordinate parenting with the other parent?

11. How does each parent characterize the other parent's ability to coordinate parenting with him or her?

12. What are the observational and collateral data about each parent's ability to coordinate parenting?

13. How effective have the parents been at establishing a consistent set of parenting rules across two households?

14. What has helped/hindered the establishment and consistent application of these household rules?

15. How has each parent helped/hindered the children's need for an ongoing relationship with the other parent?

16. How has each parent helped/hindered the children's court-ordered time with the other parent?

17. How has each parent helped/hindered the children's ongoing contact with the other parent (e.g., phone calls informing of school plays, sporting events, teacher conferences)?
18. How do you characterize the level of hostility between the parents?
19. How has the intensity and focus of hostility changed over time for each parent?
20. How do the children perceive each parent's attitude toward the other parent?

displayed disengaged parenting. Three-and-a-half years postseparation, that figure rose to 41%. It appears that a significant percentage of couples reporting conflicted coparenting at T2 resolved their conflicts by avoiding the other parent at T3. That is, some high-conflict parents resolved their disputes by disengaging from each other and establishing separate, independent households.

Moderate to Severe Parental Conflict

By the time many parents complete a custodial evaluation, there is a high probability that they are among those considered in at least moderate conflict. Therefore, consideration of factors associated with high-conflict postdivorce parenting may be useful.

Johnston (1994) has suggested that one critical factor is the *type* of postseparation conflict in which the parents have been involved. Recent research has provided information about how different types of parental conflict and cooperation affect parenting and children's adjustment to divorce. This section reviews recent research examining parental patterns of conflict and cooperation in a postdivorce context. It may be helpful for the evaluator to ponder the conceptual distinctions presented below when considering the development of parenting plans.

Dimensions of Conflict

Johnston (1994) suggests that divorce conflict has at least three important dimensions: domain, tactics, and attitude. Domain conflict refers to in which areas of life, or *where*, the conflict exists. Domain conflict may involve one or more issues about finances and support, property division, custody, access to children, or parental values and behaviors.

The tactics dimension refers to *strategies* each parent has used in attempting to resolve conflicts. Tactics may include informal, face-to-face discussions; avoidance; verbal aggression; physical coercion; or physical intimidation. Formal tactics may include mediation, litigation, or attorney-driven negotiation.

The attitudinal dimension refers to the *attitudes* and *feelings* involved in attempts to resolve the conflict. Important aspects of this dimension are the degree of negative emotional feelings, mistrust, hostility, and the degree to which these feelings are manifested overtly or covertly.

Domain, tactic, and attitudinal dimensions are often not independent of each other. The evaluator needs to explore how each conflict dimension may influence other dimensions.

Another important aspect of a conflict domain analysis is where one party perceives a specific conflict to exist and the other party does not. These conflict dimensions are not always symmetrical; that is, when one parent holds negative feelings about visitation, the other parent may feel comfortable. The evaluator should not presume symmetry in conflict domain.

Divorcing couples may have different emphases on different aspects of these conflict dimensions. For example, one party may avoid contact, whereas the other initiates litigation. One party may feel hostile, whereas the other party has moved on with his or her life.

Understanding how each of these dimensions may interact with each other is critical. Furthermore, understanding how each of these interacting dimensions may influence children's adjustment is also crucial.

Duration and Development of Conflict Patterns

A final set of variables is the duration and pattern of conflict. Looking at conflict along a time continuum helps to determine its character. For example, couples for whom there was little preseparation marital conflict may display high conflict during divorce. This lack of conflict history may be predictive of more short-term disruption, as opposed to couples for whom high conflict existed during their marriage (Johnston, 1994).

Couples who tended to resolve most preseparation marital difficulties through discussions and negotiation may be more likely to reengage positive communications after the custodial dispute. These parents may be predicted to be less likely to negatively affect their children's adjustment over time.

Conversely, couples who tended to have poor preseparation communication, avoid conflict resolution, or engage in physical aggression during their marriage may be more likely to continue their poor communication after divorce. The result is a greater likelihood of adversely affecting their children's postseparation adjustment.

QUICK REFERENCE **Questions Useful in Assessing Parental Conflict**

1. What are the domain conflicts in this custody dispute?
2. What are the tactical or strategic dimensions used in each of the domain conflicts?
3. What are the attitudinal variables for each party for each domain conflict?
4. How has the conflict developed over time?
   a. When did the conflict begin?
   b. Who initiated the conflict?
   c. What is each party's definition and understanding of the conflict?
   d. What is each party's perception of the underlying cause of the conflict?
5. What other external or internal factors or parties may be contributing to the conflict?
6. Where do you assess the conflict's duration, pattern, and nature to lie along a continuum of normal to pathological?
7. How is the children's adjustment affected by each area of conflict?
8. How has the parents' ability to coordinate parenting been affected by each conflict?
9. How does one parent's conflict style differ from the other's?
10. What is the quality of each parent-child relationship within the family?

Who initiates conflict may also be critical. If postseparation conflict is most often associated with attorney-initiated negotiations, it may be that the degree of conflict is more likely associated with the influence of third-party involvement than with the parties themselves.

Another way to explore patterns of conflict is to examine the step-by-step evolution of their origin. Understanding how the issue of conflict was defined and understood by each party may be useful. Exploring how each party interpreted the meaning and timing of the issue generating the conflict may also be helpful. Finally, learning how the particular issue may be associated with other related concerns may help place the emerging pattern of conflict into a sensible framework.

For example, a conflict over increasing visitation from Sunday at 5 p.m. to Monday at 8 a.m. may yield information about how the proposed increase in time with the parent affects state child support guidelines resulting in a change in financial contribution to the children's support. In some states, for example, demonstrating that a child spends more than 122 days per year with the nonresidential parent may significantly reduce the custodial parent's child support.

It is essential that the relationship among conflict dimensions is understood. The extent to which conflict in one area affects or triggers conflict in another domain is critical to examine. Particular focus should be on the degree to which postmarital hostility decreases the extent of parental cooperation involving the needs of the children (Johnston, 1994; Maccoby & Mnookin, 1992).

Distinguishing Factors Among High-Conflict Parents

Maccoby and Mnookin (1992, pp. 238-239) reported few factors that reliably distinguished high-conflict from low-conflict coparenting. They reported no significant differences between high- and low-conflict parents for socioeconomic status, parents' educational level, income, or ethnicity. Conflicted coparenting was as likely to be reported in remarried families as for children who resided with only the mother or the father. Quality of corparenting was not related to the families' economic resources or the father's education. Cooperation was higher and conflict lower when mothers were better educated.

Children's Age and Family Size

Families with very young children were more likely to report high levels of conflict in day-to-day parenting. Parents of preschoolers and kindergarten-aged children reported more frequent negotiations with each other about the children. This increased frequency of communication resulted in more conflicts but *not* more cooperation. These parents also were more likely to report higher incidence of legal conflict.

Conflicted coparenting was also reported in families with many children. These families appeared somewhat more likely to have coparenting conflict compared to families with one child, and less likely to display cooperation.

> The effects of family size and children's age are essentially independent, but they do combine, so that the highest incidence of a conflicted interparental pattern was found in families with three or more children where at least one of the children was still of preschool age. We interpret these findings to mean that co-parental conflict is sparked (at least in part) by the greater amounts of parental investment (effort) required when children are young or families large; the more difficult the total parenting task, the more difficulty sep-

arated parents have in allocating the parental responsibilities. (Maccoby & Mnookin, 1992, p. 239)

Disengagement was reported more likely in families with older children. Children of grade-school age or older may serve the function of conveying information between the parents, resulting in less parental contact. This reduced parental contact appears to result in reduced parental conflict. Another reason is that older children are better able to care for themselves and require less coordination of parental supervision. Parents of younger children appear more concerned about the children's well-being in the other parent's house. Parents of older children had fewer concerns in this area, presumably because older children have better established coping skills to aid them during their visits.

Level of Parental Hostility

It is commonly assumed that the amount of hostility expressed by either mother or father is related to each parent's ability to cooperatively parent. Maccoby and Mnookin (1992) reported that level of conflict was predictive of coparental patterns. Parents who displayed high levels of hostility at the time of separation tended to display similar levels of hostility more than 3 years later. Parents reporting lower levels of hostility at the point of separation tended to have a greater chance of developing cooperative parenting patterns. Maccoby and Mnookin concluded, "We have seen that couples who are highly conflicted at one period are unlikely to be cooperative at the next period" (p. 240). They further noted that the most significant decrease in reported hostility toward the other parent appeared between time of separation and 18 months later. No significant reduction in reported hostility was found between the 18-month and $3\frac{1}{2}$-year postseparation intervals. The authors reported that most of the variance in the amount of coparental discord found 3 years postseparation is accounted for by hostility level measured at the 18-month interval, which itself is quite strongly related to the level of hostility at the time of separation. Even for parents whose anger has cooled over time, subsequent support for each other's parenting never was restored to the level found among couples who were initially less angry (Maccoby & Mnookin, 1992).

Maccoby and Mnookin (1992) reported that although ongoing legal conflict contributes to parental discord, the more significant variable is level of parental hostility. Apparently, if mothers remain hostile, there is less chance of coparenting than if fathers remain equally hostile. Mothers with strong hostile feelings 18 months postseparation are likely to contribute more to coparental discord over time than are fathers.

Preseparation Involvement
With Children

Different views concerning each parent's *relative* contribution to his or her children's lives during the marriage were more likely to result in legal conflict postseparation. The greater the discrepancy, the greater the likelihood for conflict and reduced cooperation. In contrast, parents who agreed about their relative contribution or who held minor discrepancies about their preseparation roles were more likely to engage in coparenting (Maccoby & Mnookin, 1992).

Concerns expressed about the other parent's household at the time of separation was predictive of lower levels of cooperative parenting 18 months later. Maccoby and Mnookin (1992) found that parental distrust of the other parent's child-rearing environment—particularly the mother's distrust of the father—made a unique contribution to coparental conflict beyond that accounted for by parental level of hostility. They concluded, "In short, when a mother believes that the father is not an adequate parent, it is difficult for the parents to cooperate in post-separation child rearing, regardless of how much hostility they harbor toward each other" (p. 245). Depner, Cannata, and Simon (1992) also reported that distrust of the other parent's ability to care for the children typified parents in high-conflict divorce.

Parenting Plans for
High-Conflict Divorce

Garrity and Baris (1994) make a point of distinguishing between "normal" versus "conflict" visitation. Normal visitation considerations are applied when parents are able to reach agreement regarding fundamental aspects about visitation.

Until recently, judges and mental health professionals have assumed that the more contact children have with each parent, the better off they will be. However, in cases of high-conflict divorce, frequent contact may have an adverse effect on children. Johnston and Campbell (1988) have reported that frequent visitation may often intensify parental conflict and place the children in the middle of conflict more often. As discussed earlier in this chapter, the degree and type of conflict is emerging as a significant factor to consider in the formulation of visitation plans.

Moderate Parental Conflict

Couples who remain in moderate conflict often function well separately but appear unable to disengage from conflict when around each other

(Garrity & Baris, 1994). These parents often consider flexible parenting plans, thinking they can overcome their anger with the other parent in favor of a plan better suited to the child's increased access. The negative interactional style these couples have developed over the years prevents them from effectively implementing their well-intentioned flexible parenting plan.

Typically, these couples will initially agree upon flexible parenting plans. They will attempt to trade weekends or reschedule pick-up times. It is the interaction when the couple is together that produces the difficulties. When they need to communicate with the other parent about the children's needs, schedules, or activities, they are likely to be tense and will move easily toward open hostility (Garrity & Baris, 1994). It appears as if the slightest word sets each parent off into a formidable form of fault-finding. Each word, each gesture is examined for its possibility to do harm.

Children who witness these tense and often explosive exchanges tend to react with fear and confusion and, depending upon their age, may believe that the increase in parental conflict is their fault. Children may also feel a strong loyalty bind, feeling that they must take sides when their parents begin to fight.

Garrity and Baris (1994) recommend that parenting plans for moderate-conflict parents, as well as those with more pronounced conflict, be developed around the concept of *disengagement*. The less direct contact the parents have with each other, the lower the chances that conflict will occur. Although many of these parents maintain that they can overcome their conflict and coparent effectively, parenting arrangements should "require strategies that minimize interparental contact and communications" (Garrity & Baris, 1994, p. 129).

Ideas to consider are the use of a neutral drop-off point that would allow a calm transition from one parental home to the other. Rather than verbally exchanging information about the children, the parents may keep a journal or log in which child-related issues are itemized and discussed.

Joint parental attendance at school, recreational, or religious events tends to place great pressure on children in their anticipation of parental conflict. Therefore, joint attendance is often unwise. However, if the event is scheduled ahead of time and plans are made to keep parents separate from each other, then joint attendance may be appropriate.

Parents of moderate conflict will be well served by learning to parent separately and from a distance.

Moderately Severe Parental Conflict

Garrity and Baris (1994) believe that parents displaying moderately severe and severe parental conflict "are likely to have some characterological problem or disorder that threatens the children's emotional or physical well-being" (p. 130). There is a significant increase in the incidence of parental alienation; the threat of physical, sexual, or emotional violence toward the children; and spousal abuse.

The primary goal of the parenting plan is to ensure the safety of the children. Garrity and Baris (1994) suggest the active participation of a parent coordinator (described in Chapter 8). These parents have a difficult time placing the health and welfare of their children ahead of their need to do battle with the other parent. Such parents often are highly narcissistic or display borderline qualities, making the ability to design a parenting plan they would view as effective and fair virtually impossible.

Summary

This chapter provided information about how to develop parenting plans for parents with different levels of parental conflict. A conceptual model of types of parental conflict, severity of parental conflict, and types of parental coparenting were discussed.

Note

1. Depner et al. (1992) reported that 65% of families alleged domestic violence by one or both of the parents. Johnston and Campbell (1988) reported that physical aggression occurred in 75% of high-conflict parents. Johnston (1992) reported the number to be closer to 70%. In the Johnston and Campbell study, 25% termed the physical agression as moderate, and 35% termed the aggression as severe. In the Johnston study, the percentages were 20% and 48%, respectively.

THIRTEEN

Data-Organizing Tools

> Good definitions are necessary but not sufficient bases for answering fundamental questions. Broader conceptual understanding is needed.
>
> *Stanley L. Brodsky (1991, p. 49)*

The ability to organize data into a coherent, logically integrated, written report lies at the heart of all forensic evaluations. Too often, custody evaluators have to gather reams of data without the benefit of a data-organizing tool. In this chapter, four data-organizing tools will be discussed. Each provides the evaluator with a means to categorize and order data around salient concepts relevant to custodial determination.

Challenges to Self-Report and Interview Data

Self-report and clinical interview data form the foundation for much of the information used both in clinical and forensic evaluations. The importance of using a standard interview format has been discussed earlier. A standard interview format, however, does not address significant questions about the quality of information gained through self-report and interview formats. Self-report is an essential component of all child custody evaluations. Yet the information produced in a self-report or interview needs to be treated somewhat skeptically until collateral resources confirm its veracity.

Self-report and interview data have many problems. People do not like to admit that they engage in socially inappropriate or undesirable behaviors. They also tend to provide inaccurate or less-than-complete information about sensitive issues or potentially embarrassing concerns. Finally, memory plays a role in the accuracy of self-report and clinical interview data. Often, people do not remember events because they were viewed as unimportant at

---

QUICK REFERENCE   **Limitations of Self-Report and Interview Data**

- People do not like to admit to their shortcomings or that they engage in socially undesirable behavior.
- People tend to provide less complete information about sensitive or embarrassing behavior.
- People often believe in the accuracy of their memory despite it being wrong.
- Memory is best when events are unique, stimulating, and emotionally meaningful; however, child care activities are typically routine, uneventful, and unexciting.
- Memory for specific events declines over time.
- Often, data important to the custody evaluation was deemed unimportant at the time of occurrence; therefore, it was never stored in memory, became distorted over time, or could not be retrieved.

---

the time. The data may never have been properly stored. Sometimes, the stored memory becomes distorted, or the relevant information cannot be retrieved (Azar, 1997).

Memory Factors

Human memory is fallible, and self-report data are filled with the possibilities of error because "the brain does not function as a video recorder" (Borum et al., 1993, p. 38). Memories are stored in a constructive and nonsequential manner, yet parents undergoing a custody evaluation may be asked to provide information about their caretaking behaviors in the 6 months prior to the couple separating. Each parent indicates involvement as a primary caretaker in at least 75% of daily activities. Who is right? Is one parent lying? Some parents intentionally distort historical data about caretaking involvement as a means of influencing the evaluation process. Other parents recall events of minor importance at the time of their occurrence (e.g., who helps dress the children) and interpret these memories in light of their current need to view themselves and have others view them in a particular way.

There are conditions where self-report and interview data should be readily accepted and times when the evaluator needs to be skeptical, nlot only because of faking good or bad tendencies, but also because the parent may be convinced of the accuracy of the memory despite it being wrong. For example, when parents were asked to remember which immunizations their children had received as they left an immunization clinic, parents' memories of what had just occurred was not much better than chance (Azar, 1997). Parents' poor recall resulted from the relative insignificance of the event. The event was not very memorable and therefore was unlikely to have been encoded into memory.

Memory is best when the event is unique, stimulating, and emotionally meaningful. However, there are many child care activities that are not unique, stimulating, or emotionally meaningful. It may be impossible to remember accurately how often a parent has helped with bedtime, reading, bathing, school, and sports involvement. Parents may be able to describe their involvement in broad categories such as "seldom . . . often . . . all the time." However, assigning percentage of time engaged in child care activities may be a purely speculative exercise with little or no basis in the reality of the parents' predivorce life. The conclusion is that evaluators need to carefully weigh the meaning assigned to self-report and interview data for those unexciting events that parents are not likely to encode into memory (Azar, 1997).

Another reason to be careful with self-report and interview data is that memory for specific events declines over time. People often recall events in chronological order for about 10 days. After 10 days, memory for an experience is often recalled in relationship to other events in one's life. Data may be more reliable when they are reported in relation to other important events rather than specific dates. For example, a parent may recall an event that occurred sometime around Christmas more accurately than if it occurred on December 20th. Evaluators may focus the interviewee less on specific dates and times and concentrate more on contextual or other types of general cues to assist in the recall of events (Azar, 1997).

> Therefore, an over reliance on memory in forensic evaluations can result not only in a decrease in information with which to make a judgement, but also in an increase in judgement bias. . . . Thus unusual features, striking events, or extraordinary circumstances may stand out in our memory and make more complete and accurate recall of more mundane but potentially relevant details less likely. (Borum et al., 1993, p. 38)

Judgment Calls

People tend to shy away from telling the truth if questions involve personally sensitive or potentially embarrassing information (Azar, 1997). The questions posed in a typical custody assessment interview may be perceived as personally sensitive or potentially embarrassing. For example, a previously uninvolved father who has embraced the role of an active father since the marital separation may feel embarrassed by his previous relative lack of involvement in child care activities. Therefore, the data he provides to the evaluator may overestimate his involvement because of his desire to *view himself* as a more involved father. The data may be an overestimate because he wishes to *influence the examiner to view him* as a more involved father. The data may be an underestimate because the father wants to *highlight how he has changed* since his father-involved rebirth. The data may be an underestimate because he honestly *views himself* as not being involved at all. The events were relatively unimportant; therefore, the little amount he contributed is not accurately recalled. Finally, the data may be accurate and show him to have been uninvolved. The challenge for the evaluator is to find external sources of information that may help to confirm one of the above hypotheses. The lesson drawn from this research is to be wary of self-report and interview data that are not confirmed by alternative, externally obtained data sources.

Having provided a warning about the limitations of self-report and interview data, the remainder of this chapter describes tools useful in the gathering and organization of data around salient variables to be explored in custodial determinations.

Custody Assessment Tools

There are many different custody evaluation tools described in the literature. The two presented here are reported to be the most frequently used tests designed specifically for custody (Ackerman & Ackerman, 1996, 1997). The first is Marc Ackerman's ASPECT (Ackerman & Schoendorf, 1992), a 56-item questionnaire yielding a score purporting to measure overall parenting effectiveness. The second is the Bricklin Perceptual Scales (Bricklin, 1984), a 64-item test purporting to measure the goodness of fit between a child's perception of his or her parents' behavior and what the child perceives that he or she needs. As validation data on each of these instruments become increasingly more available, their use should be evaluated more thoroughly. (See Melton et al., 1997, for critiques of each tool.)

Ackerman-Schoendorf Scales for Parent Evaluation of Custody

The Ackerman-Schoendorf Scales for Parent Evaluation of Custody (ASPECT; Ackerman & Schoendorf, 1992) is designed to assess parental fitness for custody. The test attempts to identify those characteristics reported in the behavioral science literature as determinative of custodial fitness (Ackerman, 1995). The ASPECT is reported to be the most frequently used of the custody tests for adults (Ackerman & Ackerman, 1997).

The ASPECT is composed of three scales: Observational, Social, and Cognitive-Emotional. The Observational scale purports to measure the quality of a parent's self-presentation during the examination process (Ackerman,

1995). It assesses self-presentation and appearance. Items on the scale measure (a) the parent's physical appearance; (b) the manner of interaction with the examiner, child, and other parent; (c) the parent's initial understanding and discussion of the effects of the divorce on the children; and (d) the parent's perception of his or her parenting competencies.

The Social scale is designed to measure interpersonal relationships as well as social and intrafamilial factors. It examines parental social conduct and interaction with others, including the children, the other parent, and the community. Most items are focused on the parent-child relationship. Three domains are assessed. The parent-child relationship is observed directly. The child's perception of the parent and the social environment the parent provides for the child are also explored. Several additional areas are examined, including the parent's ability to recognize present and future needs of the child, parent's ability to provide discipline and self-care, and the parent's motivation for seeking custody (Ackerman, 1995).

The Cognitive-Emotional scale explores a parent's cognitive and emotional competencies in relationship to child rearing. The psychological health and emotional maturity of each parent are assessed using psychological tests such as the MMPI, WAIS-R, WRAT3, and Rorschach. These measures are weighted evenly and allow comparison between parents upon dimensions such as defensiveness (MMPI or MMPI-2 K scale or signs of guardedness on the Rorschach) and intellectual functioning (WAIS-III).

Ackerman and Schoendorf (1992) also require children to receive (a) an age-appropriate intelligence test, (b) the Draw-A-Family Test, and (c) either the Thematic Apperception Test (TAT) or the Children's Apperception Test (CAT).

The purpose of the ASPECT is to integrate clinical data, self-report data, and objective and projective psychological test data into a cohesive picture of overall parental effectiveness. The ASPECT is considered to be content valid (Ackerman, 1995). There are studies exploring its predictive and construct validity, and data have been reported for its internal consistency and interrater reliability (Ackerman & Schoendorf, 1992).

Ackerman and Schoendorf (1992) combine the Observational and Social scales into an overall measure of "overt" parental effectiveness. The Cognitive-Emotional scale is viewed as a measure of the "underlying cognitive and affective capacities for parenting and is therefore seen as a 'covert' measure" (Ackerman, 1995, p. 120). A quantitative score combining measures of significant characteristics, relationships, and interactions is provided in the Parent Custody Index (PCI), a value purporting to be an indicator of overall parental effectiveness (Ackerman, 1995).

Each parent completes a Parent Questionnaire composed of questions exploring preferred custody arrangements, living and child care arrangements, perception of children's development and education, parent-child relationship, and parent-parent relationship. Information is also obtained about parental background and past and present psychiatric, legal, and substance abuse history.

The examiner completes a separate 56-item questionnaire for each parent. Twelve of the questions are considered critical items because they are highly significant indicators of deficit parenting (Ackerman, 1995). The examiner completes the questionnaire by accumulating data from three sources: (a) observations and clinical interviews of the parents, the children, and the parents with the children; (b) several psychological tests and inventories; and (c) parent's responses to the Parent Questionnaire.

Scoring the ASPECT results in a weighted average of all three ASPECT scales, yielding a PCI score used to compare one parent to another. Subscale scores can be compared to reveal specific ways in which parents differ. Ackerman (1995) notes that "although the subscale scores are used to explain PCI differences, it is the PCI that is used to guide custody recommendations, which are not made based on subscale differences alone" (p. 121).

Bricklin Perceptual Scales

The Bricklin Perceptual Scales (BPS; Bricklin, 1984) provide information about the child's perception of each parent's behavior in four areas: competence, supportiveness, follow-up consistency, and possession of admirable character traits. The child's perception of parental behavior may or may not match the parent's real-life behavior. The BPS evaluates the goodness of fit between a child's perception of his or her needs and the child's perception of how well the parent meets those needs (Bricklin, 1984).

The BPS is the most frequently used custody test for children (Ackerman & Ackerman, 1997). The BPS can be administered to children 6 years and older. The 64 items are equally divided between those relating to mother and those relating to father. Items for each parent are identical except for the words "mother" and "father." The BPS alternates between questions about mother and father, but the content of these questions is rotated so that two items describing the same behavior are not in sequence. Each item asks the child to provide a verbal and nonverbal response. The nonverbal response is based upon the child's endorsement of a marking on a card containing a black line. The line contains the words *very well* printed on the right and *not so well* printed on the left. The child punches a hole with a stylus in the place on the line that corresponds to his or her perception of how well the parent is able to deal with the situation described in the question.

Only nonverbal answers are scorable. The child's nonverbal responses yield scores for mother and father for each of the four factors described above. Bricklin (1984) provides a means for additional analyses by calculating item differences and point differences scores. These scores provide information about the interparental similarities and differences in a child's perception. Bricklin (1984) also suggests that the child's verbal responses, which are not scored, may provide useful data similar to those obtained from structured interviews.

BPS results are particularly useful when a child rates one parent as significantly better than the other. The more extreme the scores between a child's perception of mother and father, the clearer the child appears to be about custodial preference. Bricklin (1984) refers to children who provide extreme scores for different parents as the "mind made up" profile.

There is a slowly emerging psychometric database about the BPS. There are some reliability data, particularly in the area of rater agreement. For example, Bricklin (1984) reported an agreement rate of 89% between BPS choice and the parent chosen by a judge. A similar percentage agreement was reported between BPS choice and the psychologist's custodial decision. Validity data are sparse. One reason why solid psychometric data on the BPS may be difficult is the test's highly subjective nature (Ackerman, 1995). Children's perceptions of themselves and their relationship to the world changes continuously. Developing a standardized test that can account for changes in both the child's perception of self and the child's perception of parent would be a near-impossible task to undertake.

Perception of Relationships Test

Bricklin (1990) also has developed the Perception of Relationships Test (PORT), consisting of seven subjective tasks designed to identify the child's perception of the parent of choice. Bricklin notes that the PORT does not have great reliability because of the changing nature of a child's life.

Additional Custody Assessment Tools

There are a variety of other tools. Few, however, provide solid psychometric data. Fewer still have been developed specifically for use in custodial determinations. Among the tests used by custody evaluators are the Parent Awareness of Skills Survey (PASS), the Parent Perception of Child Profile (PPCP), the Parent-Child Relationship Inventory (PCRI), and the Custody Quotient. The Custody Quotient was the first of the custody measures to be published. Ackerman and Ackerman (1997) report that it remains experimental today and is unlikely to be revised.

Structured Questionnaire Formats

There are also a variety of structured questionnaires used to guide a custodial evaluation. Three interview formats will be described. Greenberg's Parenting

History Survey contains about 100 questions, and the companion Forensic History Questionnaire, Part I & Part II provide follow-up data. Schutz et al. (1989) provide three interview tools: the Parent Questionnaire, the Parent Interview, and the Child Interview. Munsinger and Karlson (1994) produced a multistep custody evaluation system for which they have created interview structures or checklists for each step of their evaluation process.

The Parenting History Survey

The Parenting History Survey[1] (PHS) is a written interview that asks the litigant to briefly present basic background information about the parenting of his or her children, his or her caretaking, and previous and current living situations. The PHS is intended to give a litigant the opportunity to answer questions in private, outside the stress of an interview. There is no time limit. Individuals to whom I have given the PHS have taken as little as 1 hour and as much as 15 hours to complete the survey.

The PHS is an evolving work, being continuously updated and revised. The authors welcome the submission of new questions that may be considered for inclusion in the form. The result is a continuously modified instrument, responsive to current changes in evaluation theory, practice, and research.

A sampling of the thoroughness and breadth of scope of the PHS is provided here. It goes beyond typical parent and child questionnaires by addressing issues such as potential to move away, level and frequency of conflict, degree to which attorneys have been involved in parenting conflict resolution, assessment of primary caretaker, and many other factors that are addressed in the behavioral science literature.

In my judgment, the PHS and its companion questionnaires provide among the most comprehensive pictures of parent-child factors of all currently available structured interview formats. Its major limitations are that the questions are not organized around a specific theoretical framework (e.g., systems theory), and some parents complain about the length of time needed to complete it.

Parent Questionnaire and
Child Questionnaire

The Parent Questionnaire (Schutz et al., 1989) contains 59 questions provided to each parent. The Child Questionnaire (Schutz et al., 1989) contains 21 questions. The forms are designed to provide basic information and history relevant to the evaluation with the parent to complete the forms in the evaluator's office. They contain questions about a litigant's health, family, education, work, relationships, and marriage. They also ask about each child

---

QUICK REFERENCE   **Sample Areas Assessed Using the Parent History Survey**

- Strengths or significant assets existing in relationship with other parent
- List of concerns about other parent
- Summary of major aspects of current situation
- Summary of major concerns other parent is likely to raise about litigant
- Description of how current parenting arrangements were decided
- Summary of documents the litigant wants reviewed for evaluation
- Family history data, personal history data, relationship data, employment history, educational history, physical health history, mental health history, alcohol and substance use history, collateral information resources
- Chronology of relationship history with current parent
- How litigant contributed to current difficulty
- How other parent contributed to current difficulty
- Description of parenting tasks and responsibilities, estimate of specific parenting functions within marriage

---

and request a description of the legal situation regarding custody and visitation. These questionnaires are appropriate for basic information gathering. They do not provide opportunities for litigants to discuss factors such as move away, parental alienation, primary caretaker, current conflicts, and efforts to resolve conflict, among others.

When I use the Child Interview format, it serves a twofold purpose. It is a structured way to gather data and allows me to ask the same general set of questions of each child. I also use it as a relationship- and trust-building tool. The questions are preloaded in my laptop computer. I power up the computer and sit on the floor next to the child. I invite the child to sit next to me and help me answer the questions. I indicate that I will be asking questions and entering the child's answers into my computer. I state that I would welcome his or her help in making sure that the information I am typing into the computer is exactly what the child wants me to tell the judge. I have yet to find a child who does not become involved in the process. I believe that the child becomes aware of the importance of the accuracy of his or her answers and of the care taken by the evaluator in precisely and accurately recording the answers to each question.

QUICK REFERENCE   **Sample Areas Assessed Using the Child Interview**

- Description of the family
- Description of important celebrations
- Description of which social, school, and play activities are important and who participates
- Description of who provides medical care
- Description of religious participation
- Description of daily routine and parental involvement
- Description of each parent, parental social activities, and alcohol use
- Description of discipline and rules
- Description of current perspective of separation and custody arrangement
- List of alternative caretakers (i.e., baby-sitters)

Uniform Child Custody Evaluation System

Psychological Assessment Resources (PAR) publishes a comprehensive system of interview forms, checklists, and questionnaires aimed at helping the examiner better organize the evaluation process called the Uniform Child Custody Evaluation System (UCCES; Munsinger & Karlson, 1994). Twenty-five forms are placed into three categories, and they are summarized here.

The UCCES provides a useful structure for organizing custodial examinations. The parent and child questionnaires are more extensive than those offered by Schutz et al. (1989) but not as extensive as the PHS. According to Ackerman and Ackerman (1996, 1997), few evaluators use the system despite its apparently well-organized structure.

The checklists and forms are organizing aids, *not* diagnostic tools, and they should not be used as such. For example, the abuse/neglect checklist does not purport to be a valid means of assessing abuse or neglect. It is a way of summarizing observations, *not* concluding whether abuse or neglect occurred. Similarly, there are no validity data presented for the Suitability for Joint Custody checklist or the Analysis of Response Validity Checklist. Although the questions on each checklist appear to be logically related either to concerns about joint custody or response validity, logical analysis does not mean that they are psychometrically sound.

I have found the organizing aspects of the UCCES helpful. The checklists may serve to guide interview direction, stimulating discussions about critical variables in custody evaluation. However, the UCCES is not a simple, one-

QUICK REFERENCE **General Data and Administrative Forms**

- Checklist of all steps involved in the UCCES process
- Initial referral form
- Chronological record of all case contacts
- Case notes form
- Consent for psychological services form for children
- Authorization to release information form
- Suitability for joint custody checklist
- Collateral interview form
- Consent for evaluation of minors form
- UCCES summary chart

QUICK REFERENCE **Parent Forms**

- Parent's family/personal history questionnaire
- Parent interview form
- Parenting abilities checklist
- Suitability for joint custody interview
- Analysis of response validity checklist
- Behavioral observations of parent-child interaction form
- Home visit observation form
- Agreement between parent and evaluator form
- Explanation of procedures for parents and attorneys

QUICK REFERENCE **Child Forms**

- Child history questionnaire
- Child interview form
- Child abuse interview form
- Abuse/neglect checklist
- Child's adjustment to home and community checklist
- Parent-child goodness-of-fit observation form and checklist

step process. Its effective use requires, as do all forensic evaluations, skillful application of specialized knowledge in child custody assessments.

Note

1. Copyright 1984-1994 by Stuart A. Greenberg, PhD. All rights reserved. Copies of the Parenting History Survey are available for professional use by sending a check for $20 to Stuart A. Greenberg, PhD, Diplomate in Forensic Psychology, American Board of Professional Psychology, 605 Marsh & McLennan Building, 720 Olive Way, Seattle, WA 98101-1853. 24-hour telephone 206-442-9600.

FOURTEEN

Providing Testimony in Court

> The experience of being an expert witness gives the evaluator
> some small sense of what the parents in a custody case go
> through. On the stand, every single aspect of her (or his) pro-
> fessional conduct will be under intense and public scrutiny.
>
> *Schutz et al. (1989, p. 97)*

The final step in the custody evaluation process often is providing testimony in court. As discussed earlier, the Federal Rules of Evidence (FRE) and their state equivalents provide avenues for the presentation of experts and their information into the legal record of a trial. There are criteria for establishing yourself as an expert and the relevance of the information as it relates to the case at bar (FRE 702), as welll as criteria for testimony as a treating therapist (FRE 701). There are also standards that assist in determining whether the methods, procedures, and data that form the basis of an opinion are admissible as scientific evidence (FRE 703). There are evidentiary rules guiding the admissibility of testimony about the ultimate issue (FRE 704). There are criteria for establishing what is relevant evidence (FRE 401) and distinguishing between what information is probative and what may inappropriately sway the trier of fact (FRE 403).

All of these rules help to define how we present ourselves and our data to the court. However, the rules do not automatically allow for the admission of an expert who has conducted an evaluation. The evaluator needs to offer evidence showing how specific training, education, knowledge, skill, or experience has resulted in development of competencies that the court may determine may be helpful in understanding the evidence or determining a fact.

Too often, the process of voir dire allows for the qualification of experts who are not. Attorneys often question potential experts about their degrees and training at general levels of knowledge. Instead, they should be asking specific, targeted questions about training and education specific to the task at hand. In this chapter, several categories of inquiry will be presented. These queries may be useful either in preparation for voir dire or examination and cross-examination.

Qualifying as an Expert
With Unique Skills

When presenting credentials to the court as an expert in child custody evaluations, there are several areas of expertise that should distinguish your credentials from those other professionals who are not specifically trained in the custody evaluation process. The minimum level of competency may be inferred from a description of your graduate training and subsequent professional activities. However, there are ways to distinguish yourself from other, more generally trained evaluators.

One approach is to organize your training and experience around the primary methodological components of a comprehensive evaluation. For example, demonstration of training and experience in forensic interviewing, civil forensic use of psychological tests, and forensic ethics are but three areas for which there are specific forensic training and continuing education workshops (e.g., APA Division 41 workshops, APSAC workshops). The competent forensic examiner should be able to demonstrate professional training, education, and experience in each component of the evaluation process.

This chapter focuses on preparation for expert testimony by organizing questions around the Child Custody Guidelines (APA, 1994) and the Specialty Guidelines (Committee on Ethical Guidelines, 1991). Nonpsychologists may find that guidelines and standards of professional practice from other professional organizations lead to other organizational ideas and questions more relevant to your particular practice.

APA's Custody Guidelines, Section 2.5, states, *"The psychologist gains specialized competence."* Specialized knowledge may include developmental psychology; adult development; child, adult, and family psychopathology; and the separation and divorce literature. Specialized knowledge also includes familiarity with applicable legal standards and procedures (Section 2.5a). The evaluator needs to be current in his or her knowledge of the behavioral science literature pertaining to divorce and separation as well as the civil forensic use of psychological tests and other assessment tools (Section 2.5b). Finally, evaluators need to possess expertise in areas of child maltreatment and abuse, domestic violence, and other issues that may be revealed during an evaluation. When confronted with issues outside of his or her particular expertise, the competent examiner seeks additional consultation, supervision, and/or specialized training (Section 2.5c).

Evaluators need to know whether their testimony is to the ultimate issue. They also need to know whether testimony to the ultimate issue is appropri-

---

QUICK REFERENCE **Sample Qualifying Questions**

1. Describe your most recent training/continuing education seminars applied to child custody evaluation.
2. Beyond that described above, describe what additional training you have obtained in the area of the forensic interview of the child.
3. Describe your training in the forensic interview of the adult.
4. Describe your training in the civil forensic use of psychological tests as they apply to custodial assessment (i.e., MMPI-2, MCMI II, and MCMI III).
5. Describe your training in ethics applied to forensic child custody evaluations.
6. Describe your training in how to provide expert witness testimony.
7. Describe your training in the evaluation of child sexual abuse within the context of custody examinations. Also be prepared to discuss training in areas such as children's adjustment to divorce, domestic violence, divorce conflict, and child maltreatment.
8. Describe your training in the evaluation of adult personality disorders as they relate to child custody evaluations. Also be prepared to discuss training in areas such as adult psychopathology.
9. Describe your training in the application of current behavioral science literature about separation and divorce to child custody evaluations. Also be prepared to discuss training in areas such as parental conflict during and after divorce, developmental factors in predicting children's adjustment to divorce, and gender differences in parenting during and after divorce.
10. Describe your training in understanding forensic decision-making factors as they affect forensic evaluations.

---

ate, both in theory as well as within the specific jurisdiction in which they are testifying. Expanded more fully in the Specialty Guidelines (Committee on Ethical Guidelines, 1991), the APA Custody Guidelines discuss limitations imposed on evaluators in their role as experts to the court. Thus, a firm grasp of the forensic ethical concerns is necessary. Also, skill in applying and discussing how various decision-making factors may influence data gathering, data interpretation, or the final recommendations is critical.

These are just a few of the areas of inquiry that may profile the unique competencies you bring to the custody evaluation process. When you prepare for trial, spend time creating a list of questions to be asked by attorneys that

QUICK REFERENCE   **Sample Questions for**
                   Testimonial Experience

1. How many custody evaluations have you conducted in which you found for the father? For the mother?

2. How many custody evaluations have you conducted in which you recommended joint custody? Sole custody?

3. Name the case citations of some of the cases in which you have been involved as a custody evaluator.

4. Approximately how often are you hired by one side to conduct an evaluation?

5. When you have evaluated only the father (mother), how often have you found for the father (mother)?

6. Approximately how often are you appointed by the court to conduct an evaluation?

7. What is the difference between a custody evaluation and a parental competency examination?

8. Who is paying your fee for conducting the evaluation? For testifying today?

9. How much do you charge for a typical evaluation? For testifying?

10. Provide your records detailing the number of phone and face-to-face contacts you have had both with the litigants, their children, and their attorneys.

will help the court to understand the specific, unique knowledge and skills you bring to the custody evaluation process.

Testimonial Experience

Seasoned evaluators have often testified in court. The expectation of testifying may bring a sense of anxiety. This is not uncommon. Even experienced evaluators feel nervous before testifying. The witness chair is an infrequent place for most mental health professionals. A useful way to gently wash away nervousness is to have the attorney conducting the voir dire walk you through your resumé. Because most of us can sleepwalk through our credentials, taking the time to refamiliarize yourself with being on the stand while addressing relatively nonthreatening questions may help to prepare you for testimony.

QUICK REFERENCE **Primary Purpose of Child Custody Evaluation**

Section 1.1 of the Custody Guidelines states, "The primary purpose of the evaluation is to assess the best psychological interests of the child" (APA, 1994, p. 677). Questions that may be relevant to Section 1.1 of the APA Guidelines include the following:

1. What is the primary purpose of a child custody evaluation?
2. What are the fundamental components of a competent child custody evaluation?
3. What is the definition of "psychological interests"?
4. Describe each factor that comprises the child's "psychological interests."
5. How are these factors measured?
6. Are different psychological interests measured for different children? If yes, how can meaningful comparisons be made if different measures are being reported about different children?
7. How is the determination of "best" psychological interests determined?
   a. Is it objectively determined? If yes, how?
   b. Is it subjectively determined? If yes, how?
8. Why is the "best psychological interests of the child" important?
9. If the primary purpose of a child custody evaluation is to assess the best psychological interests of the child, what are some secondary purposes?
10. How are these secondary purposes determined? By whom? How are they measured?

A common area of exploration is to describe your courtroom experience. These questions may focus on the number of evaluations you have completed, the number of times you have testified, or the amount you have been paid for your evaluations.

Many of these questions can be somewhat unnerving. However, they are fair game for attorneys. Federal Rule of Evidence 26 calls for documentation of the cases in which we have participated that have reached court. Inquiring about fees and implying that testimonial conclusions are driven by who pays is common. A simple, clear response, such as "I am paid for my time, not my testimony," often will suffice.

Questions exploring your history of decision making are also fair game. If an attorney is able to find a trend in your custodial determinations (e.g., find-

---

QUICK REFERENCE   **Questions Defining Child's**
                       Interests and Well-Being

Section 1.2 of the Custody Guidelines states, "The child's interests and well-being are paramount" (APA, 1994, p. 677). Questions that may be relevant to Section 1.2 may include the following:
1. How do you define the child's "well-being"?
2. How is well-being measured?
3. What is the difference between the child's "interests" and the child's "well-being"?

---

ing often for mothers), your responsibility is to be prepared to explain the reasons behind the trend.

Preparing for Examination About
the Purpose of Custody Evaluations

Using APA's Custody Guidelines as a structure to direct your preparation for examination may prove useful. Below, many of the specific sections from the Custody Guidelines are discussed, and questions are offered that may help in preparing for court testimony. An important area is understanding the purpose and focus of a comprehensive child custody evaluation. The APA Custody Guidelines provide a reasonable definition of the purpose and focus of an evaluation.

Further defining the purpose and scope of the evaluation, Section 1.3 states, "The focus of the evaluation is on parenting capacity, the psychological and developmental needs of the child, and the resulting fit" (APA, 1994, p. 678). These concepts set the focus on three broad areas of inquiry. However, each is somewhat poorly defined, with limited research upon which to base valid predictions about future behavior. Despite these limitations, inferring from these shaky data to future behavior is precisely the task of the evaluator.

A reading of Section 1.3 reveals many potential questions that may be somewhat difficult to answer without having considered answers prior to being examined. For example, Section 1.3 (a) describes a child custody evaluation as including "an assessment of the adults' capacities for parenting, including whatever knowledge, attributes, skills, and abilities, or lack thereof, are present" (APA, 1994, p. 678).

The first area of possible inquiry may focus on questions involving the dimensions of parenting capacity and its scientific assessment. You need to be

QUICK REFERENCE **Questions Defining the Purpose and Scope of the Evaluation**

1. What is the definition of parenting capacity?
2. Describe the most relevant factors to be assessed in determining parenting capacity.
3. How is each parenting capacity factor measured?
4. When examining parenting capacity, how do you account for gender differences?
5. How do you account for differences in caretaking style that have no impact on the child's best psychological interests?
6. How do you determine the degree to which a specific parenting capacity factor influences a child's best psychological interests?
7. How do you determine what is directly attributable to parenting capacity and what is associated with the chaos of the family transition from intact to divorced?
8. How do you determine the developmental needs of a child? How are they measured?
9. What is the definition of "psychological parent"? How did you determine who is the psychological parent? (Be prepared to describe the discussion in the literature concerning the usefulness of the psychological parent concept.)
10. What is the definition of a "primary caretaker"? How did you determine who is the primary caretaker? (Be prepared to describe the discussion in the literature concerning the usefulness and allegations of inherent bias in the primary caretaker concept.)
11. How do you weigh the wishes of each child? At what age does the child's wishes play a more (less) significant role in the decision-making process? (Recall Ackerman and Ackerman's [1996, 1997] recent results indicating that evaluators tend to weigh most heavily the wishes of children age 15 and older. If you use a different standard, be prepared to defend that choice.)
12. Did you observe the children with each parent? If yes, what specific factors were being measured? How were they measured?
13. If parent-child observations were structured, why? If parent-child observations were unstructured, why? What are the benefits/costs associated with structured versus unstructured observation sessions?
14. Was each child observed with each parent over a similar amount of time and under the same types of condition(s)?
15. Who brought each child for each visit? Why is this important to note?

16. If psychological testing was conducted on each parent, why? What specific factors were being assessed, and what was their relevance to parenting capacity?

17. How did you determine the parents' values? How are values related to parenting capacity?

18. How did you assess each parent's capacity to provide a stable and loving home?

19. How did you assess each parent's potential for inappropriate behavior that may influence the child negatively? How much confidence do you have in predicting potential for inappropriate behavior?

20. How did you define the parents' functional ability to meet the needs of each child? How were these abilities measured?

21. How do you assess "resulting fit" between parent and child?

22. How did you assess each parent's knowledge of the child?

23. How did you determine which parent better provides for the child's best psychological interests?

24. What are the advantages/limitations of this conclusion?

25. What forensic decision-making factors may have affected your interpretation of the data? What steps did you take to control for these factors?

---

prepared to discuss anything from the universe of definable, measurable factors identified as dimensions of parenting capacity that were chosen as most relevant for the present evaluation. Once defined, you need to be able to describe, as well as defend in court, how each dimension was measured reliably and validly. You also need to be able to demonstrate, either through empirical research or logical analysis (the former is preferred), how each measurable parenting dimension identified as appropriate to the current evaluation is directly related (read: relevant) to meeting the child's psychological, emotional, and developmental needs.

Another area of possible ambiguity lies in defining "whatever knowledge, attributes, skills and abilities . . . are present." Most parents know much about their children. Even parents who have little direct contact with their child may possess important information unique to their relationship with that particular child. How do we as evaluators define which knowledge domains are (a) present and (b) relevant? For example, a commonly asked set of questions often focuses on the parent's knowledge of the child's developmental milestones. Presumably, knowledge of when a child crawled, walked, and talked informs the evaluator about some aspect of parenting capacity. You need to be prepared to address which aspect such knowledge addresses within the parental capacity domain. You may also be asked to demonstrate *how* you know such knowledge is directly or indirectly related to present parenting capacity. Does the lack of knowledge of historically important developmental milestones indicate poor parenting? Conversely, does accurate, detailed knowledge of historically important developmental milestones reveal something about present parental capacity? If yes, then what? If no, why not?

During voir dire, direct or cross-examination, or questioning by a judge, such questions are acceptable areas of inquiry exploring the scientific basis and relevance (FRE 702 and 703) of your evaluation methodology and procedures. You need to be prepared to defend how you operationally defined the factors evaluated in the report. You need to be prepared to defend how you chose one set of operationally defined factors rather than another set. You need to be prepared to defend how this particular set of parenting capacity factors is related to measurement of factors relevant to this particular evaluation. In light of the ethical obligation to consider alternative hypotheses, you may also need to explain how a different set of factors chosen may have been appropriate and then defend the reasons and research that supports the particular approach you chose to pursue.

A similar logic and set of questions may be pursued in discussing the concepts of "attributes," "skills," and "abilities." Each of these domains of parenting capacity may sound relevant to the overall objective of finding the best possible fit between parent and child. However, behavioral science research often lags behind the ability to conceptualize and develop logical models of human behavior. Such is the case with the major concepts identified in Section 1.3 of the APA Custody Guidelines.

There is little professional disagreement that a parent's knowledge, attributes, skill, and abilities are salient components of competent parenting. The challenge is at least threefold. The first challenge is to identify what knowledge and attributes and which skills and abilities are salient not only to competent parenting in general (most likely to be reported in research studies) but to the particular needs expressed by this specific child. The second challenge is to demonstrate how scientifically we can reliably and validly measure both factors of parenting capacity as well as relevant factors pertaining to this particular child's specific developmental needs. The third challenge is to show some predictive usefulness. We may be able to define the domain of relevant variables and measure them with precision. However, evaluators need to accurately predict, within a reasonable degree of psychological certainty, how a particular set of measurable parenting capacities, in combination with a particular set of measurable child developmental needs, informs us of future behavior. As of today's writing, the behavioral science literature is short on quality research that address this critical and complex question.

Controlling for Personal
and Society Biases

A final area of inquiry drawn from Section 1.3 lies in the definition of the "values of the parents relevant to parenting" (APA, 1994, p. 678). Clearly defining the parameters of a custody evaluation may sometimes result in a hornets' nest of problems. Identifying parenting values relevant to successful child rearing is one such potential hornets' nest. The first challenge in defining which parenting values are relevant to examine is to control for the imposition of your personal values or those of the surrounding culture. There are many adult values with which great disagreement may exist with society at large. One task for the evaluator is to know the behavioral science literature pertaining to such values and to present these results properly within the report.

This concept is also stated in Section 2.6: "The psychologist is aware of personal and societal biases and engages in nondiscriminatory practice" (APA, 1994, p. 678). An important and somewhat common dilemma is basing a custodial recommendation upon behavioral science research that runs counter to the prevailing cultural and social values of the community in which the evaluator practices. One aspect of the dilemma is that by being true to the science, the evaluator may so anger the local community or judges that his or her services will never be used again.

For example, as I write this chapter, the North Carolina Supreme Court is hearing arguments about whether a gay father—who was originally granted primary custody of his children but whose custody was subsequently revoked because of the alleged influence of his homosexual lifestyle on his children—may regain custody of his children. The behavioral science literature speaks clearly to the issue of how sexual preference and lifestyle influences child's development (see Chapter 7 for discussion). Within the city of Charlotte, there is an extraordinary debate occurring about whether to provide funding for cultural/artistic activities that may convey a message supportive (or at least tolerant) of an alternative lifestyle inconsistent with regional values and beliefs. How does an evaluator balance the need to accurately reflect the science behind a recommendation if the recommendation runs counter to prevailing social and moral beliefs? The ethical answer is simple: Follow the science. The practical answer is not as simple. Evaluators usually live in the communities in which they work. Their children go to school in those same communities. Politically incorrect decisions—even if they are scientifically accurate—may have significant effects on the personal and social life of the evaluator. How will these concerns be controlled in ways that allow the examiner to perform his or her task in an ethical, honorable, and fair manner?

6

QUICK REFERENCE **Questions About Dual Relationships**

1. Have you been involved in counseling or any other therapeutic activity with any member of the parties?
2. Have you been involved in some other forensic role, such as mediator?
3. Have you provided interim recommendations to the parties about how to resolve minor disputes prior to the conclusion of the evaluation (e.g., deciding what time a child may be picked up by a parent)?
4. In what ways does your social relationship with Attorney A affect your conclusions? Conversely, in what ways does your lack of a social relationship with Attorney B affect your conclusions?

Within the prevailing social culture, some evaluators may impose their personal values about homosexuality upon the conceptual framework of their custody examination and provide a recommendation to the court that has a strong basis in their personal religious or moral conviction rather than science. Adding to the error, these opinions are seldom discussed with the court as personal opinions but are presented as having their basis in science. I propose that such evaluator behavior undermines our entire profession by violating what I believe to be the central maxim of our professional obligation to the court: To ensure fairness and justice (Grisso, 1986) and not threaten or diminish the civil rights of a litigant (Committee on Ethical Guidelines, 1991).

Exploration of Dual Relationships

A frequently asked set of questions focuses on the relationship of the evaluator to the parties involved in the litigation. Section 2.7 states, "The psychologist avoids multiple relationships." Multiple or dual relationships may influence the ways in which the evaluator interprets the data and/or the nature of the recommendations offered to the court. Mental health professionals should avoid any mixing of therapeutic and evaluative roles. This rule applies not just to the period of time encompassing the evaluation, but for all time. Especially in custody evaluations, in which there is always a possibility of a party filing for a modification or reconsideration, the evaluator must maintain his or her neutrality.

In smaller communities, mental health professionals, attorneys, and judges often sit on the same committees, participate in the same professional and social events, and may even socialize. Understanding how such dual relationships may influence the quality of data and conclusions drawn from those data as well as the perception of evaluator neutrality is critical.

A critical issue is the degree to which your extralegal relationships with attorneys or judges may give the *perception* of impropriety. Once a shadow has been cast upon either your credibility or the objectivity of the data, it is difficult to rehabilitate the external perception of your neutrality.

Who Determines the Focus of the Evaluation?

In a court-ordered evaluation, the judge's order should contain a list of questions that the court wants answered by an evaluation. Typically, these questions are not formulated in a language useful to empirical investigation. The evaluator may need to rewrite the evaluation questions into psycholegal questions that serve two purposes. First, the questions must adequately address the legally relevant issues set forth in the present case. Second, the formulation of psycholegal questions helps to define operationally what needs to be assessed.

Section 3.8 of the Custody Guidelines states, "The scope of the evaluation is determined by the evaluator, based on the nature of the referral question" (APA, 1994, p. 678). The evaluator is responsible for defining the limits and scope of the evaluation. This is a critical step because the precision of our evaluation questions is directly related to the degree to which our data may be helpful to the court. As discussed in a previous chapter, a primary complaint among attorneys and judges is that evaluators often answer questions *not* being asked by the court. Therefore, it is incumbent upon evaluators to ensure the precision and clarity of their questions *before* beginning an evaluation.

Informed Consent and Confidentiality

There is some professional disagreement about the appropriateness of having parents who are ordered by the court to participate in an evaluation sign an informed consent. The reasoning is that a court order requires the parents to participate. How can they give informed consent to participate in an evaluation when thay are ordered by the court to participate? If a parent refuses to participate, it becomes a violation of the court order, and the parent may be subject to sanctions imposed by the court.

In discussing dimensions of confidentiality, the APA Custody Evaluation Guidelines clearly state that "a waiver of confidentiality from all adult participants or from their authorized legal representatives" is required (p. 679). Although not as clearly stated in Section 9, the spirit of the Guidelines also

QUICK REFERENCE **Questions About Determining Focus of Evaluation**

1. How did you determine the scope and focus of the evaluation?
2. Who assisted you in determining the psycholegal questions you investigated?
3. If the attorneys helped craft the focus of the evaluation, then did each attorney have equal input into the formulation of the psycholegal questions?
4. If you sought no assistance from the court or attorneys in formulating the scope and focus of the evaluation, upon what set of criteria did you base your questions?
5. How are the evaluation questions related to the legal questions being asked by the court?

appears to support obtaining a signed informed consent form from each adult.

Standard practice is to have each parent sign an informed consent document that outlines the nature, purpose, and scope of the evaluation. The evaluator should review each step of the evaluation process with each parent. The following issues need to be addressed in the informed consent document and discussed during the initial visit.

As evaluator you describe the purpose, nature, and methods of the evaluation (Section 3.9a) and clarify who ordered the evaluation (Section 3.9b). The recommendation in this book is to never begin a court-ordered evaluation without the court order in your files. In this way, you can discuss the specific statements contained in the court order with the parents. Providing a means of discussing the focus of the evaluation as ordered by the court allows each parent to describe his or her understanding of the order. Clarifying the nature and purpose of the evaluation with the parents, as well as with the attorneys and the court, often increases the chances of compliance among all involved. Finally, the court order should specify who will be responsible for fees and in what proportion (Section 9.3c).

Finally, the evaluator is responsible for discussing the procedures to be used in the assessment with parents and children alike. The examiner should provide easy-to-understand explanations of the interview process, self-report measures, psychological tests, and use of collateral resources. Questions should be addressed clearly and directly to increase the examinee's understanding of the evaluation process.

During the informed consent discussion, it is common to talk about issues related to confidentiality (Section 10). As described in an earlier chapter, the

---

QUICK REFERENCE **Questions About Informed Consent and Interview Struture**

1. Do you use a standard informed consent form?
2. What are its primary components?
3. How do you structure the initial interview?
4. Are both parents present? If yes, how does this assist the evaluation process? If no, what data are lost by not seeing the parents together?
5. How often do you see the parents together for the initial interview?
6. How often do you see the parents separately for the initial interview?
7. What factors led you to make the decision you made in this particular evaluation? In what ways did this decision influence your understanding of the parents' relationship?

---

court-appointed evaluator has the court as the client. Thus, the litigant has no privileged relationship to the evaluator. The privilege is held by the court and maintained by the evaluator. This means that all information gathered by the evaluator is subject to the court's decisions.

Multiple Methods of Data Gathering

Frequently described throughout this book is the need for all forensic examinations to include multiple data-gathering techniques. Mental health professionals who engage in forensic work only occasionally may not know the rationale behind the use of multiple data-gathering techniques. Several questions may be generated from Section 11 of the Guidelines that address the need for multiple data-gathering techniques.

Additional Areas of Inquiry

Among the remaining areas of inquiry that may arise during testimony are questions about outside influence upon the final conclusions, offering of conclusions logically derived from within a context of the derived data rather than personal beliefs or other confounding factors, providing opinions only about individuals who have been directly assessed, providing recommendations that are based on what is in the child's best psychological interests, and the need to maintain adequate records of all contacts. Each of these areas may generate a list of questions useful in preparation for testimony. As discussed throughout the book, each of these areas has a significant basis in the behav-

QUICK REFERENCE **Questions About Confidentiality**

1. How did you describe the nature of confidentiality?
2. Please show the court the signed document advising my client of the limits of confidentiality.
3. Did any party to this evaluation disclose information to you and ask you to keep it secret (confidential)?
4. Did you promise any child you interviewed that you would not tell the judge (or parents) what his or her true feelings (thoughts) were?
5. Did you disclose to the litigants that all their information may be open to the court's examination?

ioral and forensic science literature. Each has specific ethical guidelines to follow. The competent evaluator will be prepared to discuss each area, displaying knowledge of current research, professional debate, and applied case law.

If you have been able to answer most, if not all, of the questions posed in this chapter, you will be well prepared for your day in court.

State Guidelines

Over the past decade, several state mental health associations have developed custody evaluation guidelines to be used by those licensed in each state. Most state guidelines parallel those of the American Psychological Association. For example, in the early 1990s, a committee from the Pennsylvania Psychological Association (PPA) began work on a draft proposal of custody evaluation guidelines. As the initial draft of the proposal was distributed for comment to the membership of PPA, the APA Custody Guidelines were published. The result was that Pennsylvania decided to use the APA guidelines and abandoned development of an independent set of state guidelines. Alternatively, at about the same time, a committee from the North Carolina Psychological Association began work on a document about child custody evaluation guidelines. The document closely paralleled the APA guidelines, but the committee added information and expectations about the scope of an evaluation specific to the professional practice of psychology in North Carolina. Recently, a committee from NCPA has begun to revise these guidelines for use by NCPA membership. The lesson from these two examples? Know your state professional association, and follow changes in professional practice guidelines.

QUICK REFERENCE   **Questions About Data-**
————————————— **Gathering Techniques**

1. Describe how you conducted the adult forensic interviews. The child interviews?

2. Did you use a standard forensic interview protocol? If yes, why? If no, why not? What is standard practice in the field of child custody evaluations?

3. If you used a clinical interview technique, please describe the difference between a clinical and a forensic interview.

4. What are the reliability and validity of the interview protocol you used?

5. What other data-gathering techniques did you use?

6. Focusing on the standard psychological tests, were these tests developed for use in a child custody evaluation? If no, upon what basis are you able to use these tests within the present context?

7. What self-report measures did you use?

8. Were they developed for use in a child custody context? If yes, which specific factors are measured?

9. Did you follow a standard assessment protocol gathering the same data from each individual using the same measures? If yes, why? If no, why not?

10. Did you use collateral interview sources? If yes, why? If no, why not?

11. In conducting collateral interviews, did you obtain informed consent from each interviewee? If yes, how? If no, why not?

12. List the names of the collateral information sources who provided records for your review. How did this information affect your final decision?

13. What weight did you place on each collateral source in reaching your final decision?

14. Who should you have interviewed and did not? How would these data have changed your judgment?

15. Who administered the psychological tests?

16. How were the tests scored? If by hand, what are the limitations of using hand-scored methods? If by computer, what are the limitations of using computer-scored services?

17. How could the present results be interpreted differently?

18. What other tests could have been administered that may have resulted in different conclusions?

19. How do you determine which data-gathering technique (or set of techniques) is more important than any other in reaching your conclusions? If you weighed each factor differently, would you have reached different results?

20. What information would have been useful that you did not obtain? Would this information change your final conclusions?

Specialty Guidelines

Besides knowing the details of your state and national association guidelines, increasingly there are guidelines for specialty areas in different areas of mental health care. As discussed throughout this book, the "Specialty Guidelines for Forensic Psychologists" (Committee on Ethical Guidelines, 1991) is but one document that has been developed in response to the growing need for greater professional policing of professional practice standards. Should you belong to a professional association that has published specific guidelines for forensic evaluations in general, or forensic child custody evaluations in particular, you may examine these guidelines for potential questions to be offered in court examination.

Creating a Powerful Curriculum Vita

One of the first impressions an evaluator will make upon attorneys and judges is conveyed through his or her curriculum vita. Using the questions posed in this chapter, you should be able to construct a vita that distinguishes your qualifications in the eyes of the court.

The vita should have the usual information about educational training, degrees, and licenses. You may wish to include work history, publications, academic appointments, and training you have conducted in areas related to child custody, as well as public talks to professional groups, professional associations, memberships, awards and distinctions, and other professional honors.

Including a listing of the jurisdictions in which you have been admitted as an expert is helpful. You may wish to organize your testimonial history around the type of admitted expert (e.g., psychology, custody, sexual abuse, child development).

Another distinguishing aspect of a powerful forensic vita is to list all recent workshops, seminars, and continuing education experiences address-

---

QUICK REFERENCE   **Questions From the**
                   Specialty Guidelines

1. What is a forensic psychologist (mental health professional)?

2. When does work become forensic compared with when it remains clinical?

3. What is the primary ethical responsibility of a forensic psychologist as stated in the *Guidelines*?

4. Competency is defined as providing "services only in areas . . . in which they have specialized knowledge, skill, experience, and education." Describe to the court your specialized knowledge in (fill in the blank).

5. What is the current legal standard that governs your participation as an expert in today's proceedings?

6. How have you presented to the court a description of the limitations of the data and the conclusions drawn from those data?

7. There is a standard that forensic psychologists maintain current knowledge in the field. Describe the three most recent forensic workshops or continuing education seminars you attended that focused on aspects of child custody evaluation.

8. Which professionals do you turn to when faced with a forensic dilemma? Are they trained in forensic mental health? If yes, at what level? If no, why do you seek their guidance?

9. Did you provide the court with all the data that you collected during the evaluation? If yes, where are your records? If no, which data did you leave out and why? In what ways may the data not included alter the final conclusions offered to the court?

10. How are the conclusions rendered in your report related to the legal questions before the court?

---

ing specific aspects of forensic training. For example, if you have attended a specialized workshop in forensic training, you may indicate the specific names of the workshops as a way to demonstrate proficiency in each aspect of the child custody evaluation process (e.g., Civil Forensic Use of the MMPI-2, Forensic Interviewing of the Child, Child Sexual Abuse Evaluations, Ethical Expert Testimony, Current Case Law and Research in Child Custody Evaluation).

Inclusion of such forensic-specific training will help attorneys and judges see the unique qualities that you bring to the task of a civil forensic assessment.

Summary

This chapter has explored ways in which evaluators might prepare themselves for the process of voir dire, examination, and cross-examination. Using the guiding principles of APA's Custody Guidelines, questions were posed that should aid the examiner in exploring his or her preparation to undertake a comprehensive child custody evaluation as well as identifying areas of forensic practice that may be explored during testimony.

FIFTEEN

Report Writing

Report writing is a craft unto itself. A well-written report provides a narrative of the evaluation journey, taking the reader from the initial contact through the record review and collateral interviews into discussions of interview data and psychological testing woven around salient behavioral science variables that are relevant to the psycholegal question. At the end, there should be little chance that the reader does not understand how the data are directly tied to the interpretation, which itself is directly tied to the conclusions and recommendations. The report should be written clearly, with little jargon. It should be thorough enough to explain the necessary data in a logical, integrated manner.

The data reported in a forensic child custody report should also be replicable. The methods and procedures should be organized around standard data-gathering tools. The assumption is that another evaluator using the same methods and procedures should discover the same data. This is not to say that all evaluators will reach the same conclusions. Although different evaluators may reach different conclusions, the use of standard data-gathering methods and procedures helps to ensure that the same areas of examination are explored with the parties.

Introduction to the Report

All court orders provide a strange looking notation such as "93-CVD-12305." This is the court's reference number, and it tells you three things. The "93" provides information about when the case began litigation. In this case, the case began in 1993. The first hypothesis drawn from this is that the parties have been litigating a long time. The evaluator may wish to inquire about the history of litigation, with particular interest on obstacles to settlement.

The "CVD" indicates that the case is in domestic or family court, and "12305" is the case number assigned by the court administrator. In some jurisdictions, the letters of the presiding judges also appears after the case number (e.g., LBE). This introductory information quickly identifies the case to be discussed.

General Case Information Drawn From Custody Evaluation
Psychological Evaluation

Smith v. Jones   August 1, 1997
93 CVD 2527 (LBE)

The Reason for Referral Section

The next step is to provide a description of the referral concerns. This section may take various forms. It may contain direct statements drawn from the court order, narrative from the parties, or your understanding of the reasons for referral. An example of a referral section in which the party's description served as the point of departure, and an example of how the court's concerns were the defining element are provided.

Example of Referral Section From Party's Allegations
Reason for Referral

Mr. Smith brought this action, in part, because he believes that Ms. Jones is attempting to influence their children to view him in a negative light, to view Mr. Jones as their father, and to control the amount of time he has with his children. Mr. Smith stated that "everything was going fine until (my marriage to) Paula." Once married, he believes that Ms. Jones felt threatened that Mr. Smith would sue for custody because "I am better off financially. . . . She tried to split me and Carole by writing Carole a letter about me, she contacted Carole's ex-husband and her parents. Karen alleged to Carole's parents that I was being investigated for sexual abuse. Carole's parents showed up with a shotgun. Karen has also manipulated people to call DSS [Department of Social Services] alleging that I beat my child and was neglectful."

Mr. Smith stated that he would not have taken this action to pursue custody had Ms. Jones appropriately respected his relationship and protected his visitation time with his children.

Example of Referral Section From Court Order

On September 3, 1996, Judge Evans entered an order in which Mr. Smith's visitation privileges were modified. Among the modifications, Mr. Smith was ordered to maintain supervised visitation at all times.

On September 19, 1996, an Order appointing Gena Custer as *Guardian Ad Litem* and Cheryl Bennett as volunteer CLC custody advocate was entered. Among other issues, Ms. Custer and Ms. Bennett were directed to "investigate and determine the facts."

On December 30, 1996, Ms. Custer issued a letter to Plaintiff's and Defendant's attorneys summarizing her investigation. Ms. Custer and Ms. Bennett concluded no abuse had occurred. They recommended that "the restrictions on Ray's visitation be lifted. . . . We believe that supervision is not necessary and should no longer be required."

On January 6, 1997, a Motion for Psychological Examination was offered to the Court by Ms. Becker in which she challenged the investigative report completed by Ms. Custer and Ms. Bennett. Upon hearing arguments, Judge Evans ordered Psychological Evaluations to be completed on the Plaintiff and Defendant as well as Ashley and Joe. "Laurie Reed is appointed to evaluate the minor children Ashley and Joe. Jonathan Gould is appointed to evaluate the Plaintiff and Defendant."

After a series of letters in which the psycholegal questions guiding this evaluation were clearly articulated, Ms. Becker forwarded a March 12, 1997 letter in which four clearly defined *psycholegal questions* were posed. Subsequently, an additional question was added by the examiner.

Psycholegal Questions Section

The purpose of this section is to formulate questions that guide the evaluation. Specific psycholegal questions provide a means of not only selecting the focus of the evaluation but also determining the methodology and procedures to be used. Two examples of psycholegal questions of differing complexity follow.

Example of Generally Defined Psycholegal Questions
Psycholegal Questions Guiding This Evaluation

This evaluation was ordered by the Honorable Judge William White on December 9, 1996. Judge White posed three questions to be pursued by the evaluation. These questions are the following:

1. Is Mr. Smith (Plaintiff) a fit and proper person to have the care and custody of the minor children?
2. Is Ms. Jones (Defendant) a fit and proper person to have the care and custody of the minor children?
3. What recommendations does the psychologist make to the court with respect to the issues of custody and visitation between these parents and the minor children?

Example of Specifically Defined Psycholegal Questions
Psycholegal Questions Guiding the Evaluation

1. What is the ability of Mr. and Mrs. Smith to parent Mrs. Jones' two children effectively and safely?
2. What are the parental competencies of Mr. and Mrs. Smith?
3. What are the behavior management strategies used in parental discipline of children?
4. What are the risks of possible abusive behavior upon the minor children by Mr. and Mrs. Smith?
5. If a risk does exist, what safety measures need to be put into place to ensure the children's safety?
6. What is the present mental health and emotional stability of Mr. and Mrs. Smith?
7. What concerns exist of the capability of Mr. and Mrs. Smith to parent a 7-year-old and a 13-year-old child?
8. Are the children afraid of Mr. Smith? If yes, why?
9. What is the health and stability of Mr. and Mrs. Smith's marriage?
10. What effects, if any, may be of concern regarding parental competencies, mental health, or emotional stability resulting from the marriage of second cousins?

Methods and Procedures Section

The report should accurately reflect the methods and procedures used in the evaluation process. There should be a brief discussion of what steps you took and with whom. Some evaluators also indicate the amount of time they spend on each step. The examples that follow indicate the individuals who participated in the evaluation and in what procedures they were involved. The first example describes the methods and procedures used in an evaluation of two remarried families who were contesting the custodial placement of the biological parents' two children. Note how many different types of interviews were needed for a thorough evaluation.

Example of Methods and Procedures Section
Methods and Procedures

The current literature addressing appropriate methods and procedures in civil forensic evaluations identifies the following to be included in a competently conducted examination: forensic interview data using a structured interview format (Ackerman, 1995; Grisso, 1988; Schutz et al., 1989); self-report data (Greenberg, 1996; Grisso, 1989; Schutz et al., 1989); standardized psychological tests that have appropriate basis and relevance to the psycholegal questions posed (Brodzinsky, 1993; Committee on Ethical Guidelines, 1991; Greenberg, 1996); direct observational data (Ackerman, 1995; APA, 1994; Committee on Ethical Guidelines, 1991; Greenberg, 1996; Greenberg & Shuman, 1997; Grisso, 1988; Schutz et al., 1989; Stahl, 1994); and collateral interview data and record review (Ackerman, 1995; Greenberg, 1996; Greenberg & Shuman, 1997; Grisso, 1988; Schutz et al., 1989; Shapiro, 1984).

The observations and standardized assessments that contributed to forming opinions about these questions followed these procedures:

1. Psychological evaluation of Sally Jones
2. Psychological evaluation of Ernie Jones
3. Psychological evaluation of Rick Smith
4. Psychological evaluation of Lisa Smith
5. Psychological evaluation of Joe Smith
6. Psychological evaluation of Ashley Smith
7. Forensic interview of Sally Jones
8. Forensic interview of Ernie Jones
9. Forensic interview of Rick Smith
10. Forensic interview of Lisa Smith
11. Behavioral observation of Ms. Jones with each child (Joe and Ashley)
12. Behavioral observation of Ms. Jones with all children (Joe and Ashley)
13. Behavioral observation of Mr. Jones with Joe and Ashley
14. Behavioral observation of Ms. Jones with Joe and Ashley
15. Behavioral observation of Mr. Smith with each child (Joe and Ashley)
16. Behavioral observation of Mr. Smith with all children (Joe and Ashley)
17. Behavioral observation of Mrs. Smith with Joe and Ashley
18. Behavioral observation of Mr. and Mrs. Smith with Joe and Ashley
19. Review of court records
20. Collateral interviews and record reviews
    a. Ms. Laurie Skinner, MSW, Joe's therapist
    b. Ms. Jan Watson, MSW, Ashley's therapist
    c. Mr. David Evans, MA, school psychologist for Ashley
    d. Ms. Nicely, school psychologist for Joe

As revealed in this example, the report reflects a somewhat academic bent toward explaining the behavioral science support for the use of each evaluation procedure. Other evaluators consider the inclusion of literature citations to be inappropriate in a custody evaluation, but I believe that evaluators need to educate the court about the conceptual and empirical underpinnings of our methods and procedures. An introductory paragraph such as that shown in the example clearly indicates the empirical and/or conceptual foundation for the structure of the evaluation and provides little room for an examining attorney to allege that you did not follow standard civil forensic methods and procedures.

Also in the Methods and Procedures section is a description of the tests, inventories, and other data-gathering tools used. The next example shows how simply the instrumentation and interview protocols can be summarized.

Example of Instrumentation Section

Psychological Tests Administered

Minnesota Multiphasic Personality Inventory—2	(MMPI-2)
Millon Clinical Multiaxial Inventory—II	(MCMI-II)
Wechsler Intelligence Scale for Children—3rd Edition	(WISC-III)

Interview Techniques Administered

The Parenting History Survey	(PHS)
Forensic History Questionnaire, Parts 1 and 2	(FHQ)

Background and History Section

The background and history of the parties are described in this section. In the beginning of the section, I typically include a statement indicating that the information represented in this section is drawn directly from interview and self-report data provided by the litigant. There is no attempt to present the data as factual or supported by the evidence. It is information based upon the story provided by the litigant.

I include this qualifier to indicate that these background and history data do not include the evaluator's inferences or interpretations. The section provides data from the party's view only and is not intended to be presented as information that has yet to be supported through external validation.

There are a number of variables that are described in this section. The variables serve to organize the volumes of data typically provided in custody evaluations. Provided here is an example of a family-of-origin variable that typically is presented in the body of a report. The next example describes a partial listing of variables discussed in the Background and History section.

Example of Background/History Variable
Background and History

(The information contained within this section and the comparable section describing Mr. Smith's interview data is reported by the litigant on the PHS, FHQ, and interview data. There is no attempt to present it to the court as factual or as supported by the evidence. The background and history information is based upon self-report data completed by the party. It is not intended to represent either my opinion or opinions provided by collateral sources.)

Family of Origin: Ms. Jones was born on June 11, 1959 to Charlotte and Edward Mitchell. She is 38 years old and the oldest of four daughters: Debbie (33), Sheryl (32), and Lynn (26). Mr. and Mrs. Mitchell were described as having "a good relationship for most of my childhood. The latter end my dad's drinking caused a lot of problems. They separated after my high school year and divorced in 1986-1987. They moved back in together (in 1988) and remarried in 1991." Mr. Mitchell died in 1991.

Mr. Mitchell was a "local truck driver" who worked approximately 40 hours a week. He also attempted to run a family drug store. He was described as "usually home, informed, stable, consistent, reliable, orderly, open, trusting, restrictive, having rigid rules and considerate." He was also described as "misusing alcohol, critical and disrespectful." She indicated that her father had been emotionally mistreated by his alcoholic father. She also indicated that three times during her childhood, Mr. Mitchell lost his job because the company for which he worked went bankrupt. She described getting along with her father "average to better than average" and also indicated that her father emotionally mistreated the family.

Ms. Jones described her mother as a homemaker. She worked outside the family home about 25 to 30 hours a week. The last grade she completed in school was 6th grade. She was described as "usually home, informed, resilient, consistent, stable, a victim, trusting, open, thoughtful, rarely emotional, warm, accepting and honest." She was also viewed as "easy to respect, (providing) rigid rules and easy to confide in." She indicated that she got along "average" with her mother.

Results of Clinical Interviews Section

The results of hours of forensic interviewing should be summarized in this section. The section should be organized first by describing with whom you spoke, when, and for how long. Typically, this section will include informa-

---

QUICK REFERENCE   **Partial Listing of Variables Included in Background and History Section**

- Family of origin
- Educational history
- Employment history
- Residential history
- Legal history
- Military history
- Alcohol history
- Drug history
- Physical/medical health history
- Mental health history
- Relationship history
- Premarital history
- Marital history
- Postseparation history
- Concerns about other parent
- Concerns about children
- Concerns about self

---

tion gained through individual, parent-child, and family interviews. Also included may be information gained from self-report inventories. When I use self-report data, they are usually direct quotes taken from a document or questionnaire that contains the parent's own description.

There is no right way to organize this section. I prefer including information about the parent's parenting philosophy, behavior management style, and direct behavioral observations of parent-child interaction, and I use a systems framework to guide the choice of variables. The following gives examples from each of these three content areas.

Example of Results of Interview Section

Parenting Philosophy

Ms. Jones has described a significant change in her parenting over the past several years. She described having been significantly influenced by the ideas of her parents. She maintained that she has struggled to free herself from most of their influences. She stated, "The husband was the head of the household, his job was to tell everyone what the rules were and to financially provide food, clothing and shelter. The wife was to submit, her job was the home, children and husband. If I wanted to do anything outside of home (i.e., work, exercise, socialize) I had to hire sitters. Which I did."

Ms. Jones describes having made a significant change in her lifestyle that positively affected her children. "I was getting myself healthier. Was taking care of myself, separating myself. Saying no to being involved in my past limits. . . . I was weakened and had beliefs that were not healthy. . . . I was looking at words and not looking at the actions, this set the stage where I enabled the physical, verbal and emotional abuse of myself and my children. I did not take assertive action and became emotionally beat down."

Approach to Behavior Management

Historically, Ms. Jones has used a wooden spoon as a means of behavioral control. Over the past 2 to 3 years, she has recognized the inappropriateness of this disciplinary technique. She now uses a combination of discussion, time out, and other verbally based, limit-setting techniques.

Observations of Parenting Capacity

Ms. Jones was observed with each child as well as with all her children. Observations were consistent across each condition. She demonstrated patience and good communication skills, and she allowed each child to direct the activity. She readily entered into their play world and participated in a comfortable, easy, and emotionally loving manner.

No concerns were noted. Her play with the children was fluid, natural, supportive, loving, and overall excellent. Compared to other parents I have evaluated, I would characterize her as among the more involved, relaxed, and nonjudgmental. Yet she did not allow activity to become out of control nor lose sight of her responsibility as a parent.

Results of Psychological Tests Section

A discussion of results of the psychological test data is presented in this section. It should provide information about the party's emotional and psychological well-being, any indications about possible psychopathology and its effect on parenting, and a discussion of how the psychological test data are relevant to the parenting competencies questions important to the court.

It is important to remind the reader that the forensic use of psychological test data is different from its clinical use. It is wise to include a statement about using test results as a means of hypothesis generation rather than as confirmatory or diagnostic conclusions. It may also be prudent to remind the reader that the results are probabilistic in nature and reflect characteristics of people who have provided test responses similar to those of the current individual (Greenberg, 1996).

Example From Results of Psychological Tests Section

Results of Psychological Tests

NOTE: The psychological test interpretations presented below are hypotheses and should not be considered in isolation from other information in this matter. The interpretive statements are actuarial and expert predictions based upon the results of the tests. Personality test results reflect characteristics of people who have provided test response patterns similar to those of the current individual. Although test results are presented in an affirmative manner, they are probabilistic in nature. Furthermore, the reader should interpret these findings cautiously. From test results alone, it is impossible to tell if these patterns and/or deficits are directly or indirectly related to parental competencies. Therefore, the reader should examine the test interpretation for general trends and put limited weight on any one specific statement. In the integration and presentation of test data, where results were unclear or in conflict, I used clinical judgment to select the most likely hypotheses for presentation.

MMPI-2. This test compares Ms. Jones to a clinical population. Therefore, her test scores may appear somewhat distorted because she has taken this test for nonclinical purposes. The MMPI-2 highlights psychopathological characteristics and dynamics rather than strengths and positive attributes under the assumption that the clinician is performing diagnostic and treatment planning functions for an individual requesting psychological intervention rather than custody evaluation. Therefore, the assumptions of the test and the inferences drawn from the data may overstate behavioral and attitudinal characteristics.

According to this standard of comparison, Ms. Jones scores on the MMPI-2 suggest a reasonably well-adjusted individual. Her approach to the MMPI-2 was open and cooperative. Validity scales suggest this to be a valid profile. Her scores suggest a tendency to be somewhat open and uncritical of others ($F = 44$; $K = 56$). She appears somewhat interested in presenting herself in a favorable light.

Ms. Jones's MMPI-2 clinical scales are within normal limits. She appears to hold an average interest in being with other people. She does not display signs of inappropriate withdrawal or social isolation. She appears to have a relatively average need to follow rules and respect the need for other imposed structure. However, she may struggle to maintain compliance with those in authority, although she may often work hard at keeping her frustration from becoming public.

Current research on the viability of remarriages reveals that there is a significantly higher rate of divorce among remarried couples than among first-time married couples. When remarried couples with children divorce, the children are subject to another round of confusion, instability, and insecurity. Thus, it may be useful to explore present marital distress as part of this custodial evaluation. The MMPI-2 purports to measure level of marital distress (MDS). Ms. Jones's score on the MDS scale was within normal limits ($MDS = 55$).

There is a general social concern about the use of drugs and alcohol in family systems. In light of Ms. Jones's family of origin having some foundation in alcoholism, it was deemed appropriate to explore scores related to the use and abuse of alcohol and drugs.

Collateral Data Section

The purpose of collateral data is to provide external support to the party's allegations. Earlier, I described how collateral information is introduced in the body of the report. Provide here is an example of information contained in a summary of a collateral phone interview, as well as an example of information contained in a summary of a collateral record review.

Example of Collateral Interview Summary

Laurie Skinner, MSW, was interviewed on July 3, 1997 for about 75 minutes. Ms. Skinner has been Joe's treating therapist since March 18, 1996. She stated that she saw Joe weekly from March through June 1996 and then less frequently, averaging once every 3 weeks.

Ms. Skinner stated that Ms. Jones brought Joe to all sessions. Ms. Skinner indicated that Joe was being brought by his mother with the expressed goal of "helping Joe express his feelings. . . . I don't have the perception that [Sally] puts words in [Joe's] mouth. . . . I don't see Sally coming in to 'Rick-bash.'"

She stated that Joe "is not alone in sessions . . . Sally serves as an organizer of information for Joe to talk with me." Ms. Skinner explained that she finds it difficult to understand some of Joe's verbal descriptions of events and has found Ms. Jones helpful in assisting in understanding Joe.

She stated that initially Ms. Jones was "persuaded that Rick was a danger. That he showed abusive and intrusive behavior." She stated that, in hindsight, she may have unintentionally accepted some of Ms. Jones's ideas about Mr. Smith that were then reinforced when Mr. Smith "showed up uninvited" during one of Joe's sessions. "This was viewed as intrusive."

Ms. Skinner stated that she and Joe discussed her interest in talking with Mr. Smith on April 15, 1996. On April 18, she met with Mr. Smith to discuss treatment issues. She met again with Mr. Smith and his wife on February 4, 1997. Both meetings were described as "productive."

Mr. Smith is reported to have asked Ms. Skinner for greater involvement in Joe's treatment. He is reported to have asked for "weekly phone check-ins or check-ins on an as-needed basis or monthly and a meeting with Joe and Rick. Rick mentioned he wanted to read Joe's records."

Ms. Skinner indicated that she found Mr. Smith somewhat inconsistent. "What transpires in session does not carry over. My experience of the session does not often match his. There is little, or no, carryover from session to real world." For example, "Rick has not taken advantage of having a session with Joe."

She described Ms. Jones's parenting behavior as "very loving, comfortable with Joe, but parent-child boundaries are very clear. She sets limits well. She has developed consequences for following these limits. She seeks to teach but not in an overtly didactic manner. It is appropriate parenting mode. There are underlying principles to her parenting: responsibility, honesty, and consideration of others. . . . Sally is more structured during day activities and that is positive. When there are [behavior] problems at school, Sally gives Joe consequences. . . . [She displays a] child-centered activity, but the parents are in charge. When Rick has the kids, [Joe and Sally report that] activities are less structured."

Example of Collateral Record Review Summary

The information reviewed was submitted by both Ms. Graham and Ms. Sumrall. Each separate packet of material contained the same material. The collateral information reviewed in this section included the following documents:

1. Case history prepared by Rhonda Smith of CDSS
2. Medical examination report prepared by Anthony Nelson, MD
3. Summary of investigation report prepared by Betsy Ross of CDSS
4. CDSS CPS Referral Form
5. Charlotte-Mecklenburg Police Department Supplemental Report describing interview with Ben Franklin conducted by SD Henry CMDSS
6. Charlotte-Mecklenburg Police Department Supplemental Report describing interview with G. Washington conducted by SD Henry of CMDSS

The Case History submitted by Ms. Smith contains information about four interviews conducted in 1995. The records indicate that the histories were written about 6 months after the interviews took place. The first interview reports that Marlee was tearful and withdrawn.

Results of Children's Interviews and Testing

After each parent has been discussed in the report, it is time that each child is thoroughly discussed following a structure similar to that described above. Each child's individual and parent-child interviews are described. Psychological and educational data are presented in a manner similar to the above. Typically, there is a greater emphasis on describing the quality of the parent-child relationship in this section. It is important to keep the data sections distinct from each other. Describe the child's individual qualities in a subheading separate from the discussion of the parent-child observations. The example provided here describes a typical summary of a child data section.

Example of Summary for Child Interview and Test Data Section

Interview With Ashley Smith

Ashley Smith was interviewed individually on April 10, 1997 for about 90 minutes. She was observed with her mother on the same date for about 1 hour. She was observed with her father on June 24, 1997 for about 1 hour. All other parent-child observations are similar to those reported for her brother Joe.

Ashley is an engaging, high-energy, playful little girl who displayed immediate comfort in creating a positive, warm, and enjoyable interview. She talked openly about each parent and stepparent. She described feeling strongly positive about each parent. She enjoys time at each parent's home. Similarly, she described feeling positively about each stepparent.

Relationship With Parents

Similar to her brother's positive relationship with each parent and stepparent, Ashley displayed an ease and comfort with each parent. She was verbally interactive with each parent, inviting of their involvement in her activities, and generally happy in her exchanges with each parent.

Ashley displayed a closer, more verbally interactive relationship with her mother than with her father. Mother and daughter appeared to enjoy laughing together and playing with traditionally female toys such as dolls and dollhouse. Father and daughter appeared to enjoy each other, too. Their interaction was a bit more structured and less spontaneous than that observed with Ms. Jones. However, both observations revealed positive, healthy, close relationship qualities.

Ashley spoke about feeling frustrated that she cannot see her half-sister, Marie, when she visits her father. She does not appear to understand why Marie does not visit Mr. Smith any more.

Ashley was able to clearly and consistently distinguish Mr. Smith as her "real" father from Mr. Jones as her stepfather.

Academic Data

During the initial meeting on April 10, 1997, Ashley was administered the verbal scale of the Wechsler Intelligence Scale for Children—3rd Edition (WISC-III) as much as an opportunity to build rapport under somewhat structured and safe circumstances as to gain an estimate of her intellectual functioning. She readily engaged in the testing process.

Results reveal cognitive strengths in areas of verbal abstract reasoning (Var = 11), arithmetic (Ari = 13), and vocabulary (Voc = 14). She displayed some limited cognitive skill in general social knowledge (Inf = 8) and short-term memory functioning (DS = 8). There is no psychometric evidence supporting concern for attentional difficulties (Freedom from Distractibility Index = 104).

Summary

Ashley displayed a comparable level of comfort and ease with each parent, similar to that observed with her brother. Although there are slight differences in how she interacted with each parent, differences were relatively irrelevant to the overall positive quality of her relationship with each parent.

Interpretation of Results Section

The Interpretation of Results section is where the evaluator is able to integrate the separate data sections into a coherent whole. This is where the individual interview data, self-report information, psychological testing, collateral interviews, and direct observations are compared and contrasted. This is where our ability to analyze and synthesize the mountains of data helps the reader tie the disparate data into a comprehensive story that argues for the best psychological interests of the children.

Reflecting my interest in anchoring reports in the behavioral science literature, I recommend that the Interpretation of Results section is organized around salient variables in the developmental literature. Schutz et al. (1989) provide a conceptual framework that guides some of this section. The systems framework described by Kirkpatrick et al. (1994) also serves as a useful data-organizing model.

Provided here is an example of some of the variables around which the Interpretation of Results section is organized, as well as an example of how the data are integrated in a discussion of one of the variables.

Example of Interpretation of Results Discussion—Single Variable

Accurate perceptions of child. There is evidence based upon observation of Ms. Jones and her children that she accurately understands the educational, physical, emotional, and social needs of each child. Direct observation of Ms. Jones and her children supports the view that Ms. Jones holds an accurate perception of her children's current developmental needs. Discussions with Ashley and Joe reveal that both feel well-understood by their mother. Collateral interview sources also support the view that Ms. Jones historically has had a clear, healthy understanding of her children's needs, wants, interests, and desires. Collateral data also support Ms. Jones's contention that she has been consistently involved in the educational and special needs of Joe and Ashley.

The data gathered in this evaluation reveal a somewhat less accurate picture of the children held by Mr. Smith. He appears to understand his children and their physical and emotional needs. Yet he has been relatively uninvolved in their counseling, schoolwork, and other extracurricular activities. There is also

---

QUICK REFERENCE   **Partial List of Organizing Variables for Interpretation of Results Section**

- Family-of-origin factors
- Positive emotional attachment
- Differentiation of self
- Accurate perception of child
- Communication skills
- Impulse control
- Thought disorders
- Moral/social judgment
- Primary caretaker
- Psychological parent
- Ability to support other parent's relationship with child
- Child developmental variables specific to each child's age (e.g., developmental tasks, intellectual, emotional, social, psychological, special needs, educational, etc.)
- Type of parental conflict
- Level of parental conflict
- Type of parenting/coparenting style
- Intergenerational support
- Community resources
- Interparental communication

---

collateral data supporting the view that Mr. Smith's increased interest in his children has occurred over the past few years, compared with Ms. Jones's involvement since the children's infancy.

It is unclear how well Mr. Smith understands the unique challenges facing his son. According to collateral data sources, Mr. Smith has had relatively little contact with his son's school and therapist. Although there may be legitimate reasons for Mr. Smith having some discomfort in interactions with school personnel or the treating therapists, the apparent lack of consistent follow-through on invitations to become more involved raises questions about motivation, sincerity, or other factors unrelated to his children's well-being.

Conclusions Section

The final section of a report is the conclusions section. It contains direct answers to the psycholegal questions posed at the beginning of the report.

The example provided shows how the conclusions are organized directly around each psycholegal question. It is here that mental health professionals offer their opinions to the court. Each opinion should be framed as a probability statement. It should begin with words similar to, "Within a reasonable degree of psychological certainty, I conclude . . ." Framing the conclusionary statement within a reasonable degree of certainty helps to remind the reader that the conclusions are *hypotheses* drawn from data. There may be errors in the data, errors in the interpretation of the data, or errors in the conclusions drawn from the interpretations. Thus, our conclusions are statements based upon somewhat tentative, and at times uncertain, data with a limited ability to accurately predict the efficacy of our recommendations to future behavior. Our conclusions are educated guesses, based upon research, experience, and training. But they are educated guesses. Never present your conclusions to the court as anything other than judgments extrapolated from data yielding probability predictions.

The second important aspect is to frame the degree of certainty in a manner that accurately reflects the certainty you hold about your conclusions. There will be some conclusions where you have the highest degree of certainty, others in which you may hold a moderate degree of certainty, and still others in which you may be speculating. It is often helpful to express to the court the relative degree of certainty you hold for each conclusion. In that way, the trier of fact is able to understand the confidence you have in your conclusions and draw proper inferences about which decisions need closer scrutiny than others.

Example of a Conclusion Section

Conclusions

Three psycholegal questions guided this evaluation. This section will be organized around each of these questions.

Question 1:   Is Mr. Smith a fit and proper person to have the care and custody of the minor children?

Answer: Within a reasonable degree of psychological certainty, I conclude that Mr. Smith is a competent parent who has established a positive, caring relationship with his children. There are some historical data to support the view that he has been somewhat inconsistent in the degree and level of involvement in his children's daily life. There is no doubt, however, that Mr. Smith has demonstrated high-quality parenting, communication, and interpersonal relationship skills in observed interactions with his children.

Similarly, his children feel strongly and positively about the quality of their relationship with him. Allegations by Ms. Jones that Joe and/or Ashley feel threatened or fearful of their father were not supported by interview data, direct behavioral observations, or collateral data from Ms. Skinner and Ms. Watson.

Mr. Smith's wife, Lisa, provides a complementary set of parenting skills. She was observed to have developed a positive, healthy, and warm relationship with each child.

There are no data that support the concern that Joe and Ashley feel unsafe, insecure, and/or fearful of time with their father.

The majority of the data argue for the view that Joe and Ashley have a healthy, positive, emotionally supportive, and physically close relationship with their father and stepmother.

There are also considerable direct observational data as well as self-report data that Joe and Ashley accept their stepsister, Meredith, as a full-fledged family member.

Summary

This chapter has provided a step-by-step description of the components of a child custody evaluation report. This model is but one of several available to evaluators. No matter what model of report writing and presentation you use, there are some universal recommendations.

The first is to always present information that clearly distinguishes the data from the inferences you draw from that data, and then distinguishes the interpretations from the conclusions. In this way, readers will be able to glean the data and make judgments about conclusions based upon their analysis as well as yours. When the data, inferences, and interpretations are intertwined, it becomes impossible for a third party to independently examine the meaning of your data or understand the logic supporting your results.

Another important element is to always use multiple data-gathering sources. As discussed throughout this book, all reports should include interview data, self-report data, collateral data, test data, and direct behavioral observations. The multitrait-multimethod technique helps to ensure the accuracy of your results by requiring confirmation of observed behavior from at least two data sources.

Finally, a report to the court should anchor results to the behavioral science literature. One does not need to provide citations in the body of the text or a reference list at the end of the report. However, there should be clear references to how the observed behavior reflects what we know about child and developmental psychology, adjustment to divorce factors, parental conflict, and parenting styles, among other salient factors. Your report should appear to be crafted within the science of behavioral science research and literature, not as some creative fiction based upon years of clinical experience.

Each report you prepare is an opportunity for you to demonstrate to the court the wisdom of using an expert mental health professional. When the report provides a scientifically crafted answer to the court's questions, it will reflect well upon all evaluators and remind the court of the value of mental health experts. If your report provides opinions that are not anchored in behavioral science literature, and the judge is scratching his or her head trying to figure out how your conclusions were derived from your data, the court is reminded of the wasted time and money spent on expert mental health opinions.

Each report you submit is a reflection on each of us. It is a means of influence. A good report teaches the court about the utility of behavioral science research in application to serious family problems seeking resolution before the court. It is an opportunity for mental health professionals to make a difference in the lives of people whose families are in great turmoil, through the professional application of our knowledge in child custody evaluations.

A bad report, poorly written and poorly integrated, hurts us all and diminishes the chances for the court system to use the wonderfully extensive research database available in mental health to better serve the children of families of divorce.

References

Abbott, D. A., & Brody, G. H. (1985). The relation of child age, gender, and number of children to the marital adjustment of wives. *Journal of Marriage and the Family, 47,* 77-84.

Ackerman, M. J. (1995). *Clinician's guide to child custody evaluations.* New York: John Wiley.

Ackerman, M. J. (1997). *Does Wednesday mean Mom's house or Dad's? Parenting together while living apart.* New York: John Wiley.

Ackerman, M. J., & Ackerman, M. (1996). Child custody evaluation practices: A 1996 survey of psychologists. *Family Law Quarterly, 30,* 565-586.

Ackerman, M. J., & Ackerman, M. (1997). Custody evaluation practices: A survey of experienced professionals (revisited). *Professional Psychology: Research and Practice, 28*(2), 137-145.

Ackerman, M. J., & Schoendorf, K. (1992). *The Ackerman-Schoendorf Parent Evaluation of Custody Test (ASPECT).* Los Angeles: Western Psychological Services.

Adkerson v. MK-Ferguson Co., Mich. Ct. App., No. 120434, 12/16/91, 58 Empl. Prac. December. P 41, 401, 1919 Mich. App. 129, 477 N. W. 2d 465 (1991).

Ahrons, C. R., & Rodgers, R. H. (1987). *Divorced families: A multidisciplinary developmental view.* New York: Norton.

Ainsworth, M. D. (1979). Infant-mother attachment. *American Psychologist, 34,* 932-937.

Ainsworth, M. D. S., Blehar, M. C., Waters, E., & Wall, S. (Eds.). (1978). *Patterns of attachment: A psychological study of the Strange Situation.* Hillsdale, NJ: Lawrence Erlbaum.

Amato, P. (1987). Family processes in one-parent, stepparent and intact families. *Journal of Marriage and the Family, 49,* 327-337.

American Academy of Child and Adolescent Psychiatry. (1988). Guidelines for the clinical evaluation of child and adolescent sexual abuse. *Journal of the American Academy of Child and Adolescent Psychiatry, 27,* 655-657.

American Academy of Child and Adolescent Psychiatry. (1997). Practice parameters for the forensic evaluation of children and adolescents who may have been physically or sexually abused. *Journal of the American Academy of Child and Adolescent Psychiatry, 36*(3), 423-442.

American Professional Society on the Abuse of Children. (1990). *Guidelines for psychosocial evaluation of suspected sexual abuse in young children.* Chicago: Author.

American Professional Society on the Abuse of Children. (1995a). *Practice guidelines: Use of anatomical dolls in child sexual abuse assessments.* Chicago: Author.

American Professional Society on the Abuse of Children. (1995b). *Psychosocial evaluation of suspected psychological maltreatment in children and adolescents.* Chicago: Author.

American Psychiatric Association. (1994). *Diagnostic and statistical manual of mental disorders* (4th ed.). Washington, DC: Author.

American Psychological Association. (1992). Ethical principles of psychologists and code of conduct. *American Psychologist, 47,* 1597-1611.

American Psychological Association. (1994). Guidelines for child custody evaluations in divorce proceedings. *American Psychologist, 49,* 677-680.

Applied Innovations, Inc. v. Regents of the University of Minnesota, 867 F2. d 626 (8th Cir. 1989).

Arendell, T. (1995). *Fathers and divorce.* Thousand Oaks, CA: Sage.

Azar, B. (1997). Poor recall mars research and treatment. *APA Monitor, 28*(1), 1, 29.

Baris, M. A., & Garrity, C. N. (1988). *Children of divorce: Guidelines for residence and visitation.* DeKalb, IL: Psytec, Inc.

Baumrind, D. (1971). Current patterns of parental authority. *Developmental Psychology Monograph, 4*(1, Pt. 2).

Beazley v. Davis, 92 Nev. 81, 545 P2d 206 (1976).

Ben-Porath, Y. S., Graham, J. R., Hall, G. C. N., Hirschman, R. D., & Zaragoza, M. S. (Eds.). (1995). *Forensic applications of the MMPI-2.* Thousand Oaks, CA: Sage.

Berliner, L., & Conte, J. R. (1993). Sexual abuse evaluations: Conceptual and empirical obstacles. *Child Abuse & Neglect, 17,* 111-125.

Bigner, J., & Jacobson, R. D. (1989). Parenting behaviors of homosexual and heterosexual fathers. *Journal of Homosexuality, 18*(1-2), 173-186.

Black, J. C., & Cantor, D. J. (1989). *Child custody.* New York: Columbia University Press.

Blankenhorn, D. (1995). *Fatherless America: Confronting our most urgent social problem.* New York: Basic Books.

Block, J., Block, J. H., & Gjerde, P. F. (1988). Parental functioning and the home environment in families of divorce: Prospective and concurrent analyses. *Journal of the American Academy of Child and Adolescent Psychiatry, 27*(2), 207-213.

Borum, R., Otto, R., & Golding, S. (1993, Spring). Improving clinical judgement and decision making in forensic evaluation. *Journal of Psychiatry & Law,* pp. 35-76.

Bowlby, J. (1969). *Attachment and loss: Vol. 1. Attachment.* London: Hogarth.

Bowlby, J. (1980). *Attachment and loss: Vol. 2. Loss.* New York: Basic Books.

Brainerd, C. J., Reyna, V. F., & Brandse, E. (1995). Are children's false memories more persistent than their true memories? *Psychological Science, 6*(6), 359-364.

Bray, J. H. (1991). Psychosocial factors affecting custodial and visitation arrangements. *Behavioral Sciences and the Law, 9,* 419-437.

Bricklin, B. (1984). *Bricklin Perceptual Scales.* Furlong, PA: Village Publishing.

Bricklin, B. (1990). *Perception of Relationships Tests (PORT).* Furlong, PA: Village Publishing.

Brodsky, S. L. (1991). *Testifying in court: Guidelines and maxims for the expert witness.* Washington, DC: American Psychological Association.

Brodzinsky, D. M. (1993). On the use and misuse of psychological testing in child custody evaluations. *Professional Psychology: Research and Practice, 24,* 213-219.

Brownstone, H. (1980). The homosexual parent in custody disputes. *Queen's Law Journal,* 199-238.

Buchanan, C., Maccoby, E., & Dornbusch, S. (1991). Caught between parents: Adolescents' experience in divorced homes. *Child Development, 62,* 1008-1029.

Burgess v. Burgess, 1996 WL 174116 (Cal.).

Butcher, J., & Pope, K. (1993). Seven issues in conducting forensic assessments: Ethical responsibilities in light of new standards and new tests. *Ethics & Behavior, 3*(3/4), 267-288.

Camera, K., & Resnick, G. (1988). Interparental conflict and cooperation: Factors moderating children's post-divorce adjustment. In E. M. Hetherington & J. D. Arasteh (Eds.), *Impact of divorce, single parenting, and stepparenting on children* (pp. 169-196). Hillsdale, NJ: Lawrence Erlbaum.

Campbell, D. T., & Fiske, D. W. (1959). Convergent and discriminant validation by the multitrait-multimethod matrix. *Psychological Bulletin, 56,* 81-105.

Campbell v. Pommier, 5 Conn. App. 29, 496 A2d 975 (1985).

Carlson v. Carlson, 229 Cal. App. 3d 1330, 280 Cal. Rptr. 840 (1991).

Cartwright, G. F. (1993). Expanding the parameters of Parental Alienation Syndrome. *American Journal of Family Therapy, 21,* 205-215.

Ceci, S. J., & Bruck, M. (1993). The suggestibility of the child witness: A historical review and synthesis. *Psychological Bulletin, 113,* 403-439.

Ceci, S., & Bruck, M. (1995). *Jeopardy in the courtroom.* Washington, DC: American Psychological Association.

Cherlin, A. (1978). Remarriage as an incomplete institution. *American Journal of Sociology, 84,* 634-650.

Childs v. Williams, 1992 WL 15253 (Mother. App.).

Clingempeel, W. G., & Reppucci, N. D. (1982). Joint custody after divorce: Major issues and goals for research. *Psychological Bulletin, 91*(1), 101-127.

Committee on Ethical Guidelines for Forensic Psychologists. (1991). Specialty guidelines for forensic psychologists. *Law and Human Behavior, 15,* 655-665.

Commonwealth v. Monico, 396 Mass. 793, 488 NE2d 1168 (1986).

Daubert v. Merrell Dow Pharmaceuticals, 113 S. Ct. 2786 (1993).

Depner, C. E., & Bray, J. H. (1990). Modes of participation for nonresidential parents: The challenge for research, policy, education and practice. *Family Relations, 39,* 378-381.

Depner, C. E., Cannata, K. V., & Simon, M. B. (1992). Building a uniform statistical reporting system: A snapshot of California Family Court Services. *Family and Conciliation Courts Review, 30,* 185-206.

Derdeyn, A. P., et al. (1982). *Child custody consultation: Report of the Task Force on Clinical Assessment in Child Custody.* Washington, DC: American Psychiatric Association.

Doris, J. (1991). *The suggestibility of children's recollections: Implications for eyewitness testimony.* Washington, DC: American Psychological Association.

Dudley, J. R. (1996). Noncustodial fathers speak about their parental role. *Family and Conciliation Courts Review, 34,* 410-426.

Duncan, G. D., & Hoffman, S. D. (1985). A reconsideration of the economic consequences of marital disruption. *Demography, 22,* 485-498.

Ellsworth, P., & Levy, R. (1969). Legislative reform of child custody adjudication: An effort to rely on social science data in formulating legal policies. *Law and Society Review, 4,* 167-233.

Emery, R. (1982). Interparental conflict and the children of discord and divorce. *Psychological Bulletin, 92,* 310-330.

Emery, R. (1994). *Renegotiating family relationships: Divorce, child custody, and mediation.* New York: Guilford.

Faigman, D. L. (1995). The evidentiary status of social science under Daubert: Is it "scientific," "technical," or "other" knowledge. *Psychology, Public Policy & Law, 1,* 960-979.

Faller, K. C. (1993). Research on false allegations of sexual abuse in divorce. *APSAC Advisor, 6*(3), 1, 7-10.

Faller, K. C. (1996). Interviewing children who may have been abused: A historical perspective and overview of controversies. *Child Maltreatment, 1*(2), 83-95.

Federal Rules of Evidence. United States Code. Title 28.

Fischer, K. W. (1980). A theory of cognitive development: The control of hierarchies of skill. *Psychological Review, 87,* 477-531.

Fisher, R., Ury, W., & Patton, B. (1991). *Getting to yes: Negotiating agreement without giving in.* New York: Houghton Mifflin.

Fisher, S., & Fisher, R. L. (1986). *What we really know about parenting.* Northvale, NJ: Jason Aronson.

Fisher v. Johnson, 508 N.W.2d 352 (N.D. 1993).

Flavell, J. H. (1975). *The development of role-taking and communication skills in children.* Huntington, NY: Krieger.

Folberg, J., & Taylor, A. (1984). *Mediation: A comprehensive guide to resolving conflicts without litigation.* San Francisco: Jossey-Bass.

Friedrich, W. N., Grambsch, P., Damon, I., Hewitt, S. K., Koverola, C., Lang, R., & Wolfe, V. (1992). The Child Sexual Behavior Inventory: Normative and clinical comparisons. *Psychological Assessment, 4,* 303-311.

Frye v. United States, 293 F. 1013 (D.C. Cir. 1923).

Furstenberg, F. F., & Cherlin, A. J. (1991). *Divided families: What happens to children when parents part.* Cambridge, MA: Harvard University Press.

Furstenberg, F. F., Nord, C. W., Peterson, J. L., & Zill, N. (1983). The life course of children of divorce: Marital disruption and parental contact. *American Sociological Review, 48,* 656-668.

Gaines, R., Sandgrund, A., Green, A. H., & Power, E. (1978). Etiological factors in child maltreatment: A multi-variate study of abusing, neglecting, and normal mothers. *Journal of Abnormal Psychology, 87,* 531-540.

Garbino, J., & Gilliam, G. (1980). *Understanding abusive families.* Lexington, MA: Lexington Books.

Gardner, R. A. (1985). Recent trends in divorce and custody litigation. *Academy Forum (A Publication of the American Academy of Psychoanalysis), 29*(2), 3-7.

Gardner, R. (1986). *Child custody litigation.* Creskill, NJ: Creative Therapeutics.

Gardner, R. A. (1989a). Differentiating between bona fide and fabricated allegations of sexual abuse of children. *Journal of the American Academy of Matrimonial Lawyers, 5,* 1-26.

Gardner, R. A. (1989b). *Family evaluation in child custody, mediation, arbitration, and litigation.* Cresskill, NJ: Creative Therapeutics.

Gardner, R. (1992). *The Parental Alienation Syndrome.* Cresskill, NJ: Creative Therapeutics.

Gardner, R. (1997, June). Recommendations for dealing with parents who induce a parental alienation syndrome in their children. *Addendum IIIa.* Cresskill, NJ: Creative Therapeutics.

Gardner, R. (in press). *The Parental Alienation Syndrome and the evaluation of child abuse accusations.* Cresskill, NJ: Creative Therapeutics.

Garibaldi v. Dietz, 752 S.W.2d 771 (Ark. Ct. App. 1988).

Garrity, C., & Baris, M. (1994). *Caught in the middle: Protecting the children of high-conflict divorce.* New York: Lexington Books.

Gibbs, E. D. (1988). Psychosocial development of children raised by lesbian mothers: Review of research. *Women and Therapy, 8,* 65-75.

Gindes, M. (1995). Guidelines for child custody evaluations for psychologists: An overview and commentary. *Family Law Quarterly, 29*(1), 39-62.

Gindes, M., & Otto, R. (1997). Communicating the results of the evaluation with attorneys, courts, parties, or others. In *Children, divorce and custody: Lawyers and psychologists working together* (pp. 1353-1371). Chicago: American Bar Association.

GIW S Valve Co v. Smith, 471 So 2d 81 (Fla. Dist. Ct. App. 1985).

Glueck, S., & Glueck, E. (1950). *Unraveling juvenile delinquency.* Cambridge, MA: Harvard University Press.

Golding, S. L. (1992). Increasing the reliability, validity and relevance of psychological expert evidence: An introduction to the Special Issue on Expert Evidence. *Law and Human Behavior, 16,* 253-256.

Golding, S. L. (1994, November). The ethics of forensic expertise: Negotiating the gauntlet of law, ethics and professional practice. *AAFP Workshop Series,* Portland, OR.

Goldstein, J., Freud, A., & Solnit, A. (1979). *Beyond the best interests of the child.* New York: Free Press.

Goldwater, A. (1991). Le syndrome d'alienation parentale. In *Developpements recents en droit familial* (pp. 121-145). Cowansville, Quebec: Les Editions Yvon Blais.

Goodman-Delahunty, J. (1997). Forensic psychological expertise in the wake of *Daubert*. *Law and Human Behavior, 21*, 121-140.

Gordon, B. N. (1996, November 26). *A framework for assessing children's allegations of sexual abuse in juvenile, criminal and custody cases*. Workshop presented at the Charlotte Area Health Education Center Continuing Professional Education Program, Charlotte, NC.

Gordon, B. N., Schroeder, C. S., Ornstein, P. A., & Baker-Ward, L. E. (1995). Clinical implications of research on memory development. In T. Ney (Ed.), *True and false allegations of child sexual abuse: Assessment and case management* (pp. 99-124). New York: Brunner/Mazel.

Gottfredson, M. R., & Hirschi, T. (1990). *A general theory of crime*. Stanford, CA: Stanford University Press.

Gould, J. W., & Gunther, R. E. (1993). *Reinventing fatherhood*. Blue Summit Mountain, PA: TAB/McGraw-Hill

Greenberg, S. (1996, June). *Child-custody evaluations*. Workshop sponsored by the American Board of Professional Psychology Summer Institute, Post Graduate Study in Psychology, Portland, OR.

Greenberg, S., & Moreland, K. (1996, April). *Civil forensic use of the MMPI 2*. Workshop sponsored by the American Academy of Forensic Psychology, Las Vegas.

Greenberg, S. A., & Shuman, D. W. (1997). Irreconcilable conflict between therapeutic and forensic roles. *Professional Psychology: Research & Practice, 28*, 50-57.

Griggs v. Duke Power, 401 US 424 (1971).

Grisso, T. (1986). *Assessing competencies: Forensic assessment and instruments*. New York: Plenum.

Grisso, T. (1988). *Competency to stand trial evaluations: A manual for practice*. Sarasota, FL: Professional Resource Exchange.

Gruber v. Gruber, Super. Ct. No. 00204, 17 F.L.R. 1099 (1990).

Hagen, M. A. (1997). *Whores of the court: The fraud of psychiatric testimony and the rape of American justice*. New York: Regan Books.

Heilbrun, K. (1992). The role of psychological testing in forensic assessment. *Law and Human Behavior, 16*, 257-272.

Heilbrun, K. (1995). Child custody evaluations: Critically assessing mental health experts and psychological tests. *Family Law Quarterly, 29*, 63-78.

Henry, R. K. (1991, Spring). Primary caretaker: Is it a ruse? *Family Advocate*, pp. 53-56.

Hetherington, E. M. (1991). The role of individual differences and family relationships in children's coping with divorce and remarriage. In P. A. Cowan & M. Hetherington (Eds.), *Family transitions* (pp. 165-194). Hillsdale, NJ: Lawrence Erlbaum.

Hetherington, M. E., & Camera, K. A. (1984). Families in transition: The process of dissolution and reconstitution. In R. Parke (Ed.), *Review of child development research* (Vol. 4, pp. 398-439). Chicago: University of Chicago Press.

Hetherington, E. M., & Clingempeel, W. G. (1992). Coping with marital transitions: A family systems perspective. *Monographs of the Society for Research in Child Development, 57*(2-3), Serial No. 227.

Hetherington, E. M., Cox, M., & Cox, R. (1978). The aftermath of divorce. In J. H. Stevens & M. Matthews (Eds.), *Mother/child father/child relationships* (pp. 149-176). Washington, DC: National Association for the Education of Young Children.

Hetherington, E. M., Cox, M., & Cox, R. (1982). Effects of divorce on parents and children. In M. E. Lamb (Ed.), *Nontraditional families: Parenting and child development* (pp. 223-288). Hilldale, NJ: Lawrence Erlbaum.

Hetherington, E. M., & Hagan, M. S. (1986). Divorced fathers: Stress coping and adjustment. In M. E. Lamb (Ed.), *The father's role: Applied perspectives* (pp. 103-134). New York: John Wiley.

Hetherington, E. M., Stanley-Hagan, M., & Anderson, E. R. (1989). Marital transitions. *American Psychologist, 44,* 303-312.

Hoffman, M. S. (1991). *The world almanac and book of facts.* New York: Pharos.

Horn, W. F. (1995). *Father facts.* Lancaster, PA: National Fatherhood Initiative.

Horne v. Goodson, 349 S.E.2d 293, Ct. of App. NC (1986).

Howle v. PYA/Monarch, Inc., 288 SC 586, 344 SF.2d 157, 161 (Ct. App. 1986).

Illinois Psychological Assn. v. Falk, 638 F. Supp. 876 (ND Ill. 1986), *aff'd,* 818 F.2d 1337 (7th Cir. 1987).

In re A.V., 849 S.W.2d 393 (Tex. Ct. App. 1993).

In re Lifschutz, 2 Cal. 3rd 415, 467 P.2d 557 (1970).

In re Marriage of L.R., 559 N.E.2d 779 (Ill. Ct. App. 1st Dist. 1990).

In re Marriage of Luckey, WL 58252 (Wash. Ct. App. March 1, 1994).

Jenkins v. U.S. 307 F.2d 637, No. 16306, U.S. Ct. of Appeals, District of Columbia (1962).

Johnston, J. R. (1994). High-conflict divorce. *Children and Divorce, 4,* 165-181.

Johnston, J. R. (1995). Children's adjustment in sole custody compared to joint custody families and principles for custody decision making. *Family and Conciliation Courts Review, 33,* 415-425.

Johnston, J. R., & Campbell, L. E. G. (1988). *Impasses of divorce: The dynamics and resolution of family conflict.* New York: Free Press.

Johnston, J. R., & Campbell, L. E. G. (1993). Parent-child relationships in domestic violence families disputing custody. *Family and Conciliation Courts Review, 31,* 282-298.

Keilin, W. G., & Bloom, L. J. (1986). Child custody evaluation practices: A survey of experienced professionals. *Professional Psychology: Research and Practice, 17,* 338-346.

Kelly, J. (1982). Divorce: The adult perspective. In B. Wolman & G. Stricker (Eds.), *Handbook of developmental psychology* (pp. 734-750). Englewood Cliffs, NJ: Prentice Hall.

Kelly, J. B. (1988). Longer-term adjustment in children of divorce: Converging findings and implications for practice. *Journal of Family Psychology, 2,* 119-140.

Kelly, J. B. (1992, Winter). Parental conflict: Taking the higher road. *Family Advocate,* p. 17.

Kelly, J. B. (1993). Current research on children's postdivorce adjustment: No simple answers. *Family and Conciliation Courts Review, 31,* 29-49.

Kelly, J. B. (1994). The determination of child custody. *Children and Divorce, 4,* 121-142.

Kelly, J. B. (1996). A decade of divorce mediation research: Some answers and questions. *Family and Conciliation Courts Review, 34,* 373-385.

Kelly, J. B., & Wallerstein, J. S. (1976). The effects of parental divorce: Experiences of the child in early latency. *American Journal of Orthopsychiatry, 46,* 20-32.

Kirkpatrick, D., Arendshorst, D., Burlingame, B., Clarke, P., Edwards, J., Friedlander, L., Long, L., Melcher, B., Neel, D., Sage, C., Smith, P., Smoot, D., & Tadeusik, C. (1994). *Child custody guidelines.* Raleigh, NC: North Carolina Psychological Association.

Kline, M., Johnston, J. R., & Tschann, J. M. (1991). The long shadow of marital conflict. *Journal of Marriage and the Family, 53,* 297-309.

Kropinski v. World Plan Executive Council, 853 F.2d 948, 272 U.S. App. D.C. 17 (1988).

Lamb, M. E. (1987). Predictive implications of individual differences in attachment. *Journal of Consulting and Clinical Psychology, 55,* 817-824.

LAMBDA Legal Defense & Education Fund. (1994). *Co-parents rights packet: Issues and court briefs.* New York: LAMBDA.

LAMBDA Legal Defense & Education Fund. (1996). *Lesbians and gay men seeking custody and visitation: An overview of the state of the law.* New York: LAMBDA.

Lees-Haley, P. (1992). MMPI-2 F and K scores of personal injury malingerers in vocational neuropsychological and emotional distress claims. *American Journal of Forensic Psychology, 9,* 5-14.

Lerman, R., & Ooms, T. J. (1993). *Young unwed fathers: Changing roles and emerging policies.* Philadelphia: Temple University Press.

Litwack, T., Gerber, G., & Fenster, A. (1979-1980). The proper role of psychology in child custody disputes. *Journal of Family Law, 18,* 269-300.

Lowery, C. (1984). The wisdom of Solomon: Criteria for child custody from the legal and clinical points of view. *Law and Human Behavior, 8,* 371-380.

Maccoby, E. E., & Mnookin, R. H. (1992). *Dividing the child: Social and legal dilemmas of custody.* Cambridge, MA: Harvard University Press.

Main, M. (1996). Introduction to the Special Section on Attachment and Psychopathology: 2. Overview of the field of attachment. *Journal of Consulting and Clinical Psychology, 64,* 237-243.

Main, M., & Solomon, J. (1990). Procedures for identifying infants as disorganized/disoriented during the Ainsworth Strange Situation. In M. T. Greenberg, D. Cicchetti, & E. M. Cummings (Eds.), *Attachment in the preschool years* (pp. 121-160). Chicago: University of Chicago Press.

Marafiote, R. A. (1985). *The custody of children: A behavioral assessment model.* New York: Plenum.

Marriage of Woffinden, 33 Wn. App. 326, 654 P.2 1219 (1982).

McCann, J. T., & Dyer, F. J. (1996). *Forensic assessment with the Millon Inventories.* New York: Guilford.

McFadden v. United States, 814 F.2d 144 (3d Cir. 1987).

McGoldrick, M., & Gerson, R. (1985). *Genograms in family assessment.* New York: Norton.

Melton, G. B., Petrila, J., Poythress, M. G., & Slobogin, C. (1987). *Psychological evaluations for the courts: A handbook for mental health professionals and lawyers.* New York: Guilford.

Melton, G. B., Petrila, J., Poythress, M. G., & Slobogin, C. (1997). *Psychological evaluations for the courts: A handbook for mental health professionals and lawyers* (2nd ed.). New York: Guildford.

Meyers, R. G. (1993). *Preparation for board certification and licensing examinations in psychology.* Louisville, KY: Monkestee.

Miller, S. (1985). Rights of homosexual parents. *Journal of Juvenile Law, 7,* 155-159.

Millon, T. (1969). *Modern psychopathology.* Philadelphia: W. B. Saunders.

Millon, T. (1981). *Disorders of personality: DSM-III: Axis II.* New York: John Wiley.

Millon, T. (1983). *Millon Clinical Multiaxial Inventory manual* (3rd ed.). Minneapolis, MN: National Computer Systems.

Millon, T. (1987). *Manual for the Millon Clinical Multiaxial Inventory-II (MCMI-II).* Minneapolis, MN: National Computer Systems.

Millon, T. (1993). *Millon Adolescent Clinical Inventory (MACI) manual.* Minneapolis, MN: National Computer Systems.

Millon, T. (1994). *Millon Clinical Multiaxial Inventory-III (MCMI-III) manual.* Minneapolis, MN: National Computer Systems.

Millon, T. (Ed.). (1997). *The Millon inventories: Clinical and personality assessment.* New York: Guilford.

Morin, S. F., & Garfinkle, E. M. (1978). Male homophobia. *Journal of Social Issues, 34,* 29-45.

Munsinger, H. L., & Karlson, K. W. (1994). *Uniform Child Custody Evaluation System.* Odessa, FL: Psychological Assessment Resources.

Myers, J. E. B. (1994). Can we believe what children say about sexual abuse? *APSAC Advisor, 7*(1), 5-6, 33.

Myers, J. E. B. (1996). Expert testimony. In J. Briere, L. Berliner, J. A. Bulkley, C. Jenny, & T. Reid (Eds.), *The APSAC handbook on child maltreatment* (pp. 319-340). Thousand Oaks, CA: Sage.

Nastasi, B. K. (1988). *Family and child stressors: Research findings from a national sample.* Paper presented at the annual meeting of the American Orthopsychiatry Association, San Francisco.

National Commission on Children. (1991). *Speaking of kids: A national survey of children and parents.* Washington, DC: Government Printing Office.

Ney, T. (1995). *True and false allegations of child sexual abuse: Assessment and case management.* New York: Brunner/Mazel.

Oberlander v. Oberlander, 460 N.W.2d 400 (N.D. 1990).

Oglogg, J. R. P. (1995). The legal basis of forensic applications of the MMPI-2. In Y. S. Ben-Porath, J. R. Graham, G. C. N. Hall, R. D. Hirschman, & M. S. Zaragoza (Eds.), *Forensic applications of the MMPI-2* (pp. 18-47). Thousand Oaks, CA: Sage.

Okpaku, S. (1976). Psychology: Impediment or aid in child custody cases? *Rutgers Law Review, 29,* 1117-1153.

Otto, R. K., & Collins, R. P. (1995). Use of the MMPI-2/MMPI-A in child custody evaluations. In Y. S. Ben-Porath, J. R. Graham, G. C. N. Hall, R. D. Hirschman, & M. S. Zaragoza (Eds.), *Forensic applications of the MMPI-2* (pp. 222-252). Thousand Oaks, CA: Sage.

Palmore v. Sidoti, 466 U.S. 429 (1984).

People v. McDarrah, 175 Ill. App. 3d 284, 529 N.E.2d 808 (1988).

People v. Stoll, 49 Cal. 3d 1136, 265 Cal. Rptr. 111, 783 P.2d 698 (1989).

Peterson, J. L., & Zill, N. (1986). Marital disruption, parent-child relationships, and behavior problems in children. *Journal of Marriage and the Family, 48,* 295-307.

Piaget, J. (1965). *The moral judgment of the child.* New York: Free Press.

Pope, K. S., & Brown, L. S. (1996). *Recovered memories of abuse: Assessment, therapy, forensics.* Washington, DC: American Psychological Association.

Pope, K. S., Butcher, J. N., & Seelen, J. (1993). *MMPI, MMPI-2 & MMPI-A in court: A practical guide for expert witnesses and attorneys.* Washington, DC: American Psychological Association.

Prater v. Arkansas, 307 Ark. 180, 820 S. W. 2d 429 (1991).

Raisner, J. K. (1997). Family mediation and never married parents. *Family and Conciliation Courts Review, 35,* 90-101.

Regents of the University of Minnesota v. Applied Innovations, Inc. 685 F. Supp. 698 (D.C. Minn. 1987).

Robin, M. (1991). *Assessing child maltreatment reports: The problem of false allegations.* New York: Haworth.

Roe v. Roe, 324 S.E.2d 691 (Va. 1985).

Rogers, R. (1988). Structured interviews and dissimulation. In R. Rogers (Ed.), *Clinical assessment of malingering and deception* (pp. 250-268). New York: Guilford.

Rogers, R. (1995). *Diagnostic and structured interviewing: A handbook for psychologists.* Odessa, FL: Psychological Assessment Resources.

Rohman, L. W., Sales, B. D., & Lou, M. (1987). The best interests of the child in custody disputes. In L. A. Weithorn (Ed.), *Psychology and child custody determinations: Knowledge, roles, and expertise* (pp. 59-105). Lincoln: University of Nebraska Press.

Rutter, M. (1971). Parent-child separation: Psychological effects on children. *Journal of Child Psychology and Psychiatry and Allied Disciplines, 12,* 233-260.

Rutter, M. (1987). Psychosocial resilience and protective mechanisms. *American Journal of Orthopsychiatry, 57,* 316-331.

Santrock, J. W., & Warshak, R. A. (1987). Development of father custody relationships and legal/clinical considerations in father custody families. In M. E. Lamb (Ed.), *The father's role: Applied perspectives* (pp. 112-125). New York: John Wiley.

Santrock, J. W., Warshak, R. A., & Elliott, G. L. (1982). Social development and parent-child interaction in father-custody and step-mother families. In M. E. Lamb (Ed.), *Nontraditional families* (pp. 289-314). Hillsdale, NJ: Lawrence Erlbaum.

Santrock, J. W., & Yussen, S. R. (1987). *Child development.* Dubuque, IA: William C. Brown.

Saywitz, K. J. (1992, Summer). Enhancing children's memory with the cognitive interview. *APSAC Advisor,* pp. 9-10.

Scallen, R. M. (1981). An investigation of paternal attitudes and behaviors in homosexual and heterosexual fathers. *Dissertation Abstracts International, 42,* 3809B.

Schetky, D. H., & Benedek, E. P. (Eds.). (1980). *Child psychiatry and the law.* New York: Brunner/Mazel.

Schutz, B. M., Dixon, E. B., Lindenberger, J. C., & Ruther, N. J. (1989). *Solomon's sword: A practical guide to conducting child custody evaluations.* San Francisco: Jossey-Bass.

Seligman, M. E. P. (1995). *The optimistic child: A revolutionary program that safeguards children against depression and builds lifelong resilience.* New York: Houghton Mifflin.

Seman, C. H., & Baumgarten, D. (1995). Improvement of clinical and legal determinations in cases of alleged child sexual abuse. *Family and Conciliation Courts Review, 33,* 472-483.

Shapiro, D. L. (1984). *Psychological evaluation and expert testimony: A practical guide to forensic work.* New York: Van Nostrand Reinhold.

Shear, L. E. (1996). Life stories, doctrines and decision making: Three high courts confront the move-away dilemma. *Family and Conciliation Courts Review, 34,* 439-458.

Skafte, D. (1985). *Child custody evaluations: A practical guide.* Beverly Hills, CA: Sage.

Skidmore, S. (1994, November). *Conducting competent, ethical child custody evaluations.* Workshop presented by the American Academy of Forensic Psychology, Portland, OR.

Stahl, P. M. (1994). *Conducting child custody evaluations: A comprehensive guide.* Thousand Oaks, CA: Sage.

Stahl, P. (1997, September). *Evaluation issues re: Parental Alienation Syndrome.* Paper presented at the Third International Symposium on Child Custody Evaluations, Breckenridge, CO.

State v. Lafferty, 749 P.2d 1239 (Utah 1988).

State v. Milbrandt, 756 P.2d 620 (Or. 1988).

State v. Perkins, 518 A.2d 715 (Me. 1986).

State v. Perry, 502 So 2d 543 (La. 1986).

Steward, M. S., Bussey, K., Goodman, G. S., & Saywitz, K. J. (1993). Implications of developmental research for interviewing children. *Child Abuse & Neglect, 17,* 25-37.

Sullivan, M. (1997, September). *Parent alienation: Assessing and addressing the challenge.* Workshop presented at the Third International Symposium on Child Custody Evaluations, Breckenridge, CO.

Susoeff, S. (1985). Assessing children's best interest when a parent is gay or lesbian: Toward a rational custody standard. *UCLA Law Review, 32,* 832-903.

Thoennes, N., & Ijaden, P. G. (1990). The extent, nature, and validity of sexual abuse allegations in custody/visitation disputes. *Child Abuse & Neglect, 14,* 151-163.

Thompson, L., & Walker, A. J. (1989). Gender in families: Women and men in marriage, work and parenthood. *Journal of Marriage and the Family, 51,* 873-893.

Tipton v. Marion County Department of Public Welfare, WL 59326 (Ind. App. Ct. March 2, 1994).

Trad, P. V. (1990). *Conversations with preschool children.* New York: Norton.

Tucker v. Tucker, 14 Wash. App. 454, 542 P.2d 789 (1975).

Uniform Marriage and Divorce Act (UMDA) Sec. 402 (1970).

United States v. Shorter, 618 F. Supp. 255 (1985).

U.S. Bureau of the Census. (1992). *Statistical abstracts of the United States, 1988: National data book and guide to sources.* Washington, DC: Government Printing Office.

Vogeltanz, N. D., & Drabman, R. S. (1995). A procedure for evaluating young children suspected of being sexually abused. *Behavior Therapy, 26,* 579-597.

Walker, L. (1984). *The battered woman syndrome.* New York: Springer.

Wallerstein, J., & Blakeslee, S. (1989). *Second chances: Men, women and children, a decade after divorce.* New York: Houghton Mifflin.

Wallerstein, J. S., Corbin, S. B., & Lewis, J. M. (1988). Children of divorce: A 10-year study. In E. M. Hetherington & J. D. Arasteh (Eds.), *Impact of divorce, single parenting & stepparenting on children* (pp. 198-214). Hillsdale, NJ: Lawrence Erlbaum.

Wallerstein, J., & Kelly, J. (1980). *Surviving the breakup: How children and parents cope with divorce.* New York: Basic Books.

Ward, P., & Harvey, J. C. (1997, September). *Family wars: The alienation of children.* Paper presented by the Third International Symposium on Child Custody Evaluations, Breckenridge, CO.

Warshak, R. A. (1992). *The custody revolution: The father factor and the motherhood mystique.* New York: Poseidon.

Warshak, R. A. (1993). *The primary parent presumption: Primarily meaningless.* Dallas: Clinical Psychology Associates.

Warshak, R. A., & Santrock, J. W. (1983). The impact of divorce in father-custody and mother-custody homes: The child's perspective. In L. A. Kurdek (Ed.), *Children and divorce* (pp. 29-46). San Francisco: Jossey-Bass.

Weiner, I. B. (1995). Psychometric issues in forensic applications of the MMPI-2. In Y. S. Ben-Porath, J. R. Graham, G. C. N. Hall, R. D. Hirschman, & M. S. Zaragoza (Eds.), *Forensic applications of the MMPI-2* (pp. 48-81). Thousand Oaks, CA: Sage.

Weissman, H. N. (1991a). Child custody evaluations: Fair and unfair professional practices. *Behavioral Sciences and the Law, 9,* 469-476.

Weissman, H. N. (1991b). Forensic psychological examination of the child witness in cases of alleged sexual abuse. *American Journal of Orthopsychiatry, 61,* 48-58.

Weissman, H. N. (1994). Psychotherapeutic and psycholegal considerations: When a custodial parent seeks to move away. *American Journal of Family Therapy, 22,* 176-181.

Weissman, H. N. (1996, March). *Child custody evaluations: Concepts, methods, and complications.* Workshop presented by the American Academy of Forensic Psychology, Hilton Head, S.C.

Weithorn, L. A. (Ed.). (1987). *Psychology and child custody determinations: Knowledge, roles, and expertise.* Lincoln: University of Nebraska Press.

Wiggins, J. (1966). Substantive dimensions of self-report in the MMPI item pool. *Psychological Monographs, 80*(22, Whole No. 630).

Ziskin, J. (1995). *Coping with psychiatric and psychological testimony* (5th ed.). Los Angeles: Law and Psychology Press.

Ziskin, J., & Faust, D. (1988). *Coping with psychiatric and psychological testimony* (4th ed.). Los Angeles: Law and Psychology Press.

Specialty Guidelines for Forensic Psychologists[1]

Committee on Ethical Guidelines for Forensic Psychologists[2]

The *Specialty Guidelines for Forensic Psychologists,* while informed by the *Ethical Principles of Psychologists* (APA, 1990) and meant to be consistent with them, are designed to provide more specific guidance to forensic psychologists in monitoring their professional conduct when acting in assistance to courts, parties to legal proceedings, correctional and forensic mental health facilities, and legislative agencies. The primary goal of the *Guidelines* is to improve the quality of forensic psychological services offered to individual clients and the legal system and thereby to enhance forensic psychology as a discipline and profession. The *Specialty Guidelines for Forensic Psychologists* represent a joint statement of the American Psychology-Law Society and Division 41 of the American Psychological Association and are endorsed by the American Academy of Forensic Psychology. The *Guidelines* do not represent an official statement of the American Psychological Association.

The *Guidelines* provide an aspirational model of desirable professional practice by psychologists, within any subdiscipline of psychology (e.g., clinical, developmental, social, experimental), when they are engaged regularly as experts and represent themselves as such, in an activity primarily intended to provide professional psychological expertise to the judicial system. This would include, for example, clinical forensic examiners; psychologists employed by correctional or forensic mental health systems; researchers who offer direct testimony about the relevance of scientific data to a psycholegal issue; trial behavior consultants; psychologists engaged in preparation of amicus briefs; or psychologists, appearing as forensic experts, who consult with, or testify before, judicial, legislative, or administrative agencies acting in an adjudicative capacity. Individuals who provide only occasional service to the legal system and who do so without representing themselves as *forensic experts* may find these *Guidelines* helpful, particularly in conjunction with consultation with colleagues who are forensic experts.

While the *Guidelines* are concerned with a model of desirable professional practice, to the extent that they may be construed as being applicable to the advertisement

Committee on Ethical Guidelines for Forensic Psychologists. (1991). Specialty guidelines for forensic psychologists. *Law and Human Behavior, 15*(6), 655-665. Reprinted by permission of Plenum Publishing Corporation.

of services or the solicitation of clients, they are intended to prevent false or deceptive advertisement or solicitation, and should be construed in a manner consistent with that intent.

I. PURPOSE AND SCOPE
    A. Purpose
        1. While the professional standards for the ethical practice of psychology, as a general discipline, are addressed in the American Psychological Association's *Ethical Principles of Psychologists,* these ethical principles do not relate, in sufficient detail, to current aspirations of desirable professional conduct for forensic psychologists. By design, none of the *Guidelines* contradicts any of the *Ethical Principles of Psychologists;* rather, they amplify those *Principles* in the context of the practice of forensic psychology, as herein defined.
        2. The *Guidelines* have been designed to be national in scope and are intended to conform with state and Federal law. In situations where the forensic psychologist believes that the requirements of law are in conflict with the *Guidelines,* attempts to resolve the conflict should be made in accordance with the procedures set forth in these *Guidelines* [IV(G)] and in the *Ethical Principles of Psychologists.*
    B. Scope
        1. The *Guidelines* specify the nature of desirable professional practice by forensic psychologists, within any subdiscipline of psychology (e.g., clinical, developmental, social, experimental), when engaged regularly as forensic psychologists.
            a. "Psychologist" means any individual whose professional activities are defined by the American Psychological Association or by regulation of title by state registration or licensure, as the practice of psychology.
            b. "Forensic psychology" means all forms of professional psychological conduct when acting, with definable foreknowledge, as a psychological expert on explicitly psycholegal issues, in direct assistance to courts, parties to legal proceedings, correctional and forensic mental health facilities, and administrative, judicial, and legislative agencies acting in an adjudicative capacity.
            c. "Forensic psychologist" means psychologists who regularly engage in the practice of forensic psychology as defined in I(B)(1)(b).
        2. The *Guidelines* do not apply to a psychologist who is asked to provide professional psychological services when the psychologist was not informed at the time of delivery of the services that they were to be used as forensic psychological services as defined above. The *Guidelines* may be helpful, however, in preparing the psychologist for the experience of communicating psychological data in a forensic context.
        3. Psychologists who are not forensic psychologists as defined in I(B)(1)(c), but occasionally provide limited forensic psychological services, may find the *Guidelines* useful in the preparation and presentation of their professional services.

C. Related Standards

1. Forensic psychologists also conduct their professional activities in accord with the *Ethical Principles of Psychologists* and the various other statements of the American Psychological Association that may apply to particular subdisciplines or areas of practice that are relevant to their professional activities.

2. The standards of practice and ethical guidelines of other relevant "expert professional organizations" contain useful guidance and should be consulted even though the present *Guidelines* take precedence for forensic psychologists.

II. RESPONSIBILITY

A. Forensic psychologists have an obligation to provide services in a manner consistent with the highest standards of their profession. They are responsible for their own conduct and the conduct of those individuals under their direct supervision.

B. Forensic psychologists make a reasonable effort to ensure that their services and the products of their services are used in a forthright and responsible manner.

III. COMPETENCE

A. Forensic psychologists provide services only in areas of psychology in which they have specialized knowledge, skill, experience, and education.

B. Forensic psychologists have an obligation to present to the court, regarding the specific matters to which they will testify, the boundaries of their competence, the factual bases (knowledge, skill, experience, training, and education) for their qualification as an expert, and the relevance of those factual bases to their qualification as an expert on the specific matters at issue.

C. Forensic psychologists are responsible for a fundamental and reasonable level of knowledge and understanding of the legal and professional standards that govern their participation as experts in legal proceedings.

D. Forensic psychologists have an obligation to understand the civil rights of parties in legal proceedings in which they participate, and manage their professional conduct in a manner that does not diminish or threaten those rights.

E. Forensic psychologists recognize that their own personal values, moral beliefs, or personal and professional relationships with parties to a legal proceeding may interfere with their ability to practice competently. Under such circumstances, forensic psychologists are obligated to decline participation or to limit their assistance in a manner consistent with professional obligations.

IV. RELATIONSHIPS

A. During initial consultation with the legal representative of the party seeking services, forensic psychologists have an obligation to inform the party of factors that might reasonably affect the decision to contract with the forensic psychologist. These factors include, but are not limited to

1. the fee structure for anticipated professional services;
2. prior and current personal or professional activities, obligations, and relationships that might produce a conflict of interests;
3. their areas of competence and the limits of their competence; and
4. the known scientific bases and limitations of the methods and procedures that they employ and their qualifications to employ such methods and procedures.

B. Forensic psychologists do not provide professional services to parties to a legal proceeding on the basis of "contingent fees," when those services involve the offering of expert testimony to a court or administrative body, or when they call upon the psychologist to make affirmations or representations intended to be relied upon by third parties.

C. Forensic psychologists who derive a substantial portion of their income from fee-for-service arrangements should offer some portion of their professional services on a *pro bono* or reduced fee basis where the public interest or the welfare of clients may be inhibited by insufficient financial resources.

D. Forensic psychologists recognize potential conflicts of interest in dual relationships with parties to a legal proceeding, and they seek to minimize their effects.

1. Forensic psychologists avoid providing professional services to parties in a legal proceeding with whom they have personal or professional relationships that are inconsistent with the anticipated relationship.
2. When it is necessary to provide both evaluation and treatment services to a party in a legal proceeding (as may be the case in small forensic hospital settings or small communities), the forensic psychologist takes reasonable steps to minimize the potential negative effects of these circumstances on the rights of the party, confidentiality, and the process of treatment and evaluation.

E. Forensic psychologists have an obligation to ensure that prospective clients are informed of their legal rights with respect to the anticipated forensic service, of the purposes of any evaluation, of the nature of procedures to be employed, of the intended uses of any product of their services, and of the party who has employed the forensic psychologist.

1. Unless court ordered, forensic psychologists obtain the informed consent of the client or party, or their legal representative, before proceeding with such evaluations and procedures. If the client appears unwilling to proceed after receiving a thorough notification of the purposes, methods, and intended uses of the forensic evaluation, the evaluation should be postponed and the psychologist should take steps to place the

client in contact with his/her attorney for the purpose of legal advice on the issue of participation.

2. In situations where the client or party may not have the capacity to provide informed consent to services or the evaluation is pursuant to court order, the forensic psychologist provides reasonable notice to the client's legal representative of the nature of the anticipated forensic service before proceeding. If the client's legal representative objects to the evaluation, the forensic psychologist notifies the court issuing the order and responds as directed.

3. After a psychologist has advised the subject of a clinical forensic evaluation of the intended uses of the evaluation and its work product, the psychologist may not use the evaluation work product for other purposes without explicit waiver to do so by the client or the client's legal representative.

F. When forensic psychologists engage in research or scholarly activities that are compensated financially by a client or party to a legal proceeding, or when the psychologist provides those services on a *pro bono* basis, the psychologist clarifies any anticipated further use of such research or scholarly product, discloses the psychologist's role in the resulting research or scholarly products, and obtains whatever consent or agreement is required by law or professional standards.

G. When conflicts arise between the forensic psychologist's professional standards and the requirements of legal standards, a particular court, or a directive by an officer of the court or legal authorities, the forensic psychologist has an obligation to make those legal authorities aware of the source of the conflict and to take reasonable steps to resolve it. Such steps may include, but are not limited to, obtaining the consultation of fellow forensic professionals, obtaining the advice of independent counsel, and conferring directly with the legal representatives involved.

V. CONFIDENTIALITY AND PRIVILEGE

A. Forensic psychologists have an obligation to be aware of the legal standards that may affect or limit the confidentiality or privilege that may attach to their services or their products, and they conduct their professional activities in a manner that respects those known rights and privileges.

1. Forensic psychologists establish and maintain a system of record keeping and professional communication that safeguards a client's privilege.

2. Forensic psychologists maintain active control over records and information. They only release information pursuant to statutory requirements, court order, or the consent of the client.

B. Forensic psychologists inform their clients of the limitations to the confidentiality of their services and their products (see also Guideline IV E) by providing them with an understandable statement of their rights, privileges, and the limitations of confidentiality.

C. In situations where the right of the client or party to confidentiality is limited, the forensic psychologist makes every effort to maintain confidentiality with regard to any information that does not bear directly upon the legal purpose of the evaluation.

D. Forensic psychologists provide clients or their authorized legal representatives with access to the information in their records and a meaningful explanation of that information, consistent with existing Federal and state statutes, the *Ethical Principles of Psychologists,* the *Standards for Educational and Psychological Testing,* and institutional rules and regulations.

VI. METHODS AND PROCEDURES

A. Because of their special status as persons qualified as experts to the court, forensic psychologists have an obligation to maintain current knowledge of scientific, professional and legal developments within their area of claimed competence. They are obligated also to use that knowledge, consistent with accepted clinical and scientific standards, in selecting data collection methods and procedures for an evaluation, treatment, consultation or scholarly/empirical investigation.

B. Forensic psychologists have an obligation to document and be prepared to make available, subject to court order or the rules of evidence, all data that form the basis for their evidence or services. The standard to be applied to such documentation or recording *anticipates* that the detail and quality of such documentation will be subject to reasonable judicial scrutiny; this standard is higher than the normative standard for general clinical practice. When forensic psychologists conduct an examination or engage in the treatment of a party to a legal proceeding, with foreknowledge that their professional services will be used in an adjudicative forum, they incur a special responsibility to provide the best documentation possible under the circumstances.

1. Documentation of the data upon which one's evidence is based is subject to the normal rules of discovery, disclosure, confidentiality, and privilege that operate in the jurisdiction in which the data were obtained. Forensic psychologists have an obligation to be aware of those rules and to regulate their conduct in accordance with them.

2. The duties and obligations of forensic psychologists with respect to documentation of data that form the basis for their evidence apply from the moment they know or have a reasonable basis for knowing that their data and evidence derived from it are likely to enter into legally relevant decisions.

C. In providing forensic psychological services, forensic psychologists take special care to avoid undue influence upon their methods, procedures, and products, such as might emanate from the party to a legal proceeding by financial compensation or other gains. As an expert conducting an evaluation, treatment, consultation, or scholarly/empirical investigation, the forensic psychologist maintains professional integrity by examining the issue at hand from all reasonable perspectives, actively seeking information that will differentially test plausible rival hypotheses.

D. Forensic psychologists do not provide professional forensic services to a defendant or to any party in, or in contemplation of, a legal proceeding prior to that individual's representation by counsel, except for persons judicially determined, where appropriate, to be handling their representation *pro se*. When the forensic services are pursuant to court order and the client is not represented by counsel, the forensic psychologist makes reasonable efforts to inform the court prior to providing the services.

1. A forensic psychologist may provide emergency mental health services to a pretrial defendant prior to court order or the appointment of counsel where there are reasonable grounds to believe that such emergency services are needed for the protection and improvement of the defendant's mental health and where failure to provide such mental health services would constitute a substantial risk of imminent harm to the defendant or to others. In providing such services the forensic psychologist nevertheless seeks to inform the defendant's counsel in a manner consistent with the requirements of the emergency situation.

2. Forensic psychologists who provide such emergency mental health services should attempt to avoid providing further professional forensic services to that defendant unless that relationship is reasonably unavoidable [see IV(D)(2)].

E. When forensic psychologists seek data from third parties, prior records, or other sources, they do so only with the prior approval of the relevant legal party or as a consequence of an order of a court to conduct the forensic evaluation.

F. Forensic psychologists are aware that hearsay exceptions and other rules governing expert testimony place a special ethical burden upon them. When hearsay or otherwise inadmissible evidence forms the basis of their opinion, evidence, or professional product, they seek to minimize sole reliance upon such evidence. Where circumstances reasonably permit, forensic psychologists seek to obtain independent and personal verification of data relied upon as part of their professional services to the court or to a party to a legal proceeding.

1. While many forms of data used by forensic psychologists are hearsay, forensic psychologists attempt to corroborate critical data that form the basis for their professional product. When using hearsay data that have not been corroborated, but are nevertheless utilized, forensic psychologists have an affirmative responsibility to acknowledge the uncorroborated status of those data and the reasons for relying upon such data.

2. With respect to evidence of any type, forensic psychologists avoid offering information from their investigations or evaluations that does not bear directly upon the legal purpose of their professional services and that is not critical as support for their product, evidence or testimony, except where such disclosure is required by law.

3. When a forensic psychologist relies upon data or information gathered by others, the origins of those data are clarified in any professional product. In addition, the forensic psychologist bears a special responsibility

to ensure that such data, if relied upon, were gathered in a manner standard for the profession.

G. Unless otherwise stipulated by the parties, forensic psychologists are aware that no statements made by a defendant, in the course of any (forensic) examination, no testimony by the expert based upon such statements, nor any other fruits of the statements can be admitted into evidence against the defendant in any criminal proceeding, except on an issue respecting mental condition on which the defendant has introduced testimony. Forensic psychologists have an affirmative duty to ensure that their written products and oral testimony conform to this Federal Rule of Procedure (12.2[c]), or its state equivalent.

1. Because forensic psychologists are often not in a position to know what evidence, documentation, or element of a written product may be or may lend to a "fruit of the statement," they exercise extreme caution in preparing reports or offering testimony prior to the defendant's assertion of a mental state claim or the defendant's introduction of testimony regarding a mental condition. Consistent with the reporting requirements of state or federal law, forensic psychologists avoid including statements from the defendant relating to the time period of the alleged offense.

2. Once a defendant has proceeded to the trial stage, and all pretrial mental health issues such as competency have been resolved, forensic psychologists may include in their reports or testimony any statements made by the defendant that are directly relevant to supporting their expert evidence, providing that the defendant has "introduced" mental state evidence or testimony within the meaning of Federal Rule of Procedure 12.2(c), or its state equivalent.

H. Forensic psychologists avoid giving written or oral evidence about the psychological characteristics of particular individuals when they have not had an opportunity to conduct an examination of the individual adequate to the scope of the statements, opinions, or conclusions to be issued. Forensic psychologists make every reasonable effort to conduct such examinations. When it is not possible or feasible to do so, they make clear the impact of such limitations on the reliability and validity of their professional products. evidence, or testimony.

VII. PUBLIC AND PROFESSIONAL COMMUNICATIONS

A. Forensic psychologists make reasonable efforts to ensure that the products of their services, as well as their own public statements and professional testimony, are communicated in ways that will promote understanding and avoid deception, given the particular characteristics, roles, and abilities of various recipients of the communications.

1. Forensic psychologists take reasonable steps to correct misuse or misrepresentation of their professional products, evidence, and testimony.

2. Forensic psychologists provide information about professional work to clients in a manner consistent with professional and legal standards for

the disclosure of test results, interpretations of data, and the factual bases for conclusions. A full explanation of the results of tests and the bases for conclusions should be given in language that the client can understand.

a. When disclosing information about a client to third parties who are not qualified to interpret test results and data, the forensic psychologist complies with Principle 16 of the *Standards for Educational and Psychological Testing*. When required to disclose results to a nonpsychologist, every attempt is made to ensure that test security is maintained and access to information is restricted to individuals with a legitimate and professional interest in the data. Other qualified mental health professionals who make a request for information pursuant to a lawful order are, by definition, "individuals with a legitimate and professional interest."

b. In providing records and raw data, the forensic psychologist takes reasonable steps to ensure that the receiving party is informed that raw scores must be interpreted by a qualified professional in order to provide reliable and valid information.

B. Forensic psychologists realize that their public role as "expert to the court" or as "expert representing the profession" confers upon them a special responsibility for fairness and accuracy in their public statements. When evaluating or commenting upon the professional work product or qualifications of another expert or party to a legal proceeding, forensic psychologists represent their professional disagreements with reference to a fair and accurate evaluation of the data, theories, standards, and opinions of the other expert or party.

C. Ordinarily, forensic psychologists avoid making detailed public (out-of-court) statements about particular legal proceedings in which they have been involved. When there is a strong justification to do so, such public statements are designed to assure accurate representation of their role or their evidence, not to advocate the positions of parties in the legal proceeding. Forensic psychologists address particular legal proceedings in publications or communications only to the extent that the information relied upon is part of a public record, or consent for that use has been properly obtained from the party holding any privilege.

D. When testifying, forensic psychologists have an obligation to all parties to a legal proceeding to present their findings, conclusions, evidence, or other professional products in a fair manner. This principle does not preclude forceful representation of the data and reasoning upon which a conclusion or professional product is based. It does, however, preclude an attempt, whether active or passive, to engage in partisan distortion or misrepresentation. Forensic psychologists do not, by either commission or omission, participate in a misrepresentation of their evidence, nor do they participate in partisan attempts to avoid, deny, or subvert the presentation of evidence contrary to their own position.

E. Forensic psychologists, by virtue of their competence and rules of discovery, actively disclose all sources of information obtained in the course of their professional services; they actively disclose which information from which source was used in formulating a particular written product or oral testimony.

F. Forensic psychologists are aware that their essential role as expert to the court is to assist the trier of fact to understand the evidence or to determine a fact in issue. In offering expert evidence, they are aware that their own professional observations, inferences, and conclusions must be distinguished from legal facts, opinions, and conclusions. Forensic psychologists are prepared to explain the relationship between their expert testimony and the legal issues and facts of an instant case.

Notes

1. The *Specialty Guidelines for Forensic Psychologists* were adopted by majority vote of the members of Division 41 and the American Psychology-Law Society. They have also been endorsed by majority vote by the American Academy of Forensic Psychology. The Executive Committee of Division 41 and the American Psychology Law Society formally approved these *Guidelines* on March 9, 1991. The Executive Committee also voted to continue the Committee on Ethical Guidelines in order to disseminate the *Guidelines* and to monitor their implementation and suggestions for revision. Individuals wishing to reprint these *Guidelines* or who have queries about them should contact either Stephen L. Golding, Ph.D., Department of Psychology, University of Utah, Salt Lake City, UT 84112, 801-581-8028 (voice) or 801-581-5841 (FAX) or other members of the Committee listed below. Reprint requests should be sent to Cathy Osizly, Department of Psychology, University of Nebraska-Lincoln, Lincoln, NE 68588-0308.

2. These Guidelines were prepared and principally authored by a joint Committee on Ethical Guidelines of Division 41 and the American Academy of Forensic Psychology (Stephen L. Golding, [Chair], Thomas Grisso, David Shapiro, and Herbert Weissman [Co-chairs]). Other members of the Committee included Robert Fein, Kirk Heilbrun, Judith McKenna, Norman Poythress, and Daniel Schuman. Their hard work and willingness to tackle difficult conceptual and pragmatic issues is gratefully acknowledged. The Committee would also like to acknowledge specifically the assistance and guidance provided by Dort Bigg, Larry Cowan, Eric Hams, Arthur Lerner, Michael Miller, Russell Newman, Melvin Rudov, and Ray Fowler. Many other individuals also contributed by their thoughtful critique and suggestions for improvement of earlier drafts which were widely circulated.

Guidelines for Child Custody Evaluations in Divorce Proceedings

Introduction

Decisions regarding child custody and other parenting arrangements occur within several different legal contexts, including parental divorce, guardianship, neglect or abuse proceedings, and termination of parental rights. The following guidelines were developed for psychologists conducting child custody evaluations, specifically within the context of parental divorce. These guidelines build upon the American Psychological Association's *Ethical Principles of Psychologists and Code of Conduct* (APA, 1992) and are aspirational in intent. *As guidelines, they are not intended to be either mandatory or exhaustive. The goal of the guidelines is to promote proficiency in using psychological expertise in conducting child custody evaluations.*

Parental divorce requires a restructuring of parental rights and responsibilities in relation to children. If the parents can agree to a restructuring arrangement, which they do in the overwhelming proportion (90%) of divorce custody cases (Melton, Petrila, Poythress, & Slobogin, 1987), there is no dispute for the court to decide. However, if the parents are unable to reach such an agreement, the court must help to determine the relative allocation of decision making authority and physical contact each parent will have with the child. The courts typically apply a "best interest of the child" standard in determining this restructuring of rights and responsibilities.

Psychologists provide an important service to children and the courts by providing competent, objective, impartial information in assessing the best interests of the child; by demonstrating a clear sense of direction and purpose in conducting a child custody evaluation; by performing their roles ethically; and by clarifying to all

Copyright © 1994 by the American Psychological Association. Reprinted with permission.

These guidelines were drafted by the Committee on Professional Practice and Standards (COPPS), a committee of the Board of Professional Affairs (BPA), with input from the Committee on Children, Youth, and Families (CYF). They were adopted by the Council of Representatives of the American Psychological Association in February 1994.

COPPS members in 1991-1993 were Richard Cohen, Alex Carballo Dieguez, Kathleen Dockett, Sam Friedman, Colette Ingraham, John Northman, John Robinson, Deborah Tharinger, Susana Urbina, Phil Witt, and James Wulach; BPA liaisons in 1991-1993 were Richard Cohen, Joseph Kobos, and Rodney Lowman; CYF members were Don Routh and Carolyn Swift.

Correspondence concerning this article should be addressed to the Practice Directorate, American Psychological Association, 750 First Street, NE, Washington, DC, 2002-4242.

involved the nature and scope of the evaluation. The Ethics Committee of the American Psychological Association has noted that psychologists' involvement in custody disputes has at times raised questions in regard to the misuse of psychologists' influence, sometimes resulting in complaints against psychologists being brought to the attention of the APA Ethics Committee (APA Ethics Committee, 1985; Hall & Hare-Mustin, 1983; Keith-Spiegel & Koocher, 1985; Mills, 1984) and raising questions in the legal and forensic literature (Grisso, 1986; Melton et al., 1987; Mnookin, 1975; Ochroch, 1982; Okpaku, 1976; Weithorn, 1987).

Particular competencies and knowledge are required for child custody evaluations to provide adequate and appropriate psychological services to the court. Child custody evaluation in the context of parental divorce can be an extremely demanding task. For competing parents the stakes are high as they participate in a process fraught with tension and anxiety. The stress on the psychologist/evaluator can become great. Tension surrounding child custody evaluation can become further heightened when there are accusations of child abuse, neglect, and/or family violence.

Psychology is in a position to make significant contributions to child custody decisions. Psychological data and expertise, gained through a child custody evaluation, can provide an additional source of information and an additional perspective not otherwise readily available to the court on what appears to be in a child's best interest, and thus can increase the fairness of the determination the court must make.

Guidelines for Child Custody Evaluations in Divorce Proceedings

I.   Orienting Guidelines: Purpose of a Child Custody Evaluation

1.   *The primary purpose of the evaluation is to assess the best psychological interests of the child.* The primary consideration in a child custody evaluation is to assess the individual and family factors that affect the best psychological interests of the child. More specific questions may be raised by the court.

2.   *The child's interests and well-being are paramount.* In a child custody evaluation, the child's interests and well-being are paramount. Parents competing for custody, as well as others, may have legitimate concerns, but the child's best interests must prevail.

3.   *The focus of the evaluation is on parenting capacity, the psychological and developmental needs of the child, and the resulting fit.* In considering psychological factors affecting the best interests of the child, the psychologist focuses on the parenting capacity of the prospective custodians in conjunction with the psychological and developmental needs of each involved child. This involves (a) an assessment of the adults' capacities for parenting, including whatever knowledge, attributes, skills, and abilities, or lack thereof, are present; (b) an assessment of the psychological functioning and developmental needs of each child and of the wishes of each child where appropriate; and (c) an assessment of the functional ability of each parent to meet

these needs, including an evaluation of the interaction between each adult and child.

The values of the parents relevant to parenting, ability to plan for the child's future needs, capacity to provide a stable and loving home, and any potential for inappropriate behavior or misconduct that might negatively influence the child also are considered. Psychopathology may be relevant to such an assessment, insofar as it has impact on the child or the ability to parent, but it is not the primary focus.

II.   General Guidelines: Preparing for a Child Custody Evaluation

4. *The role of the psychologist is that of a professional expert who strives to maintain an objective, impartial stance.* The role of the psychologist is as a professional expert. The psychologist does not act as a judge, who makes the ultimate decision applying the law to all relevant evidence. Neither does the psychologist act as an advocating attorney, who strives to present his or her client's best possible case. The psychologist, in a balanced, impartial manner, informs and advises the court and the prospective custodians of the child of the relevant psychological factors pertaining to the custody issue. The psychologist should be impartial regardless of whether he or she is retained by the court or by a party to the proceedings. If either the psychologist or the client cannot accept this neutral role, the psychologist should consider withdrawing from the case. If not permitted to withdraw, in such circumstances, the psychologist acknowledges past roles and other factors that could affect impartiality.

5. *The psychologist gains specialized competence.*

A. A psychologist contemplating performing child custody evaluations is aware that special competencies and knowledge are required for the undertaking of such evaluations. Competence in performing psychological assessments of children, adults, and families is necessary but not sufficient. Education, training, experience, and/or supervision in the areas of child and family development, child and family psychopathology, and the impact of divorce on children help to prepare the psychologist to participate competently in child custody evaluations. The psychologist also strives to become familiar with applicable legal standards and procedures, including laws governing divorce and custody adjudications in his or her state or jurisdiction.

B. The psychologist uses current knowledge of scientific and professional developments, consistent with accepted clinical and scientific standards, in selecting data collection methods and procedures. The *Standards for Educational and Psychological Testing* (APA, 1985) are adhered to in the use of psychological tests and other assessment tools.

C. In the course of conducting child custody evaluations, allegations of child abuse, neglect, family violence, or other issues may occur that are not necessarily within the scope of a particular evaluator's expertise. If this is so, the psychologist seeks additional consultation, supervision, and/or specialized knowledge, training, or experience in child abuse, neglect, and family violence to address these complex issues. The psychologist is familiar with the laws of his or her state addressing child abuse, neglect, and family violence and acts accordingly.

6. *The psychologist is aware of personal and societal biases and engages in nondiscriminatory practice.* The psychologist engaging in child custody evaluations is aware of how biases regarding age, gender, race, ethnicity, national origin, religion, sexual orientation, disability, language, culture, and socioeconomic status may interfere with an objective evaluation and recommendations. The psychologist recognizes and strives to overcome any such biases or withdraws from the evaluation.

7. *The psychologist avoids multiple relationships.* Psychologists generally avoid conducting a child custody evaluation in a case in which the psychologist served in a therapeutic role for the child or his or her immediate family or has had other involvement that may compromise the psychologist's objectivity. This should not, however, preclude the psychologist from testifying in the case as a fact witness concerning treatment of the child. In addition, during the course of a child custody evaluation, a psychologist does not accept any of the involved participants in the evaluation as a therapy client. Therapeutic contact with the child or involved participants following a child custody evaluation is undertaken with caution.

A psychologist asked to testify regarding a therapy client who is involved in a child custody case is aware of the limitations and possible biases inherent in such a role and the possible impact on the ongoing therapeutic relationship. Although the court may require the psychologist to testify as a fact witness regarding factual information he or she became aware of in a professional relationship with a client, that psychologist should generally decline the role of an expert witness who gives a professional opinion regarding custody and visitation issues (see Ethical Standard 7.03) unless so ordered by the court.

III. Procedural Guidelines: Conducting a Child Custody Evaluation

8. *The scope of the evaluation is determined by the evaluator, based on the nature of the referral question.* The scope of the custody-related evaluation is determined by the nature of the question or issue raised by the referring person or the court, or is inherent in the situation. Although comprehensive child custody evaluations generally require an evaluation of all parents or guardians and children, as well as observations of interactions between them, the scope of the assessment in a particular case may be limited to evaluating the parental capacity of one parent without attempting to compare the parents or to make recommendations. Likewise, the scope may be limited to evaluating the child. Or a psychologist may be asked to critique the assumptions and methodology of the assessment of another mental health professional. A psychologist also might serve as an expert witness in the area of child development, providing expertise to the court without relating it specifically to the parties involved in a case.

9. *The psychologist obtains informed consent from all adult participants and, as appropriate, informs child participants.* In undertaking child custody evaluations, the psychologist ensures that each adult participant is aware of (a) the purpose, nature, and method of the evaluation; (b) who has requested the psychologist's services; and (c) who will be paying the fees. The psychologist informs adult participants about the nature of the assessment instruments and techniques and informs those participants about the possible disposition of the data collected. The psychologist provides this information, as appropriate, to children, to the extent that they are able to understand.

10. *The psychologist informs participants about the limits of confidentiality and the disclosure of information.* A psychologist conducting a child custody evaluation ensures that the participants, including children to the extent feasible, are aware of the limits of confidentiality characterizing the professional relationship with the psychologist. The psychologist informs participants that in consenting to the evaluation, they are consenting to disclosure of the evaluation's findings in the context of the forthcoming litigation and in any other proceedings deemed necessary by the courts. A psychologist obtains a waiver of confidentiality from all adult participants or from their authorized legal representatives.

11. *The psychologist uses multiple methods of data gathering.* The psychologist strives to use the most appropriate methods available for addressing the questions raised in a specific child custody evaluation and generally uses multiple methods of data gathering, including, but not limited to, clinical interviews, observation, and/or psychological assessments. Important facts and opinions are documented from at least two sources whenever their reliability is questionable. The psychologist, for example, may review particularly relevant reports (e.g., from schools, health care providers, child care providers, agencies, and institutions). Psychologists may also interview extended family, friends, and other individuals on occasions when the information is likely to be useful. If information is gathered from third parties that is significant and may be used as a basis for conclusions, psychologists corroborate it by at least one other source wherever possible and appropriate and document this in the report.

12. *The psychologist neither overinterprets nor inappropriately interprets clinical or assessment data.* The psychologist refrains from drawing conclusions not adequately supported by the data. The psychologist interprets any data from interviews or tests, as well as any questions of data reliability and validity, cautiously and conservatively, seeking convergent validity. The psychologist strives to acknowledge to the court any limitations in methods or data used.

13. *The psychologist does not give any opinion regarding the psychological functioning of any individual who has not been personally evaluated.* This guideline, however, does not preclude the psychologist from reporting what an evaluated individual (such as the parent or child) has stated or from ad-

dressing theoretical issues or hypothetical questions, so long as the limited basis of the information is noted.

14. *Recommendations, if any, are based on what is in the best psychological interests of the child.* Although the profession has not reached consensus about whether psychologists ought to make recommendations about the final custody determination to the courts, psychologists are obligated to be aware of the arguments on both sides of this issue and to be able to explain the logic of their position concerning their own practice.

If the psychologist does choose to make custody recommendations, these recommendations should be derived from sound psychological data and must be based on the best interests of the child in the particular case. Recommendations are based on articulated assumptions, data, interpretations, and inferences based upon established professional and scientific standards. Psychologists guard against relying on their own biases or unsupported beliefs in rendering opinions in particular cases.

15. *The psychologist clarifies financial arrangements.* Financial arrangements are clarified and agreed upon prior to commencing a child custody evaluation. When billing for a child custody evaluation, the psychologist does not misrepresent his or her services for reimbursement purposes.

16. *The psychologist maintains written records.* All records obtained in the process of conducting a child custody evaluation are properly maintained and filed in accord with the APA *Record Keeping Guidelines* (APA, 1993) and relevant statutory guidelines.

All raw data and interview information are recorded with an eye toward their possible review by other psychologists or the court, where legally permitted. Upon request, appropriate reports are made available to the court.

References

American Psychological Association. (1985). *Standards for educational and psychological testing.* Washington, DC: Author.

American Psychological Association. (1992). Ethical principles of psychologists and code of conduct. *American Psychologist, 47,* 1597-1611.

American Psychological Association. (1993). *Record keeping guidelines.* Washington, DC: Author.

American Psychological Association, Ethics Committee. (1985). *Annual report of the American Psychological Association Ethics Committee.* Washington, DC: Author.

Grisso, T. (1986). *Evaluating competencies: Forensic assessments and instruments.* New York: Plenum.

Hall, J. E., & Hare-Mustin, R. T. (1983). Sanctions and the diversity of ethical complaints against psychologists. *American Psychologist, 38,* 714-729.

Keith-Spiegel, P., & Koocher, G. P. (1985). *Ethics in psychology.* New York: Random House.

Melton, G. B., Petrila, J., Poythress, N. G., & Slobogin, C. (1987). *Psychological evaluations for the courts: A handbook for mental health professionals and lawyers.* New York: Guilford Press.

Mills, D. H. (1984). Ethics education and adjudication within psychology. *American Psychologist, 39,* 669-675.

Mnookin, R. H. (1975). Child-custody adjudication: Judicial functions in the face of indeterminacy. *Law and Contemporary Problems, 39,* 226-293.

Ochroch, R. (1982, August). *Ethical pitfalls in child custody evaluations.* Paper presented at the 90th Annual Convention of the American Psychological Association, Washington, DC.

Okpaku, S. (1976). Psychology: Impediment or aid in child custody cases? *Rutgers Law Review, 29,* 1117-1153.

Weithorn, L. A. (Ed.). (1987). *Psychology and child custody determinations: Knowledge, roles, and expertise.* Lincoln: University of Nebraska Press.

Other Resources

State Guidelines

Georgia Psychological Association. (1990). *Recommendations for psychologists' involvement in child custody cases.* Atlanta, GA: Author.

Metropolitan Denver Interdisciplinary Committee on Child Custody. (1989). *Guidelines for child custody evaluations.* Denver, CO: Author.

Nebraska Psychological Association. (1986). *Guidelines for child custody evaluations.* Lincoln, NE: Author.

New Jersey State Board of Psychological Examiners. (1993). *Specialty guidelines for psychologists in custody/visitation evaluations.* Newark, NJ: Author.

North Carolina Psychological Association. (1993). *Child custody guidelines.* Unpublished manuscript.

Oklahoma Psychological Association. (1988). *Ethical guidelines for child custody evaluations.* Oklahoma City, OK: Author.

Forensic Guidelines

Committee on Ethical Guidelines for Forensic Psychologists. (1991). Specialty guidelines for forensic psychologists. *Law and Human Behavior, 6,* 655-665.

Pertinent Literature

Ackerman, M. J., & Kane, A. W. (1993). *Psychological experts in divorce, personal injury and other civil actions.* New York: Wiley.

American Psychological Association, Board of Ethnic Minority Affairs. (1991). *Guidelines for providers of psychological services to ethnic, linguistic, and culturally diverse populations.* Washington, DC: American Psychological Association.

American Psychological Association, Committee on Women in Psychology and Committee on Lesbian and Gay Concerns. (1988). *Lesbian parents and their children: A resource paper for psychologists.* Washington, DC: American Psychological Association.

Beaber, R. J. (1982,Fall). Custody quagmire: Some psycholegal dilemmas. *Journal of Psychiatry & Law,* 309-326.

Bennett, B. E., Bryant, B. K., VandenBos, G. R., & Greenwood, A. (1990). *Professional liability and risk management.* Washington, DC: American Psychological Association.

Bolocofsky, D. N. (1989). Use and abuse of mental health experts in child custody determinations. *Behavioral Sciences and the Law, 7*(2), 197-213.

Bozett, F. (1987). *Gay and lesbian parents.* New York: Praeger.

Bray, J. H. (1993). What's the best interest of the child? Children's adjustment issues in divorce. *The Independent Practitioner, 13,* 42-45.

Bricklin, B. (1992). Data-based tests in custody evaluations. *American Journal of Family Therapy, 20,* 254-265.

Cantor, D. W., & Drake, E. A. (1982). *Divorced parents and their children: A guide for mental health professionals.* New York: Springer.

Chesler, P. (1991). *Mothers on trial: The battle for children and custody.* New York: Harcourt Brace Jovanovich.

Deed, M. L. (1991). Court-ordered child custody evaluations: Helping or victimizing vulnerable families. *Psychotherapy, 28,* 76-84.

Falk, P. J. (1989). Lesbian mothers: Psychosocial assumptions in family law. *American Psychologist, 44,* 941-947.

Gardner, R. A. (1989). *Family evaluation in child custody mediation, arbitration, and litigation.* Cresskill, NJ: Creative Therapeutics.

Gardner, R. A. (1992). *The parental alienation syndrome: A guide for mental health and legal professionals.* Cresskill, NJ: Creative Therapeutics.

Gardner, R. A. (1992). *True and false accusations of child abuse.* Cresskill, NJ: Creative Therapeutics.

Goldstein, J., Freud, A., & Solnit, A. J. (1980). *Before the best interests of the child.* New York: Free Press.

Goldstein, J., Freud, A., Solnit, A. J., & Goldstein, S. (1986). *In the best interests of the child.* New York: Free Press.

Grisso, T. (1990). Evolving guidelines for divorce/custody evaluations. *Family and Conciliation Courts Review, 28*(1), 35-41.

Halon, R. L. (1990). The comprehensive child custody evaluation. *American Journal of Forensic Psychology, 8*(3), 19-46.

Hetherington, E. M. (1990). Coping with family transitions: Winners, losers, and survivors. *Child Development, 60,* 1-14.

Hetherington, E. M., Stanley-Hagen, M., & Anderson, E. R. (1988). Marital transitions: A child's perspective. *American Psychologist, 44,* 303-312.

Johnston, J., Kline, M., & Tschann, J. (1989). Ongoing postdivorce conflict: Effects on children of joint custody and frequent access. *Journal of Orthopsychiatry, 59,* 576-592.

Koocher, G. P., & Keith-Spiegel, P. C. (1990). *Children, ethics, and the law: Professional issues and cases.* Lincoln: University of Nebraska Press.

Kreindler, S. (1986). The role of mental health professions in custody and access disputes. In R. S. Parry, E. A. Broder, E.A.G. Schmitt, E. B. Saunders, & E. Hood (Eds.), *Custody disputes: Evaluation and intervention.* New York: Free Press.

Martindale, D. A., Martindale, J. L., & Broderick, J. E. (1991). Providing expert testimony in child custody litigation. In P. A. Keller & S. R. Heyman (Eds.), *Innovations in clinical practice: A source book* (Vol. 10, pp. 481-497). Sarasota, FL: Professional Resource Exchange.

Patterson, C. J. (in press). Children of lesbian and gay parents. *Child Development.*

Pennsylvania Psychological Association, Clinical Division Task Force on Child Custody Evaluation. (1991). *Roles for psychologists in child custody disputes.* Unpublished manuscript.

Saunders, T. R. (1991). An overview of some psycholegal issues in child physical and sexual abuse. *Psychotherapy in Private Practice, 9*(2), 61-78.

Schutz, B. M., Dixon, E. B., Lindenberger, J. C., & Ruther, N. J. (1989). *Solomon's sword: A practical guide to conducting child custody evaluations.* San Francisco: Jossey-Bass.

354   SCIENTIFIC CHILD CUSTODY EVALUATIONS

Stahly, G. B. (1989, August 9). *Testimony on child abuse policy to APA Board.* Paper presented at the meeting of the American Psychological Association Board of Directors. New Orleans, LA.

Thoennes, N., & Tjaden, P. G. (1991). The extent, nature, and validity of sexual abuse allegations in custody/visitation disputes. *Child Abuse & Neglect, 14,* 151-163.

Wallerstein, J. S., & Blakeslee, S. (1989). *Second chances: Men, women, and children a decade after divorce.* New York: Ticknor & Fields.

Wallerstein, J. S., & Kelly, J. B. (1980). *Surviving the breakup.* New York: Basic Books.

Weissman, H. N. (1991). Child custody evaluations: Fair and unfair professional practices. *Behavioral Sciences and the Law, 9,* 469-476.

Weithorn, L. A., & Grisso, T. (1987). Psychological evaluations in divorce custody: Problems, principles, and procedures. In L. A. Weithorn (Ed.), *Psychology and child custody determinations* (pp. 157-158). Lincoln: University of Nebraska Press.

White, S. (1990). The contamination of children's interviews. *Child Youth and Family Services Quarterly, 13*(3), 6, 17-18.

Wyer, M. M., Gaylord, S. J., & Grove, E. T. The legal context of child custody evaluations. In L. A. Weithorn (Ed.), *Psychology and child custody determinations* (pp. 3-23). Lincoln: University of Nebraska Press.

Permissions

Committee on Ethical Guidelines for Forensic Psychologists. (1991). "Specialty Guidelines for Forensic Psychologists." *Law & Human Behavior, 15 (6),* pp. 655-665. Copyright © 1991 by Plenum Publishing Corporation. Reprinted with permission.

American Psychological Association. (1994). "Guidelines for Child Custody Evaluations in Divorce Proceedings." *American Psychologist, 49 (7),* pp. 677-680. Copyright © 1994 by the American Psychological Association. Reprinted with permission.

Association of Family and Conciliation Courts. (1995). *Model Standard of Practice for Child Custody Evaluations.* Madison, WI: Association of Family and Conciliation Courts. Copyright © 1995 by the Association of Family and Conciliation Courts. Reprinted with permission.

The American Professional Society on the Abuse of Children. (1995). *Use of Anatomical Dolls in Child Sexual Abuse Assessments.* Chicago, IL: American Professional Society on the Abuse of Children. Copyright © 1995 by the American Professional Society on the Abuse of Children. Reprinted with permission.

"This was published by the American Professional Society on the Abuse of Children (APSAC), the nation's largest interdisciplinary professional society for those who work in the field of child maltreatment. APSAC's aim is to ensure that everyone affected by child maltreatment receives the best possible professional response. APSAC provides ongoing professional education in the form of publications and conferences and, through media and legislative advocacy, educates the public about the complex issues involved in child maltreatment. For further information contact APSAC at 407 S. Dearborn St., Suite 1300, Chicago, IL. 60605. Phone: 312-554-0166; fax: 312-554-0919; or e-mail: APSACPubisWaol.com."

Association of Family and Conciliation Courts

Model Standards of Practice for Child Custody Evaluation

Introduction

The following Standards of Practice for Child Custody Evaluation have been formulated for members of the Association of Family and Conciliation Courts who conduct evaluations in custody/access matters. These members include both court-connected and private practice evaluators in many areas of the world with significant variations in practice and philosophy. It is recognized that local jurisdictional requirements influence the conduct of the custody evaluation; however, the goal of these standards is to highlight common concerns and set standards of practice that are applicable regardless of local circumstances.

Preamble

Child custody evaluation is a process through which recommendations for the custody of, parenting of, and access to children can be made to the court in those cases in which the parents are unable to work out their own parenting plans. Evaluation may be requested by the parents or their attorneys or ordered by the court. Evaluations may be performed by qualified mental health professionals who are part of a family court system or carried out privately by qualified individuals or teams. Evaluators always serve impartially, never as an advocate for one parent or the other.

The primary purpose of a child custody evaluation is to assess the family and provide the courts, the parents, and the attorneys with objective information and recommendations. The assessment goals of a child custody evaluation shall be to (a) identify the developmental needs of the child(ren), (b) identify the strengths, vulnerabilities, and needs of all other members of the family; (c) identify the positive and negative family interactions; (d) develop a plan for custody and access utilizing the strengths of each individual that will serve the best interests of the child(ren) and within those parameters, the wishes and interests of the parents, and in most situations provide them with an opportunity to share in the upbringing of their child(ren), and (e) through

Reprinted with permission of the Association of Family and Conciliation Courts. For additional copies or further information contact AFCC, 329 W. Wilson St., Madison, WI 53703, (608) 251-4001.

a written report, provide the court, parents, and attorneys with these recommendations and supporting data.

These standards are intended to assist and guide public and private evaluators. The manner of implementation and evaluator adherence to these standards will be influenced by local law and court rule.

I.   INITIATING THE PROCESS

A.   Appointing or choosing an evaluator

If there is a court-connected office of evaluation and conciliation, the evaluation shall be referred to that office for assignment to a qualified evaluator. If there is no such related office or if the evaluation is to be handled privately, the court shall appoint an evaluator or one must be agreed to by both parties and approved by the court.

Informed written consent of all parties must be obtained. Parties shall have the right to suspend or terminate an evaluation pending the consultation of an attorney regarding the advisability of continued participation if the evaluation is not court ordered.

B.   Arrangements with the parties

1a. The evaluator shall clarify with all parties, perhaps at a joint meeting, the evaluation procedures, license and credentials of the evaluator or team, the costs (if the evaluation is private or if there is an agency fee), the mutual responsibilities of the evaluator and the parties, and the limits of confidentiality. The evaluator shall assure the parties and their attorneys that no prior relationship existed or exists between the evaluator and any of the parties.

1b. If some previous relationship exists, however insignificant, it should be raised at this point and discussed in order to assure each party that objectivity will not be compromised by any prior contact. A decision whether to proceed or not will be made at the conclusion of this discussion or following discussion between the parties and their attorneys.

2.   During the orientation process, if preevaluation informational meetings are held, similar meetings shall be offered to all of the parents and potential caretakers and to all of their attorneys. Parties and/or their attorneys shall be free to ask questions. The evaluator shall provide information on any inherent bias(es) (e.g., joint custody, shared physical custody, mediation, lifestyle, and/or religion, etc.) that he or she holds, prior to the commencement of any evaluation.

3.   Communication between the evaluator and the attorneys shall be conducted so as to avoid any question of ex parte communication. Communication of significant matters between evaluator and attorneys may be best accomplished by conference call or in writing with copies to both attorneys.

II. EVALUATOR STANDARDS

A.   Education and training

Custody evaluators shall have a minimum of a master's degree in a mental health field that includes formal education and training in child development, child and adult psychopathology, interviewing techniques, and family systems. In addition, by formal training or work experience, the evaluator should have a working understanding of the complexities of the divorce process, awareness of the legal issues in divorce in the evaluator's jurisdiction of practice, and an understanding of the many issues, legal, social, familial, and cultural involved in custody and visitation.

B. Supervision and consultation for the evaluator

In addition, for evaluators in either public or private settings who have less than 2 years of experience conducting custody evaluations, it is recommended that ongoing supervision and consultation be available and utilized while the evaluator strengthens his or her skills.

C. Knowledge of statutes

The evaluator shall be familiar with the statutes and case law governing child custody. These will vary from jurisdiction to jurisdiction, and the evaluator must be completely knowledgeable concerning the criteria for original determination of custody, criteria for change of custody, the use of custody evaluation, qualifications for custody evaluators, and the legal requirements of the custody evaluation process of the jurisdiction in which the evaluation is to be conducted.

D. Psychological testing

If the evaluator is not licensed or certified to perform and interpret psychological testing, any psychological testing that is to be included as part of the custody evaluation must be referred to a licensed/certified psychologist who has the training and experience to understand the issues in custody evaluations.

III. EVALUATION PROCEDURES

A. Evaluation elements

The evaluator shall determine the scope of each evaluation, including who is to be included other than the litigants. In general, as diverse a number of procedures for data collection as possible and feasible to the specific evaluation is encouraged. These may include interviewing, observation, testing, use of collaterals, and home visits. It is important that the evaluator maintain a constant sense of balance, that is, obtaining similar types of information about each parent (when applicable) and spending similar amounts of time with each parent under similar circumstances.

B. Procedures during an evaluation

Each evaluator or team may use different procedures relative to joint and/or individual interviews, the necessity of a home visit, and the circumstances in which the children are interviewed. It is desirable that all parties to a dispute, as well as any other significant caretakers, be evaluated by the same evaluator or team. In cases where domestic violence is an issue, joint interviews may not be advisable.

C. Evaluations in two separate jurisdictions

In those cases in which the patients or caretakers reside in geographically separated jurisdictions, different evaluators may be necessary for the evaluations of each parent or caretaker. When such is the case, it is the responsibility of the requesting evaluator to be as specific as possible with the details and information requested from the courtesy evaluator, in order that the returning information is as near as possible to the quality and type of information that the requesting evaluator would have elicited. It is also the responsibility of the originating evaluator to help with the interpretation of the courtesy evaluation for the court. Where feasible, however, it is preferable for all parties to be interviewed by the same evaluator.

D. Interviewing and testing

Each adult shall be evaluated individually, and comparable evaluation techniques shall be used with all of the significant adults. If special procedures, such as psychological testing, are used for general evaluative purposes of one parent or potential caretaker, that procedure or those procedures shall be used for all significant adults involved in the evaluation. However, if a special technique is used to address a specific issue raised about one of the significant adults, it may not be necessary to use that same technique on all other significant adults.

E. Procedures with child(ren)

Each child shall be evaluated individually with procedures appropriate to the developmental level of the child. These procedures may include observation, verbal or play interview, and formal testing. It is not appropriate to ask children to choose between their parents because, in most families, children need good access to both parents following the divorce and should not be placed in the position of having to choose. Information about the child(ren)'s feelings, thoughts, and wishes about each parent can be obtained through techniques that will not be harmful and guilt inducing. The children shall be observed with each parent or potential caretaker in the office or home setting.

F. Psychological testing
1. Any psychological testing is to be conducted by a licensed/certified psychologist who adheres to the ethical standards of the jurisdiction in which he or she is licensed.
2. If testing is conducted with adults or children, it shall be done with knowledge of the limits of the testing and should be viewed only within the context of the information gained from clinical interviews and other available data. Conclusions should take into account the stresses associated with the divorce and the custody dispute.
3. If psychological test data are used as a significant factor in the final recommendations, the limitations of psychological testing in this regard should be outlined in the report.

4. The results of psychological testing shall be discussed with the significant adult participants in the evaluation, especially if the results indicate the need for psychological treatment or counseling. Whatever the outcome of the testing, of primary concern to the evaluator should be the parenting skills and abilities of the individual parents. Diagnostic considerations shall be considered secondary to parenting and treatment considerations.

G. Collaterals

1. Information from appropriate outside sources, such as pediatricians, therapists, teachers, health care providers, and day-care personnel, shall be obtained where such information is deemed necessary and related to the issues at hand. Prior to the seeking or gathering of such information releases signed by the parents shall be obtained; these releases shall specifically indicate the areas in which the information is sought and limit the use of this information to use by the evaluator in the preparation of the evaluation report.

2. Interviewing of family and/or friends shall be handled with great care given its potential for increasing divisiveness and resulting in harm to the children. It is possible, however, that family friends and neighbors may be able to present valuable information and/or leads to the evaluator. The use of such information shall be related to the circumstances of a particular evaluation, used only when the evaluator is convinced of its usefulness, and obtained in a manner that discourages conflict.

H. Home visits

When home visits are made, they shall be made in similar ways to each parent's or potential caretaker's home. Care shall be exercised so that temporary inequality in housing conditions does not lead to bias on the part of the evaluator. Economic circumstance alone shall not be a determining factor in a custody evaluation.

I. Interpretive conferences

The evaluator may hold an interpretive conference with each of the parties, either separately or conjointly. This is not a conference that attorneys need attend. The purpose of this conference is to discuss with each party the recommendations that are to be made and the rationale for each of these recommendations. It should be made clear to each party that these are the recommendations that are to be presented to the court in the evaluation report; acceptance and use by the court cannot be guaranteed.

IV. AREAS OF EVALUATION

A. Quality of relationship between parent or caretaker and the child

This shall include assessment of the strength and quality of the relationship, emotional closeness, perceptions of each other, and the ability of the parent or potential caretaker to support appropriate development in the child(ren) and to understand and respond to the child(ren)'s needs. The evaluator shall consider ethnic, cultural, lifestyle, and/or religious factors where relevant.

B. Quality of relationship between the contesting parents or potential caretakers

This shall Include assessment of each parent's or potential caretaker's ability to support the child(ren)'s relationship with the other parent and to communicate and cooperate with the other parent regarding the child(ren). The evaluator shall consider the relevancy of ethnic, cultural, lifestyle, and/or religious factors in assessing these relationships. Also, some consideration of the contribution of each parent to the marital and subsequent discord might be helpful in this regard.

C. Ability of each parent or caretaker to parent the child

This shall include assessment of the parent's or potential caretaker's knowledge of the child(ren), knowledge of parenting techniques, awareness of what is normal development in children, ability to distinguish his or her own needs from the needs of the child(ren), and ability to respond empathically to the child(ren). The evaluator shall consider the relevancy of ethnic, cultural, lifestyle, and/or religious factors in assessing these relationships.

Also to be taken into account is the ability and/or willingness of the parent, who perhaps has not had the opportunity to learn these skills, to learn them, to demonstrate an interest in learning them, and to try to use them in whatever time he or she has with the child.

D. Psychological health of each parent or potential caretaker

This shall include assessment of the parent's adaptation to the divorce, ability to develop relationships, ability to provide a stable home for the child(ren), ability to encourage development in the child(ren), and ability to support the child(ren)'s relationship with the other parent or caretaker. Assessment should also be made of factors that might affect parenting, such as alcohol or drug use, domestic violence, or a history of becoming involved in brief or harmful relationships.

E. Psychological health of each child

This shall include assessment of special needs of each child, for example, health or developmental problems. It shall also include assessment of the child(ren)'s adjustment to school, friends, community, and extended family. Children shall not be asked to choose between parents. Their overt and covert wishes and fears about their relationships with their parents shall be considered but shall not be the sole basis for making a recommendation.

F. Patterns of domestic violence

In cases in which domestic violence is alleged or a pattern of domestic violence exists and the evaluator, or evaluation team, does not possess expertise in this area, outside personnel with specialized training and experience in this area shall be consulted. In such cases the recommendation made by the evaluator, after consultation, shall take into consideration both the danger to the other parent or caretaker and the potential danger to and effect on the children.

V. THE EVALUATION REPORT

A. Style

The evaluation report shall be written clearly and without jargon so that it can be understood by the court, attorneys, and clients. It shall convey an attitude of understanding and empathy for all of the individuals involved, adults and children, and shall be written in a way that conveys respect for each individual.

B. Contents

In preparing reports, evaluators shall be aware that their own professional observations, opinions, recommendations, and conclusions must be distinguished from legal facts, opinions, and conclusions. The report shall include identifying information, reasons for the evaluation, procedures used, family history, evaluation of each child and each parent and caretaker, and evaluation of the relationships among parents and children and among the adults. Conclusions about the individuals and the relationships shall lead logically to the recommendations for custody, access, and visitation. It is helpful, and in some jurisdictions required, to spell out clearly how the data, the conclusions, and the recommendations are related to the statutory requirements.

C. Distribution

1. The evaluation report shall be distributed according to the rules established by each jurisdiction.
2. After the report has been distributed and considered, the court may order or it may be deemed wise for either or both parties to participate in therapy and/or counseling. The professional counselor/therapist may be an appropriate recipient of the report or that portion of the report relating to his or her client with approval of the court.

VI. ETHICAL PRINCIPLES

A. Ethical principles of professions

Evaluators are to adhere to the ethical principles of their own professions above the needs of the parties, the attorneys, or the courts. When there is a conflict between these ethical principles and others' needs, the evaluator shall try to explain the conflict to the parties and the attorneys and shall try to find ways of continuing the evaluation that will minimize or remove the conflict. If that is not possible, the evaluator shall withdraw from the process with notice to all parties and their attorneys in writing.

B. Prior relationships

An evaluator must disclose any prior relationship between the evaluator and any member of the family and, in most cases, should not perform a custody evaluation if there is a prior relationship of any kind. In addition, a person who has been a mediator or a therapist for any or all members of the family should not perform a custody evaluation because the previous knowledge and relationship may render him or her incapable of being completely neutral and incapable of having unbiased objectivity.

C. Post-relationships

After the completion of an evaluation, the evaluator should similarly be cautious about switching roles to that of either mediator or therapist. Such a change of roles would render future testimony and/or reevaluations invalid by virtue of the change in objectivity and neutrality. If all parties, including the evaluator, wish the evaluator to change roles following an evaluation, it is important for the evaluator to inform the parties of the impact that such a change will have in the areas of possible testimony and/or reevaluation.

D. Issues beyond the evaluator's expertise

In cases where issues arise that are beyond the scope of the evaluator's expertise, the evaluator shall seek consultation with a professional in the area of concern.

E. Limitations on evaluator's recommendations

Evaluators shall make every effort to include all parties involved in the custody dispute in the evaluation process itself. Evaluators shall not make statements of fact or inference about parties whom they have not seen. On occasion, evaluators will be unable to see all parties in a custody evaluation dispute, either because of refusal of one party to participate or because of logistical factors such as geography. In these cases the evaluator may perform a limited evaluation, but must limit his or her observations and conclusions. For example, if only one parent is seen, the evaluator must not make statements about the other parent and must not make a recommendation for custody because the other parent has not been seen. The evaluator may report on those individuals who have been seen and on their interactions with each other and may draw conclusions regarding the nature of those relationships, such as whether they should continue, not continue, or be modified in some way. The evaluator may also make comments or state opinions about the need for a more expanded evaluation. Prior to undertaking such an evaluation the evaluator may want to inform the court of the circumstances of the evaluation as well as determine that the party who brings the child for a limited evaluation has the legal right to provide consent for the evaluation.

Conclusion

Responsibility and authority for final decisions regarding custody and access rest with the court. As the conclusions of the evaluator are but one piece of the evidence before the court, these conclusions are to be framed as recommendations.

APSAC Practice Guidelines

Use of Anatomical Dolls in Child Sexual Abuse Assessments

I.   USES AND LIMITATIONS OF GUIDELINES

These Guidelines have been developed to reflect current knowledge and generally accepted practice concerning the use of anatomical dolls in interviewing children during assessments of suspected child sexual abuse. The Guidelines are offered to encourage appropriate use of anatomical dolls and to provide direction in the development of training for professionals. The Guidelines are not intended to establish a legal standard of care or a rigid standard of practice to which professionals are expected to adhere. Interviewers must have the flexibility to exercise judgment in individual cases. Laws and local customs may influence accepted methods in a given community. Professionals should be knowledgeable about various constraints on practice and prepared to justify their decisions about particular practices in specific cases. As experience and scientific knowledge expand, further revision of these Guidelines is expected.

These Guidelines apply to the use of anatomical dolls in investigative and diagnostic interviews of children in cases of alleged or suspected child sexual abuse. Such interviews are designed to determine whether an allegation is likely true, and if so, the nature of the abuse. Investigative interviews are typically conducted by child protective services and law enforcement professionals and by child interview specialists in specialized child abuse programs. Diagnostic interviews are typically conducted by mental health or health care professionals as a part of psychological or medical evaluations (American Medical Association,

Copyright © 1995 by the American Professional Society on the Abuse of Children. All rights reserved.

This was published by the American Professional Society on the Abuse of Children (APSAC), the nation's largest interdisciplinary professional society for those who work in the field of child maltreatment. APSAC's aim is to ensure that everyone affected by child maltreatment receives the best possible professional response. APSAC provides ongoing professional education in the form of publications and conferences and, through the media and legislative advocacy, educates the public about the complex issues involved in child maltreatment. For further information contact APSAC at 407 S. Dearborn St., Suite 1300, Chicago, IL 60605. Phone: 312-554-0166; fax: 312-554-0919; or e-mail: APSACPubls@aol.com.

1985). Diagnostic interviews often go beyond the focus of investigative interviews in also assessing the child's psychological status and the possible need for psychological treatment.

These Guidelines are not designed to address the use of anatomical dolls in psychotherapy. Furthermore, these Guidelines do not address the broad issue of questioning techniques during investigative or diagnostic interviews. These Guidelines have the narrower purpose of providing direction on the use of dolls as an adjunct to the questioning process. It is also not the purpose of these Guidelines to provide a comprehensive discussion of the clinical and empirical rationale for the use of anatomical dolls in child sexual abuse assessments.[1]

II. INTRODUCTION

Anatomical dolls are widely used as interview aids by professionals involved in the investigation and evaluation of child sexual abuse (Boat & Everson, 1988a; Conte, Sorenson, Fogarty & Dalla Rosa, 1991; Kendall-Tackett & Watson, 1992). Nevertheless, concern has been expressed about possible harm through the use of anatomical dolls in this context. One concern is that anatomical dolls may suggest sexual material, encouraging false reports from non-abused children. Another is that the dolls may be overstimulating or even traumatizing to non-abused children by introducing them prematurely to sexual ideas and body parts. A final concern is that interviewers using the dolls may be poorly trained and overzealous in their search for sexual abuse, eliciting unreliable, if not erroneous, evidence of abuse.

Research does not support the concern that anatomical dolls are inherently too suggestive or sexually stimulating (Everson & Boat, 1994). Follow-up interviews of parents whose young children had previously been exposed to anatomical dolls do not support the concern that the dolls are traumatizing to non-abused children or may induce them to become preoccupied with sexual issues (Boat, Everson & Holland, 1990; Bruck, Ceci, Francoeur & Renick, 1995; Dawson, Vaughn & Wagner, 1992). Research suggests that the level of training among interviewers using the dolls has increased substantially over the last several years (Boat & Everson 1988a; Kendall-Tackett & Watson, 1992). The actual skill level of interviewers, however, has only recently become the focus of systematic study and empirical findings on this topic are still limited (Boat & Everson, 1995).

When used by a knowledgeable and experienced professional, anatomical dolls can be an effective tool to aid in interviewing children to determine (1) whether an allegation of sexual abuse is likely true, and (2) if so, the nature of the abuse. Anatomical dolls are, however, only one of many useful interview tools (e.g. drawing materials, puppets, anatomical drawings) and cannot take the place of sound, child-sensitive interview skills and reasoned clinical judgment. Professionals should be able to describe how the dolls were used in the particular case and how this use conforms to accepted practice (Myers & White, 1989). Professionals should also be familiar with current research on the dolls.

III. SUMMARY OF RESEARCH FINDINGS

A. SUGGESTIBILITY

1. The majority of available research does not support the position that the dolls are inherently too suggestive and overly stimulating to be useful in sexual abuse investigations and evaluations (see review by Everson & Boat, 1994; Everson & Boat, 1990). Specifically, there is little empirical evidence that exposure to the dolls induces non-abused, sexually naive children to have sexual fantasies and to engage in sex play that is likely to be misinterpreted as evidence of sexual abuse.

2. Although analogue studies of children's memory and suggestibility find children four and younger more suggestible than older ones (see review by Ceci & Bruck, 1993), anatomical dolls have not generally been found to be a significant source of increased suggestibility and recall error. Three studies using anatomical dolls as interview aids with children in the 3- to 7-year-old range have found that the dolls increased recall accuracy with little are no increase in false reports of genital touching (Katz, Schonfeld, Carter, Leventhal & Cicchetti, 1995; Saywitz, Goodman, Nicholas & Moan, 1991; Steward & Steward, in press). In contrast, one study reported high rates of false assertions and false denials of genital touching among children under age 3-1/2 years when the dolls were used as interview aids in conjunction with direct, leading and misleading questions (Bruck et al, 1995).

B. INTERPRETING BEHAVIOR WITH DOLLS

Young children suspected or known to be sexually abused are statistically more likely than presumably non-abused children to engage in explicit sexualized interactions with dolls. However, many victims of sexual abuse do not display such behavior, and some non-abused children may display such behavior (White, Strom, Santilli & Halpin, 1986; Jampole & Weber, 1987; August & Forman, 1989). Following are empirical findings that provide some guidance for interpreting sexual behavior with the dolls:

1. Explicit sexual positioning of dolls (e.g., penile insertion in vaginal, oral, and anal openings) is uncommon among non-referred, presumably non-abused young children (see review by Everson & Boat, 1990). When allowed to manipulate the dolls, especially in the absence of adults, a small percentage of presumably non-abused children demonstrate explicit sexual intercourse between dolls or, more rarely, attempt to enact apparent sexual acts between themselves and a doll. Such behavior with the dolls appears to be related to prior sexual exposure (Glaser & Collins, 1989; Everson & Boat, 1990) and to age, gender, socioeconomic status, and possibly race, with four- and five-year-old boys from lower socioeconomic status families somewhat more likely to enact explicit sexual acts with dolls than younger children, girls, or children from higher socioeconomic status families (Boat & Everson, 1994; Everson & Boat, 1990). Therefore, while explicit demonstrations of sexual intercourse with anatomical dolls always deserve further exploration, such activities among younger children and children without known prior sexual exposure are of particular concern.

2. Among non-referred, presumably non-abused children, mouthing or sucking a doll's penis is very rare prior to about age four and infrequent after age four (Sivan, Schor, Koeppl & Noble, 1988; Glaser & Collins, 1989; Everson & Boat, 1990). This finding suggests that penises on dolls do not encourage most young children to seek oral gratification by sucking them. Sucking a doll's penis therefore should raise serious concerns about possible prior sexual exposure.

3. When a young child's positioning of the dolls indicates detailed knowledge of the mechanics of sexual acts, the probability of sexual abuse is increased, and further investigation of the source of the child's sexual knowledge is warranted. This is especially true for children under approximately four years of age and for children displaying knowledge of oral and anal intercourse (Everson & Boat, 1990).

4. Manual exploration of a doll's genitalia, including inserting a finger in the doll's vaginal or anal openings, is fairly common behavior among young, presumably non-abused children (Boat & Everson, 1994; Glaser & Collins, 1989). Such behavior is likely to be more concerning if it is accompanied by distress reactions (e.g., anxiety, fear), behavioral regression, or displays of anger and aggression (Gordon, Schroeder, & Abrams, 1990a, 1990b), or by obsessive repetition (Terr, 1981).

C. THE EFFICACY OF ANATOMICAL DOLLS

1. When compared to reliance solely on verbal communication, the use of anatomical dolls has been shown to enhance children's ability to recall and describe events (Katz et al, 1995; Leventhal, Hamilton, Rekedal, Tebanao-Micci & Eyster, 1989; Saywitz et al, 1991; Steward & Steward, 1995). However, the dolls may not necessarily be superior to other interview aids such as anatomical drawings or regular dolls (Britton & O'Keefe, 1991; Goodman & Aman, 1990; Steward & Steward, in press). Additional research is needed, especially examining the various functions anatomical dolls can serve in the assessment process among children of different developmental levels.

IV. APPROPRIATE USES

A. No predetermined amount of time must expire before dolls are introduced, nor must a predetermined number or type of questions be asked before using dolls. Every child is unique and interviewers should use their judgment to determine when, and if, dolls may be useful.

B. If possible, the interviewer should be aware of the extent and nature of the child's possible prior exposure to anatomical dolls. This information is important for assessing the likely usefulness of the dolls in the current interview and for better understanding the child's reaction to and behavior with the dolls. Such information is especially important in cases in which children may have had multiple, prior doll interviews or may have been exposed to the dolls in a play therapy format in which fantasy play was encouraged.

C. The number of dolls presented (e.g., individual dolls vs. set of two, three, or four) depends upon their specific use in the interview.

D. When sexual abuse is suspected, dolls can be used as part of the assessment process in the following ways (Everson & Boat, 1994):

1. Anatomical Model: The dolls can function as anatomical models for assessing a child's labels for parts of the body, understanding of bodily functions, and possible precocious knowledge of the mechanics of sexual acts. The interviewer may point to sexual and non-sexual body parts and ask questions like, "What do you call this part?," "What is it for?," and, "Is it for anything else?"

   The dolls can also serve as visual aids for direct inquiries about the child's personal experiences with private parts. This may include questions such as, "Do you have one (vagina)?," "Has anything ever happened to yours?," and "Has it ever been hurt?"

   If the child uses a non-standard term, such as "kitty cat," to refer to a body part, the dolls can be used to clarify the child's meaning. It is appropriate to use the child's terms for body parts.

2. Demonstration Aid: The dolls can serve as props to enable children to "show" rather than "tell" what happened, especially when limited verbal skills or emotional issues, such as fear of telling or embarrassment about discussing sexual activities, interfere with direct verbal description. This function of the dolls also includes their use to clarify a child's statement after a disclosure of abuse has been made. Whether or not a child experiences difficulty communicating about sexual abuse, dolls are sometimes useful to confirm an interviewer's understanding of a child's description of abuse and to reduce the likelihood of miscommunication between the child and the interviewer.

   Interviewers should be cautious in using anatomical dolls as demonstration aids with children under approximately age 3-1/2 years. This caution is based on questions about the cognitive ability of young preschoolers to use dolls to represent themselves in behavioral reenactments (DeLoache, 1995) and on concerns about the potential of the dolls to distract very young children (e.g., Goodman & Aman, 1990). These concerns do not preclude other uses of the dolls with young children. Furthermore, young children may use an anatomical doll to represent someone other than themselves and may, for example demonstrate with a doll on their own bodies what they experienced.

3. Memory Stimulus: Exposure to the dolls, and especially to such features as secondary sexual characteristics, genitalia, and articles of clothing, may be useful in stimulating or triggering a child's recall of specific events of a sexual nature. Supporting this use is research suggesting that props and concrete cues may be more effective in prompting memories in young children than are verbal cues or questions (e.g., Nelson & Ross, 1980). To encourage recall, it may be appropriate for the interviewer to ask questions such as, "Have you seen one (penis)?," or "Do the dolls help you remember anything else that happened?"

4. Screening Tool: This function, which sometimes overlaps with the Memory Stimulus use, is based on the premise that exposure to the dolls in a non-threatening setting may provide an opportunity for the child to spontaneously reveal his/her sexual interests, concerns, or knowledge. Typically, the child is given the opportunity freely to examine and manipulate the dolls while the interviewer observes the child's play, reaction, and remarks. The interviewer can be either present or absent (observing through a one-way mirror) during this time, although children are likely to be less inhibited in their manipulations of the dolls without an adult present. After a period of uninterrupted manipulation and exploration of the dolls, the interviewer asks follow-up questions about the child's behavior with, or reaction to, the dolls (e.g., "What were the dolls doing?" "Where did you learn about that?"). Graphic sexual behavior, unusual emotional responses, as well as spontaneous "suspicious" statements made by the child (e.g., "Daddy's pee-pee gets big sometimes") should be the focus of follow-up questions to the child.

5. Icebreaker: The dolls can serve as a conversation starter on the topic of sexuality by focusing the child's attention in a non-threatening, non-leading manner on sexual issues and sexual body parts. This may be especially important in the case of younger children and children with less well developed language skills who may require very direct cueing to understand what, from the universe of possibilities, the interviewer wants the child to talk about (Steward & Steward, in press). Dolls can also be useful in helping a child feel comfortable about talking about body parts, sexuality, etc., and in conveying tacit permission for the child to describe or demonstrate sexual knowledge and experience.

D. Sexually abused children are not always able to give a coherent verbal account of sexual abuse for a variety of reasons, including developmental level, language limitations, fear, embarrassment, and guilt. When a child's characteristics allow it, however, interviewers should generally attempt to obtain a verbal description from the child before asking the child to demonstrate with the dolls.

E. Generally accepted practice is to present the dolls clothed, but exceptions exist. For example, it may be appropriate to present the dolls unclothed when they are being used as a demonstration aid with a child who has already indicated that the individuals in his/her account were naked.

F. Depending upon individual child characteristics, anatomical dolls can be appropriately used in interviews with children from a wide age range, including with some adolescents. Some uses, however, such as screening tool and icebreaker, are less common among older children (Boat & Everson, 1995; Kendall-Tackett & Watson, 1992).

V.   INAPPROPRIATE USES

A. The use of anatomical dolls as a diagnostic test for child sexual abuse is not supported by the empirical evidence (Everson & Boat, 1994). Specifically, it is not appropriate to draw definitive conclusions about the likelihood of abuse based solely upon interpretations of a child's behavior with the dolls. There is no known behavior with the dolls that can be considered a definitive marker of sexual abuse in the absence of other factors, such as the child's verbal account or medical evidence (Everson & Boat, 1990; Realmuto, Jensen & Wescoe, 1990; Boat & Everson, 1994).

B. Interviewers should refrain from making statements that might encourage the child to view the dolls as toys or objects for fantasy play. This includes the use of words such as "play," "pretend," or "make believe." Interviewers should also be cautious in the use of conjecture in questioning with the dolls because of the possibility of encouraging fantasy (e.g., "If someone were to touch a girl in a way she didn't like, show me how they would do it."). The interviewer should consider giving the child the clear admonition that the dolls are used to help talk about and show "things that really happened."

C. The practice of the interviewer placing the dolls in sexually explicit positions and asking the child to relate the depiction to the child's experience (e.g., "Did this ever happen to you?") is leading and should be avoided.

D. Like any interview tool or technique, anatomical dolls can be misused. For example, dolls can be used in conjunction with inappropriately suggestive questions. Interviewers should monitor themselves to avoid improperly suggestive use of dolls (White & Quinn, 1988; Quinn, White & Santilli, 1989).

VI. DOLL SPECIFICATIONS

A. The utility of dolls in the interview process depends in large measure on the presence of certain physical features of the dolls. The following are considered to be important features:
   1. Genitalia and breasts that are proportional to body size and appropriate to the gender and age of the given doll.
   2. Oral, vaginal, and anal openings that will accommodate the adult male doll's penis.
   3. Facial expressions that are at least reasonably attractive and devoid of negative emotions, such as fear or anxiety.
   4. A size that can reasonably be manipulated by young children.
   5. Sturdy construction that can withstand rough handling.
   6. Clothes that can be easily removed.
   7. Clothes, including underwear, that are appropriate to the doll's represented age and gender.

B. The impact of the racial features and skin color of the dolls on the child's response has not been empirically examined. Preferred practice is to match the dolls with the race of the child. If it is likely that the alleged perpetrator is a different race from the child, the interviewer should consider presenting dolls of both races or a set of race non-specific dolls with neutral skin tones.

VII. TRAINING AND SKILL LEVEL OF INTERVIEWERS

A. Professionals using dolls should possess the training and/or knowledge and experience required to conduct forensic investigative or diagnostic interviews with children suspected of having been sexually abused. Refer to the APSAC Guidelines for Psychosocial Evaluation of Suspected Sexual Abuse in Young Children for general requirements regarding training, skill level, and supervision for interviewers.

B. Before using the dolls, the interviewer should acquire the requisite skills through familiarity with the research literature and applicable guidelines, consultation with colleagues, and/or clinical supervision. The interviewer should be familiar with developmental issues in the use of the dolls, appropriate and inappropriate uses of the dolls, and potential problems caused by using leading questions or other suggestive techniques with the dolls.

C. A formal, structured protocol detailing the use of dolls in interviews is not required and, given the state of our knowledge and the need for flexibility in individual cases, rigid protocols are probably not advisable. However, these guidelines and other general guidelines on the use of anatomical dolls in sexual abuse evaluations are available and may be helpful (e.g., Boat & Everson, 1986, 1988b; Levy, Kalinowski, Markovic, Pittman, & Ahart, 1991; Morgan, 1995; White, 1991).

VIII. DOCUMENTATION

A. Detailed documentation of the interview process should be provided. Because of the potential subtlety and richness of the child's behavior with anatomical dolls, videotape recording of the interview may offer advantages. If videotaping is impracticable or contraindicated, the interviewer's questions and the child's verbal, non-verbal, and affective responses regarding sexual abuse allegations or concerns should be documented. This can be done in writing or using a combination of audiotape and written notes.

B. It is desirable to prepare a verbatim record of all portions of the interview specifically relating to the issue of possible sexual abuse. This includes a description of the child's behavior with dolls, including the child's positioning of the dolls, critical verbal statements, and any verbal, non-verbal, or affective behavior with the dolls, such as avoidance, anxiety, fear, anger, or regression.

IX. CONCLUSIONS

A. Anatomical dolls are a useful and accepted tool for investigative and diagnostic interviews of children in cases of possible sexual abuse.

B. Professionals using anatomical dolls in child sexual abuse assessments should be knowledgeable and experienced in conducting forensically sound interviews with children and in the specific use of anatomical dolls.

C. Interviewers should be prepared to describe how they used anatomical dolls in each specific case and how this use conforms to accepted practice.

D. Interviewers should be aware of the limitations in the use of anatomical dolls. Specifically, anatomical dolls should not be considered to be a diagnostic test of sexual abuse, nor be over-emphasized in the assessment process to the exclusion of broader interview techniques and sound clinical reasoning.

References

American Medical Association (1985). AMA diagnostic and treatment guidelines concerning child abuse and neglect. *Journal of the American Medical Association, 254*, 796-803.

American Professional Society on the Abuse of Children (1990). *Guidelines for psychosocial evaluation of suspected sexual abuse in young children.* Chicago: Author.

August, R. L., & Forman, B. D. (1989). A comparison of sexually and nonsexually abused children's behavioral responses to anatomically correct dolls. *Child Psychiatry and Human Development, 20,* 39-47.

Boat, B. W., & Everson, M. D. (1995). *Interview errors in the use of anatomical dolls in child protective services investigations.* Paper presented at the Biennial Conference of the Society for Research in Child Development, April.

Boat, B. W., & Everson, M. D. (1994). Anatomical doll exploration among non-referred children: Comparisons by age, gender, race, and socioeconomic status. *Child Abuse & Neglect, 18,* 139-153.

Boat, B. W., & Everson, M. D. (1988a). Use of anatomical dolls among professionals in sexual abuse evaluations. *Child Abuse & Neglect, 12,* 171-179.

Boat, B. W., & Everson, M. D. (1988b). Interviewing young children with anatomical dolls. *Child Welfare, 67,* 337-351.

Boat, B. W., & Everson, M. D. (1986). *Using anatomical dolls: Guidelines for interviewing young children in sexual abuse investigations.* Chapel Hill, NC: University of North Carolina.

Britton, H., & O'Keefe, W. A. (1991). Use of anatomical dolls in the sexual abuse interview. *Child Abuse & Neglect, 15,* 567-573.

Bruck, M., Ceci, S. Francoeur, D., & Renick, A. (1995). Anatomical detailed dolls do not facilitate preschoolers' reports of a pediatric examination involving genital touching. *Journal of Experimental Psychology: Applied, 1,* 95-109.

Ceci, S. J., & Bruck, M. (1993). Suggestibility of the child witness: A historical review and synthesis. *Psychological Bulletin, 113,* 403-439.

Conte, J. R., Sorenson, E., Fogarty, L., & Dalla Rosa, J. (1991). Evaluating children's reports of sexual abuse: Results from a survey of professionals. *American Journal of Orthopsychiatry, 61,* 3:428-437.

DeLoache, J. (1995). The use of dolls in interviewing young children. In M. S. Zaragoza, J. R. Graham, G. H. Hall, R. Hirschman, & Y. S. Ben-Porath, (Editors). *Memory and testimony in the child witness.* Thousand Oaks, CA: Sage Publications.

Everson, M. D., & Boat, B. W. (1990). Sexualized doll play among young children: Implications for the use of anatomical dolls in sexual abuse evaluations. *Journal of the American Academy of Child & Adolescent Psychiatry, 29,* 736-742.

Everson, M. D., & Boat, B. W. (1994). Putting the anatomical doll controversy in perspective: An examination of the major uses and criticisms of the dolls in child sexual abuse evaluations. *Child Abuse & Neglect, 18,* 113-129.

Glaser, D., & Collins, C. (1989). The response of young, non-sexually abused children to anatomically correct dolls. *Journal of Child Psychology & Psychiatry, 30,* 547-560.

SCIENTIFIC CHILD CUSTODY EVALUATIONS

Goodman, G., & Aman, C. (1990). Children's use of anatomically correct dolls to report an event. *Child Development, 61,* 1859-1871.

Gordon, B. N., Schroeder, C., & Abrams, J. M. (1990a). Children's knowledge of sexuality: A comparison of sexually abused and nonabused children. *American Journal of Orthopsychiatry, 60,* 250-257.

Gordon, B. N., Schroeder, C., & Abrams, J. M., (1990b). Age and social class differences in children's knowledge of sexuality. *Journal of Clinical Child Physiology, 19,* 33-43.

Jampole, L., & Weber, M. K. (1987). An assessment of the behavior of sexually abused and non-sexually abused children with anatomically correct dolls. *Child Abuse & Neglect, 11,* 187-192.

Katz, S., Schonfeld, D. J., Carter, A. S., Leventhal, J. M., & Cicchetti, D. V. (1995). The accuracy of children's reports with anatomically correct dolls. *Developmental and Behavioral Pediatrics, 16(2),* 71-76.

Kendall-Tackett, K. A., & Watson, M. W. (1992). Use of anatomical dolls by Boston-area professionals. *Child Abuse & Neglect, 16,* 423-428.

Koocher, G. P., Goodman, G. S., White, S., Friedrich, W. N., Sivan, A. B., & Reynolds, C. R. (1995). Psychological science and the use of anatomically detailed dolls in child sexual abuse assessments: Final report of the American Psychological Association Anatomical Doll Task Force. *Psychological Bulletin, 118,* 2.

Leventhal, J. M., Hamilton, J., Rekedal, S., Tebano-Micci, A., & Eyster, C. (1989). Anatomically correct dolls used in interviews of young children suspected of having been sexually abused. *Pediatrics, 84,* 900-906.

Levy, J., Kalinowski, N., Markovic, J., Pittman, M., & Ahart, S. (1991). *Victim-sensitive interviewing in child sexual abuse.* Chicago, IL: Mount Sinai Hospital Medical Center.

Morgan, M. (1995). *How to interview sexual abuse victims.* Thousand Oaks, CA: Sage.

Myers, J. E. B., & White, S. (1989). Dolls in court? *The APSAC Advisor, 2(3),* 5-6.

Nelson, K., & Ross, G. (1980). The generalities and specifics of long-term memory in infants and young children. In M. Perlmutter (Ed.), *New directions for child development, 10: Children's memory,* 87-101. San Francisco: Jossey-Bass.

Realmuto, G. M., Jensen, J. B., & Wescoe, S. (1990). Specificity and sensitivity of sexually anatomically correct dolls in substantiating abuse: A pilot study. *Journal of the American Academy of Child and Adolescent Psychiatry, 29(5),* 743-746.

Sivan, A., Schor, D., Koeppl, G. K., & Noble, L. D. (1988). Interactions of normal children with anatomically correct dolls. *Child Abuse & Neglect, 12,* 295-304.

Steward, M., & Steward, D. (in press). Interviewing young children about body touch and handling. *Monograph Series for the Society for Research in Child Development.*

Terr, L. (1981). Forbidden games: Post-traumatic child's play. *Journal of the American Academy of Child Psychiatry, 20,* 740-759.

White, S. (1991). Using anatomically detailed dolls in interviewing preschoolers. In C. Schaefer, K. Gitiund, & D. Sandgrund (Eds.), *Play diagnosis and assessment* (pp. 317-330). New York: Wiley & Sons.

White, S., & Quinn, K. (1988). Investigatory independence in child sexual abuse evaluations: Conceptual considerations. *Bulletin of the American Academy of Psychiatry Law, 16,* 269-278.

White, S., Strom, G., Santilli, G., & Halpin, B. (1986). Interviewing young children with anatomically correct dolls. *Child Abuse & Neglect, 19,* 519-529.

Additional Resources on Interviewing

American Professional Society on the Abuse of Children. (1990). *The APSAC Advisor, 3,* 2. (Special issue dedicated to child interviewing).

Faller, K. C. (1995). *APSAC Study Guide: Interviewing children suspected of having been sexually abused.* Thousand Oaks, CA: Sage.

Faller, K. C. (1990). *Understanding child sexual maltreatment.* Newbury Park, CA: Sage.

Garbarino, J., & Stott, F. M. (1990). *What children can tell us.* San Francisco: Jossey-Bass.

Jones, D. P. H., & McQuiston, M. (1985). *Interviewing the sexually abused child.* Denver: C. Henry Kempe National Center for the Prevention and Treatment of Child Abuse and Neglect.

MacFarlane, K., & Waterman, J. (1986). *Sexual abuse of young children.* New York: Guilford.

Myers, J. E. B. (1992). *Legal issues in child abuse and neglect.* Newbury Park, CA: Sage.

Perry, N. W., & Wrightsman, L. S. (1991). *The child witness.* Newbury Park, CA: Sage.

Acknowledgments

These Guidelines are the product of APSAC's Task Force on the Use of Anatomical Dolls in Child Sexual Abuse Assessments chaired by Mark D. Everson, Ph.D., John E. B. Myers, J. D., and Sue White, Ph.D. The first draft was published for comment in *The APSAC Advisor* in Spring, 1993. In addition, four open Task Force meetings were held to request input on early drafts of the Guidelines: at the San Diego Conference on Responding to Child Maltreatment in January 1993; at the First National APSAC Colloquium in Chicago, June 1993; at the Second National APSAC Colloquium in Cambridge, Massachusetts, May 1994; and at the San Diego Conference on Responding to Child Maltreatment in January, 1995. The current version of the Guidelines reflects the experience and expertise of a large number of APSAC members as well as the APSAC Board of Directors. We gratefully acknowledge the many individuals who contributed their time and expertise to make these Guidelines possible and especially to Kathleen Coulborn Faller, Ph.D., A.C.S.W.

These Guidelines will be updated periodically. Any comments or suggestions should be directed to Mark D. Everson, Ph.D. through APSAC, 407 S. Dearborn St., Suite 1300, Chicago, IL 60605.

Note

1. For such a discussion, the reader is referred to the final report of the American Psychological Association's Task Force on Anatomical Dolls (Koocher et al., 1995).

Index

About the Author

Jonathan W. Gould, Ph.D., received his undergraduate degree from Union College and his doctorate from the State University of New York at Albany. He completed a post-doctoral year at the Marriage Council of Philadelphia. Currently, he is a partner in Charlotte Psychotherapy & Consultation Group. He specializes in forensic assessments as well as child, adolescent, marriage, and family therapy. He serves on a number of family court subcommittees in his home town and is active in its local forensic association as well as the state psychological association. He is senior author of the book, *Reinventing Fatherhood* (1993) and is completing a book for the Family Law Section of the American Bar Association pertaining to child custody evaluations. He is married to Debra, his guiding light, and has three children.